W9-BIQ-228

Mark 2:9

AT THE CROSS

Where Healing Begins

By Rod Parsley

CREATION
HOUSE PRESS

AT THE CROSS: WHERE HEALING BEGINS by Rod Parsley
Published by Creation House Press
A Part of Strang Communications Company
600 Rinehart Road
Lake Mary, FL 32746
www.creationhouse.com

This book or parts thereof may not be reproduced in any form,
stored in a retrieval system or transmitted in any form by any
means—electronic, mechanical, photocopy, recording or
otherwise—without prior written permission of the publishers,
except as provided by United States of America copyright law.

Unless otherwise noted, the Scripture quotations are from The
King James Version of the Bible.

Scripture quotations marked NIV are from the Holy Bible, New
International Version. Copyright © 1973, 1978, 1984, International Bible Society. Used by permission.

Scripture quotations marked NKJV are from the New King James
Version of the Bible. Copyright © 1979, 1980, 1982 by Thomas
Nelson, Inc., publishers. Used by permission.

Scripture quotations marked RSV are from the Revised Standard
Version of the Bible. Copyright © 1946, 1952, 1971 by the
Division of Christian Education of the National Council of the
Churches of Christ in the USA. Used by permission.

Cover design by Doug Martin
Interior design by David Bilby

Copyright © 2003 by Rod Parsley

Library of Congress Control Number: 2003104167
International Standard Book Number: 1-59185-228-5

This book was previously published as *The Backside of Calvary:
Where Healing Stained the Cross* by Results Publishing, ISBN 1-
880244-01-2, copyright © 1991.

03 04 05 06 07 — 8 7 6 5 4 3 2 1
Printed in the United States of America.

To my sister, Debbie.

When I think of God's healing power, you are the first example that comes to mind. From the car accident that almost took your life, on through the months of recovery that followed, your quiet strength and unshakable faith was—and remains— living proof that healing is not a fable, but fact.

Contents

FOREWORD

In our desperate, imperfect world, its assistance is critical. The need for this valuable commodity spans every social, economic, racial, and age barrier. Everyone, at some point in his life, is faced with the urgency of choosing whether or not to believe in the existence of divine healing.

The majority of the books I have read on this topic usually deal more with how to build your faith rather than exploring the actual ingredients of healing itself. This book breaks the mold and gives you the background necessary to better comprehend the reasons behind healing, thereby making it easier to understand and believe.

What event made healing necessary? When did this terrible incident take place? How did mankind figure in? What role did God play in this drama? How did He remedy the situation? Where does healing fit into God's salvation plan? Who is eligible to receive it?

All of these questions can be answered by simply pointing to one place, one incident, one moment in time. Suffice it to say that everything is made clear *at the cross*.

—ROD PARSLEY
COLUMBUS, OHIO

The Creator Himself knelt on the muddy banks of earth's freshly formed shore and carved out a figure in His own image. It was the shape of a man.

chapter one

PARADISE QUARANTINED

One single exposure to Satan was all that was needed to transmit the communicable disease of sin into the bloodline of all humanity.

We live in a temporal, imperfect world. Nothing in this physical environment goes unscarred by the weathering hands of time. Flowers wither, rocks crumble, iron rusts, and even our fragile human bodies slowly, but surely, deteriorate. Everything about this physical sphere is in a state of decay; nevertheless, our world was not created with this affliction. The disease was contracted.

In the beginning, God spoke, and out of the void of space something marvelous was created—life! With just a word, He invented the sun for the day shift and put the moon and stars on night duty. By His spoken thought, rivers began to flow and mountains rose to the sky. On and above earth's greening landscape, He scattered a diversity of living things. Along the shore, He ordered the seven seas to their respective boundaries.

> And God said, "Let there be light"…
> And God said, "Let there be a firma-
> ment"…And God said, "Let the waters
> under the heavens be gathered together
> into one place"…And God said, "Let the
> waters bring forth swarms of living crea-
> tures, and let birds fly above the earth
> across the firmament of the heavens."
>
> —GENESIS 1:3, 6, 9, 20, RSV

Although He had created a vast, global
menagerie, God discovered that there was no one
in the world for Him to talk to. In those early
moments of time, the Lord realized that He
desired someone with whom He could commune,
fellowship. Therefore, the Creator Himself knelt
on the muddy banks of earth's freshly formed
shore and lovingly carved out a figure in His Own
image. It was the shape of a man.

> And God said, Let us make man in our
> image, after our likeness…And the
> LORD God formed man of the dust of the
> ground, and breathed into his nostrils
> the breath of life; and man became a liv-
> ing soul.
>
> —GENESIS 1:26; 2:7

God "made" a man. He did not speak humanity into existence, as He had with the stars, the earth, and all other living things. When it came to the creation of His special companion, God took an unusual interest and "physically" involved Himself in the process.

By the Creator's hands-on approach, it is obvious that the Lord desired a unique relationship with man. What an extraordinary creation he was!

The moment God's divine breath entered man, he became superior to all other forms of earthly life. Not only was Adam's complex physical structure a work of divine craftsmanship, he was capable of such feats as abstract thought, original concepts, and the all-important attribute of free will.

Man was a one-of-a-kind combination of flesh and spirit, a creation that could actually have fellowship with the Almighty! Within him, the Lord placed the mind and emotions of a soul and the priceless gift of an eternal spirit. The Creator housed this rare combination in a clay "earthsuit" called the body.

After six busy days of creating, God stepped back and surveyed the length and breadth of His handiwork. Seeing that it was good, He gave Adam and Eve, the first man and woman, total dominion over it all.

MUTINY IN THE MIDST OF BOUNTY

It was a world of perfection, a garden paradise where the concepts of need, worry, and pain were unknown. Abundance was commonplace. Daily conversations with God were as natural and ordinary as the breeze that rustled through the fruit-filled trees.

Man had been granted control of all that he surveyed—that is except for one small patch of ground.

> And the LORD God commanded the man, saying, Of every tree of the garden thou mayest freely eat: But of the tree of the knowledge of good and evil, thou shall not eat of it: for in the day that thou eatest thereof thou shalt surely die.
> —GENESIS 2:16–17

It seems reasonable that if Adam could be faithful with the "little things" of this world, in time, humanity would be "made rulers over many" worlds throughout the Creator's vast domain.

But Satan slithered into the picture.

Enraged by God's fellowship with man and covetous of the world which the Lord had graciously given to His creation, the devil set his sights on paradise.

Why was Satan so opposed to the new world and its inhabitants? In actuality, humanity and its surroundings meant very little to him. The devil's motivation was not to get to man necessarily, but rather, to get back at God. Satan wanted revenge.

Once before, Lucifer had tried to gain control of God's property. Supposing himself to be "like the most High," Satan attempted a heavenly coup. The prophet Isaiah recounts the story this way:

> How art thou fallen from heaven, O Lucifer, son of the morning! How art thou cut down to the ground, which didst weaken the nations! For thou hast said in thine heart, I will ascend into heaven, I will exalt my throne above the stars of God: I will sit also upon the mount of the congregation, in the sides of the north: I will ascend above the heights of the clouds; I will be like the most High. Yet thou shalt be brought down to hell, to the sides of the pit.
>
> —ISAIAH 14:12–15

Satan's selfish scheme backfired, and he, along with his deceived followers, were banished for eternity. The New Testament concludes the episode with the postscript:

> And he [Jesus] said unto them, I beheld
> Satan as lightning fall from heaven.
>   —LUKE 10:18

Having been summarily booted out of Glory, it
is safe to presume that Satan was on the lookout
for a chance to strike back. Upon seeing how
pleased God was with His "new" creation, the
devil found a fresh target.

This time, however, Lucifer did not voice his
intentions aloud. He approached his objective
under the subtle guise of a serpent. Using the same
infectious words he had used to woo a third of
heaven's angels into hell, the serpent struck back
and sank his venomous fangs into the bloodstream
of humanity. (See Revelation 12:4.)

SELFISHNESS: REACHING FOR THE TREE

Slipping into the Garden, the devil approached
Eve and slyly drew her attention to the one and
only restriction God had imposed:

> And he said unto the woman, Yea, hath
> God said, Ye shall not eat of every tree of
> the garden? And the woman said unto the
> serpent, We may eat of the fruit of the
> trees of the garden: But of the fruit of the
> tree which is in the midst of the garden,

God hath said, Ye shall not eat of it, neither shall ye touch it, lest ye die. And the
serpent said unto the woman, Ye shall not
surely die: For God doth know that in the
day ye eat thereof, then your eyes shall be
opened and ye shall be as gods, knowing
good and evil. And when the woman saw
that the tree was good for food, and that
it was pleasant to the eyes, and a tree to
be desired to make one wise, she took of
the fruit thereof, and did eat, and gave
also unto her husband with her, and he
did eat.

—GENESIS 3:1–6

That single exposure to Satan was all that was
needed to transmit the communicable disease of
sin into the bloodline of all humanity. That initial
contact quarantined mankind. It forced a wedge
between the Creator and His creation.

SATAN'S STRATEGY

That fateful day in the Garden, Satan dangled
before man the most basic of temptations—selfish
desire. "Ye shall be as Gods" (Genesis 3:5).
Although Adam had it all, the serpent easily
enticed him with the notion of MORE.

Satan's attack was aimed at the two weakest

parts of man's makeup: the soul, wherein resides the uniquely human attribute of free will, and the flesh, housing the sensory feelings that constantly influence the soul to do its physical bidding. These two elements are governed by man himself, thereby rendering them easily accessible to the serpent's vengeful ploy.

However, the third and most important ingredient of man, the spirit, was protected against Lucifer's game. This rare component of humanity was—and remains—the property of the Creator Himself. It is God's timeless means of communication with His creation.

The human spirit can be compared to a piano string which is perfectly tuned to a particular note. When another instrument sounds the exact same pitch, the tuned string will vibrate on its own. Likewise, when God sounds out His perfect will, man's eternal spirit acknowledges the communication. Humanity's created spirit always vibrates to the will of its Creator.

Nevertheless, this heavenly force does not override man's own free will. It allows humanity to make its own choices, right or wrong.

Although the spirit constantly, gently reverberates God's wishes, it never assumes control until man freely relinquishes that authority.

Realizing this, Satan quickly seized the physical side of Adam and put up a smoke screen of fleshly desire to distract his attention away from God's gentle call. To this day, Lucifer's diversions of pleasure (lust of the eye, lust of the flesh, pride of life) and pain (mental and physical disease) remain his only defense against man's free-will choice to follow God.

That extraordinary gift of free will not only separated Adam from earth's lower life forms, it now sadly severed his special bond of fellowship with God.

If that was not enough, his decision to disobey the Lord's one and only rule disqualified humanity's rights to God's perfect physical world, and by default, dominion fell into the corrupt hands of Lucifer.

In that regrettable instant, everything changed. The world that had once rumbled to life began to show signs of age. Everything about this physical sphere was suddenly in a state of decay.

> Cursed is the ground for thy sake; in sorrow shalt thou eat of it all the days of thy life; Thorns also and thistles shall it bring forth to thee; and thou shalt eat the herb of the field; In the sweat of thy face shalt thou eat bread, till thou return

> unto the ground; for out of it wast thou
> taken: for dust thou art, and unto dust
> shalt thou return.
>
> —GENESIS 3:17–19

Flowers began to wither, rocks started to crumble and man's human body began to grow fragile with need, worry, and pain. For Adam, Eve, and the rest of mankind, the prognosis was all too obvious: Separation from God was indeed separation from life.

It seemed that Paradise was forever lost.

Nevertheless, though Satan's invasion gained him a piece of ground, the war that he started was far from over. Despite it all, the Creator (who never changes) still desired a relationship with His creation. God's divine breath still resided within man's eternal spirit.

That day, the combat perimeters were drawn: God on one side, Satan on the other. And the scrimmage line dividing the two ran across the very heart of man; for within this one-of-a-kind creation resided the domains of both warring factions—spirit (the gift of God) and flesh (the physical realm man relinquished to Satan).

Therefore, a divine strategy for humanity's rescue was conceived, and battle plans were drawn. On that decisive day, the voice of the omniscient

God spoke, and declared throughout the Garden
the first of many prophecies and promises
designed to give mankind hope and the serpent a
reason to fear:

> I will put enmity between thee and the
> woman, and between thy seed and her
> seed; it shall bruise thy head and thou
> shall bruise his heel.
>
> —GENESIS 3:15

That day the war between spirit and flesh
began.

*What began as a selfish act under a tree
... ended with a selfless act on a tree.*

chapter two

GOD'S RESCUE PLAN

*Through the filter of the blood covering,
God, our Physician, treated the
symptoms for sin.*

Although God was displeased with the way man had used the gift of free will, He still loved His one-of-a-kind creation. The Lord knew that if things remained status quo, man would be lost forever and would ultimately suffer the same fate that awaited Satan and his band of defectors. Yet for divine fellowship to be restored, mankind had to be cleansed of the corruption it had contracted.

Therefore, God devised a two-phased purification process that would 1) initially allow Him closer contact to His tainted creation that He might tend to the physical symptoms of sin, and 2) introduce a cure which would totally annihilate sin itself and all of its diseased properties. The one element common to both of these purification phases was the shedding of blood.

This liquid-like substance is the main ingredient

18

of every living, breathing creation of God. Its vein-pulsing flow is what invigorates and sustains the very gift of physical existence. Its presence inside a body is the ultimate evidence of life.

However, if enough of the blood's potent ingredients are allowed to spill out of the body, the tangible presence of life itself also escapes. To put it in modern terms: blood, like gasoline, keeps the body's "motor" running. Without it, man's "earth-suit" is nothing but a lifeless shell.

Simply put, the substance of blood is the ultimate common denominator. Its presence, as well as its absence, affects the vital functions of both the body AND the spirit.

> For the life of all flesh is the blood.
> —LEVITICUS 17:14

Realizing the eternal value of this life-giving flow, God chose the element of blood as the "currency" (a promissory note of an agreed transaction) for His arrangements with man.

PHASE ONE:
THE COVERING COVENANT

The first phase of the Creator's rescue plan was to narrow the breach that Satan had forged between

God and man. Effecting this reconciliation would, by definition, require the two parties to come together. To achieve such a union, there had to be a measure of mutual agreement. Therefore, the Creator established a covenant with His creation and sealed it with the blood of a slaughtered animal.

It was necessary for man to agree with God and confess his disobedience. (Honesty makes mistakes easier to tolerate.) It was also important for humanity to understand that "the wages of sin is death" (Romans 6:23). To accomplish this, God creatively employed a "visual aid" that graphically illustrated both the peril of sin and His divine promise to cover its corruption from His sight.

Upon tasting Eden's forbidden fruit, Adam and Eve immediately realized that they were naked. Their corruption to sin was exposed. Seeing their sad condition, God Himself slaughtered a beast and made coats of skin for the couple to wear. The Lord shed the blood of an animal to provide a covering for humanity's transgression.

> Unto Adam also and to his wife did the LORD God make coats of skins, and clothed them.
>
> —GENESIS 3:21

That event instituted the practice of animal

sacrifice. Its purpose was to act as a temporary blood covering for man's transgressions. However, its effectiveness was so inadequate that our Old Testament forefathers had to repeat the process each time they brought a petition to the Lord. In effect, the shedding of animal blood was a means of "momentarily sterilizing" man's sin infection, that he might reestablish limited contact with His Creator.

> An altar of earth thou shalt make unto me, and thou shalt sacrifice thereon thy burnt offerings and thy peace offerings, thy sheep and thine oxen: in all places where I record my name I will come unto thee, and I will bless thee.
>
> —EXODUS 20:24

God desired a one-on-one relationship with humanity. He longed to supply all of man's needs: spirit, soul, and body. Through the covering of animal sacrifice, mankind was able to achieve a glimpse into the vast range of blessings the Father yearned to share.

In Exodus 15, the Israelites discovered that God was not only capable of rescuing them from the clutches of Pharaoh's army; He was also willing and able to supply their physical needs.

> So Moses brought Israel from the Red
> Sea, and they went out into the wilder-
> ness of Shur; and they went three days in
> the wilderness and found no water. And
> when they came to Marah, they could
> not drink of the waters of Marah, for
> they were bitter...And the people mur-
> mured against Moses, saying. What shall
> we drink? And he [Moses] cried unto the
> LORD; and the LORD showed him a tree,
> which when he had cast into the waters,
> the waters were made sweet.
>
> —EXODUS 15:22–25

Through that episode, Israel got a glimpse into the character of the Lord. On that day, they heard the voice of God, through Moses, declare "I am the Lord that healeth thee" (Exodus 15:26). That powerful proclamation in the original Hebrew is translated *Jehovah-Rapha*, which is to say, "God Our Physician."

By such acts, it is obvious that the Lord wanted to be our helper and healer, but man's infection of sin impeded His efforts. Our exposure to Satan kept God at a distance. The Lord's holy nature will not "cohabitate" with corruption. Therefore, the blood covering, the first step in the restoration process, became the temporary "filter" through which God worked.

Although He was unable to dwell eternally within the heart of man, the Lord still found a way to use the blood covering's limited access to His advantage. The Almighty God of the universe moved His living quarters "next door."

> And let them make me a sanctuary; that
> I may dwell among them.
>
> —EXODUS 25:8

From the tabernacle's holy of holies, the Almighty was able to keep His distance yet still disperse His miracle-working power. This was accomplished through His use of chosen, anointed (purified) individuals.

> And Aaron [the High Priest] lifted up
> his hand toward the people, and blessed
> them, and came down from offering of
> the sin offering, and the burnt offering,
> and the peace offerings...And there
> came a fire out from before the LORD,
> and consumed upon the altar the burnt
> offering and the fat: which when all the
> people saw, they shouted, and fell on
> their faces.
>
> —LEVITICUS 9:22, 24

On another occasion when serpents entered Israel's camp and attacked the population, causing many to perish, God answered their cries for mercy through His servant Moses.

> And the LORD said unto Moses, Make thee a fiery serpent, and set it upon a pole: and it shall come to pass, that every one that is bitten, when he looketh upon it, shall live. And Moses made a serpent of brass, and put it upon a pole, and it came to pass, that if a serpent had bitten any man, when he beheld the serpent of brass, he lived.
>
> —NUMBERS 21:8–9

Throughout the Old Testament, God miraculously touched His people through the consecrated hands of His proxy representatives. The prophet Elijah, for instance, displayed his Master's desire to heal in a most dramatic way.

> And it came to pass...that the son of the woman, the mistress of the house, fell sick; and his sickness was so sore, that there was no breath left in him. And she said unto Elijah, What have I to do with thee, O thou man of God? Art thou come unto me to call my sin to remembrance, and to slay my son?
> And he said unto her, Give me thy son. And he took him out of her bosom,

and carried him up into a loft, where he
abode, and laid him upon his own bed...
And he stretched himself upon the child
three times, and cried unto the LORD and
said, O LORD my God, I pray thee, let this
child's soul come into him again.

And the LORD heard the voice of
Elijah, and the soul of the child came
into him again, and he revived ...And
the woman said to Elijah, Now by this I
know that thou art a man of God, and
that the word of the LORD in thy mouth
is truth.

—1 KINGS 17:17–19, 21, 22–24

Just as God's healing power was displayed
through Elijah, the authority of God was likewise
demonstrated through His messenger Isaiah. This
prophet's example was nothing short of earth-
moving:

Standing over King Hezekiah's sickbed, Isaiah
bluntly announced, "Set thine house in order; for
thou shalt die, and not live" (2 Kings 20:1). Upon
hearing these shocking words, the king turned his
face to the wall and began to beseech God in
tears.

Having delivered the Lord's message, the
prophet was about to leave when suddenly God
spoke to him and said:

> Turn again, and tell Hezekiah...I have
> heard thy prayer, I have seen thy tears:
> behold, I will heal thee...and I will add
> unto thy days fifteen years.
>
> —2 KINGS 20:5–6

Hearing Isaiah deliver this unexpected reprieve, the sick king became understandably doubtful. Realizing this, the prophet stated:

> This sign shalt thou have of the LORD,
> that the LORD will do the thing that he
> hath spoken: shall the shadow go for-
> ward ten degrees, or back ten degrees?

And Hezekiah answered:

> It is a light thing for the shadow to go
> down ten degrees: nay, but let the shad-
> ow return backward ten degrees.
>
> And Isaiah the prophet cried unto the
> LORD: and he brought the shadow ten
> degrees backward, by which it had gone
> down in the dial of Ahaz.
>
> —2 KINGS 20:9–11

Even through the "filter" of the blood covering and the use of His "go-betweens," the prophets, God was able to push back the shadow of sickness and death for all who recognized His authority. Nevertheless, this first phase of the

Lord's purification process was nothing more than a "Band-Aid." As a matter of fact, the New Testament book of Hebrews describes this first blood covenant as being, in a word, inadequate.

> For if that first covenant had been fault-less, then should no place have been sought for the second. For finding fault with them, he saith, Behold, the days come, saith the LORD, when I will make a new covenant with the house of Israel and with the house of Judah.
>
> —HEBREWS 8:7–8

Man's free-will decision changed God's paradise into Satan's partition. The corruption of sin which Adam allowed to infest the world restricted mankind's access to his Maker. Although the Lord longed for direct companionship with His creation, the first blood covenant could do very little to affect the barrier.

Through the filter of that covering, God, our Physician, treated the symptoms of sin. But being merciful, He desired to do more than simply cover the corruption. God intended, from the foundation of the world, to cure the infestation!

From the beginning, His strategy was to break through Satan's barrier, eradicate sin and its puny arsenal of disease, and restore man to his rightful place of dominion.

However, this portion of God's rescue plan demanded a sacrificial covering far more potent than the blood of a soulless animal. To eradicate the disease of sin, it would require a dose of pure blood from the same species that was originally infected—man.

PHASE TWO:
THE SUBSTITUTE SACRIFICE

But man did not qualify. Humanity's bloodline was tainted from the very start by Adam's sin. The only alternative was to exchange man with a substitute that harbored the same rare combination of flesh and spirit. This replacement had to possess the qualities of a pure, sinless bloodline; and, as God so graphically illustrated with the first slaughtered animal, this alternative also had to shed its blood.

The sacrifice of this pure substitute would not have to be repeated. Its potent flow would supply, once and for all, the ultimate covering for all of humanity's transgressions.

Man's sin required a death. Man's sicknesses needed a cure. Yet, ironically, the only one who could possibly fulfill all of these sanctified qualifications was the one, and the only, Son of God!

Therefore, seeing that there was no other way to reconcile the earth and the creation He loved, the Father Himself offered His Only Begotten to be the ultimate sacrifice.

Possessing the very Spirit of the Almighty, the Son honored the will of His Father. Clothing Himself in man's flesh through a virgin birth, Jesus Christ came to earth and became the sole supplier of what this temporal, imperfect world needed most: the healing balm of divine blood.

*Sin-infected humanity needed the kind of
transfusion that only God could provide.
And the only way such a divine exchange
could be made was if God Himself
provided the blood.*

chapter three

THE IMMUNIZED BLOOD OF JESUS

That morning in Gethsemane's garden,
Christ, like the first Adam, faced
a hard choice.

In today's modern society, the general public protects itself against the threat of disease by going to a family doctor for a vaccination. By exposing their bodies to the painful point of a syringe, they voluntarily allow their bloodstream to be injected with a portion of the very illness that they wish to avoid. The process is called immunization.

Modern medical science has learned that to fight a disease, it is sometimes necessary to be "infected" with it. Through this ironic process, the treated are rendered immune to the effects of a given illness.

Although this unusual method of prevention and healing is commonly used today, modern medicine is not the first to put its unique principles into practice. The process of "deliberate infection to bring about immunity" was described in graphic detail over 2,700 years ago, by a man who never heard the word *vaccination*:

> He was wounded for our transgressions, he was bruised for our iniquities: the chastisement of our peace was upon him; and with his stripes we are healed...the LORD hath laid on him the iniquity of us all.
> —ISAIAH 53:5–6

Isaiah's emotional words painted a vivid portrait of an event that would ultimately take place some seven hundred years after his time. The old prophet looked into the future and described the torture and crucifixion of God's own Son.

Not only do his words evoke an image of a painful death, they also provide a glimpse into the inner workings of the Creator's strategy. Although it was God's will to "immunize" the world against the contamination of Satan, the Lord knew that both His plan's success and Isaiah's prophecy would hinge on the outcome of yet another decision made in a garden, this time by a man called Jesus.

THE GARDEN BATTLEGROUND

Long before the Garden of Gethsemane, in the Garden of Eden, Satan dangled before Adam the most basic of temptations, selfish desire. The blind, self-serving choice he made that day lured him into a grave, and eventually, all humanity stumbled in after him. Freely choosing to eat of the Tree of the Knowledge of Good and Evil, Adam got just what he asked for: the knowledge of every evil disease and atrocity, and the awareness of every good and perfect gift, which lay just beyond his infected reach.

But then Jesus entered the scene, armed with the mandate to "be about My Father's business" (Luke 2:49).

One hundred percent man, one hundred percent God—He came to earth with the power to heal and forgive. He spoke words of "life" and light to those who had none. And He gave to all who would heed His words the will and the faith to climb out of their graves of despair.

However, when all was said and done, the paramount purpose of Jesus Christ was to be the substitutionary sacrifice for man's disobedience. It was His mission to administer the blood antidote for sin and disease to all of mankind.

Simply put, for God's plan to succeed, His only Son had to die.

In the early morning hours of that terrible and triumphant day, Jesus knowingly awaited His fate in the Garden of Gethsemane. Being the Son of God, He was aware of the torturous death He would soon face. Yet also being a man, and "in all points tempted like as we are" (Hebrews 4:15), Jesus naturally wanted to avoid the whole painful situation.

Recalling Isaiah's graphic prophecy—"He was wounded for our transgressions...bruised for our iniquities: the chastisement of our peace was upon him: and with his stripes we are healed...the Lord hath laid on him the iniquity of us all" (Isaiah 53:5–6)—the Son of God's physical mind contested the notion.

Within this "Second Adam," the domains of spirit and flesh also resided. There a battleground once again unfolded: God's plan on one side, Satan's selfish desire on the other.

That morning in Gethsemane's garden, Christ, like the first Adam, faced a hard choice. However, unlike the decision made in Eden, the alternatives that confronted Jesus would not only affect the world of the present and future, it would determine the ultimate fate of everyone, all the way back to Adam himself.

> And he went a little farther, and fell on
> his face and prayed saying, O my Father,
> if it be possible, let this cup pass from me.
> —MATTHEW 26:39

But instantaneously, His Spirit, in tune with the Father, voiced its rebuttal. In almost the same breath, Christ immediately added "nevertheless, not as I will, but as thou wilt" (Matthew 26:39).

There in that pivotal moment (as He had throughout His earthly life), Jesus did not allow His temporal, physical body to make His decisions. He was indeed, "tempted like as we are" (Hebrews 4:15)—yet without sin.

Instead of giving in to His physical, short-term desires, instead of surrendering to Satan's smoke screen of selfishness, Jesus listened to the Spirit of God within Him and chose the path that would ultimately benefit both man and God for all eternity. Instantly, Christ gathered Himself and turned His attention back to the hour which He, Himself, said would come.

> For he shall be delivered unto the Gentiles, and shall be mocked, and spitefully entreated, and spitted on; And they shall scourge him, and put him to death: and the third day he shall rise again.
>
> —LUKE 18:32–33

CALVARY'S VACCINATION

Just as Christ prophesied, He was indeed delivered into the hands of the Gentiles. He was mocked and spat upon. After His robe was stripped from His shoulders, the snap of a Roman whip filled the morning air.

Just as the prophet Isaiah envisioned, the Son of God willingly endured the flesh-tearing strokes of a leather cat-o'-nine-tails. With each blood-letting incision, Jesus bore upon His back the nau-seating agony of every disease mankind would ever know. He suffered through the intense tor-ment of those forty lashes minus one, so we could boldly proclaim, "with his stripes, we are healed" (Isaiah 53:5).

Led by His executioners up the steep incline of Calvary's hill, He was made to lie down on the long beam of the cross. There, He was forced to press the raw, open wounds of His back against the rough, splintery wood of a tree. His pain must have been excruciating.

However, at the cross, miraculous healing began to flow. As His wounds bled against the skin of the tree, a crimson stain marked the post, thereby initiating God's definitive, redeeming Passover of man's sicknesses and transgressions.

Then, without warning, there came the sudden thud of a hammer. The nails that pounded into Christ's hands and feet that day "injected" Him with every blatant iniquity, every subtle sin, every vile act that mankind had ever or would ever commit.

> The LORD hath laid on him the iniquity
> of us all.
>   —ISAIAH 53:6

Hanging from those nails, Jesus was also deliberately infected with all manner of sickness and sin, so to bring about salvation and healing, through His divine, immunized blood.

For this purpose, Jesus came into the world. Humanity needed the kind of transfusion that only God could provide. The only way such a divine exchange could be made was if God Himself provided the blood.

The Son of God became our substitute. He suffered the penalty for our sins and died in our place. He endured the ill effects of Calvary's "vaccination" so that we wouldn't have to. By simply believing in Him and the power of His blood, we can be cleansed from our unrighteousness AND healed of all manner of sickness and disease.

The apostle Peter put it this way:

> Christ also suffered for us...who his own
> self bare our sins in his own body on the
> tree, that we, being dead to sins, should
> live unto righteousness: by whose stripes
> ye were healed.
>
> —1 Peter 2:21, 24

Notice that Peter said that you "were" healed, and Isaiah said that you "are" healed. Therefore, if you were and you are, that means that your body is already healed, present tense!

If you will only believe in the power of His blood and accept what Christ has done for you on the cross, YOU CAN BE HEALED right now, present tense! TODAY!

AT THE CROSS

Before Calvary, man had to approach the Lord through the "filter" of animal blood and the veil of God's "go-betweens," the Temple High Priest and prophets. There was no direct contact. Although God wanted, and man needed, this separation to end, the original blood covenant could not fulfill that purpose.

However, at the cross, when the blood of Christ's sacrifice stained the rough skin of that tree, all the sin and sickness which Adam had brought into the world by touching God's forbidden tree, were COVERED. With His sacrifice, there is no more need for the old covenant; Christ's selfless act took care of it all.

> Neither by the blood of goats and calves, but by his own blood he entered in once into the holy place having obtained eternal redemption for us.
> —HEBREWS 9:12

The sin infection Adam contracted by his selfish act under a tree was covered for all time by Christ's selfless act on a tree.

Through the ultimate sacrifice of Christ, all the barriers came tumbling down. With His triumphant cry, "It is finished" (John 19:30), the breach which Satan had thrust between man and God was destroyed, and the temple veil of the holy of holies was ripped in two.

> Jesus, when he had cried again with a loud voice, yielded up the ghost. And behold, the veil of the temple was rent in twain from the top to the bottom; and the earth did quake, and the rocks rent.
> —MATTHEW 27:50–51

Satan was once again booted out, and no barrier of separation, save man's own free will, now stood between the Creator and His creation.

> There is therefore now no condemna-
> tion to them which are in Christ Jesus,
> who walk not after the flesh, but after
> the Spirit…For what the law could not
> do, in that it was weak through the flesh,
> God sending His own Son in the like-
> ness of sinful flesh, and for sin, con-
> demned sin in the flesh.
>
> —ROMANS 8:1, 3

Now, safe at the cross, our sin and sicknesses are covered once and for all, for Christ took all of our corruption with Him to the grave. When He rose to life again, our Savior left our sins buried there, covered for time and eternity!

At the cross, there's no reason to endure the condemnation of your past or suffer the discomfort of your physical maladies. By simply believing in the redeeming "transfusion" power of Christ's blood, you can bury it all and be resurrected again, to a renewed life: body, soul, and spirit.

The apostle Paul put it this way:

> Therefore if any man be in Christ, he is
> a new creature: old things are passed
> away; behold, all things are become new.
>
> —2 CORINTHIANS 5:17

Jesus Christ accomplished everything that God the Father started at the creation, and that includes total health, and a fulfilled one-on-one relationship with the Creator Himself. All you need to do to acquire these gifts is exercise your free will.

If healing was available to those separated by the old covenant, just think how much more accessible it is now that we've been at the cross of Calvary. Now, all that is needed to apply this heavenly balm is pure and simple faith.

When you go to your family doctor and expose your body to the prick of a vaccination needle, you are blindly trusting that the disease he is injecting into your bloodstream will keep you from illness…that's faith!

With just a portion of that "believing power" (even as small as a mustard seed), you not only can have the assurance of health, but you can also have the promise of eternal life.

If Adam changed the entire world with a decision, and Christ, by choosing the way of the Spirit, repaired the damage, just think how your world could change if you would only choose.

All you have to do is simply believe that:

He was wounded for our transgressions, he was bruised for our iniquities: the chastisement of our peace was upon him; and with his stripes we are healed.

—ISAIAH 53:5

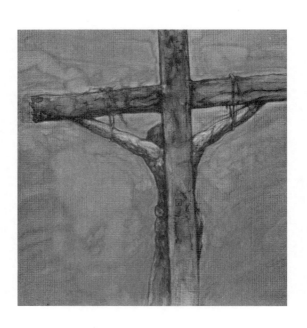

*As the wounds on His back pressed
against the rough wood of the tree,
a crimson stain marked the post,
thereby initiating God's Passover
of man's sicknesses and
transgressions.*

chapter four

SIMPLY BELIEVE

*God did not lay down His Son's life so
that our beat-up "earthsuits" could sit in
heaven's front yard and rust.*

Although most Christians understand
what took place in the Garden of Eden,
and though the majority comprehend
God's sacrificial plan to save mankind, there are
still those today who fail to grasp that healing
was—and is—a part of God's divine design.

Salvation and healing are two gifts wrapped
up in the same package. For God, it is just as
easy to forgive sin as it is to dissolve a cancerous
growth. To Him, healing is just as important and
necessary as Salvation.

The apostle Mark brought this point into
vivid focus in his retelling of the day Jesus
healed the man with the palsy:

> And they come unto him [Jesus], bring-
> ing one sick of the palsy, which was
> borne of four. And when they could not
> come nigh unto him for the press, they

uncovered the roof where he was: and when they had broken it up, they let down the bed wherein the sick of the palsy lay. When Jesus saw their faith, he said unto the sick of the palsy, Son, thy sins be forgiven thee. But there were certain of the scribes sitting there, and reasoning in their hearts, Why doth this man thus speak blasphemies? Who can forgive sins but God only?

...when Jesus perceived in his spirit that they so reasoned within themselves, he said unto them, Why reason ye these things in your hearts? Whether is it easier to say to the sick of the palsy, Thy sins be forgiven thee; or to say, Arise, take up thy bed, and walk? But that ye may know that the Son of man hath power on earth to forgive sins, (he saith to the sick of the palsy), I say unto thee, Arise, and take up thy bed, and go thy way into thine house.

And immediately he arose, took up the bed, and went forth before them all; insomuch that they were all amazed, and glorified God, saying, We never saw it on this fashion.

—Mark 2:3–12

Thanks to the displayed power of God's Son,

the man who came in with his back on his bed left with his bed on his back! The only thing the scribes could do was grumble.

Like oil and water, Jesus and religion have never mixed well. Back in the New Testament days, when Christ held out a healing hand, the scribes and Pharisees squirmed uncomfortably. Although they didn't like what He was doing, they could not publicly challenge His work, for the evidence of opened eyes and straightened limbs was widespread and irrefutable.

However, when Jesus spoke of forgiving sin, the religious community presumed that it finally had Him cornered. But as always, Christ was one step ahead of the devil's game.

To display the full range of His authority, the Son of God pointed a loaded question at His adversaries, "Is it easier to say...thy sins be forgiven thee; or to say, Arise, and take up thy bed, and walk?" (Mark 2:9).

Knowing that religion always needs tangible proof, Jesus did not wait for an answer. Immediately, He turned to the palsied man and spoke, "Arise and take up thy bed" (Mark 2:11).

Christ's words spoke power and life to the palsied man's limbs. When he stood to his feet, religion had its tangible proof that not only could

Jesus heal, but by extension, His words possessed the power to forgive as well.

Although twenty centuries have passed, Jesus and religion still do not mix. Christ hasn't changed; man has. In the New Testament days, the theological world conceded that the power of healing existed and balked at the forgiveness of sin. But today, it's the other way around. The church doesn't seem to mind preachers talking about salvation and forgiveness of sin, but they are adamant against any positive reference to the subject of divine healing.

It's a sad commentary on today's Bible believers, but a large portion of them do not receive the healing they need, simply because they are too busy wondering, "Is it God's will to heal?"

That question was voiced only once in the New Testament. The inquiry was posed by a humble leper, kneeling at the feet of God's Son, during the first year of His ministry.

"If Thou wilt," the man submissively bowed, "Thou canst make me clean" (Mark 1:40).

Looking down at the man's white, flaky skin, Jesus was moved with compassion. Stretching out His hand, Christ gently touched the leper and answered, "I will; be thou clean" (Mark 1:41).

Instantly, as the man rose to his feet, the surface

of his tainted skin became as soft and pure as a baby's. So with great excitement,

> He went out, and began to publish it much, and to blaze abroad the matter, insomuch that Jesus could no more openly enter into the city, but was without in desert places: and they came to him from every quarter.
>
> —MARK 1:45

After that day, the overwhelming crowds that surrounded Jesus made it obvious why the question of healing was only asked once. The news of His compassion and power was indeed "blazed abroad."

However, these days, it seems there are still churches that haven't grasped the Good News. These worthless institutions are so busy expounding their own agenda that they fail to even bring up the subject of healing, much less practice it.

If that's not bad enough, there are sermons being preached from today's pulpits that proclaim the validity of salvation by the blood, yet simultaneously reduce the experience of healing to mere coincidence.

Looking at the results of such unproductive congregations, it's no wonder that there are still those who ask, "Is God even able to heal?"

Able?! He flung the stars into place and traced
out the course of rivers with His finger. He set the
world spinning upside down and commanded the
oceans not to spill a drop.

Is He able? He walked on the water. He turned
water into wine and commanded the wind and the
waves to be still. He fed five thousand with a few
loaves and fishes and drove out devils with a single word.

Is Jesus able? Ask blind Bartimaeus to describe
the Savior's smile. Ask the widow if her tainted
blood is still an issue. Ask Lazarus what it's like to
be called back from the other side.

He took up another man's cross and placed on
His shoulders the weight of the entire world's sin
and disease. He willingly allowed His immunized
blood to be spilled for our salvation and healing.
He rose again that we, too, might be transformed
by His power and grace.

Is Jesus able? A man once brought his demon-
tortured son to the disciples for healing. But
despite their collective, diligent efforts, Christ's
apostles were powerless to control the convulsing
lad. Finally, just as the boy's disappointed father
was about to turn for home, Jesus (who is always
right on time), came on the scene.

Assessing the situation, the Son of God instantly

took control: "Bring him unto me…" (Mark 9:19).

That's good advice! When the doctors can't help you; when your lawyer's hands are tied; when the deacons shrug their shoulders; and the bank president shakes his head no, bring your problems to Jesus. He is more than willing; He is able to repair the damage.

It amazes me that in the midst of a crisis, people compulsively grab at every fad, fable, and "snake-oil remedy" within reach and totally ignore the spiritual power that is at their disposal. Such disabled people remind me of an old nursery rhyme:

> Humpty-Dumpty sat on a wall.
> Humpty-Dumpty had a great fall.
> All the King's horses,
> And all the King's men
> Couldn't put Humpty together again.

Why was the repair job given to the King's horses and men? Why wasn't the matter brought directly to the King? He's the one with the power.

Likewise, Jesus is "the way" to the Father, the Creator of all things. When your body isn't functioning correctly, who better is there to turn to than the One who created you?

The watch on my arm is proof positive that somewhere there is a watchmaker. If my timepiece suddenly stops or requires replacement parts, the best thing for me to do is to find the man who made the watch. He is the one best able to fix the damage. Just the same, the healing power of Christ's immunized blood was designed specifically to repair whatever malady keeps you from ticking.

No matter how desperate your situation seems to be, don't grab for fads, fables, or a quick fix; like the man with the demon possessed son, bring your problems to Jesus.

> And they brought him unto him: and when he [Jesus] saw him [the boy], straightway the spirit tare him; and he fell on the ground, and wallowed foaming. And he [Jesus] asked his father, How long is it ago since this came unto him? And he said, Of a child. And ofttimes it hath cast him into the fire, and into the waters, to destroy him: but if thou canst do anything, have compassion on us, and help us.
>
> Jesus said unto him, If thou canst believe, all things are possible to him that believeth.
>
> And straightway the father of the child cried out, and said with tears, Lord, I believe; help thou mine unbelief.
>
> When Jesus saw that the people came running together, he rebuked the foul

> spirit, saying unto him, Thou dumb and
> deaf spirit, I charge thee, come out of
> him, and enter no more into him. And
> the spirit cried, and rent him sore, and
> came out of him: and he was as one dead;
> insomuch that many said, He is dead.
> But Jesus took him by the hand, and lift-
> ed him up; and he arose.
>
> —MARK 9:20–27

That day, Jesus displayed to the people that He
was not only available and willing to heal, but
that He was also indeed "able." Furthermore, if
you look at this episode closely, you'll also discover that Christ clearly gave us a glimpse of our own
capabilities, as well. He said,

> If thou canst believe, all things are
> possible.
>
> —MARK 9:23

If you can simply believe in the power of God,
there is nothing—absolutely *no* thing—that you
cannot do. There is no problem you cannot influence. There is no circumstance you cannot
change.

If God can speak and create an entire world out
of the vacuum of space, there is no reason to doubt
that He can call into existence whatever you need.

The only limitations God has are the ones that you place on Him. If you question His willingness; if you doubt His ability, or even your own worthiness; you are constricting the flow of His miracle-working power.

His willingness was illustrated when He voluntarily hung on the cross. Your worthiness was exhibited plainly by the blood He shed there. Jesus Christ's unlimited ability was demonstrated profoundly when He emerged from a tomb of death triumphant, alive forever more!

When Mom and Dad can't seem to find the answer; when husbands and wives can offer no hope or comfort; when it seems that your Humpty-Dumpty world has shattered into thousands of irreplaceable pieces; when everything that can be done has been done—have faith and bring your problems to the Master Watchmaker, the King of kings.

When you get right down to the heart of the matter, it's not a question of what He can do, but rather a question of what YOU can believe. The Old Testament story of the Shunammite woman is a perfect example of this kind of faith.

This elderly woman wanted to be so close—so dependent—on God that she asked her husband to build a room onto their house for the traveling prophet, Elisha.

> I know this is a holy man of God, who
> passes by us regularly. Please, let us make
> a small upper room on the wall; and let
> us put a bed for him there, and a table
> and a chair and a lampstand; so it will
> be, whenever he comes to us, he can
> turn in there.
>
> —2 KINGS 4:9–10, NKJV

The Shunammite's idea seemed good to her husband. They had often heard Elisha speak during his regular visits to town. In fact, gradually, over the years, it had become a steady practice for the prophet to go home with the couple for dinner and fellowship.

Elisha was his generation's link to God. Naturally, with that kind of divine connection, the old couple wanted him near. So they knocked down a wall, hung a door and constructed an adjoining room to their house for the prophet.

By doing so, this family in Shunem (which means "double resting place") joined their house to the house of God. By attaching their home to God's, they not only had a place to rest, they could also "rest assured" (have faith) that no matter what may come, the Lord God Almighty was able and available to help them, because He was right next door!

When the Shunammites presented Elisha with his comfortable quarters, the prophet was moved. Lying on his new bed, he pondered what could be done to show his appreciation. Nevertheless, after much thought and consideration, no solution seemed adequate. Eventually running out of ideas, the prophet then turned to his servant, Gehazi:

> And he said, What then is to be done for her? And Gehazi answered, Verily, she hath no child, and her husband is old.
> —2 KINGS 4:14

The house was indeed empty. There were no children. Noting his servant's keen observation, Elisha immediately called for the old woman:

> And he said, Call her. And when he had called her, she stood in the door. And he said, About this season, according to the time of life, thou shalt embrace a son. And she said, Nay, my lord, thou man of God, do not lie to thine handmaid.
> —2 KINGS 4:15–16

Her initial reaction should not be interpreted as doubt, but more appropriately, as total surprise. The woman's words were a genuine response to a statement that definitely seemed "unnatural." She was indeed far past the natural time for motherhood. Likewise, there was no denying that her husband was an old man.

Nevertheless, when God decides to do something, the standard rules of creation are suspended. When He says a certain thing will occur, nature voluntarily relinquishes its jurisdiction and bows its authority to the Creator's wishes, thereby making mere nature super-natural!

Mankind could take some pointers from nature: If we would simply believe and likewise relinquish ourselves to God's wishes, the supernatural could be our everyday nature too. Remember, it's not a question of what God can do; it's a question of what you can believe.

> And the woman conceived, and bare a son at that season that Elisha had said to her, according to the time of life. And when the child was grown, it fell on a day, that he went out to his father to the reapers. And he said to his father, My head, my head. And he [the father] said to a lad, Carry him to his mother. And when he had taken him, and brought him to his mother, he [the boy] sat on her knees till noon, and then died.
>
> —2 KINGS 4:17–20

In that devastating instant, the Shunammite woman had every reason to cry out and question God; her miracle son was dead. However, instead of erupting into an understandable display of motherly remorse, she chose to handle her problem a different way.

> And she went up, and laid him on the bed of the man of God, and shut the door upon him, and went out.
>
> —2 KINGS 4:21

This stalwart woman took her problem to the Lord and left it there.

> And she called unto her husband, and said, Send me, I pray thee, one of the young men, and one of the asses, that I may run to the man of God, and come again. And he said, Wherefore wilt thou go to him today? It is neither new moon, nor sabbath. And she said, It shall be well.
>
> —2 KINGS 4:22–23

The old woman had such faith, that she didn't even bother to tell her husband the devastating news. She had places to go, appointments to keep. She had to see a certain Watchmaker about repairing one of His custom creations.

Unlike the man who brought his devil-tormented son to the disciples, the Shunammite did not waste time or energy with those who could do nothing about her problem. No snake-oil cures for her; she was taking the broken pieces of her dilemma straight to the King Himself.

I like what she told her husband: "It shall be well" (2 Kings 4:23). It's not a question of what God can do; it's a question of what *you* can believe.

> Then she saddled an ass, and said to her servant, Drive, and go forward; slack not thy riding for me, except I bid thee. So she went and came unto the man of God to Mount Carmel. And it came to pass, when the man of God saw her afar off, that he said to Gehazi his servant, Behold, yonder is that Shunammite: Run now, I pray thee, to meet her, and say unto her, Is it well with thee? Is it well with thy husband? Is it well with the child?
>
> —2 KINGS 4:24–26

Any other time, Gehazi's question would have been considered polite banter between old friends, but on this occasion, his inquiry had the same volatile potential as a keg of dynamite—with a short fuse. But again, the woman's strong, stubborn faith sustained her. She answered, "It is well"

(2 Kings 4:26).

> And when she came to the man of God
> to the hill, she caught him by the feet:
> but Gehazi came near to thrust her away.
> And the man of God said, Let her alone;
> for her soul is vexed within her: and the
> Lord hath hid it from me, and hath not
> told me.
>
> Then she said, Did I desire a son of
> my lord? did I not say, Do not deceive
> me?
>
> Then he [Elisha] said to Gehazi, Gird
> up thy loins, and take my staff in thine
> hand, and go thy way: if thou meet any
> man, salute him not; and if any salute
> thee, answer him not again: and lay my
> staff on the face of the child.
>
> And the mother of the child said, As
> the Lord liveth, and as thy soul liveth, I
> will not leave thee. And he arose, and
> followed her.
>
> —2 KINGS 4:27–30

Having joined her house to the house of God,
the Shunammite knew what God could do. After
all, He was the One who gave her the miracle
child. Therefore, she was not about to entrust her
son to Gehazi, Elisha's staff, or to any of the King's
horses or men. She stubbornly clung to the feet of

God's earthly representative and demanded nothing short of a command performance. Her faith compelled Elisha to follow.

> And Gehazi passed on before them, and laid the staff upon the face of the child; but there was neither voice, nor hearing. Wherefore he [Gehazi] went again to meet him [Elisha], and told him, saying, The child is not awaked. And when Elisha was come into the house, behold, the child was dead, and laid upon his bed.
>
> He went in therefore, and shut the door upon them twain, and prayed unto the Lord. And he went up, and lay upon the child, and put his mouth upon his mouth, and his eyes upon his eyes, and his hands upon his hands: and he stretched himself upon the child; and the flesh of the child waxed warm.
>
> —2 KINGS 4:31–34

When your faith allows God to get involved in your situation, His healing flow always has a way of warming things up.

> Then he [Elisha] returned, and walked in the house to and fro; and went up, and stretched himself upon him [the boy]: and the child sneezed seven times, and

the child opened his eyes.

And he called Gehazi, and said, Call this Shunammite. So he called her. And when she was come unto him, he said, Take up thy son. Then she went in, and fell at his feet, and bowed herself to the ground, and took up her son, and went out.

—2 KINGS 4:35–37

I admire that old woman for not only did she display a monumental faith, she also exhibited a great capacity for praise. If this tragedy had happened to one of my children, Ashton or Austin, and the prophet had announced, "Here's your child," I would have immediately rushed to the bed and wrapped my arms around him—first. But that's not what the Shunammite did. She fell down at Elisha's feet, bowed herself to the ground and gave thanks to God for giving her miracle child life once again. Then she picked up her boy.

Furthermore, throughout her ordeal, the old woman proclaimed, "It shall be well." That powerful statement did not question the situation; it did not evaluate God's ability or His willingness to intervene. It simply proved that the old Shunammite woman indeed lived in a "double resting place." She was able to "rest assured" that

God was just as available to her as if He lived next door, and that her miracle was not predicated by what He could do, but rather on what she was willing to believe.

The old woman simply displayed her faith and left the hard part up to God.

THE HARD PART

It has been said that religion is the practice of making simple things hard. Never has that theology been more in vogue than it is today. It seems that our modern world finds it increasingly difficult to comprehend that God will supply our every need—if we but simply ask and believe.

The fact is that Satan (still trying to get back at God) has slyly placed the notion in the collective rationale of modern man that to receive anything from God we must go through the torturous mechanics of meaningless rituals. That old serpent has perpetuated the idea that to gain God's ear one must articulate certain words, dance a pre-choreographed jig, and fulfill a specific set of rules. But my friends, that evil notion is the farthest thing from the truth!

There is no need to go through the rituals and formulas of man or the sacrifices of religion. It isn't difficult to get to God. In fact, He has already taken care of the hard part for you.

Through the death of Jesus Christ, we can be reconciled to God and actually have an intimate, personal relationship with the Creator. The only requirement is faith in the fact that Christ accomplished this for you.

Through the blood Jesus sacrificed on Calvary's tree, you can be cleansed of every physical sickness, discomfort, and disease; every form of mental anguish and torture; and all manner of infirmity. The only prerequisite is to believe.

It is that simple. The hard part has already been tackled. If God didn't want to heal you, He should not have done it! Remember, by His stripes, you WERE healed! Your cure has already been appropriated, through the immunized blood of His Son.

Whether you accept God's gift or not is up to you. All it takes is faith—which is the absolute absence of doubt.

When you question the notion of healing, you're not wondering if God will heal you, you're wondering if He's lying. That's unbelief. The Bible says that "I am the LORD that healeth thee" (Exodus 15:26). That's not a denomination's word—it's God's Word.

Why would He put into motion a battle plan to redeem you from sin and not make provisions to cleanse you of sin's disrepair? Why would God sacrifice His Only Son to rectify His relationship with a sickly, diseased creation?

A man does not lay down good money for a rusty, beat-up jalopy unless he knows he can tune it up, shine it up, and get it back on the road. Likewise, God did not lay down His Son's life so that our beat-up "earthsuits" could sit in heaven's front yard and rust.

If you are saved by the blood of Jesus Christ and you know it, you're redeemed! You are on your way to heaven. Sin's curse is broken. Therefore, if you believe God's Word on salvation, there's no reason why you should not believe that you are also healed.

The same immunized blood that saved your soul was shed as well for the healing of your body. This is not just a factual promise; it's a Bible truth.

What is the difference between fact and truth? Facts are temporal; they can falter. The scientific community is always updating their information. More often than not, when their influx of data is amended and the details of their studies are analyzed, the house of cards they've built with facts usually falls.

On the other hand, truth is eternal, an absolute. It is a reality of fixed law which has been established from the beginning of time itself.

"Forever, O Lord," Psalm 119:89 proclaims, "thy word is settled in heaven."

God's Word never changes. He is the Way, the Truth, and the Life. Every syllable of prophecy in the scriptures has been fulfilled. Everything that God said would happen up to this day has happened without fail.

His words are life. When He speaks, it is always the truth and the truth cannot be changed.

If your doctor tells you that you have only six weeks to live, don't worry; he's just reporting the temporal facts. Instead of panicking, you should start praising, for temporal facts can never stand up to God's eternal Word.

> I create the fruit of the lips; Peace, peace
> to him that is far off, and to him that is
> near, saith the LORD; and I will heal him.
> —ISAIAH 57:19

In the midst of adversity, you can have peace. No matter where you are, near or far, in a church pew or lying on a surgeon's table, God's words of truth and healing are potent and available.

> He sent his word, and healed them, and
> delivered them from their destructions.
> —PSALM 107:20

If you will simply listen to God's truth rather than to man's facts, you can easily tap into His heavenly healing benefits.

This gift from God requires only our simple participation to gain its benefits. Though you are not responsible to perform your healing, it is a basic requirement, however, that you initiate your miracle by displaying your belief. Faith will not work without corresponding actions.

ACTION = EXPECTATION

Throughout both the Old and New Testaments, God demanded that the sick act on their belief in His healing power, so that His supernatural flow might be released. A good example of this process is found in the story of Naaman.

As the victorious captain of Syria's armies, Naaman was a tough man and held great favor with his king. However, Naaman was also a leper. Upon hearing of Israel's God, he was sent by his king to visit the nation and inquire if anything could be done to relieve his malady. Hearing about Naaman's plight, the prophet Elisha sent a message to the Syrian captain. The prophet simply told Naaman to...

Go and wash in Jordan [river] seven

times, and thy flesh shall come again to
thee, and thou shalt be clean.

—2 KINGS 5:10

Just like many in today's society, Naaman was
somewhat put out by Elisha's uncomplicated
request. To this Syrian captain, the prophet's
informality was confusing.

> I thought, He will surely come out to me,
> and stand, and call on the name of the
> LORD his God, and strike his hand over
> the place, and recover the leper. Are not
> Abana and Pharpar, rivers of Damascus,
> better than all the waters of Israel? May
> I not wash in them, and be clean? So he
> turned and went away in a rage.
>
> —2 KINGS 5:11–12

The muddy state of the Jordan River had nothing to do with Naaman's healing. The real issue
here was his stubborn state of mind. It took one of
his own servants to finally show him that he was
making something easy into something hard.

> If the prophet had bid thee do some
> great thing, wouldest thou not have
> done it? How much rather then, when
> he saith to thee, Wash, and be clean?
>
> —2 KINGS 5:13

Seeing his servant's logic, Naaman calmed down and turned toward the river.

> Then went he down, and dipped himself seven times in Jordan, according to the saying of the man of God: and his flesh came again like unto the flesh of a little child, and he was clean.
>
> —2 KINGS 5:14

Coming up out of the muddy water that first time, nothing changed. Likewise, breaking the surface a second time didn't seem to make any difference. Three, four, five, even six times more Naaman immersed himself in the Jordan, but nothing happened. However, when he broke the water line the seventh and final time, something miraculous took place; he was clean! The Syrian captain's healing came only after he obeyed.

To obey someone, you have to believe in him. Therefore, the act of obedience is a form of faith, and faith is God's only requirement for healing.

When we act on our faith, we display our expectation that healing is on the way.

Christ's healing of the man's withered hand, in Matthew 12:13, was manifested only after the man took an active role—and did some stretching.

Remember, the atmosphere of expectation is the birthplace of miracles. Never was that atmosphere

more highly charged than the day Jesus passed by
an ailing woman who suffered with an issue of
blood.

Like the man with the deformed hand, this
woman's protracted predicament had long since
withered away all hope for her recovery. The
woman's situation seemed terminal, irreversible—
up until that day Jesus passed by.

> And a woman having an issue of blood
> twelve years, which had spent all her liv-
> ing upon physicians, neither could be
> healed of any, came behind him and
> touched the border of his garment: and
> immediately her issue of blood stanched.
> And Jesus said, Who touched me?. . .
> I perceive that virtue is gone out of me
> . . . and falling down before him, she
> declared unto him before all the people
> for what cause she had touched him,
> and how she was healed immediately.
> And He said unto her, Daughter, be of
> good comfort: thy faith hath made thee
> whole; go in peace.
>
> —LUKE 8:43–48

Using what little energy she had, this woman
fought a large crowd just to touch the clothes of
Jesus. What made this frail woman do such a

thing? *Expectation.*

Watching Christ and His large group of follow-ers pass by, the ailing woman began to think on all that she had heard about this Man of Miracles. She recalled how He had opened blind eyes and caused the lame to walk. As she thought on these things, the notion began to well up in her spirit that if He could do those things for others, Jesus could change her circumstances, too.

Sparked by that belief, she sprang to her feet, and acted on it. Stepping into the passing crowd, the woman began to push and shove her way through the pack. With each step, her faith increased. Ignoring twelve painful years of disap-pointment, she fixed her eyes on the Man up front, and elbowed her way forward.

Finally, the sick woman came within reach of God's Son. Extending her arm toward Him through the bump and jostle of the crowd, the woman with the issue of blood strained and stretched until her spindly fingers caught hold of Christ's garment.

Upon contact, her twelve-year-old disorder immediately disappeared. In that instant, the dis-ease which had tainted her blood was no longer an issue.

You don't reach out for something unless you

expect to get it.

This determined woman stretched out her hand, and by that act, she communicated to her situation her strong belief in the power of Jesus Christ. By that demonstration of faith, her irreversible circumstances changed.

One hand reached for a tree . . .
another was nailed to it.

chapter five

SPEAK THE WORD

If the Lord and His Word never change,
and if He created life with a spoken
thought, then He is still able
to speak into existence
whatever you need today.

Satan never relinquishes his stronghold over you just because you are uncomfortable. You have to show him who's boss. And nothing gets your message across faster than when you reach out, speak the name of Jesus and expect an answer.

In the middle of a tempestuous, wave-crashing storm, the apostle Peter called on Christ's name. However, the extraordinary thing about this particular petition is that he actually believed that Jesus would answer it!

> The boat was already a considerable distance from land, buffeted by the waves because the wind was against it. During the fourth watch of the night Jesus went out to them, walking on the lake. When the disciples saw him walking on the

> lake, they were terrified. "It's a ghost,"
> they said, and cried out in fear.
>
> But Jesus immediately said to them:
> "Take courage! It is I. Don't be afraid."
>
> "Lord, if it's you," Peter replied, "tell
> me to come to you on the water."
>
> "Come," He said. Then Peter got
> down out of the boat, walked on the
> water and came toward Jesus.
>
> —MATTHEW 14:24–29, NIV

Hearing the answer to his incredible request, Peter threw his leg over the side of the wind-tossed ship and lowered himself onto the sea. His actions were simple, yet powerful.

Having faith in Jesus, Simon Peter ignored the roaring waves and literally acted as if it were a common, everyday occurrence to do the impossible.

He didn't dance a jig or offer up an animal sacrifice; Peter simply threw his leg over the side—as if he were actually going somewhere!

His faith, coupled with the Son of God's one word, "Come," pushed all indecision out of the picture. Instantly, all of the necessary elements locked into place to allow a mere human being to walk on water.

The power of faith is simply concentrating more on what you and God can do to the waves, than what the waves can do to you.

Take, for example, Craig and Judy Bickle. For this young couple, it seemed the waves were far too high. The storm they faced almost pulled them under. As a matter of fact, the doctor's report claimed that Craig was, "...drowning from the inside out."

BELIEVING IS CONCEIVING

A stabbing pain in his lungs yanked him from his sleep. In an instant, Craig was sitting straight up in bed.

Awakened by the commotion, Judy opened her eyes and slowly became aware of her husband's strange gasping. In their two years of marriage, he had never shown any sign of illness. In fact, Craig had never been sick a day in all of his twenty-five years, that is, until that moment.

At the Emergency Room, a chaotic parade of doctors, nurses, tubes, and needles surrounded the young man. In the waiting room, Judy was likewise encompassed by her concerned family. In the wee hours of that morning, they held each other and hoped.

Evaluating their results, the medical staff considered a number of possibilities, but eventually the prognosis was clear—young Craig Bickle had fallen victim to acute pneumonia.

Under normal conditions, such news would have been tragic, but for this twosome, the diagnosis was especially crushing. For close to three months, the Bickles had been attending our church, where divine healing is proclaimed in every service.

In fact, only two weeks before the appearance of Craig's illness, the couple had publicly experienced the baptism of the Holy Spirit in the church's sanctuary. Therefore, when the doctor calmly stated, "You're drowning from the inside out; you are not going to make it," the Bickles' natural reaction was despair, questions, and doubt.

"Here we are, Lord," Judy whispered, "we've given our lives to You; we've been filled with Your Spirit—and now this happens to my husband?"

When they exchanged their dry, denominational background for the faith-filled atmosphere of World Harvest Church, the Bickles felt they had been given a new lease on life. There they had witnessed firsthand unexplainable miracles. They had taken to heart the Spirit-led messages that were preached every time the doors were opened.

But now in the hospital, it seemed that the doctor's devastating words echoed louder than

God's Word. It looked as though the small print in their new lease on life concealed a clause of "early eviction."

Medically, the only recourse was to drain the pneumatic fluid from Craig's infected lungs. This continual process kept him alive, but it also weakened his respiratory system. In no time, Judy's once robust husband was seventy pounds thinner.

Although I frequently visited his hospital bedside with words of expectation and encouragement, the tangible evidence of Craig's dwindling condition could not—and would not—be ignored.

With each labored breath, the ailing young Christian and his wife found it harder to conceive the notion of Simon Peter's kind of faith. It was a struggle.

Alone one Wednesday evening, Judy entered the sanctuary of the church. Late for the service, she slipped into a space on the back pew and listened to the upbeat choruses resounding over the clapping, hand-waving crowd. Having spent so many hours in the antiseptic solitude of a hospital, she felt good to be in such an energetic, positive atmosphere.

Suddenly the music stopped. As the reverberations faded, the young housewife recognized a familiar voice coming thorough the sanctuary speakers. After a moment, she realized that the voice was speaking to—her!

"Judy!" I called out from the platform, "Judy Bickle, come down here!"

Disoriented momentarily, she felt her heart beat faster. Then without thinking, she instinctively stepped into the aisle and made her way down front, where I stood waiting.

As Judy approached, I informed the congregation of her husband's situation, and a swell of prayers began to rise throughout the church. Likewise, I raised my voice in prayer, speaking words of faith for Craig's immediate healing.

Then suddenly, the Spirit spoke to me. Placing my hand over the microphone, I leaned down to Judy's ear and whispered, "Have you and Craig been wanting children?"

I could see the surprise and confusion in her eyes. But after a moment, she wrinkled her brow and slowly nodded yes.

Then out of nowhere, I again felt the Spirit's leading. Raising the microphone, I heard my voice blare over the sanctuary's speakers, "You are going to conceive!"

As my words echoed throughout the building, Judy's mind raced. "My husband is lying at death's door…and I-I-I'm gonna have a b-b-baby?"

Though I was surprised by my statement, I could see that she was stunned. "I'm sorry," I recalled whispering in her direction, "I can't believe I'm telling you this." Yet before I could even inhale my next breath, I raised the microphone once again and declared, "By the way, it will be a girl."

As the crowded church erupted in praise, I felt a wave of prophetic words begin to flow, "She will be a mighty warrior for God...Many will be her fruits...and many will eat of her fruits...Even the world will be amazed at the things she will do..."

In that instant, Judy Bickle conceived the notion of faith. Listening to those words spoken with conviction, she no longer struggled to believe. Although Craig lay in a bed fighting for breath, she clung to what she had heard, and believed that they were words of life—sent directly to her and Craig from the Throne of God.

"It was like a gift of faith," she remembers. "I just received it as mine. I didn't care how or when, just that it was going to happen!"

Later that evening, smiling Judy Bickle sat on her husband's bed and lovingly announced, "I went to church tonight. Pastor Parsley prayed for you. And guess what? God told him and me and everyone in the church that we are going to have a baby!"

Looking up from his pillow, Craig simply drew in a breath and grinned...

Eight months later, everyone was breathing easier—especially Craig Bickle. Accomplishing what the doctors said could not be done, he was now 100 percent fully recovered and back to work.

The couple's simple belief in God's healing Word conceived the notion of Craig's complete recovery. Their choice to listen to God, rather than to the roaring waves of man's temporal facts, set in motion events that renewed their lease on life.

Coming home from work one afternoon, Craig entered the house, tossed his keys on the counter and called out to his wife, "Judy, I'm home." But his only answer was the "r-r-ring" of the telephone. It was the doctor's office.

"Is this the Bickle residence?"

"Yes," Craig replied, controlling his apprehension.

"We just received the test results," the stoic voice on the other end began, "the doctor thought it best that you should know right away..."

Sitting down, Bickle gripped the receiver tightly in his hand.

"According to our findings, it looks like you are going...to have a baby!"

Before the last syllable was even spoken, Craig's

lungs filled to capacity and he let out a "whoopie!" that yanked him straight out of his chair.

This time, the doctor's facts harmonized with God's eternal, healing truth. And in no time, a chaotic parade of family and friends showered them with gifts for their new addition.

"God turned it all around," Craig remembers. He healed me! What God has done for us, surely He will do for all who will call on His name!"

Whatever you need: hope, help, healing, or even the patter of little feet around the house, if you put your trust in God's words of life and believe, ANY-THING you need—can be conceived.

FAITH COMETH BY... READING

Right now, specific parts of your body may be in so much pain that you would like to throw them over the side of a boat and be done with it, but that kind of attitude will only make your discomfort worse. You've got to stop focusing on the physical, and begin centering your attention on the spiritual. You'll never walk on the waves if you're sinking in despair.

To build up your faith to the level that the Bickles displayed, you have to do what Peter and the rest of the disciples did: walk and talk with

Jesus on a daily basis.

In our modern world, such a thing can still be accomplished—and no complicated ritual of man or religion is necessary. By simply applying the power of God's Word through consistent study and prayer, you can have the kind of personal, one-on-one relationship with the Creator that was originally intended back in Eden's Garden.

In a mutual relationship, both parties get to know one another. God already knows you. He knew you before you were even born. By studying the holy Scriptures, you, in turn, can learn about Him and what He is capable of doing on your behalf. Through that consistent mind-renewing process, your expectation expands.

The more you know, the more faith grows. Diligent study of the scriptures reprograms your brain to the principles of God. It fine-tunes your spirit to His holy will.

> This book of the law shall not depart out of thy mouth; but thou shalt meditate therein day and night, that thou mayest observe to do according to all that is written therein: for then thou shalt make thy way prosperous, and then thou shalt have good success.
>
> —JOSHUA 1:8

Meditating "therein day and night" is simply storing up the Word of God in your spirit. It is opening the Bible and learning the 7,000-plus promises which God has put there "in writing" just for you. It is consistently applying those promises to your condition, day and night.

Learning the Godly guarantees which deal with your situation and rehearsing them over and over in your spirit will help you, like Peter, to possess the kind of faith that makes the impossible an everyday occurrence.

> Thy faith hath made thee whole.
> —MATTHEW 9:22

> Then touched he their eyes, saying, According to your faith be it unto you. And their eyes were opened.
> —MATTHEW 9:29–30

> And all things, whatsoever ye shall ask in prayer, believing, ye shall receive.
> —MATTHEW 21:22

> If ye abide in me, and my words abide in you, ye shall ask what ye will, and it shall be done unto you.
> —JOHN 15:7

Get a word from God—and stick with it. Even

if you have to paper your walls with little yellow "stick 'em" notes, keep His words of faith and healing always before you.

> Incline thine ear unto my sayings...for they are life...and health.
> —PROVERBS 4:20, 22

God's truth-filled Word will always outlive your circumstances, because the Word, like God Himself, never changes. The apostle John put it best:

> In the beginning was the Word, and the Word was with God, and the Word was God. The same was in the beginning with God. All things were made by him; and without him was not any thing made that was made.
>
> —JOHN 1:1–3

In the beginning, He spoke the Word, and out of the nothingness of space, there was suddenly—life! Using just His Word, God invented the sun, the moon, and endless galaxies of stars. But when it came to the creation of man, the Lord lovingly formed us with His Own hands.

He fashioned us using a rare combination of earthly flesh, a soul of free will, and a priceless eternal spirit "tuned" to Him.

This loving God, who never changes, cared for us so much that when we freely chose to fall into Satan's contaminated clutch, He didn't dust us off His hands and try again; He declared war and put into motion a purification plan.

Reading His Word, it is obvious that God took upon Himself "the hard part" and willingly sacrificed His Own Son, so that through Christ's immunized blood, we are forgiven, purified, and able to choose again.

Even today, because of the cross, Satan's authority is broken. The serpent's puny arsenal of sickness is now nothing but a pesky fly, which we could easily swat—if we would simply choose to believe.

Like Christ in the Garden of Gethsemane, we must stop focusing on the physical and turn our attention to the Spirit of God within us. By doing so, we can easily overcome Satan's smoke screen of disease and selfish desire. All it takes is faith—an unwavering expectation in the promises of God's Word.

If through the "filter" of the old blood covenant the Lord was able to declare, "I am the God that healeth thee," then at the cross of Calvary, through the immunized blood of His Son, how much better for us is God's healing Word?

If the Lord and His Word never change, and if He created life with a spoken thought, then He is still able to speak into existence whatever you need today. Healing is not hard. It is as simple and easy as saying, "I believe Your Word, Lord. Now speak. Create new life in me."

GOD'S WORD ON HEALING
TO RECEIVE HEALING, SIN MUST BE CLEANSED

> If my people, which are called by my name, shall humble themselves, and pray, and seek my face, and turn from their wicked ways; then will I hear from heaven, and will forgive their sin, and will heal their land.
>
> —2 CHRONICLES 7:14

> I said, LORD, be merciful unto me: heal my soul; for I have sinned against thee.
>
> —PSALM 41:4

> I have seen his ways, and will heal him: I will lead him also, and restore comforts unto him and to his mourners.
>
> —ISAIAH 57:18

> Then shall thy light break forth as the morning, and thine health shall spring forth speedily: and thy righteousness

shall go before thee; the glory of the
LORD shall be thy reward.

—ISAIAH 58:8

Return, ye backsliding children, and I
will heal your backslidings. Behold, we
come unto thee; for thou art the LORD
our God.

—JEREMIAH 3:22

Heal me, O LORD, and I shall be healed;
save me, and I shall be saved: for thou art
my praise.

—JEREMIAH 17:14

For I will restore health unto thee, and I
will heal thee of thy wounds, saith the
LORD; because they called thee an
Outcast, saying, This is Zion, whom no
man seeketh after.

—JEREMIAH 30:17

Behold, I will bring it health and cure,
and I will cure them, and will reveal unto
them the abundance of peace and truth.

—JEREMIAH 33:6

Come, and let us return unto the LORD:
for he hath torn, and he will heal us; he
hath smitten, and he will bind us up.

—HOSEA 6:1

I will heal their backsliding, I will love them freely: for mine anger is turned away from him.

—HOSEA 14:4

O LORD my God, I cried unto thee, and thou hast healed me.

—PSALM 30:2

Why art thou cast down, O my soul? and why art thou disquieted within me? hope thou in God: for I shall yet praise him, who is the health of my countenance, and my God.

—PSALM 42:11

He healeth the broken in heart, and bindeth up their wounds.

—PSALM 147:3

A wicked messenger falleth into mischief: but a faithful ambassador is health.

—PROVERBS 13:17

The centurion answered and said, Lord, I am not worthy that thou shouldest come under my roof: but speak the word only, and my servant shall be healed.

—MATTHEW 8:8

And make straight paths for your feet, lest that which is lame be turned out of the way; but let it rather be healed.

—HEBREWS 12:13

Confess your faults one to another, and pray one for another, that ye may be healed. The effectual fervent prayer of a righteous man availeth much.

—JAMES 5:16

Beloved, I wish above all things that thou mayest prosper and be in health, even as thy soul prospereth.

—3 JOHN 2

Who forgiveth all thine iniquities; who healeth all thy diseases.

—PSALM 103:3

FAITH BRINGS HEALING

And when he heard of Jesus, he sent unto him the elders of the Jews, beseeching him that he would come and heal his servant.

—LUKE 7:3

For she said within herself, If I may but touch his garment, I shall be whole. But Jesus turned him about, and when he saw her, he said, Daughter, be of good comfort; thy faith hath made thee whole. And the woman was made whole from that hour.

—MATTHEW 9:21–22

And when Jesus departed thence, two blind men followed him, crying, and saying, Thou son of David, have mercy on us. And when he was come into the house, the blind men came to him: and Jesus saith unto them, Believe ye that I am able to do this? They said unto him, Yea, Lord. Then touched he their eyes, saying, According to your faith be it unto you. And their eyes were opened; and Jesus straitly charged them, saying, See that no man know it.

—MATTHEW 9:27–30

While he spake these things unto them, behold, there came a certain ruler, and worshipped him, saying, My daughter is even now dead: but come and lay thy hand upon her, and she shall live.

—MATTHEW 9:18

And when Jesus came into the ruler's house, and saw the minstrels and the people making a noise, He said unto them, Give place: for the maid is not dead, but sleepeth. And they laughed him to scorn. But when the people were put forth, he went in, and took her by

the hand, and the maid arose.
—MATTHEW 9:23–25

HIS WORD ISSUES HEALING

He sent his word, and healed them, and delivered them from their destructions.
—PSALM 107:20

And he sent them to preach the kingdom of God, and to heal the sick.
—LUKE 9:2

And they departed, and went through the towns, preaching the gospel, and healing everywhere.
—LUKE 9:6

And the people, when they knew it, followed him: and he received them, and spake unto them of the kingdom of God, and healed them that had need of healing.
—LUKE 9:11

And Jesus said unto the centurion, Go thy way; and as thou hast believed, so be it done unto thee. And his servant was healed in the selfsame hour.
—MATTHEW 8:13

Wherefore neither thought I myself
worthy to come unto thee: but say in a
word, and my servant shall be healed.

—LUKE 7:7

JESUS CHRIST IS HEALING PERSONIFIED

But he was wounded for our transgressions, he was bruised for our iniquities:
the chastisement of our peace was upon
him; and with his stripes we are healed.

—ISAIAH 53:5

And Jesus saith unto him, I will come
and heal him.

—MATTHEW 8:7

And when he had called unto him his
twelve disciples, he gave them power
against unclean spirits, to cast them out,
and to heal all manner of sickness and all
manner of disease.

—MATTHEW 10:1

And a woman having an issue of blood
twelve years…Came behind him, and
touched the border of his garment: and
immediately her issue of blood stanched.

—LUKE 8:43–44

And Jesus went forth, and saw a great multitude, and was moved with compassion toward them, and he healed their sick.

—MATTHEW 14:14

And great multitudes came unto him, having with them those that were lame, blind, dumb, maimed, and many others, and cast them down at Jesus' feet; and he healed them.

—MATTHEW 15:30

Heal the sick, cleanse the lepers, raise the dead, cast out devils: freely ye have received, freely give.

—MATTHEW 10:8

And he healed many that were sick of divers diseases, and cast out many devils; and suffered not the devils to speak, because they knew him.

—MARK 1:34

And they that were vexed with unclean spirits: and they were healed.

—LUKE 6:18

They also which saw it told them by what means he that was possessed of the devils was healed.

—LUKE 8:36

For unclean spirits, crying with loud voice, came out of many that were possessed with them: and many taken with palsies, and that were lame, were healed.

—ACTS 8:7

And as the lame man which was healed held Peter and John, all the people ran together unto them in the porch that is called Solomon's, greatly wondering.

—ACTS 3:11

And beholding the man which was healed standing with them, they could say nothing against it.

—ACTS 4:14

There came also a multitude out of the cities round about unto Jerusalem, bringing sick folks, and them which were vexed with unclean spirits: and they were healed every one.

—ACTS 5:16

And it came to pass, that the father of Publius lay sick of a fever and of a bloody flux: to whom Paul entered in, and prayed, and laid his hands on him, and healed him.

—ACTS 28:8

Who his own self bare our sins in his own body on the tree, that we, being dead to sins, should live unto righteousness: by whose stripes ye were healed.

—1 PETER 2:24

How God anointed Jesus of Nazareth with the Holy Ghost and with power: who went about doing good, and healing all that were oppressed of the devil; for God was with him.

—ACTS 10:38

HEALING IS FOR EVERYONE

And great multitudes followed him; and he healed them there.

—MATTHEW 19:2

For he had healed many; insomuch that they pressed upon him for to touch him, as many as had plagues.

—MARK 3:10

And straightway the fountain of her blood was dried up; and she felt in her body that she was healed of that plague.

—MARK 5:29

Now when the sun was setting, all they that had any sick with divers diseases brought them unto him; and he laid his hands on every one of them, and healed them.

—LUKE 4:40

And the whole multitude sought to touch him: for there went virtue out of him, and healed them all.

—LUKE 6:19

THE RESULT OF HEALING IS PRAISE

And one of them, when he saw that he was healed, turned back, and with a loud voice glorified God.

—LUKE 17:15

Now Peter and John went up together into the temple at the hour of prayer, being the ninth hour. And a certain man lame from his mother's womb was carried, whom they laid daily at the gate of the temple which is called Beautiful, to ask alms of them that entered into the temple; Who seeing Peter and John about to go into the temple asked an alms. And Peter, fastening his eyes upon him with John, said, Look on us. And he gave heed unto them, expecting to receive something of them.

Then Peter said, Silver and gold have I none; but such as I have give I thee: In the name of Jesus Christ of Nazareth rise up and walk. And he took him by the right hand, and lifted him up: and immediately his feet and ankle bones received strength. And he leaping up stood, and walked, and entered with them into the temple, walking, and leaping, and praising God.

—ACTS 3:1–8

And it came to pass on a certain day, as he was teaching, that there were Pharisees and doctors of the law sitting by, which were come out of every town of Galilee, and Judaea, and Jerusalem: and the power of the Lord was present to heal them.

And, behold, men brought in a bed a man which was taken with a palsy: and they sought means to bring him in, and to lay him before him. And when they could not find by what way they might bring him in because of the multitude, they went upon the housetop, and let him down through the tiling with his couch into the midst before Jesus.

And when he saw their faith, he said unto him, Man, thy sins are forgiven thee. And the scribes and the Pharisees began to reason, saying, Who is this which speaketh blasphemies? Who can forgive sins, but God alone?

But when Jesus perceived their thoughts, he answering said unto them, What reason ye in your hearts? Whether is easier, to say, Thy sins be forgiven thee; or to say, Rise up and walk? But that ye may know that the Son of man hath power upon earth to forgive sins, (he said unto the sick of the palsy,) I say unto thee, Arise, and take up thy couch, and go into thine house. And immediately he rose up before them, and took up that whereon he lay, and departed to his own house, glorifying God.

—LUKE 5:17–25

And he was teaching in one of the synagogues on the sabbath. And, behold, there was a woman which had a spirit of infirmity eighteen years, and was bowed together, and could in no wise lift up herself. And when Jesus saw her, he called her to him, and said unto her, Woman, thou art loosed from thine infirmity. And he laid his hands on her: and immediately she was made straight, and glorified God.

—LUKE 13:10–13

And one of them, when he saw that he was healed, turned back, and with a loud voice glorified God, And fell down on his face at his feet, giving him thanks: and he was a Samaritan.

—LUKE 17:15–16

And Jesus said unto him, Receive thy sight: thy faith hath saved thee. And immediately he received his sight, and followed him, glorifying God: and all the people, when they saw it, gave praise unto God.

—LUKE 18:42–43

OTHER BOOKS BY ROD PARSLEY

Ancient Wells, Living Water
Could It Be?
Daily Breakthrough
The Day Before Eternity
He Came First
No Dry Season (Bestseller)
No More Crumbs (Bestseller)
On the Brink (#1 Bestseller)
Repairers of the Breach

For more information about Breakthrough,
World Harvest Church,
World Harvest Bible College,
Harvest Preparatory School,
or to receive a product
list of the many books,
audio and video tapes by
Rod Parsley, write or call:

Breakthrough
P. O. Box 32932
Columbus, OH 43232-0932
(614) 837-1990 (Office)

World Harvest Bible College
P. O. Box 32901
Columbus, OH 43232-0901
(614) 837-4088
www.worldharvestbiblecollege.org

Harvest Preparatory School
P. O. Box 32903
Columbus, OH 43232-0903
(614) 837-1990
www.harvestprep.org

If you need prayer, Breakthrough Prayer Warriors
are ready to pray with you
24 hours a day, 7 days a week at:
(614) 837-3232

Visit Rod Parsley at his website address:
www.breakthrough.net

PRAISE FOR THE

"Among the best crime fiction ever written."
—*San Jose Mercury News*

The Chalk Girl

"A complex, gritty thriller. . . hard to put down."
—*Kirkus Reviews*

Find Me

"A terrific find: a tightly wrapped, expert combination of suspense, mystery, and showstopping character."
—*The New York Times*

Winter House

"Scores on all levels. A densely plotted modern gothic and police procedural in one. O'Connell keeps the tension and suspense high right through to the surprising end."
—*Detroit Free Press*

Dead Famous

"Mallory returns with a vengeance and in total control . . . blazingly original. Once again, O'Connell transcends the genre." —*Kirkus Reviews* (starred review)

continued . . .

Crime School

"Easily one of the most original and striking crime fiction protagonists to appear in the last few years . . . Multilayered, serpentine in plot . . . a rich, evocative novel."
—*St. Petersburg Times*

Shell Game

"Rich, complex, memorable . . . another superb effort from one of our most gifted writers." —*Booklist* (starred review)

Stone Angel

"A hard-edged, brilliant, and indomitable heroine. *Stone Angel*, as much Southern novel as mystery novel, is rich in people, places, and customs vividly realized, with mordant humor, terror, and sadness." —*San Francisco Chronicle*

Killing Critics

"Darkly stylish . . . highly original . . . This is great fun."
—*Chicago Tribune*

The Man Who Cast Two Shadows

"Beautifully written." —*Harper's Bazaar*

"The suspense is excruciating." —*Detroit Free Press*

Mallory's Oracle

"One of the most unique, interesting, and surprising heroines you've ever come across in any work of fiction."
—Nelson DeMille

"Wild, sly, and breathless—all the things that a good thriller ought to be."
—Carl Hiaasen

PRAISE FOR

Bone by Bone

"Ingenious . . . dizzying . . . [a] serpentine story."
—*The New York Times*

"Pulses with a gothic noir . . . this is one of those books you can't put down."
—*The Boston Globe*

PRAISE FOR

The Judas Child

"Breathtakingly ambitious suspense . . . A brilliant twist . . . mesmerizing."
—*Minneapolis Star Tribune*

"Her most stunning novel yet . . . more chilling, twisted, and intense with each page . . . [a] soul-shattering climax."
—*Booklist* (starred review)

CAROL
O'CONNELL

it happens
in the
DARK

BERKLEY BOOKS
New York

THE BERKLEY PUBLISHING GROUP
Published by the Penguin Group
Penguin Group (USA) LLC
375 Hudson Street, New York, New York 10014

USA • Canada • UK • Ireland • Australia • New Zealand • India • South Africa • China

penguin.com

A Penguin Random House Company

IT HAPPENS IN THE DARK

A Berkley Book / published by arrangement with the author

Copyright © 2013 by Carol O'Connell.
Penguin supports copyright. Copyright fuels creativity, encourages diverse voices,
promotes free speech, and creates a vibrant culture. Thank you for buying an authorized
edition of this book and for complying with copyright laws by not reproducing, scanning,
or distributing any part of it in any form without permission. You are supporting writers
and allowing Penguin to continue to publish books for every reader.

BERKLEY® is a registered trademark of Penguin Group (USA) LLC.
The "B" design is a trademark of Penguin Group (USA) LLC.

For information, address: The Berkley Publishing Group,
a division of Penguin Group (USA) LLC,
375 Hudson Street, New York, New York 10014.

ISBN: 978-0-425-27087-5

PUBLISHING HISTORY
G. P. Putnam's Sons hardcover edition / August 2013
Berkley premium edition / August 2014

PRINTED IN THE UNITED STATES OF AMERICA

10 9 8 7 6 5 4 3 2 1

Cover photograph: Stage lights © Dhoxax/Shutterstock.
Cover design by Andrea Ho.

This is a work of fiction. Names, characters, places, and incidents either are the product
of the author's imagination or are used fictitiously, and any resemblance to actual persons,
living or dead, business establishments, events, or locales is entirely coincidental.

If you purchased this book without a cover, you should be aware that this book is
stolen property. It was reported as "unsold and destroyed" to the publisher, and neither
the author nor the publisher has received any payment for this "stripped book."

A PHOTOGRAPHIC MEMORY

I have a black-and-white photograph of four children on a beach in Paradise. That's how they remembered years of their childhood in the tropics on the Isle of Pines, the setting for Robert Louis Stevenson's Treasure Island.

There are palm trees in the background, and the children wear swimsuits. Marion, grinning, perches on driftwood and cuddles her younger sister, Martha. Norman stands behind them, the oldest child, the serious one. In the foreground is little George, who tells terrible jokes, and yet he gets laughs.

A perfect day. Paradise in a snapshot.

Later, the family orange grove will be lost in a fire, and their father will work in a sugarcane factory to earn the passage money back to Boston. On the boat ride home, the children will lose all the Spanish words they knew. Still ahead of them is a global war, uniforms, guns and weddings, USO dances, jazz and jitterbug, an exciting time to be alive—so alive. An atomic bomb will fall, a mushroom cloud will bloom. Their families will grow through more wars, through an upheaval of technology and social revolution, more weddings, funerals, lots of christenings, as the four of them move through history, brothers and sisters.

One child on that beach in the photograph, Martha Olsen, died this past September. She was my aunt. She was the last. They are all gone.

ACKNOWLEDGMENTS AND
APOLOGIES TO REAL LIFE

Though downplayed in the book, Manhattan's Midtown North police are so good they won a Tony Award for service to the Theater District. Also, the local unions would have you know that they protect their artists and artisans much better than I do, and union-card holders are rarely—in fact, never—*murdered this way.*

ROLLO: To cadge a line from Blake,
"Sooner strangle an infant
in its cradle than to nurse
unacted desires." (He turns
to Susan.) Oh . . . sorry.
Did that make you nervous?
—<u>The Brass Bed</u>, Act I

1

The Theater District did not shut down for winter storms. East and west of the Great White Way, streets were electrified. Bright lights and the dazzle of animated signs hawked comedy and drama, dance and song. Up and down the sidewalks, ticket holders shielded their eyes with mittens and gloves to gawk at the gaudy marquees.

Peter Beck's bare hands were jammed into his pockets, and, head bowed, he only saw the pavement. His scarf was a crusted band of ice, feeble protection from stinging snow, but it served to hide the playwright's moving lips. His voice was low, and so there was no fair warning for passersby. If other pedestrians had seen his face, they might have found him odd, but, had they heard what he was saying, they would have given a wide berth to the mumbling man who was alternately angry and insanely sad.

The woolen cap was ripped from his scalp, and he turned back to watch it sail over a lamppost on the corner of Forty-ninth Street and Broadway. He raised one naked hand, and it was an effort to form his numb fingers into a fist. *"Thieving wind!"*

His other enemies were all theater folk.

He was done with crying, but the tears had not dried. They had frozen. Muttering, shivering, Peter walked past the theater's main entrance, where he might well be told to wait in line. Farther down the sidewalk, he paused at the stage door, but decided against the humiliation of proving his worthiness to a rent-a-cop and perhaps being turned away if his name was not on the list of those who had made the cut.

When he had rounded a corner and then another to enter a blind alley, the wind was at his back, blowing him down the narrow lane of fire escapes and Dumpsters to a dead end at the rear door. And there was the damn security guard he had hoped to avoid. The stranger in the tri-cornered cap hunched beneath a glass-caged lightbulb, smoking a cigarette.

Would this man stop him? Oh, let him *try*.

As Peter reached for the doorknob, he knew there would be no challenge. He was invisible to the guard. At best, he was perceived as insignificant. And then there was that other word, the one used by women to neuter men—*harmless*.

Well, not tonight!

After the final curtain, the whole theater company, players to grunts, would bow to him on bended knee, wet their pants and crawl away.

Once he was inside, the alley door banged shut behind him, and Peter's fingers, red as lobsters, fumbled with the buttons of his overcoat. As he made his way toward the broad scenery flats, the backstage lights flickered. Apparently, the glitches in the wiring were an ongoing thing. He looked up to see the young lighting tech, a tall stick with big feet, clambering down the catwalk ladder to stand with a pimple-faced stagehand in the wings. Neither of them gave so much as a nod to the sad man swaddled in wet, black wool.

Had he been *stark naked*, they would not have acknowledged him.

Snowflakes melted on Peter's shoulders and his hatless, almost hairless head. Unwinding his scarf as he walked, he glanced at the blackboard on the wall behind the stage manager's desk.

He stopped.

And his heart stopped—

For one beat—

Two beats.

New line changes were scrawled on the slate in white block letters. Opening night had come and gone, but the play was still evolving by an unseen hand, a chalk-wielding haunt, who gave new meaning to the word *ghostwriter*.

The playwright burped. A hiccup followed. The floor tilted and spun.

Hours ago, Peter Beck had left his apartment, dead drunk, and then lost both his gloves in two different bars twixt home and the theater. Listing to one side, he nearly toppled over when he heard the warning call, "Curtain in thirty minutes!" Threatening to pitch forward with every step, he lurched down a short flight of stairs to find his seat in the audience before—

The lobby doors opened wide, and people were coming down the aisles.

Peter found a place card on his reserved chair in the front row—but not front-row *center*. He had been shunted off toward a wall, brushed aside by a lackey's seating arrangements. More cards appeared on three neighboring seats, and these were marked for the playwright's guests, though he had invited no one.

Lacking the energy to shrug off his heavy coat, saving his strength for the final act, he sat down and fell asleep. Now and then, his watery eyes opened to catch snatches of the night. The front row was filled to his right. On his left side, the three complimentary seats remained empty, advertising that he was a man with no friends, certainly none among the cast and crew. He had missed the first performance, and not one of those bastards had thought to call and ask if he was well—or had he done them all the favor of a final exit, perhaps a long fall from some high window.

Rousing from lethargy for a slow turn of the head, he counted the house. According to the only critic in attendance last night, the play had opened to a sparse audience of twenty souls in a space built to hold more than a thousand—though not a bad turnout for foul weather, a theater with a blank marquee and a play with no advertising. Ah, but owing to that bizarre review in the *Herald*, tonight's crowd had grown. At least seventy people had braved this second night of horizontal wind and snow.

They formed a cluster in the center rows, and all of them had better views of the stage than he did.

The houselights dimmed. The curtains parted. Peter's eyelids drooped and fell. Laughter woke him in fits as the first act was drawing to a close. He came fully awake to screams from the audience, cued by an actor's swing of a baseball bat.

A *bat*? And when had *that* piece of business been added to the play?

The lights went out. *All* the lights. Curiously, even the red exit signs were turned off. Peter sweated in his thick wool coat and shifted his head to work out the crick in his neck, a quick slice of pain. His shirt collar was soaking wet, yet he felt oddly buoyant in his body, and his mind was floating elsewhere. The only sound was that of a small object striking the floor. And now, like the darkness, the silence was absolute.

When the stage lights came up, a woman seated on Peter's right was the only one to scream this time, but she was not facing the stage. She was shrieking at *him*. He turned to her and gurgled a response as his chin nodded down to his chest.

Onstage, two actors transgressed when they stepped out of character and turned to the invisible fourth wall. Peering into the audience, they saw the bloodied corpse of the playwright slumped in a front-row seat, and one thespian said to the other, "Oh, crap. Not *again*."

ROLLO: It's locked. My brothers
rarely open my window.
They're afraid the flies
might get out.

—<u>The Brass Bed</u>, Act I

2

The man from Special Crimes Unit had all the props: the salt-and-pepper hair of seniority, a gold shield on display and hooded eyes that said to everyone he met tonight, *I carry a gun. Don't piss me off.* Even so, he had to shoulder and shove his way through the mob in the lobby, where people from the audience were giving statements to uniformed officers. Regrettably, Detective Riker had tempered his drinking this evening, only two shots of booze at his niece's wedding reception, and that was hardly enough to take the edge off a theatergoer's elbow to his kidney.

A smaller man, half Riker's age, followed close behind him, yelling to be heard above the fray, identifying himself as the theater company's gopher. "I go for this, I go for that. Whatever ya need." His more formal name was Bugsy, he said, "—'cause I gotta bug people to get stuff," and then he added, "Detective Mallory's already here. She beat the local cops."

Of course she did. And the Upper West Sider had won that race with a forty-block handicap. *Vehicular maniac.* If only ambulances and fire trucks could match Mallory's speed on the streets of Manhattan. Riker had no car of his own. Faced with an easy choice of drinking or driving, he had allowed his license to expire long ago. And so he had begged a ride back to the city with a fellow wedding guest, a slower motorist than his partner, one with regard for icy roads and human life.

The detective pushed through the lobby doors, and his vista widened with a jolt of space expanding, all tricked out in Technicolor. Halfway along the aisle of lush red carpet and beyond the overhang of the balcony, Riker looked up to a ceiling painted with dancers, high-kicking jazz babies weirdly blending with wall decorations of plastered-on Grecian urns. And scores of ornate sconces illuminated row upon row of red velvet chairs. Not a Broadway kind of cop, most of his theater experience came from Hollywood films, and now he was walking around inside an old movie made before he was born. Drop-dead glamorous was not a phrase he would say aloud, but here it was.

And there *she* was.

Framed by red curtains, his young partner, Kathy Mallory, stood at the center of the stage, motionless under a single unflattering light that made her seem flat like a cardboard cutout. But now other lights were trained on her, angling down from all sides to give the blond curls a weird halo effect, to sculpt a cat's high cheekbones and round out her tall, slim body—bringing her to life.

Detective Riker had to smile.

Whoever was working the stage lights tonight, that guy was falling in love with Mallory.

A paunchy Midtown detective, Harry Deberman, stood beside her, waving his arms and ranting in shadow, clearly unloved by the lighting guy. And Mallory also ignored the man from the local copshop, though she was the interloper in this precinct.

Riker followed his guide to the end of the aisle. The gopher was quick, but not a sprinter, more of a scrambler. Years down the road, whenever the detective thought of this young man, he would forget the details of tangled sandy hair and blue eyes that were *way* too bright; he would always picture Bugsy with twitchy whiskers and a tail.

No need of directions to the corpse, the locus of the medical examiner's team and a crew from Crime Scene Unit. The local cop from Midtown North came down from the stage to stand with this small crowd, to hitch up his pants and splay his hands and yell, "Hey, let's get on with the show! Get to work here, guys!"

No one obeyed Harry Deberman. None of them moved, except to raise their eyes to Mallory, who stood in the authority of a spotlight, arms folded and so in charge of all that she surveyed. She could also win the vote for best dressed. That cashmere blazer was custom made, and even the designer jeans were tailored. Her dress code of money on the hoof said to everyone around her,

Pay attention! And they did. Her audience below, those who dressed down to the pay grade of civil servants, awaited her okay to bag the body and process the crime scene—*her* crime scene.

On her partner's account, Mallory had held up the removal of Peter Beck's bloody corpse for a solid hour.

How sweet. How thoughtful.

Riker hunkered down before the front-row seat of the balding dead man, who might be in his forties, maybe younger. The face had an unfinished look: hardly any lip, more like a pencil line for a mouth; and the nose was small, a kid's nose that had failed to grow up with the man. The black woolen coat was open to expose a shirt-front soaked with the blood of a slit throat. On the floor at the victim's feet was an old-fashioned straight-edged razor, and the corpse conveniently reeked of alcohol—liquid courage for the long, deep cut.

Well, how neat was that?

Detective Deberman bent down to Riker's ear. "What're you doin' in *my* patch? Your partner won't tell me squat."

As yet, Riker had no idea why his unit had been called in, and so he shrugged. "I go where I'm kicked. I do what I'm told."

Harry Deberman squatted on his haunches and pointed to the bloody weapon on the floor. "Odds are—that belonged to my stiff. The crew tells me this wimp used to brag about shavin' with a cutthroat razor. I got this covered. . . . You can *go* now."

The cut angled down from the victim's right.

"You said you knew this man?" Riker looked up to catch a nod from Bugsy. "Was he left-handed?"

"Yeah, yeah," said Deberman, answering for the gopher. "And the cut angle matches up with a lefty. Now take a whiff. Smell the booze? The guy had to get stinking drunk to do it. So you got no business here. Everything fits with a suicide."

"Murder," said Mallory in the tone of *Boo!*

The man from Midtown North jumped to his feet and spun around to face Riker's partner. He had never heard her step down from the stage to steal up behind him. Given a sporting chance to see her coming, the long slants of her eyes also made people jumpy. They were electric green. If a machine had eyes—

Mallory glanced at the corpse. "Deberman took a loose key from the coat pocket. The *right* pocket of a left-handed man." Turning on the local detective, she said, "You thought I wouldn't notice that?"

"*One* key." Riker snapped on latex gloves and probed underneath the corpse's winter coat to reach the pants pockets, and there he felt a bulge with the hard edges of a key ring. In New York City, most house keys traveled in fives: a mailbox key, one for a building's outer door, and three more for the deadbolts that secured the average apartment in this lockdown town. Now the loose key from the overcoat was more interesting. Riker stood up, held out one hand and said, "Gimme."

After a testy few seconds, Harry Deberman handed over an evidence bag containing a single key. Before he could be asked what else had been stolen, the man melted back through the ranks of the ME's people and the crime-scene crew. Making a show of leaving on some more urgent matter, Deberman checked his wristwatch twice as he made an escape up the aisle.

"You *better* run," said Mallory, though her voice was soft, and the departing detective was well out of earshot.

"Nice catch." Pulling off his gloves, Riker stepped back from the body and stared at the bloody weapon on the floor. "But we don't have the makings of a homicide. Not if it turns out the guy owned that razor."

Mallory held up a closed hand, showing him one corner of a twenty-dollar bill. "I say that key was planted. The coat pocket was the only one the perp could reach."

"No bet," said Riker. The black overcoat had a mangled, slept-in look about it. One of its pockets was trapped under Peter Beck's left thigh, and the most light-fingered killer could not have accessed either pocket of the tight-fitting pants. He hefted the bagged key in one hand, as if testing its weight as court evidence. There had to be more to it than this. With only the rise of one eyebrow, he managed to say to his partner, *I know you're holding out on me.*

Mallory gave a curt nod to the ME's man, the one holding a long, zippered bag sized to carry a corpse. While the body snatchers and forensic gatherers converged on the dead man, she threaded one hand under Riker's arm and led him off to the side, where she held out her bet money in plain sight. "I say the loose key fits the victim's front door, and the razor *does* belong to him. *That* makes it murder."

Cryptic brat.

He shook his head, not game enough to take her bait.

"But why call *us*?" A death like this one rarely got the attention of Special Crimes. Their unit favored a higher body count. "*I* say . . . let the local cops have it."

He smiled. She did not.

"Unless there's more to it." Riker's smile got a little wider, a signal that she should pocket her twenty and just give it up. To bring this point home, he glanced at his watch. "Why waste time on a—"

"The play opened last night," said Mallory, "but it shut down before the second act. And a city councilman was in the audience. Well, he comes back tonight to see the rest of the play. Again, it shuts down before the finish. So he calls a friend—a *good* friend. He's got the commissioner's home phone number, and Beale agrees with the councilman. *Two* dead bodies—one for each performance—that's a bit much."

"And Beale calls in Special Crimes." So it was not just his partner's reckless driving that got her to the crime scene ahead of the locals. He also understood why the Midtown cop had wanted this homicide so badly. It had all the elements of a career case for a mediocre detective like Harry Deberman.

And now they had a game.

Riker felt a tap on his shoulder and turned to face a younger man with long dark hair. If not for the clipboard and the microphone headset, the civilian might have stepped out of a photograph from the 1800s. His shirt had an old-fashioned collar, and a bolo tie was strung around his neck. The detective knew he would see pointy-toed western boots when he looked down. *Yup*. This man was good-looking, and he had movie-star teeth, but he introduced himself as the stage manager, Cyril Buckner.

The urban cowboy turned to Mallory. "I think you have the wrong idea about—"

"I've been looking for you," she said. "Where've you been for the past hour?"

"I was trapped in the lobby with the audience." Only this minute, he explained, the officers had released him with orders to report to her. And following an apology for eavesdropping, Cyril Buckner added, "This *was* a suicide. And that first death? That one doesn't count."

And Riker said, "Huh?"

"The woman who died last night had a heart attack." The stage manager freed a folded page of newsprint from his clipboard. "That's how we got this smash review." He held it up so they could both read the bold-type words, *A Play to Die For.* "The drama critic only reviewed the first thirty minutes. That's when the lady keeled over, and the cops shut us down. We didn't get past the first act tonight, either."

Mallory, the detective who did *not* need reading glasses, snatched the review from Buckner's hand. After scanning the column, she smiled, not at all troubled over one death by natural causes. "The woman who died last night *also* had a front-row seat. . . . She *also* died at eight-thirty." Mallory lifted her chin a bare inch to silently ask if her partner was a great believer in that sort of coincidence.

He was not.

A lobby door swung open, and a young officer ran down an aisle, yelling, "We talked to everybody!" With the hands-up flourish of a boy sliding into home plate, he came to a stop beside Mallory. "Nobody sat behind the dead guy. There *was* a lady in the seat next to him. She's got blood in her hair. But she didn't see a thing—not till the lights came up. The whole place was pitch-black for maybe a minute."

Mallory turned her head slowly until her eyes locked onto the small man with the designation of everyone's errand boy, and Bugsy froze in midstride. She called out to him, "Where's that lighting guy? Get him out here!"

In the hour before Riker's arrival, the gopher had come to know Mallory well enough to run for his life on command. And though his legs were short, Bugsy shot up the steps to the stage at light's speed. Once he was on the other side of the footlights, his head craned all the way back as he looked straight up to yell, "Gil, come down! She wants you!" No need to give a name; he was obviously referring to She Who Scares Me.

Sheets of dropped paper wafted down from an unseen perch high above the floorboards. Apparently, Mallory also made the lighting guy nervous. After a distant patter of feet slapping stairs, a tall youngster, gawky and shovel footed, appeared onstage, wearing jeans and a sweatshirt. He only had eyes for her—*big* eyes.

Mallory pointed to a row of small bulbs lodged at the foot of one wall and leading to the red glow of an exit sign. "When the houselights go down, how bright are those emergency lights?"

"J-j-just bright enough for people to find their way out during a performance," said Gil. "Except near the end of the first act—that was the blackout cue. *All* the lights were out for forty seconds. The lobby, too. Even the exit signs."

The stage manager yelled, "That's a violation of the fire code! What the *hell* were you—"

"I followed your instructions, okay?" Gil dropped to hands and knees, madly searching the fallen pages that littered the stage. Clutching one, he waved it like a white flag. "Here! Look for yourself. You added that cue to my—"

"No," said Cyril Buckner, "I didn't make *any* changes for lighting cues."

"So those lights were on the whole time *last* night," said Mallory, "but not tonight." She faced the stage manager, *daring* him to lie to her. "Who *else* makes changes like that?"

"The ghostwriter."

Backstage, a wooden staircase led up to a loft platform. Its railed walkway was lined with dressing rooms, and Mallory longed to see what was behind those locked doors, but the supervisor of the CSIs had taken ill and been taken away, and the detective had not yet convinced the remaining team to violate laws of search and seizure.

Maybe later.

She stood beside the gopher in the wings. Here, Cyril Buckner's desk had a view of the stage through an open doorway in a scenery flat, but Mallory faced the other way, reading words on a large blackboard bolted to a more solid wall of brick.

"That board's really old," said Bugsy. "It's been there forever. The ghostwriter's the only one who uses it. That's how he talks to us."

"He's never screwed with a change sheet before." Cyril Buckner walked into the end of this conversation, accompanied by a uniformed escort. The stage manager turned to read the message on the blackboard. "Oh, shit! Well, you *know* that's new." He flicked through pictures on his cell phone to show the detective what had been written there earlier in the evening.

Mallory confiscated the phone and gave a nod to the waiting officer, who led the stage manager away. Bugsy remained, never drifting far from her side, as if tethered by a leash. This little man was *her* creature now.

With her back turned to the blackboard, the detective looked through the door in the scenery. Amid the stage furnishings of a brass bed, a table and a wheelchair, CSIs stood on taped *X*s, standing in for actors while they reconstructed the moment when the playwright's corpse was discovered in the front row. The cast and crew members, under the watch of officers, were tucked into widely spaced theater seats. But one of these people had slipped out of captivity for a while. The theater hummed with the comings and goings of cops and techs, and none of them had noticed the escapee at work on the blackboard.

"That spook's the only one who uses chalk," said Bugsy. "The stage manager uses a computer." He unlocked a drawer in the desk and lifted a laptop to show her a stack of printouts. "Here ya go. Rehearsal notes, lighting cues, line changes. I post 'em on the callboard by the stage door."

Riker walked up behind them as the gopher explained the odd history of one play replacing another, line by line, via anonymous changes printed on the blackboard.

Was her partner listening to any of this? No, he was not. Sloughing off his winter coat, Riker sat on the edge of the desk. Though it only took a moment to read the words on the blackboard, he continued to stare at them—and Mallory stared at his suit. There were no wrinkles or stains, though he rarely resorted to dry cleaning until it was well past time to throw away his worn-out threads. A brand-new suit? Only a family wedding would rate this extreme measure; he was more lax about the funerals. She had not been invited, perhaps because she never showed up at these events. But when had he tired of asking her to come?

"Look at this." She held up the stage manager's cell phone to show him the small photograph of block letters in white chalk. "The ghostwriter was rewriting Peter Beck's play."

Because Riker would not wear bifocals in public, he only nodded, never taking his troubled eyes off the actual blackboard in front of him.

Bugsy leaned in close to look at her picture of it on the small screen. "Oh, that's the spook's line change for the second act."

Those chalked words had since been erased and replaced with a new message: GOOD EVENING, DETECTIVE MALLORY. HOW YOU INSPIRE ME. FORGIVE ME, MUSE. CRUEL, I KNOW, BUT YOU MUST LOSE YOUR LOVELY HEAD. OH, THE BLOODY THINGS I DO FOR ART.

"Very formal," said Riker. "Even for a first date."

SUSAN: A spinal injury?
ROLLO: My own carelessness. . . .
        I tripped in the blood. It
        was everywhere.
                    —The Brass Bed, Act I

3 Clara Loman walked onstage, buttoning her coat over the white coveralls of a CSI. The overhead lights deepened the frown lines of this tall, lanky woman with gray hair and rank. One rung below the commander of Crime Scene Unit, she supervised the night shift from a desk, rarely venturing into the field. Tonight was the exception, due to the burst appendix of her senior man. And so she had been late to arrive at the theater—and appalled to find Mallory issuing orders to crime-scene investigators. *That* was intolerable.

With terrifying efficiency, Loman had spent the past hour whipping her crew of CSIs in a race to bag the forensic evidence and *move on*. Now she informed the two homicide detectives that her people had business elsewhere tonight "—and your questions *will* be brief." She spread a large sheet of graph paper across the brass bed at the center of the stage.

The CSIs had diagrammed ground-floor parameters for the crime scene, though the stairs to off-limits dressing rooms were marked, as were the exits and large objects. But Riker was only interested in the initialed *X*s for the positions of cast and crew during the forty seconds when Peter Beck was being murdered in the dark.

So far no one had been caught lying in the crosscheck of statements made to CSIs when asked the key question: Where were you when the lights went out?

Loman tapped the *X*s initialed by the two stagehands. "I ruled out these kids. They were moving props and furniture around during the blackout. I clocked them myself on a run-through. There wasn't enough time to do their jobs *and* a murder in the audience."

Ruling suspects in or out was not her call, but Riker had been raised well, and he would not engage in a pissing contest with a woman who had more gray hair than he did. "What'd your guys get off our witness, the lady sitting next to Peter Beck?"

"She caught the bloodfly from the razor. No way she'd get that kind of splatter pattern if she was the slasher. Send the woman home." This was said in the unmistakable tone of an order, as if the detectives might be Loman's underlings.

They were not.

Riker's partner appeared to let this slide. Oh, no, that was wishful thinking on his part. Her smile was just a flash, a *taste* of things to come. He shot her a glance to beg, *Play nice. Please?*

The CSI supervisor pulled on a pair of woolen gloves to announce that she was leaving, and Mallory politely asked, "How much blood would've landed on our perp?"

"A few flecks or none at all. Given the angle of the wound, the killer was sitting on Beck's left and reaching across him to make the cut. The victim was a shield for the bloodfly." Loman's gloved hand penciled a quick slash on the diagram. "That downward angle and a half-cut throat—you don't see that with suicides. So it *was* murder." Not a *complete* waste of her time.

But Riker had seen many a botched suicide, and the call of murder belonged to the medical examiner, not her.

"The witness was sitting on the victim's right." Loman drew circles around three chairs to the left of the dead man's position. "The woman said these seats were empty when she sat down—still empty after the blackout."

"And she mentioned *place cards* on those seats," said Mallory—just being helpful—with a bit of attitude.

The tip of Clara Loman's pencil poked a hole in the diagram. And this could only mean—oh, shit!—her CSIs had missed something. Had they even *looked* for the place cards?

Before his partner could go to war on this woman, Riker asked, "So where did our guy come from?" He leaned over the diagram to point out the *X*s initialed by the cashier and the head usher. "These two alibi each other. They were playin' grab ass in the lobby." In a momentary departure from his only vanity, he slipped on his bifocals, then quickly pocketed them, and his finger settled on the *X*s for the wardrobe lady and the security guard. "These marks are off by a hair. Nan Cooper and Bernie Sales should be on the other side of that door. They went out in the alley for a smoke."

Loman's jaw jutted out, unhappy with this criticism of her team. She turned to the wings and called out to a young CSI, "Henry, did you check outside the rear door?"

The man nodded and held up his bag of alley trash along with a smaller bag of cigarette butts.

"Swab Miss Cooper and Mr. Sales! Make it *quick*!" Loman turned back to the detectives. "We'll run their DNA against the butts."

"Waste of time and money," said Riker. "I'd rule 'em both out. Bernie's from a rent-a-cop agency. Luck of the draw, different guys on different nights. He's got no reason to lie up an alibi for the wardrobe lady."

"What about the audience," said Mallory, "did you—"

"Did we spray *seventy-one* people with Luminol?" Done with the heavy sarcasm, Loman dismissed the younger detective with the wave of one hand. "No, my team eyeballed all of them for blood."

"Seventy-*one* people?" Mallory's tone implied another screwup in addition to the missing place cards and the diagram's error. She liked to keep score.

"That's my count," said Loman, who was not about to take any grief from a puppy cop. "Nobody got out of this theater before the patrolmen showed up, and their tally matches mine."

"She's right," said Riker, playing the peacemaker. "We

got containment." He handed his partner a witness state-ment taken from the head usher. "The guy snagged two cops off the sidewalk outside the theater. So the lobby entrance was secured right away. Then we got Nan and Bernie smokin' behind the alley door. Nobody got past 'em."

Loman bowed her head to draw a circle around small slash marks that stood for a third exit. "And the only route to the stage door was blocked by a volunteer usher. Sat-isfied?"

"Good enough," said Riker—before Mallory could say otherwise. "I bet nobody from the audience even *tried* to get out." Sudden death was considered live theater in New York City. People always formed a crowd around a crime scene, and, in this case, they had bought tickets.

His partner was unconvinced. Or maybe he only believed that because she wore half a smile that said to the woman from CSU, *I'm gonna getcha*.

Trouble? Oh, yeah.

Turning her back on Loman, Mallory looked out over the rows of empty seats to watch the bright portholes in the lobby doors go dark. And now the red exit signs ceased to glow, and so did the small bulbs along the wall.

What was that about?

Mallory raised her face to the youngster up on the catwalk, and yelled, "Gil, cut the stage lights!"

In that instant, the whole world winked out of exis-tence. Every touchstone was lost in the blackout dark, and Riker was not even sure of the floorboards beneath his feet. Stone blind, he had no sense of space, no up or down. Only isolation. Though this theater was full of CSIs, cops and civilians, there was no sound of companion voices, no shuffle of shoes onstage or backstage. Every man and woman was still as death, afraid of moving even one step into the unknown. How far did he stand from the edge of the stage and a leg-breaker fall?

Clara Loman's disembodied voice was a church whisper. "There was only one cut. *No* hesitation wounds. Even if the killer paced out the walk to Peter Beck's chair, he'd still have to find the man's throat in the dark."

"Yeah," said Riker. "You'd have to fumble around. There'd be some warning. You put your hands on a guy in the dark, he's gonna jump. He's gonna *say* somethin'. . . . But that didn't happen." In the stillness that came with total darkness, the woman seated next to the victim could not have failed to notice a struggle, not with only the width of a chair's armrest between her and Peter Beck. This would only work if they were looking for a razor-packing, killer bat—or some other freak of nature that could see in the dark.

Mallory spoke out from the void. "Loman's crew missed more than the place cards." The young detective clapped her hands. And there was light.

Riker turned to see Clara Loman's back as the woman stalked off the stage, shrugging out of her coat, *ripping* off her gloves. And now her bare hands balled into fists.

Point taken.

The actors had been asked to give up only their stage costumes, but all of the crew's clothing had been bagged by CSIs to be tested for the dead man's blood and fiber. Now the two stagehands walked up to the footlights in stocking feet and clothes borrowed from a wardrobe rack. Joe Garnet was a boy with a bad case of acne. The other teenager, Ted Randal, had a round head atop a stick-thin body. In Riker's shorthand notes, he had rechristened them as Pimples and Lollypop. And they had each earned a question mark after their names.

The theater was a limited job market, more so in hard times, and the detective had to wonder why the stagehand positions had not been filled by senior union men. A question mark also followed the name of the lighting technician, Gil Preston, another youngster with a union card.

Riker turned around to watch a uniformed officer shepherd a troupe of matrons down the aisle by the wall. These volunteer ushers wore plastic CSU booties and theater costumes. Hours ago, they had been written off as harmless theater groupies, but now there was just one more question. When they were assembled in front of the stage, the detective pointed toward four velvet chairs encircled with yellow crime-scene tape. "Did you ladies put place cards on any of those seats?" They shook their heads. "Did you at least *see* the place cards?" After more head-shaking, they were led away, all of them somewhat disappointed when told that they were not suspects. And they were sent home.

More people straggled onto the stage. No close fit of loaned clothing had been found for Bugsy. The gopher's shirt hung tent-like, and the pant-leg cuffs were triple rolled.

The wardrobe lady, Nan Cooper, had exchanged her

own muumuu for a loose black sheath that made her into a sexless stovepipe. Her red hair was teased into a frizzy ball, a lame attempt to hide balding patches. On this account, she now had Mallory's interest. The young detective stared at the woman's scalp, moving in close—closer. His partner would always stop to look at every odd thing. But the older woman only shrugged off this way too intimate inspection—and *that* got Riker's attention. Though he had yet to speak with Nan Cooper, she now had her own question mark in his notebook.

Edging down the line, he stopped to face the lone actress in the play—a young one. Nothing in her eyes, true baby blues, registered as New Yorker savvy, and her face fit his cookie-cutter idea of a corn-fed cheerleader. Alma Sutter could only be a few years off the bus from Elsewhere, America, which was any town but this one. Loose blond hair waved down to her waist, and without the garish stage makeup, she seemed childlike. Nervous, too. The actress rocked heel to toe, considering his question of place cards. "No, I didn't see them, either."

Very breathy, *very* Marilyn Monroe.

And though she bore no other likeness to that long-dead film icon, Riker was just a wee bit in love. He knew this moment was a keeper—a kind of souvenir.

He moved on down the line to stand before two short, skinny actors named in his notes as Weirdo Twins. The identical Rinaldi brothers, Hollis and Ferris, were in their early twenties. They had a slack-jawed, stupid look about them, and their hair was chopped short, the sort of cut favored by caregivers in mental institutions.

"What about you guys? See any place cards?"

Their slow-moving eyes lacked focus as they shifted their weight from one foot to the other in unison, playing idiots to perfection. Riker waited for the Rinaldi boys to realize that his partner was standing behind them. *So close.* Could they feel her breathing on them? Yeah, and they also did the startle response in tandem. The runts turned to look up at tall Mallory, who folded her arms to complete a stance of no mercy. *Damn*, she was good at this; no one could do cold-and-bloodless like her. She stared them down with machine-green eyes, no life in them now, and she spoke with an eerie lack of inflection. "The play is over. Cut the crap."

She had *out-weirded* them. *Amateurs.* The twins dropped the glazed look of brainless fools and actually stood at attention, just two ordinary guys with bad haircuts.

Riker sighed. *Actors.*

At the other end of this chorus line, Bugsy the gopher raised his hand as children do in class, and he said, "The twins like to stay in character. The roles they play—"

"Yeah, *right.*" More than likely they had only wanted to mess with him. Riker stood back from the lineup. One actor was missing, the older man, the fat one with a girth as wide as the brass bed at the center of this stage. "Where's the big guy—Rollo?"

"That's my *character's* name," said a voice from the wings. "*So* sorry." The late arrival made his barefoot entrance, belting a long black robe as he joined the lineup. He was tallest among them—and no longer three hundred pounds overweight. The body padding had been shed; his cheeks were not bulging anymore, but gone to lean hollows; and the wild brown hair had been smoothed back into an eighties-era power ponytail. Now he put on the charming bad-boy smile that was his trademark.

Man, where have you been all this time?

This actor was Riker's favorite gangster, his favorite cop and psycho killer. Before Axel Clayborne had disappeared from Hollywood, he had won critical acclaim just for leaving his house in the morning. Those famous hazel eyes were focused on Riker's partner, and the movie star so obviously liked what he saw.

With no glimmer of recognition, Mallory passed by the actor to stand before a less important member of the theater company, a younger man, whose only distinguishing feature was a crooked front tooth. "You're the head usher, right?" She held up an evidence bag. "We found this place card on Peter Beck's chair—*under* his dead body."

"Well, none of *my* people put it there." The man bent at the waist, looking down the lineup, and he pointed to the gopher. "Had to be him."

"It wasn't me," said Bugsy. "I never saw any damn place cards." He nodded toward the stage manager, who stood beside him, three inches shorter without the cowboy boots. "Cyril gave me a velvet rope. I laid it across the armrests on Peter's seat. The guy was a no-show last night. But tonight, I roped off the same chair—front-row center. I'd *never* put Peter near the wall."

Cyril Buckner rested a protective hand on the gopher's shoulder. "Maybe someone from the audience—"

"We ruled out the audience." Riker turned to the head

usher and his girlfriend, the cashier. "And you guys, too. Go home." When this pair had left the stage, the detective moseyed down the line of cast and crew, holding up a sheet of paper for all to see. "This is a statement from the lady who sat next to Peter Beck. She was one of the first people through the door tonight. Our victim was sitting on a place card, but the lady saw three more cards on seats in the front row. Somebody put 'em there *before* the audience was seated."

"To keep those chairs empty," said Mallory, "so a killer could sit down beside Peter Beck—and cut his throat. The cards disappeared before the lights came on again."

And fifteen minutes ago, Clara Loman's crew of CSIs had found them.

"They were stashed behind a trunk backstage," said Riker. "And all of you swore there was nobody back there who didn't belong. No backstage visitors allowed—*ever*." He was smiling, so amiable when he said, "We usually wait till we're asked . . . but who'd like to lawyer up first?"

No takers.

Detective Mallory faced the famous barefoot actor in the black robe, the one who had signed his statement with the name of a character from the play. *Cute.* She hated all things cute. "Axel Clayborne?"

"You're guessing, aren't you?" The movie star's smile was wry, for who among the six billion would need to ask his name? He belted the robe tighter around his lean body. "Sorry I'm late, but your people wanted my fat suit, and then they wanted autographs." He seemed younger than his thirty-eight years, the age on his driver's license. And he was entirely too relaxed.

Mallory stepped back a few paces to address the whole ensemble. "The blackout lasted forty seconds. Did any of you sense someone moving past you in the dark? Any sound or movement at all?"

Three of the actors raised their hands.

But not Axel Clayborne. "You'll never get a right answer to that one," he said. "The power of suggestion. Actors are very malleable people. We're prized above every other profession for jury duty—so easily swayed."

"I didn't see *your* hand go up."

His grin was wide. "Of course. That can only mean that *I* killed Peter. Seriously, could anyone have a better alibi? I was onstage the whole time. Me and Alma."

"That's how you made my shortlist." Mallory turned to the androgynous redhead in charge of wardrobe. "You have a spare fat suit, right?"

"Oh, yeah," said Nan Cooper. "I got two of every damn thing."

"*Get* it!"

A minute later, the balding redhead reappeared, effortlessly carrying a huge bulk of foam encased in striped pajamas, and she laid it down at Mallory's feet. The detective turned to Axel Clayborne, saying, "Put it on."

He folded his arms and smiled—no, call it a leer. "You want me to *strip*? I'm only wearing jockey shorts under this robe."

"I don't care," she said. "*Do* it!"

"*No.* I have to be . . . *seduced.*"

"Hey, Mr. Clayborne," said Riker, "just get into the damn suit, okay?"

Mister? Her partner deferred to nobody. She stared at Riker, but the film buff only shrugged and looked away.

Mallory pulled out her gold pocket watch, an inheritance from her foster father, the late Louis Markowitz, whose name was inscribed on the back below the previous owners, older generations of police. Normally, in times of trouble with superiors, she pulled out the watch as a reminder of her ties to an old cop family, almost royalty in the NYPD. But tonight, she needed its stopwatch function.

Axel Clayborne dropped his robe to the floorboards to stand nearly naked and unabashed. There were old scars on his flesh, the marks of an eventful life. Conscious of her eyes on his body, he did a slow revolve to display a few fresh rakes of abrasion on his back. A woman's claws had done that, but not in anger. His smile was still in place when he turned around to face her again. "Seen enough?" The actor leaned down to pick up the bottom half of the fat suit. He pulled on the pajama pants that gave him a belly and widened him, hip and thigh. Next, he shrugged into the thick arms of the top half. After securing the foam padding with Velcro straps, he buttoned the shirtfront over his expanded chest. Then he glanced at her pocket watch, asking, "How did I do?"

"I haven't timed you yet," said Mallory. "Go down to the audience and slit the man's throat."

With mock curiosity, he looked down at the front row, where yellow crime-scene tape ringed the area around the victim's empty chair. "If you mean the dead man . . . who *used* to be there—"

"It's called *acting*," she said. "Now go kill Peter Beck."

Axel Clayborne stood his ground. Was he waiting for her to say *please*? He flashed a sly grin, a *big* mistake. Mallory also smiled. Her blazer was slowly drawn open as her hands came to rest on her hips, every woman's wordless way of saying, *You're dead meat*. And, to back up that—*suggestion*—a large revolver, a .357 Smith & Wesson, was now on public display in her shoulder holster. Most cops carried streamlined Glocks, but this gun was more lethal in its looks, a virtual ad for stop-and-drop killing power—and playtime was *over*.

Quick to guess that smart-ass charm was not his best option here, the actor bowed to her. And then, though his limbs were thickly padded, Clayborne moved with deep grace. Light-stepping like a dancer, he descended the stairs to the audience level, where he stood before the dead man's chair and slashed the air above it with his right hand. Then he climbed the steps to take his place onstage. "Would you like to see me do it again? I'm sure I could—"

"You could've done it with your eyes closed." The pocket watch snapped shut. "That foam padding doesn't slow you down. And you had the easiest access to the dead man's chair." She stared at a taped *X* on the floorboards, a CSI's mark for Alma Sutter's position. "The actress would've had to walk around the brass bed and *you*. She couldn't go the other way. The stagehands were moving props on that side. But you had no obstacles."

"Yeah," said Riker. "No worries about bumping into stuff in the dark. Works for me."

Clayborne grinned, so pleased with himself.

No, there was more than that to the actor's expression—something like an unspoken joke. And who was he smiling at now?

Mallory whirled around to stare at the stagehands, as if she had caught them doing something wrong. They were still in their teens, a guarantee of at least one or two illegal acts. The CSU re-creation of the critical blackout seconds had cleared them from the suspect list, but they were both antsy and ready to bolt. They had done *something*. "The way I hear it, you two were moving around a lot while the lights were out. Moving furniture, collecting props. . . . Neat trick in the dark."

The pimpled stagehand shrugged, saying, "Naw, it was easy with—" And the other one elbowed him in the ribs. Those outside the teenage cult of youth, cops in particular, were considered too bone stupid to *possibly* read this as a signal to shut the hell up.

Riker graced them with an evil smile. "Easy with . . . *what?*"

"Night-vision goggles." Clara Loman walked onstage, carrying a cardboard carton under one arm. "It's easy when you've got the right toys." The CSU supervisor dipped one hand into the box and pulled out an object of bright purple plastic sealed in a clear plastic wrapper. It looked like a child's Halloween mask decked with chin straps and three green-glass eyes.

Loman pointed to the center lens positioned on the

mask's forehead. "This emits a beam of light in a spectrum invisible to the naked eye. But when you're wearing the goggles, it works like a flashlight." She turned to face the two stagehands, none too pleased with them. "You little bastards might've mentioned the goggles when we did that run-through."

Riker also shot them an angry look. "Damn kids."

The boys had only wanted to leave the theater early tonight—stuff to do, dope to smoke. And *screw* the cops. Why complicate things with helpful information that might delay their escape—*and* make them likely suspects?

Mallory glanced at her partner for a wordless conversation of her raised eyebrows and his slow shake of the head. What else might have been missed in Loman's rush to bag the evidence and run? How could the night-vision goggles have gone overlooked for *hours*?

Clara Loman held up her carton and pointed to a line of bold type that listed six headsets to the box. "We only have five." Hubris incarnate, she announced, "If the missing goggles were backstage, my crew would've found them." And now, with a special glare for Mallory, maybe anticipating fresh doubts, more insults, Loman said, "Nobody carried them out of this building tonight. Everyone from the audience took off their coats when my people checked them for blood splatter." She hefted the pair of night-vision goggles in one hand. "You can't fit this in a pocket, and I know the cops were checking purses."

"There aren't any more goggles," said Cyril Buckner. "There were only five pairs in the box when we got them."

Mallory turned to face her lineup of suspects. "Which one of you bought them?"

No one answered. Heads were turning side to side, shoulders shrugging, and finally Bugsy said, "Must've been the ghostwriter."

Yeah, *right*.

"That reminds me." Mallory turned to the woman from Crime Scene Unit. "Did you find the chalk yet?"

Chalk? What chalk? That much could be read in the graying diva's startled eyes. Had this woman's harried crew even mentioned to her what was printed on the slate before she arrived at the theater?

"Our prime suspect's the only one who uses the blackboard," said Mallory. "He left me a message tonight. I know your CSIs got pictures of it. . . . So, where's the chalk?" Even a trace of it would have been helpful, maybe a dusting in the lining of a pocket. "Your guys did *look* for it, right?" *Wrong.* Now she could read Clara Loman's thoughts as a stream of four-letter words.

SUSAN: Puddles of it? Whose blood?
ROLLO: My mother's, my aunt's.
Granny's blood and the
blood of my sisters.
                    —<u>The Brass Bed</u>, Act I

 The collar of Axel Clayborne's pajama costume was soaked with sweat as he baked in the thick foam padding. Nine times, Mallory had run him up and down stairs in the dark to murder an invisible man in an empty theater seat, all the while clocking him, prompting him to go faster. She was very thorough in all things—including payback.

The actor appealed to Detective Riker. "Am I being punished?"

"Oh, yeah."

The stagehands had also been kept late, but not just for penance. Riker had finally resolved the problem of kids in union jobs that should have gone to senior men, and it had the stink of deep financial trouble. Thanks to nepotism, the teenagers had signed on with Lollypop's uncle and Pimples's dad, a seasoned prop master. The older men had elected not to take a cut in pay, and they had found work elsewhere. Gil Preston's story was much the same. He had originally been hired as the lighting director's assistant. And Bugsy, the gopher, was also doing the job of the stage manager's laid-off assistant.

This was Broadway on a shoestring.

The crew had been cut by more than half, and so a question mark still remained after Nan Cooper's name. Why lose all those people and keep a wardrobe lady on salary?

Mallory looked up to the catwalk and yelled, "Gil! Lights!" And there was instant darkness.

Axel Clayborne resumed his blackout position on the brass bed, covering himself with a blanket that could have hidden the small murder kit of a straight-edge razor, goggles and place cards. He did this very smoothly for a man who could not see.

But she could—aided by night-vision lenses.

With the turn of her head, Mallory aimed the green light of her third eye at the blind stagehands and called out to them in the dark, "Garnet! Randal!" They stiffened up, their sightless eyes gone wide and spooked, believing that she was standing in front of them—as she softly padded around behind the boys to touch the backs of their necks and whisper, "You're dead." She ripped off her goggles, yelling, "Lights!"

Blinking at the sudden brightness, the teenagers spun around to face her.

Frightened much? Oh, *yes.*

She squared off against them. "So . . . you two are moving props on the stage. . . . A man's being murdered in the audience." One hand went to her hip. "And you don't *see* that?"

"Well, no, we wouldn't," said Garnet, the pimple-faced boy. "When we wear the goggles, we keep our eyes on the floor." He nudged his friend. "Remember that last dress rehearsal?"

"Yeah," said Randal, the thin one with the round head. "This idiot PR guy tested his camera flash during a black-out scene. The damn goggles magnified the light a zillion times. It was like lookin' into the sun. I thought I was gonna go blind."

"Another time," said Garnet, "somebody next to me lit a penlight. Messed me up for the whole scene. Your eyes need recovery time when you get blinded, and we ain't got any. It's all split-second moves. The goggles *gotta* come off before the lights come back on."

"Or we're screwed."

"Yeah. So we don't take our eyes off the floor."

Mallory turned to the actor on the brass bed. "And there goes your alibi." She hunkered down to look at the theater diagram laid out on the floor. Maybe the stage-hands had no time to do a murder in the audience, but they *knew* something, *did* something. *What?*

She waved them away. "That's all for tonight. You can leave."

As the teenagers hustled down the stairs and made a fast retreat up the aisle, Riker turned to Axel Clayborne, another offender who could have enlightened them earlier and saved them some time. "We're done with you, too. Everybody *out*!"

Her partner was no longer starstruck. He was pissed off.

When the detectives were alone on the stage, Riker sat down on the brass bed. "You *know* it wasn't just the kids. The whole pack of 'em decided not to tell us about the goggles. And they weren't protecting the stagehands. Those two couldn't have done it."

Mallory held up the folded sheet of newsprint with the only review of the first performance. "Wouldn't you think more than one critic would've turned out for the opening of a Broadway play?"

"We've had lots of canceled openings," said a soft, breathy voice from the wings. "Nobody knew if the curtain would go up last night."

Alma Sutter had been sent home an hour ago. And so it was a surprise to see her step through the open door in the scenery. The actress approached them with halting steps, a touch of fear and other guilty signs of a sin-ridden Catholic schoolgirl on her way to confession—and then, of course, straight to hell.

Flanked by her audience of two detectives, Alma sat on floorboards, her legs dangling over the edge of the stage. "Peter Beck was a very nice man. He was always good to me. Then the play changed . . . and Peter changed."

She could tell they had already heard several versions of this story tonight, and they were sick of it. By their glances and signals, Alma followed a silent conversation of cops. The man, with only the rise of one flat hand, stayed his partner's objections to going slowly. Detective Mallory's expression of ennui—and the brief opening of her blazer to expose a weapon—let him know that she would prefer to extract information at gunpoint.

The actress recoiled as if this last part had been said aloud.

The man, the *nice* detective, smiled at her. "Take your time, kid."

Kid? On this cue, Alma struck an attitude of little-girl-lost, lacing her fingers in prayer, eyes cast down. *Shy* child. "The ghostwriter's changes started with the Fat Man's Ballet. It was *wonderful*." Her lashes fluttered up, eyes wide with imitation wonder. "And Peter saw that, too. He didn't have a problem with it. But then the ghostwriter started rewriting all the lines. Every rehearsal was a screaming match until Peter walked out. He didn't even come to the opening. So I was surprised to see him out front tonight."

Detective Riker scribbled in his notebook and then asked, "What time?"

"Maybe fifteen minutes before curtain. I was standing behind the—"

Mallory leaned in close—*too* close. "You *saw* those place cards on the chairs."

Not a question.

Confession time. "Yes. . . . I should've told you. I'm so sorry." Alma looked down at her dangling shoes, aiming for shame. *Bad* little girl. "I was really nervous . . . but that wasn't the first time I saw the cards." Ah, she was out of trouble now. They liked that part.

"Okay," said Riker. "So the *first* time you looked at the audience, did you see anybody else out there?"

"There's always somebody out front. The ushers for sure. But not the stagehands. I would've remembered them. They dress in solid black so you don't see them moving props onstage. Except for that total blackout tonight, there's emergency lights and exit signs. With any light at all, white skin shows up in the—" Oh, she was losing the female cop to boredom. "Well, anyway, that's why the stagehands wear black ski masks and gloves."

Detective Mallory looked to her partner. "Loman missed that, too."

"Alma," said Detective Riker. "Cut to the good part. What's eating you?"

"A friend of mine *died* tonight."

"Your boyfriend," said Detective Mallory, who would have heard all the backstage gossip by now.

"We were *friends*, but I auditioned. It's not like Peter *gave* me the role." Was she believed? Alma turned from one cop to the other. No and no. Well, this part they would believe: "We had a falling out."

"A fight," said Riker.

"With a razor," said Mallory.

"Oh, *God*, no! Just shouting. He was so paranoid. He thought we were all against him. But that wasn't true. Everyone felt sorry for Peter. The ghostwriter destroyed him."

"By changing the play?"

"By writing a *better* play. You see? It *had* to be suicide. It wasn't the weather that wrecked our turnout. A star like Axel Clayborne would've brought out fans, even in a blizzard. But Peter had his lawyers shut down our preview and every scheduled opening night. They killed all the ads—newspapers, radio, TV. You can starve out any Broadway play without ticket sales. A lot of people got laid off. The legal fees were *huge*, and—"

"But none of you wanted Beck to *die*." Mallory's sarcasm was delivered deadpan.

"What for? Yesterday the judge sided with us. He let the play open last night. And we got a great review because of that lady in the audience. She was so scared, she had a heart attack and dropped dead."

"What a lucky break." Riker was no longer the nice detective.

"But don't you see? That's why Peter showed up tonight. If he couldn't starve the play, he could give it the ultimate kiss of death—a playwright committing suicide after the first act." Alma bowed her head for the closing line. It had taken her the better part of an hour to come up with it. "The play was *killing* Peter . . . so he killed the play."

Life could be so simple if the police would only allow it.

"All of you followed the ghostwriter's changes." Detective Mallory said this as an accusation heavy on sarcasm. "Someone you've never even met, never—"

"Oh," said Alma. "He left another message on the blackboard. It's for you."

Riker watched the actress's back as she walked away. It seemed like everyone her age was stoned on something. In her case—wandering eyes, slow reaction time—a sedative was an easy guess. It would have been helpful to know if she had popped any pills before the murder of Peter Beck, a kill that had required speed and good reflexes.

As his partner followed Alma Sutter into the wings, a sound from above made him tilt his head back to see the eavesdropper. Even without bifocals, Riker had no trouble following the track of the youngster's wide eyes. Gil Preston was fascinated by Mallory.

It was easy to forget when he was around. The lighting guy, shy string bean, kept the distance of a schoolboy with a hopeless crush. His gaze stayed locked on Mallory until she was out of sight, disappearing through the door in the stage set. And now he saw Riker watching him.

The stage lights went out.

The detective followed the glow of a lamp through the scenery door, and he joined the two women in the wings by Buckner's desk. Mallory was staring at the new message on the blackboard—written with the chalk that Loman's crew had never found. By now, it had walked out the door in somebody's pocket. But not Alma's. The actress's pockets were turned inside out when his partner returned her coat, saying, "Go home."

When Alma Sutter was out of sight, Mallory reached up to a shelf near the desk and pulled aside a canvas tarp that had covered the stage manager's laptop, all but the tiny dot of its camera lens. With taps of the keyboard, she raised the camera's view of the black slate, a moving picture of uniformed officers and CSIs walking by. She sped

up the motion to make the foot traffic faster, and then—
the screen went black.

"Damn," said Riker. "He jammed the laptop signal?"

Mallory pressed one finger over the lens. "Sticky. Our
guy's low tech. He came up on the laptop's blind side and
put tape over the lens." She turned toward the sound of
a scuffle on the stairs.

Riker heard footsteps behind the stage set. And now
Bugsy was walking toward them in the scruff-of-the-neck
custody of a uniformed officer, who said, "I caught him
coming out of a dressing room. He's got a bedroll stashed
up there."

When Riker had dismissed the officer with thanks, he
turned a smile on the nervous gopher. "It's okay, Bugsy.
You can stay the night . . . but I guess we can scratch that
flophouse address you gave us."

The little man drifted to Mallory's side, looking up to
her as his higher power. She pulled a roll of bills from a
back pocket and peeled off a twenty, saying, "Get something to eat."

Riker was touched. Would this gesture pass for empathy with the homeless gopher? Well, no. But it would have
made her foster mother so happy, this hopeful sign of
late-blooming humanity—Mallory feeding her pet.

The money disappeared into Bugsy's back pocket. His
eyes dropped to the moving picture on the laptop screen.
The camera blackout had ended, and people were passing
by the lens again. "Oh, we tried that. Tried every damn
thing to catch the spook. Nothin' worked. One time, I

sprinkled talcum powder on the floor. The ghostwriter left a message—but no footprints. I bet the guy's got his own camera planted somewhere."

"Maybe." Riker looked up to the high-hanging litter of scaffolding, pulley rigs and weights, pipes and spaghetti loops of rope, cable and wire. "But who's got a year to go look for it?" He turned his attention back to the new blackboard message. This time, no name was mentioned—or needed. It was an apt description. "What's it from? Shakespeare?"

"It's a Bible quotation." Mallory could quote scripture better than any soapbox lunatic in the city.

"Four years of Catholic school finally pays off," said Riker. Though his partner had spent much of her childhood in a Jewish household, her foster mother, the late Helen Markowitz, had given the Catholics equal time—due to a misunderstanding in Kathy Mallory's puppy days when the feral street kid had made the sign of the cross. Later, it was discovered that the little girl only used this religious gesture to ward off mad dogs and cops.

A Sunday-school dropout he might be, but Riker well understood why the actress had assumed that this love letter was meant for his partner.

WHO IS SHE THAT LOOKETH FORTH AS THE MORNING, FAIR AS THE MOON, CLEAR AS THE SUN, AND TERRIBLE AS AN ARMY WITH BANNERS?

SUSAN: (paces the length of the
room) I'm not afraid. . . .
I'm not.
ROLLO: Give it time.
　　　　　　　—<u>The Brass Bed</u>, Act I

5 Snowfall was light, a final dusting of the storm
that had paralyzed all but the city's main
arteries for two days. There were no pedestrians in sight, and gone was the twenty-four-
hour static of traffic and the drive-by blasts of music from
car radios. Manhattan by night—nothing sweeter. But
this night, the town had taken itself indoors, and Riker
found the lack of noise unsettling. Creepy. A born New
Yorker, he could only read perfect peace as the hush at
the end of the world. But then a hulking snowplow lumbered past the theater on its way to some blocked road,
and the two detectives walked down Forty-ninth Street.

Riker wrapped his scarf a little tighter against a sudden
chill wind. His partner wore a trench coat, a poor choice
in winter. It must have been the first thing that came to
hand in her flight to the crime scene. He wanted to ask if

she was cold, but this might be taken the wrong way, as though he were asking if she didn't feel the cold like a *normal* human. Mallory the Machine was her moniker, the one used behind her back in the squad room, where she kept everyone at the distance of her surname. Everyone. Even though he had watched her grow up in the care of old friends, he was not allowed to call her Kathy anymore.

After the funeral of Inspector Louis Markowitz, Riker had received a letter written against a day when Lou's foster child might be left alone in Copland. The dead man's final words had obliged him to look after her, and Riker had taken this to mean keeping her safe. Now he expanded upon that old instruction, removing his scarf and wrapping it around her neck to keep her warm.

She forgave him for this act of kindness by not acknowledging his gift, and neither did she shrug it off as she unlocked her car, a silver convertible that any passerby might take for a Volkswagen—if they never looked under the hood to see the Porsche engine of a speed freak who loved to drive—*lived* to drive. Semi-suicidal Riker was the only man on the squad who would ride with her, and so he had become her partner by default; that was the story he told, and he stuck to it whenever he was asked the question that always began with *Why in God's name*—

"One of the first cops on the scene lied to us." Mallory slid in behind the wheel. "Somebody from the audience got past them before they secured the doors."

"A *uniform* confessed to a screwup like that?"

She shot him a look that said, *Oh, sure—like that was ever going to happen.*

Then how could she know? Riker climbed in on the passenger side. Was he going to ask her? No, he knew this game too well. Contrary to what the rest of the squad believed, Mallory *did* have a sense of humor, twisted though it might be. There was never any laughter when she got to the end of a joke—only a fleeting smile to say, *Gotcha*.

But not tonight.

That was his resolve as his partner pulled away from the curb for the six-block ride to Peter Beck's residence in Hell's Kitchen. Riker double-checked the math, leafing through the officers' notes on people interviewed in the lobby. And now he consulted his own notebook. "I don't have the cashier's statement. Donna Loo? She was your interview, right?"

"Yes, she was." Mallory slowed down for a red light. Coming to a full stop was against her religion. She pulled a small evidence bag from the pocket of her trench coat and handed it over. "Donna doesn't know who left them. They were in the cashier's booth when she came to work."

Through the clear plastic, Riker read the typed note that banded a packet of four tickets: *Peter Beck and guests*. "But the lighting guy said the man came in by the alley door."

"Right," said Mallory. "Beck didn't *need* a ticket. But after that good review, our killer couldn't count on a bad turnout. He had to keep Donna from selling those seats in the front row. She handed out seventy-two tickets tonight. I checked her count with the usher's stubs."

Oh, *shit*! Only seventy-*one* people had given up their names and IDs while submitting to a CSI search for blood evidence. Clara Loman must have counted Peter Beck as ticket holder seventy-two. Another damned screwup.

"Okay," said Riker. "Maybe those cops were wrong about nobody gettin' out, but what makes you think one of 'em lied? Maybe you—"

"Read the head usher's statement. He pulled the two cops off the sidewalk outside the front entrance. Donna Loo backs him up on that. So now they're all in the lobby. The usher and the cashier have their backs to the street door—and that's when somebody flies out. The cops don't stop the runaway. They're both listening to the usher, right? They don't even know what's happened yet. Only one cop saw that ticket holder run out the door . . . and he *lied* about it."

Riker sighed. She might be making this up as she went along, but there was no fault in her logic. One ticket holder was in the wind, and one of the four people in that lobby *might* have seen the escape. "So you just worked this out with the ticket count? That's how you know one cop lied?" *Fat chance.*

"I can even tell you which cop."

He knew she was *not* doing this with tea leaves. Too easy.

"It was the younger one," said Mallory. "The rookie. I nailed him five minutes after I got to the theater. He couldn't look me in the eye when I asked if anyone got past him."

Punch line.

And well timed. They turned onto Peter Beck's side street, traveling slowly in the wake of a snowplow. The neighborhood of Hell's Kitchen had long ago lost its gangland reputation. Thanks to an infusion of wealth and an invasion of interior decorators, only pansy criminals would live here.

"I guess our guy walked to the theater," said Riker. The sidewalks were passable, shoveled by shopkeepers and building supers, but not the road ahead.

Axel Clayborne had downed many shots of Chivas Regal, but the actor was not yet hammered, not by half. He left his apartment and climbed the steps to the roof, where a door opened upon a square field of pristine snow. To the north, the Empire State Building was a needle on the skyline. Closer to home, colored holiday lights were strung on balconies, and tinny notes of song wafted up from the street. He leaned over the brick parapet to look down at the sidewalk far below, where drunken ants were singing Christmas carols by the neon glow of a bar sign.

He was surrounded on all sides by the bright windows of his TriBeCa neighborhood, though no close rooftop was higher than this one. The storm had covered the deck chairs and the table. They were unrecognizable mounds. Axel unwound his scarf and used it to whack the furniture and send the snow flying. When the tabletop was clear, he laid out two shot glasses and a whiskey bottle.

Now . . . where was Dickie Wyatt? He had so much to tell this man with whom he shared everything. Once, they had even shared a toothbrush on a red-eye flight out of Cairo.

Axel turned east. That way? No, he had bearings now, and his feet punched deep holes in the snow as he made his way to the opposite corner of the sky, shouting, "Dickie! I'm home!"

Peter Beck's doorman had a typical New Yorker's reaction to the sudden death of one of his tenants. "Well, I'll be damned." He tilted his head to one side in the attitude of *So what else is new?*

The hour was late, and the old man wore a bathrobe over his pajamas as he answered questions in the lobby of the building where he was also a resident, though his studio apartment was underground. "No windows," he complained, and their crime victim lived in the sky "—with God and the pigeons. But I haven't seen Mr. Beck for a week. Not in the daytime. There used to be a second shift, but we had budget cuts. Cheap bastards. And me? I go off duty at six-thirty." He turned from one detective to the other, the giveaway sign of awaiting a challenge.

"But tonight you left early," said Mallory.

His eyes darted right to left. Looking for a way out? He raised his hands, palms up, a prelude to coming clean. "I had a doctor's appointment."

"Okay," said Riker, "let's say that's true. What time did you leave? And before you answer that, if I think you're lyin', we'll bang on doors all over this building till we—"

"Around five o'clock, maybe quarter after."

Mallory pointed to the main entrance. "And that door was locked when you left?"

"Oh, yeah. The tenants got their own keys."

"What about Beck's visitors?" Riker waved the old man into the waiting elevator. "Anybody stand out?"

"Well, yesterday this little guy shows up. He wants to see Mr. Beck. I think his name was Bugsy. Yeah, that's it. But Mr. Beck never answered his intercom buzzer." The doorman pushed a button, and the elevator hummed as they rode upward. "The little guy was worried—said Beck wasn't taking phone calls, either. So I get the manager's key, and we go upstairs to knock on the door. No answer. But I don't use the key 'cause I hear somebody moving around in there. So this guy, Bugsy, he was satisfied, and he left."

The elevator opened, and the doorman said, "I got no keys tonight. If you want in, I have to call the—"

"Got it covered," said Riker. "Go back to sleep."

The detectives stepped out to walk down a hallway carpet that was the pale green shade of money. And when they stood before the dead man's door, the top lock, one of three, was not a fit for any keys on Peter Beck's ring, but Riker unlocked it with the loose one from the victim's coat pocket. And Mallory refrained from saying, *I told you so.*

He flicked on the light switch in the foyer, and then he whistled. "Beck must've been a *great* playwright."

In a town where success was measured in square feet of living space, the foyer was big enough to park a truck. And beyond the window glass, the Hudson River spanned the entire wall of the front room. Come morning, it would be flooded with light, another marker for wealth.

But prosperity had not brought happiness to Peter Beck.

The signs of depression were recognizable from Mallory's rare forays into her partner's apartment. Every surface and much of the floor was littered with unopened mail, empty liquor bottles, cast-off clothes and crumbs of food from take-out cartons. In Riker's place, this effect was cumulative. But here, in a neighborhood of once-a-week cleaning ladies, it was the excess of a *very* sad man. And now she noticed golden statues of theater awards, some of them broken, all of them knocked to the floor below the mantelpiece—evidence of an *angry* man.

Riker bent down to pick up a receipt with the logo of a liquor store. "Delivery charges. This address is two blocks away, but the guy got his booze delivered. Lots of it."

Mallory found another receipt, one stapled to a paper bag from a vegan restaurant.

A vegetarian drunk?

A cursory search of the room's drawers and cabinets gave up nothing more than the average hotel suite. Very neat. Too neat. This would not square with the litter trails of a man who did not bother to cart his garbage to the trash chute in the outer hallway.

Riker closed a drawer. "Let's toss the whole place. Better us than Loman's crew."

Mallory agreed. If Clara Loman saw the same evidence of a tidy vegetarian recently turned boozing slob, she might make a call of suicide by a man unhinged, and that CSI had done enough damage tonight.

The detectives moved on to the next room, Beck's den, where a handsome desk and a long table provided workspace for the playwright, but there were no writing tools in sight. And the air was stale. It smelled of abandonment. A light gray film covered every surface to mark the last visit of a cleaning woman. It outlined the rectangular shape of a recently moved, maybe stolen, laptop. An easy guess. Disconnected wires led to the desktop printer and a scanner. The lone, shallow file drawer told Mallory that Beck had been a purger of hard copy. The rest of his personal papers would have been committed to the missing computer and then to the document-shredder in the corner. Other drawers were clutter free, and their spare contents could be seen at a glance.

Thieves prized compulsive neatness in their victims; valuables were so quickly found for the taking, and so it took less than a minute to know that there were no thumb drives or any backup disks left behind. The thief's fingerprints would not be found here, either. Only the missing laptop had left a track in the dust.

A second hallway door opened onto a toilet, a sink and a wide mirror lined with vanity lights. Her foster mother, Helen, would have called this the powder room, a convenience for visitors. Farther down the hall, Mallory entered another doorway and walked past a king-size, unmade bed. The stink of booze rose off the sheets. She stepped into the master bathroom of modern luxury appointments, marble tiles and a sauna. The only old thing, a worn leather case, lay open beside the sink, and it held an incomplete set of antique barber tools. One empty well of the velvet lining was molded to fit a missing straight-edge razor. So the murder weapon *had* belonged to Peter Beck.

Her partner stood just outside the bathroom door, looking down at a week's worth of clothing strewn about the floor. Then he turned to the open closet, a contradiction of clean shirts and suits hung in an orderly row and, beneath them, shoe trees lined up like soldiers.

"Peter Beck's killer was here tonight," said Mallory. "He was here *twice*."

Riker only glanced her way to ask where this was coming from.

"Beck let him in the door," she said. "That's how our perp stole the key. He needed it so he could come back later." She held up the old barber kit to show him the razor shape of the empty well. "He couldn't get at it while Beck was in the apartment. No good reason to come in here, not with a guest bathroom outside." So far her partner was nodding in agreement—until she said, "I know Beck left the building with his killer tonight."

He folded his arms and smiled to say, *Okay, I'll bite.*

Mallory quit the bedroom, followed by Riker, her expert in all things alcoholic. "Let's say you've been drinking—a *lot*." She crossed the front room to open the foyer closet. After checking the pockets of a down parka, she moved on to other jackets and coats. "Ever have trouble threading a key in a lock?"

No need for him to answer. Mallory had been eleven years old the first time she had performed that small service for Riker. She held up the house keys and jingled them. "So

Beck's on his way out the door, and the killer snatches the keys. Just being helpful. And he locks up the apartment. Only *one* lock. Our killer slips that key off the ring before he returns it to Beck." This key ring was not a fingernail breaker. It opened easily with a simple catch, and she demonstrated a quick theft for her partner. "The perp doesn't steal a key for the street door, and that's smart. Even falling-down drunk, Beck might notice two keys missing from a ring of five. But you know that's no problem."

When the killer had returned to steal Beck's razor, he only had to wait until a tenant showed up, and then he would have followed that person through the untended door. This was the time-honored way for every burglar in town to enter a well-secured building.

Riker followed her through all the back rooms to watch her make short work of ransacking closets and drawers. "Too bad this guy did his drinking at home. We're not gonna find any helpful bartenders to tell us who he was with tonight."

"Yes we will." Mallory waited a beat, just long enough to make him a *little* crazy. "Peter Beck was on his way out, wearing his overcoat when the killer locked up."

Riker bit down on his lower lip. He was *not* going to play. He trailed her into a kitchen of many cabinets and more drawers to plunder, and finally he cracked and said, "So?"

"Let's say our perp stuffed the key ring in Beck's coat pocket. Easier to get at it again—*after* he cut the man's throat. Then he could slip the key back on the ring. That's what I'd do." She closed the last drawer, and her search was done. "Good idea. But later on, the keys got shifted to a pants pocket, and the killer couldn't get at them. Beck would've done that if he'd stopped off someplace between here and the theater—a place that checks coats. Even drunks go through their pockets before they hand a coat to a stranger."

"No way," said Riker. "Kid, you got lucky tonight. It all panned out, but don't push it, okay? Every guy in the world keeps his house keys in his pants pockets. That does *not* mean he checked his damn coat in a—"

"So where are the gloves? It's *cold* outside. We didn't find any gloves on the body, and they're not here, either."

And her partner said, *"What?"*

The wind was rising, the temperature falling. Impervious to cold, Axel Clayborne topped off his shot glass and smiled at his rooftop companion, the man in the neighboring deck chair. "So . . . Peter's dead, we covered that. . . . Oh, and I met the most extraordinary girl tonight. A blonde with a gun." The bottle was half gone when the actor looked up at the sky. The clouds had parted and the stars were out, but not many. Starlight was chintzy in New York City. "She's in her twenties. I'm pushing forty. Fancy my chances?"

Tactfully, Dickie Wyatt said nothing. But what was age to him anymore? He seemed to have grown younger with the passage of time. His brow had smoothed. The worry lines were gone.

His eyes were closed.

Good night, sweet prince.

With no fear of interrupting the man's rest, Axel raised his voice to say, "You don't *smell*, Dickie. Not a bit." He intended this as the highest of compliments. It was said that the corpses of saints did not stink, either.

Traveling along the shortest route to the theater, they found two restaurants with bars and coat-check service. The detectives got lucky when the second bartender looked at the photograph of their crime victim. The man left them for a moment and returned with a box of lost items. Passing over pairs of woolen gloves, he pulled out one of black leather lined with fur. "The guy came in alone, and this was lying on the bar when he left."

"Only *one* glove," said Mallory.

"Yeah, one glove. I saw him check all his pockets. I guess he was looking for the other one. He drank scotch. Paid cash. Tipped big. That's all I know."

In search of the second glove, they backtracked to a small saloon that had not made their shortlist for lack of a coat-check. The woman mixing drinks was Riker's dream bartender, not much on looks, more of a maternal soul, who coddled her customers by leaning on the pours for every shot of booze.

Motherlove for drunks.

She instantly recognized the dead man in the photograph, and Riker gave her points because she did not blanch at the sight of blood. The playwright had been a regular customer for the past three or four weeks. "A big tipper," she said with appropriate sadness and no need to add that, on this account, he would be missed.

Riker opened his notebook to scribble down the approximate time when Peter Beck had walked in the door. "And he had two gloves when he sat down?"

"Yeah." The bartender handed over a solitary black glove, the only one left behind. In answer to the next question, she said, "Peter came in alone. . . . At least, I think he did. He was looking around for somebody."

Mallory flashed her partner a *gotcha* smile.

Riker's pencil was stalled, as if it might have run out of lead. "Did the guy check his watch, like maybe he was lookin' to meet up with—"

"No," said the bartender, "he was surprised. It was more like he lost someone between here and the door."

This squared with the theory that Peter Beck had company when he left for the theater tonight. And now it seemed likely that the killer had ditched Beck here—to return to the apartment with the stolen key—so he could steal the victim's cutthroat razor.

And Mallory's punch lines just kept on coming.

The whiskey had a warming effect on Axel Clayborne. Or was he merely numb?

Certainly drunk.

Barehanded, he covered Dickie Wyatt's corpse with snow and smoothed this whitest of blankets until there was no trace of a mound, no sign of a grave.

Done. Hidden.

Till it be morrow.

One last toast?

No, the bottle was dry. He sent it flying across the rooftop. And only now, in Dickie's absence, Axel felt the cold.

Back in the car and on the roll, heading south through Greenwich Village, Riker slouched low in his seat. "It's late, kid. Time to pack it in."

"All right," said Mallory. "I thought we might visit the missing ticket holder, the guy who slipped past the cops in the lobby. . . . He lives in this neighborhood." After putting on some speed to pass through a red light before it could turn legal green—always a challenge—she made a left turn onto Houston. "But he didn't kill Peter Beck. So I guess that can wait till tomorrow."

Never would Riker ask how she had divined all of this from a flawed ticket count and a rookie cop's lie. He turned away from her to lightly knock his head against the passenger window.

SUSAN: (hushed) Don't they ever
            speak?
ROLLO: (loudly) My brothers
            grunt. Sometimes they gig-
            gle. And their needs are
            met. What use do they have
            for words?

                           —<u>The Brass Bed</u>, Act I

 Mallory was dressed for cold weather this morning, but the hallway was overheated by a hissing radiator, and she unbuttoned her new winter jacket, a rust-colored shearling. Riker was no fashionista. He could only guess that it was at least the price of ten topcoats like his own.

It was his turn to bang on the door of their runaway ticket holder. He could hear noises of a pet inside the apartment, one too small to bark like a real dog. Now the yappy little beast went silent. A dog with an off-switch? More likely the owner had hushed the animal—or thrown it out a window. He pictured Leonard Crippen snug in his bed, not at home to the police at this early hour.

Mallory bent down to slip a card under the door, and then Riker followed her into the elevator. He had so many questions, and he knew she would never give him straight answers. Where was the fun in that? They rode down to the ground floor in silence.

Last night, she had volunteered very little about Crippen, only mentioning that his theater seat had been surrounded by other people. And so it was easy to follow her logic for innocence. Given only forty seconds to kill a man—moving down a row of occupied seats in the blackout dark and on the run, trotting on toes without getting decked—well, that was just too tricky.

The detectives left the Greenwich Village apartment house to stand under a bright blue sky on Sixth Avenue. This was a neighborhood of human-scale structures, and a snow-covered playground across the street allowed more sunlight than other parts of town. Riker was quick to don his shades. He was not a morning person, but at least it was winter—no chirpy birdsong, only soft coos from dive-bombing pigeons that defecated on sidewalks and pedestrians all year long.

On the way to breakfast, he decided to save time and just ask Mallory how she knew the runaway's name and address. Oh, yeah, and how had she known where the guy was sitting? The police check of the audience had not included that kind of detail; because of the poor turnout, most audience members had abandoned their ticketed seats for better ones. But Riker was not inclined to ramble on with his queries, and so, as they crossed the broad avenue, he only said, "Talk to me."

Heading for a Bleecker Street café that did not keep sleepy Villagers' hours, they had walked a block or so before she said, "You remember that newspaper review, the one the stage manager—"

"'A play to die for,'" said Riker, quoting the headline, the only line he had been able to read without his bifocals.

"Last night, the *Herald*'s drama critic came back to see the rest of the play."

"That's Leonard Crippen?" Riker's loyalties lay with the *Daily News*, and he had no idea who wrote *their* theater reviews.

"It helps if you know the cashier's an actor," said Mallory.

"Of course she is." In this town, half the population was out-of-work actors, why not the cashier? "Let me guess. Donna Loo knows the critic on sight."

"Right." Mallory stopped on the corner outside the café. "And she gave him the same seat he had the night before, the best one in the house. Not the front row. Donna says the raised stage cuts off the actors' feet, and he would've missed the best part of a ballet scene."

Riker opened the door. "Got it." He could fill in the rest. When the stage manager had shown them the rave review for opening night, only Mallory had bothered to note the critic's name, one that was not on the police list for the audience. And then she had asked the cashier if Crippen had returned for the second performance.

Well, this was progress.

Most days his partner required no confirmation for ideas arrived at via telepathic transmissions from other planets. Best of all were the theories she constructed from nothing more than paranoia; they always panned out, and *that* was scary. But then there were the punch-line scenarios—

And now it was get-even time.

The air of the café was warm and rich with best-loved

smells of coffee and bacon. Because Mallory disliked any change in her routine, seats at their regular table were always empty when they walked in—thanks to Gurt, the waitress who lost tips when the young detective hovered over customers to speed up their breakfasts.

Riker was smiling when they sat down by the window. "I see Leonard Crippen as an older guy, a lot older than me." He looked out at the sidewalk, as if divining his insight from pigeon droppings in the snow. "*That's* why he ran out before the cops could stop him."

Mallory's eyes narrowed. Suspicious? Yeah, and, *bonus*, she was annoyed. Where did he get off doing *her* act? And how had he made the ageist connection to the critic's flight from the theater?

Easy. At the age of fifty-five, he had a growing sense of what it was like to be left behind—to eat a youngster's dust. "Crippen could've filed his review from the theater *if* he had a cell phone. Imagine a newspaper guy without one. So . . . no calling, no texting. And no time to stop and chat with the cops. That could take all night—and the critic had a deadline. He *had* to run for it . . . so he could turn in his review the old-fashioned, old-fart way."

Gotcha.

Streets in the SoHo precinct were small-town narrow and flanked by storefronts that changed their faces with every passing era from the factory age through the decades of squatters and artists, and then the galleries and the good-times roll of boutiques, antique stores and trendy restaurants. Now there were dark windows, here and there, with going-out-of-business posters and real estate signs signaling more changes to come.

After dropping Riker off at the station house, the only building to keep its purpose for a century, Mallory drove down to the end of the block, where she killed the engine. Snow was piled waist high between the unmarked police car and the sidewalk, and so she walked back along the slushy cobblestone roadbed—followed by footfalls, the long strides of catch-up steps.

Charles Butler spoke to her back. "You were missed at the last poker game." And now he walked alongside her, cutting an elegant figure in his long black coat, custom made for a man six-feet-four, who could not easily buy off the rack, even if he were so inclined—and he was not. Tailoring was something they had in common, that and the Louis Markowitz Floating Poker Game.

"You have to play next week," he said. "We need the money."

Mallory nearly smiled. The game was penny ante, a dollar bet was considered daring, and what were the odds that Charles could ever win? He was genetically programmed to blush in every attempt at deceit. And his smile was another accident of birth; in company with a frog's eyes and a large eagle beak, any expression of happiness made this very smart man look like a crazed clown. She almost forgot to be angry with him for chasing her down this morning.

Almost.

He had forgotten three barber appointments since she had seen him last. His brown hair had grown past his ears, and it would have covered his eyes but for a sudden gust that whipped it back and straightened out the curl. "Do you want to hear what was said behind your back?"

Not really. Her hands jammed into her pockets, head down to duck the wind, she walked faster now. He kept pace with her and kept up the fiction that this conversation was his own idea. Not annoying by nature, Charles was certainly doing the dirty work of someone else, an older man who would keep dogging her until one of them died, and so she asked, "How *is* Rabbi Kaplan?"

Her proof of conspiracy was in Charles's reddening face—that and David Kaplan's many calls stacking up on her answering machine, all invitations to the game and every one of them laced with guilt. The rabbi was ruthless in his lectures on her neglect of old friends—her crimes of the heart.

"David thinks the rules might be too hard on you," said Charles, the rabbi's emissary, his proxy *stalker.* "The others agreed. . . . I was your only defender."

A lame joke, but so was the card game. She had tired of it when she was twelve years old, long before Charles Butler had become a player. At forty, this psychologist was the youngest man in her foster father's tight circle of hand-me-down friends. Then and now, he was the anomaly in a world where cops and shrinks were natural enemies, though he had proved useful at times. Transparent Charles, who could not hide a lie of his own, had an uncanny knack for catching liars. He made a polygraph machine look like a Ouija board.

And he might be useful again.

She weighed the payoff against the attendant hassle of a predictable payment: a chair at the table in the poker game, a wasted night. *So* not worth it.

They had reached the station house. Mallory turned her back on him to pass through an opening in the snow bank, heading for the doors. She caught his reflection in the door's glass. Ephemeral. Ghosty. And now—the smile of a hopeful loon.

"Charles, I'm running late."

"The game's at my place this week. In your honor, we're dispensing with some of the rules."

The doors opened, two patrolmen stepped out, and she could see Riker waiting for her inside. "I have to go."

"Treys will *not* be wild if it snows," said Charles. "Sevens won't be wild cards, either, though it *is* an election year. And never mind the crescent moon. All cards will be dealt in a clockwise fashion."

Mallory watched his reflection as one hand reached out to tap her shoulder in a plea for her to turn around. He stopped an inch shy of touching her.

She had rules, too.

With no goodbye, she moved on through the doors, already forgetting that he was ever there.

The lieutenant in command of Special Crimes had no clear memory of how he had found his way home last night.

There had to be a better cure for high anxiety. Drink should be a last resort to keep his head from exploding. In his rookie days, Jack Coffey had spent much time in cop bars, studying under legendary drunks, but proved an unworthy acolyte with merely average ability to hold his liquor. He was also average in respect to physical features, his height and weight—ordinary everything, though the lieutenant was a better cop than most. Still in his thirties, some might say he was young to hold this command—and young to be losing his hair. The growing bald spot at the back of his head was put down to stress.

Too many murders in the house.

He held the telephone receiver to his ear and listened to a city councilman ramble on about missing night-vision goggles—like that was a sane complaint to a homicide squad. It made more sense when Councilman Perry ranted about having seen two first acts, and tonight he wanted to see the whole damn play, but how could the play go on if the police had the goggles?

It would be impolitic to explain to this man that the hierarchy of the NYPD did not include whiney bureaucrats. And so Jack Coffey said, "Goggles. Check. I'll get right on that."

Maybe next year.

Click. And the councilman was gone.

It would have been so helpful if Riker and Mallory had shown up on time to brief him on the Broadway suicide. This morning, most of his information had come from the media, and more reporters were stacking up in a row of blinking red lights for calls on hold. They would have to wait. In his present sorry state, he was sensitive to every noise, even to the sound of hair falling out of his scalp and crashing to the floor.

Leaving his private office, seeking relief from the telephone that would *not* stop ringing, the lieutenant carried
his newspaper out to the squad room, a large space with
tall windows filmed in grime to discourage sunlight. The
high ceiling was crisscrossed with pipes and ducts and
spanned by long tubes of ancient fluorescent lights that
hissed and threatened to go on the blink any minute.
Only two of the desks had empty chairs. The others were
occupied by men with cups of brew and deli bags.

No phones were ringing out here, not yet. Blessed peace.

The only holiday decoration was a small potted Christmas tree. This was a personal gift from the mayor to every
overworked squad in the city, a token of his honor's affec-
tion as he crippled the police with budget slashes. It said
to one and all, *Merry Christmas and screw you.* The tree
had turned brown, and the same apathy that denied it any
water had left it to rot on the windowsill. No, wait. Something was different today. The bright plastic decorations
were missing. Some joker had strung the brittle branches
with bullets painted black. Now doubly grim, the little
tree set the tone for morale.

Ah, his errant detectives had come through the stairwell door. They walked to the coatrack—*slowly*—as if they
were not late *enough.* He stared at Mallory as she shrugged
off her new jacket, rich suede lined with fleece. What the
hell did that thing cost? *Thousands.* It called to him across
the room, screaming, *Dirty money! Dirty money!* He
always took her wardrobe additions personally. She
wanted him to have a heart attack.

The lieutenant waited until the detectives sat down at

their facing desks by the bank of windows. Strolling up to them, he said, "Good morning. Did you guys have a nice *leisurely* breakfast?" There would be no yelling. Too much pain. He rolled his newspaper tight to the width of a beat cop's baton. "I wanna see your reports on my desk in—"

Mallory handed him a short stack of paper, and he leafed through it. She had typed up their reports and all the interviews. When did she sleep? Did she even *need* sleep?

Jack Coffey unrolled his newspaper and opened it to the entertainment section. "Let me read you a few lines from the *Herald*'s second review of the play. 'A death in the audience every night. It's a play *and* a lottery. Buy a ticket and take your chances, but get your will in order before you go.'" He crushed the paper into an unwieldy ball. "Commissioner Beale didn't bother with chain of command today. He called to ask if there was a problem with letting the play go on. CSU released your crime scene. So, unless you two have a—"

"Hey, no problem," said Riker. "Of course, if somebody dies tonight, that's gonna make us look stupid."

"Ain't gonna happen," said the lieutenant. "I called the ME. That woman who kicked off two nights ago? Dr. Slope says she had a heart attack. And the playwright's death was suicide." Jack Coffey sent his copy of the *Herald* flying ten feet to land in a corner wastebasket, a perfect shot. He was much practiced in disposing of bad press this way. And now a civilian clerk stepped up to him and handed over the preliminary autopsy reports still warm from the printer. *Nice timing.*

"Hold on," said Riker. "Even Harry Deberman knew that guy was murdered. He tried to hijack our case."

"Then I may personally hand it over to that worthless asshole." The lieutenant held up the two sheets of paper. "Prelims on your vics." He slapped them down, one on Riker's desk, "Heart attack!" and one for Mallory, "Suicide!" Softer now, he said, "Wrap it up. Make it go away."

The room temperature was chilly, the better to keep the meat from spoiling. A morgue attendant walked up to the wall of stainless steel lockers and pulled out two cold-storage drawers for the theater fatalities, Mrs. McCormick and Mr. Beck, who had died on successive evenings.

Tallest among the living and the dead was Dr. Edward Slope, a man with the ramrod posture of a general and gray hair that fit well with a countenance of unyielding stone. The wave of his hand was sufficient to send the attendant scuttling away. The doctor consulted his clipboard, scanning the autopsy findings, and—contrary to the complaint—he found nothing amiss with the work of his pathologists. Turning a cold eye on the two visitors from Special Crimes, he showed them a smile that said, *I'm going to eat you alive.*

Not every detective in the NYPD warranted a personal audience with the chief medical examiner, but he had a history with Kathy Mallory, an infrequent player in the Louis Markowitz Floating Poker Game. He had lost many a hand of cards to his old friend's foster child before the little shark was out of grade school. All these years later, he was still looking for ways to get even—and ways to keep her engaged in what passed for a relationship with another human being. Toward these ends, he employed more sophisticated challenges than cards, each encounter ending in a bloody face-off across a dead body. He did this for Louis. He did it for love.

So this was their game now. They both called it war. However, he was a gentleman, and the first strike would always be hers.

The young detective pulled the sheet back from the face of the woman's corpse. "You ruled her death as natural causes." This was said in the tone of talking down to imbeciles.

"Daring of me, wasn't it? My pathologist saw two heart valves that should've been replaced ten years ago. Then he leapt to the rash conclusion that it was heart failure, a *natural* death. And I signed off on it. *What* was I thinking?"

"There are other ways to bring on a heart attack."

"Yes, Kathy . . . there are." Oh, did that sound condescending?

"Mallory," she said—she *insisted*—so unforgiving in his use of her given name. Upon graduation from the Police Academy, she had granted him only the options of her rank or surname.

Tough.

He pulled the sheet down farther to expose crude autopsy stitches. "If you wanted to induce *this* heart attack, you'd have to cut her open, crack the rib cage, stick your hand into her chest cavity and shred two heart valves. . . ."

But my pathologist would've noticed that in the postmortem." He covered the late Mrs. McCormick. "The valves failed the heart. That's fact, not opinion. And the heart failed the woman." He turned to the neighboring drawer's steel bed with the draped corpse of the playwright, Mr. Beck. "And that one's a suicide. Exsanguination, to be precise. He bled out. I don't plan to change the cause of his death, either, *Kathy*."

This time she only glared at him for failing to address her in a more professional manner. She *had* warned him. There was always a warning before—

Riker stepped between them. "Here's the catch, Doc. These two people died in the same place, the exact same time on *two* different nights."

"I see. . . . So you assumed my staff must've missed something." *Not likely.* "Obviously, Mr. Beck *selected* the time of his death. A pity we can't ask him why he matched it to Mrs. McCormick's heart attack, but that's what happened. And *that* supports suicide."

Kathy Mallory drew back the sheet to expose the dead man's neck wound. "Very neat stitches. Dr. Pool did this one, right?"

"So he did." Eyes on the first page of the preliminary report, he paraphrased Dr. Pool's opinion. "No bruising, no defensive wounds. The *only* wound is consistent with suicide." He looked up from his reading. "So, before you ask, Mr. Beck isn't getting a broad-base tox scan, either." Slope handed his clipboard to the more reasonable detective, Riker, and pointed to a line on the top sheet. "Check out his alcohol level."

Riker donned a pair of bifocals and said, "Holy crap!"

Edward Slope nodded to second this opinion. "Rather admirable that he managed to remain upright long enough to get to the theater. Most men his size would've passed out on less alcohol. Our Mr. Beck seems to have had lots of practice." Retrieving the paperwork from Riker's hand, the doctor flipped to the next page. "Now here's an odd note—"

"He didn't have an alcoholic's liver," said Detective Mallory.

The medical examiner paused for a count of three. "Kathy, why don't we bypass the silly autopsies. Waste of my time. Just type up your own damn—"

"Hey," said Riker, "is she right?"

"No signs of long-term alcohol abuse, and Mr. Beck has indicators for a vegetarian. Stomach contents, skin coloring. High carotene levels—apparently he favored carrots. Very health-conscious diet. So the drinking jag indicates a recent change in his state of mind, but not for the better. And that *also* supports a finding of suicide. Dr. Pool's logic is flawless."

"The man's throat was *slashed*," said Kathy Mallory. "And a witness sitting next to him never noticed. Not a sound. Even if he was drunk, that wound had to—"

"There were no painkillers or sedatives—if that's where you're heading. Drugs like that would've shown up in our *standard* tox screen."

"There are drugs that don't—"

"He didn't *need* to be drugged!" Was this frustrating? Hell, *yes*. Tightening every muscle of his face, Edward

Slope looked down at his clipboard. "It appears that Dr. Pool was very thorough. He had CSU send over the weapon for wound comparison. A very sharp razor. The throat was slashed in a single stroke." He looked up at her. "It would take a while for pain to kick in . . . but he only had sixty seconds to live. *Possibly* ninety."

"Depending on the drug," she said. "There are rare—"

"Stop with the damn drugs! If we add something exotic to the alcohol in his system, he would've died before he could whip out the razor. Mr. Beck was losing a lot of blood very quickly. He was in *shock*—best painkiller known to God and man. So we're *done* with the bloodwork!"

The young detective inclined her head a bare inch, acknowledging his win—with a smile that so clearly said he had lost. And now he realized that she had never given a damn about the bloodwork. What did she—

Oh, bloody hell!

Dr. Slope stared at the final page of the report, a diagram of the wound, and then he walked around to the other side of the corpse for his first hard look at the actual trauma—and a flaw in Pool's logic.

The wound was not horizontal, not typical. It began below the right ear, angling down from there to divide the carotid artery, then crossing over to partially sever the windpipe. A half-cut throat was also atypical, but not the troublesome point. Once the body had been washed clean of blood, a more experienced pathologist would have understood the secondary injury, a minor one that had not bled, but only roughed the skin. This long abrasion ran parallel to the fatal cut.

Kathy Mallory was also staring at the corpse and leaning down close to it—kissing distance. *Such* an evil smile. The late Louis Markowitz would have been so proud of her today.

"What's this?" She touched the abrasion line below the cut. "Your pathologist missed a hesitation mark?"

She was enjoying this too much.

"No, wait," she said. "That *can't* be a hesitation mark. Even *Dr. Pool* knew the razor would've broken the skin. I say that's the drag line of a fingernail . . . on the hand that held the razor." She lifted the left hand of the corpse. Every nail had been chewed to the quick. "But I suppose suicide is . . . *possible*."

Could she be more sarcastic? He thought not.

When the detectives finally took their leave, they were carrying the chief medical examiner's *amended* report. Dr. Slope had split the difference between suicide and homicide with a call of "suspicious death."

SUSAN: They murdered all those
people? Women? Children?
ROLLO: Oh, never mind all that. Do
you like ballet?
—The Brass Bed, Act I

7

A cloudless sky. Damn sun. Come to melt the snow?

Axel Clayborne stood by the low brick wall that lined the roof, and he looked down at the street, lamenting the changes that he could see from his sky-high perch. Once, this part of town had been an enclave of entertainers who ran the gamut of broke to breakthrough money. But now the sidewalks were overrun with nannies pushing babies around in thousand-dollar strollers. Oh, TriBeCa was definitely a neighborhood in decline.

"We're sold out for tonight's performance," he said to the man who slept on his rooftop. The death was still too raw to call it anything but sleep. He knelt down to clear the snow from Dickie Wyatt's face. "You're looking well." Though the flesh was white beyond pale. And the eyes—a bit sunken? Perhaps.

The actor reached up to the parapet, where he had placed his newspapers alongside a steaming mug of coffee for himself and one for his friend, who was beyond thirst, but every good illusion required props. First, he opened the *Herald*, and when he was done reading aloud from Leonard Crippen's second review, he moved on to the next newspaper, which had sent an intrepid critic into the storm to review last night's performance. Though this woman's praise was not quite so lavish, she *had* been entertained, and, in a read with a bit of squint, it was a fairly good review. Tonight's weather forecast was free of snow, and the rest of the drama critics would certainly show up. "Dickie, the play's a hit, and no one's even seen the second act."

He looked down at his friend, who showed no joy in this.

Axel gulped the dregs of his coffee. "Sorry. Have to run. Reporters are waiting at the theater. Oh, and I promised Cyril I'd shake hands with a few politicians. He thinks that'll give us a shot at going on tonight—in case the police have other ideas."

The actor covered the sleeper's face with snow, the better to keep him fresh and fragrant, though he could not keep him for long. "What will I do when you're gone?"

Dickie Wyatt could not say.

Jack Coffey tried to concentrate on paperwork for the playwright's death, though it was hard to ignore the fact that a large bear was standing in the open doorway. He looked up to meet the slow brown eyes of his unannounced visitor, who wore a suit that fit tight across the broad shoulders. And he said to the bear, "What's up?"

Heller, the man in command of Crime Scene Unit, lumbered into the lieutenant's private office, held a small carton over the desk blotter—and dropped it.

That must be a clue.

"You caught a lucky break, Jack. All the evidence is useless. If the case ever makes it to trial, your guys won't need Clara Loman on their side in court. She hates their guts."

Now it was Jack Coffey's turn to shoot. "Yeah, I heard Loman came out of her bat cave last night. When's the last time she worked in the field? Five, six years ago?" That woman was the sacred cow of CSU, the one who had hired Heller back in his rookie days. But now this man was in charge of the whole department, and he ran errands for no one—not even her.

So what was Heller doing here?

"Your detectives had her team crawling all over that theater, looking for damn pieces of chalk. You know how many hours of overtime—"

"When did Clara Loman *ever* take orders from detectives?" That prima donna had been chained to a desk for good reason. "Did she *find* the chalk?"

Heller pretended not to hear this. "Peter Beck's fingerprints are the only ones on that razor. Some prints are smudged, but not the way I'd expect, one print layered over another."

"So you're thinking—gloves." Coffey picked up the sheet that detailed his detectives' pub crawl last night.

Peter Beck had lost his own gloves long before his throat was cut. But no one from CSU would know that.

"Yeah, gloves," said Heller. "That's what makes the razor useless. And most of the night-vision goggles had prints from the whole cast and crew. Everybody played with those things." He tapped the carton on the desk. "I can't cut 'em loose from evidence, but I bought these replacements at a toy store. Councilman Perry's been ragging my office all morning. He says the theater needs these goggles today." Heller nudged the box across the desk blotter. "Call it a present, Jack—if you wanna score a few points with the guy. He tells me he's real tight with Commissioner Beale."

Politicians had no influence on Heller, and yet here he was—playing politics.

Coffey drummed his fingers on the desk. "So . . . what about the chalk?"

Heller, the very busy man of few words, now sat down to chat for a while. "Blue chalk was found in a desk drawer. The theater people used it to mark up the stage during rehearsals. But the chalk on the blackboard was white, and it was old. Powdery, no modern binder."

"Sounds messy," said Coffey. "So Loman's crew found it."

"No, not a stick. They took samples from the writing on the blackboard. And none of the CSIs noticed chalk residue on anybody's hands. Maybe your perp wore gloves for the razor *and* the chalk. And now you got a pile of overtime on the books, all for nothing."

"But they found the gloves? Loman never said anything to my—"

"Naw, no latex, nothin' like that."

"It's winter," said Coffey. "Everybody's wearing gloves."

Oh, *crap* and *aha*!

Now he knew why Heller had come. This visit was all
about damage control—Clara Loman's damage. "Let me
guess. The CSIs only collected what people were wearing
during the blackout. Am I right? Yeah, all they'd care
about is bloodfly. Well, too bad our suspects' gloves never
got tested for blood . . . or chalk residue. I suppose the
killer's pair walked out the door with him—before Loman
even got around to hunting for the chalk. And *she's* pissed
off at *my* guys?"

Heller shrugged, and this was tantamount to waving
a flag of surrender. "Clara's off your case. She's taking
some sick days . . . and I owe you one."

Jack Coffey smiled and bit back his favorite adage for
dealings with this man: *Some days the bear gets you. And
some days you get that bear—by the balls.*

The *Herald*'s drama critic was still not at home to the
police, nor was he responding to messages left on his
answering machine. The newspaper's editor had sympathized with Riker and explained that, on principle, Leonard Crippen never opened his eyes before noon.

The detective had concluded one more follow-up call,
this one to the stage manager, and then he slammed down

the receiver of his desk phone and said to his partner, "Bugsy hasn't turned up yet."

Mallory's attention was focused on some point behind him, and he turned to see Clara Loman, queen of the CSU night shift. When the lady stepped up to the demarcation line between their two desks, she was missing her attitude of one who owns the earth beneath her feet. This morning, her place in the world seemed more tenuous.

And Loman's voice cracked when she said, "I'm not working your case anymore. Nothing personal. I'll be taking some time off." She stared at Mallory, maybe looking for some sign that the young detective had heard the other version, the rumor that Heller had removed her from the case because she had botched the job.

And yes, twenty minutes ago, that rumor had been phoned in by a snitch at CSU, and Heller's visit to Coffey's office had given it some weight. But Mallory gave away nothing. Her face was a mask.

"I don't like loose ends," said Loman. "Now . . . about the night-vision goggles. They're kids' toys, but old models, discontinued years ago. So you can scratch the toy stores, and I've already checked eBay. But the boxes were in a manufacturer's carton, and the shipping label should lead to a liquidator or a stolen-goods report." Now she laid down a thick sheaf of paper bound with a rubber band, and she did it with something approaching ceremony. "*This* is a copy of the play."

What were they supposed to do with that? *Read* it?

As for the goggles, it had taken his partner ten minutes

to match the carton to a robbery for the year when the goggles were brand-new. Mallory could even name the day when the box was boosted off the back of a delivery truck. Yet Loman stood there waiting for their thanks— thanks for nothing. However, never one to keep a lady waiting, Riker was prepared to do the gallant thing.

Mallory beat him to it. She rose from her desk and extended her hand to the older woman, saying, "Thanks."

When Clara Loman shook hands, she did not smile. No one had ever seen her do that. But she squared her shoulders and made a curt nod before marching away.

Riker watched the woman's retreating back, which was straighter now, as she passed through the stairwell door with her dignity restored—by Mallory of all people. His partner could still surprise him, and he toyed with the idea that she might have a heart.

Now you see it—now you don't.

He snapped back to reality when he saw Heller standing outside of Coffey's office—*watching*. So Mallory had only been building up currency in the CSU favor bank. That unit's commander had always looked out for Clara Loman, who, by temperament, by age and grating personality, would never find another job.

Mallory was running a game on *Heller's* heart.

Axel Clayborne saw the ground floor of the SoHo station house as a landmark from the era of Boss Tweed and Tammany Hall. *Marvelous.* Century-old molding and hardwood floors remained intact. Civilians and police walked to and fro, paying the film star no attention until he removed his dark glasses and muffler. A policewoman stopped to gape at him, and another officer thrust a pen and paper into his hand, saying, "You mind? The wife's a big fan."

Axel smiled as he personalized his autograph with the name of the officer's spouse. Then he handed the man two complimentary theater tickets. "They're for the end of the week. Tonight's performance sold out in six minutes."

After enduring profuse thanks, the actor explained the errand that had brought him here, and the officer called out to a man behind a tall desk. "Sarge? Mr. Clayborne's here for the goggles."

A visitor's card on a chain was strung around Axel's neck, and he was escorted up the staircase to Special Crimes. The stairwell door opened into a large, bleak room that smelled like a breakfast menu of various foods, though the aroma of coffee prevailed. There were cups and deli bags on every abandoned desk. The sole occupant of this space was a hulking brute in street clothes. He had the low brow of a great ape and the face of menace incarnate, yet he introduced himself in a voice of surprising softness. "I'm Detective Janos. . . . We've been *waiting* for you."

Did that sound just a bit ominous? Oh, yes. Good touch.

The actor followed the large detective to the end of a hallway, where a door was opened. With a gentle wave that was almost dainty, Axel was ushered inside a small room. The promised box of night-vision goggles sat on a small square table ringed with chairs. As he picked up the carton, the door closed behind him. His guide was gone, and a metallic click told him the door had been locked. He turned around to see his reflection in a framed mirror. All the cop roles played in his formative years had not been for naught, though it *was* clever to disguise an interrogation room with a vending machine, a refrigerator and a coffeemaker. He bowed to the audience he could only imagine on the other side of that one-way glass. And now, with no stage direction necessary, he sat down to wait for the priceless opportunity to be grilled by actual police.

And he waited.

Every few minutes, he stole glances at the clock on the wall. A half hour passed before the door opened. *At last.*

When Detectives Mallory and Riker entered the room, he had the sense that they were somehow displeased with him. The tall blonde folded her arms, and her voice was a bit testy when she said, "We were expecting Bugsy."

"And you wound up with me, the star . . . instead of the gopher. Well, *now* I understand your disappointment." Collecting the box had been a ruse. He had been asked to come here—to charm the police and sleep with whomever he must so that the play could go on. But his own incentive was purely to see her again. She had seduced him with indifference. And the gun had also made her wildly attractive.

The less lovely Detective Riker flopped down in a chair. His hooded eyes presupposed a lie before he asked the first question. "The stage manager told us he'd send Bugsy over to pick up the goggles. So where *is* the little guy?"

Axel Clayborne splayed his hands to ask, *Who knows or cares?* "He's an errand boy. He comes and goes. Everyone else is still at the press conference. The stagehands, too. So I was—"

"Yeah, yeah," said Riker. "How well do you know him?"

"Bugsy? We don't travel in the same circles. My wine bottles have corks. You need an informant in the screw-cap crowd." He turned to the mirror, imagining the amusement of watchers beyond the looking glass.

Detective Mallory was also staring at the mirror, though it was not angled to catch her reflection. She walked over to the wall and straightened the frame, as if it might be off-kilter. If so, that defect had been invisible to any *normal* human eye.

So the mirror was only that and nothing more, not a window to another place, and apparently he was sitting in a lunchroom. Axel smiled at this good joke on himself as he watched Mallory reach out to the box of goggles and shift it so that one edge was parallel with that of the table.

A tidy and meticulous detective.

And perhaps a little crazy?

He hoped so. *Great* fun.

She sat down on the other side of the table and faced him with a look so cold. To screw with a line from Byron, there was something primal in her aspect and her eye when she said, "Tell us what you know about Bugsy."

"Not much," said Axel. "Never met him till the first day of rehearsal. Our erstwhile director, Dickie Wyatt—he's the one who hired the gopher."

Riker pulled out his notebook and pen. "Where can we find Wyatt?"

Asleep beneath the snow.

"No idea. His contract expired after the third week of rehearsals. You see, three weeks is all the time most plays ever—"

"Bugsy gave his full name as Willard Albright," said Mallory.

"Seriously? Bugsy *was* Willard Albright's nickname, but he's fictional."

Riker waved his pencil in impatient circles. "We already *know* he gave us a bogus name."

"No, I mean fictional, as in—a *work of fiction.* Maybe a chicken and the egg kind of thing? What came first? The real-life Bugsy or a character from a play?"

The detectives exchanged glances, and then Riker's pencil touched down on his open notebook. "What's the name of this play?"

"I'm not sure. Could've been a film, I suppose. People are always sending me scripts for—" Axel snapped his fingers. "You know who you should talk to? Leonard Crippen. He's the theater critic for the *Herald.*" Ah, a spark of interest from Detective Mallory, and now his smile was all for her. "I'll tell you how Bugsy gets his gopher jobs. No matter what the play is—a Broadway show or a church-cellar production—if you hire Bugsy, that's a guarantee that Crippen will review it. He may pan it, but he *will* show up on opening night."

The detectives were done with him—and so quickly, both of them moving toward the door.

No kisses? No goodbyes?

ROLLO: Fetch a chair for our
        guest! (One twin opens the
        closet doors and pulls out
        a wheelchair.) A souvenir
        from my leaner days.

                    —The Brass Bed, Act I

8

His long hair was curly and bright white—it *thieved* light—a dramatic contrast to the black coat draped over his shoulders. All of his clothing was black, but not slimming. Though he had been dragged here by uniformed officers, the man with three chins stood on the threshold, politely awaiting an invitation to enter the squad room. His chest heaved with a much aggrieved sigh to let them all know that he should not be kept waiting long.

Mallory rose from her desk and called out to him, "Mr. Crippen!"

"Detective Mallory?" With a flourish, the theater critic waved the card she had left under his door. He moved down the aisle of desks, preceded by fifty pounds or so of excess weight on his belly, and he carried this paunch with grandiosity. When he stood before her, he bowed

and said, "At your service." But this did not sound ludicrous, not from a man in his seventies.

She turned to her partner, who only smiled to say,
Nailed it, didn't I? And yes, he had. The critic was indeed
old and certainly from the lost world of the low-tech
people.

"Have a seat, Mr. Crippen."

In a contest of sorts, he remained standing until she
sat down, and then he settled into the chair beside her
desk, shifting a bit, arranging his tie and his bulk. He
emitted one more sigh, as though put out by this exertion.

"Thanks for coming in," said Riker, with a touch of
sarcasm for the runaway ticket holder. "We understand
Bugsy has a lot of influence with you."

"And we think that's strange." Mallory followed her
partner's lead, forgoing threats for the critic's flight from
the theater—*and* the police. "But everything about Bugsy
is a little . . . *off*."

"I know him well, and I'd love to discuss that dear
little man. However, just this moment, I have a small
problem." Leonard Crippen paused for another sigh, and
this one should have been reserved for a death in the
family. "You see, I plan to go back for tonight's performance. However, since the theater company didn't antic-
ipate a *third* review from me, all the best seats were taken
by the time I called. The only one they had left is not very
good. . . . They put me in the back row."

The critic's slow smile was an easy translation for Mallory. She recognized it from her own repertoire, and now
she completed this blackmail transaction. "We roped off

four seats in the front row. Would you like to sit in the dead man's chair?"

"Oh, *would* I!"

Alma Sutter's long blond hair was done up in a bun and secured by two pointed sticks, her idea of weaponry. She flicked a wall switch by the stage door, and fluorescent tubes lit up the long passageway to the backstage area, where she found another switch. More light, but not much. The young actress unbuttoned her coat as she walked toward the dark side. Before rounding the back of the stage set, she stopped and stood very still, holding her breath.

Listening—to nothing.

No footsteps, no chalk scratching on slate, but did she feel safe yet? No. And she never would. Not here.

The blackboard was lit by a rectangle of weak light shining through the door in the scenery flat, but the blocky chalk words were clear enough. And Alma wrapped her coat tight around her, though there was no draft, no sudden drop in temperature—except for what shock could do to the *innards* of a body. *That* was cold.

She pulled one of the sharp sticks from the pile of hair atop her head. Stupid flimsy thing. Next to useless. What was closer, the alley door or the prop locker with the baseball bat?

No matter now. Her knees were buckling, threatening to drop her to the floor.

She turned toward the scenery door. Onstage, a single

caged bulb hung down by a wire, burning bright in an ancient custom to prevent the mischief that unworldly spirits did in the dark. The ghost light was only left on when the last living soul had left the theater.

So she was alone.

Screaming was futile.

Alma turned back to the blackboard. Cyril Buckner would never believe this. Every time she told him about a personal message from the ghostwriter, the stage manager counted it as a black mark against her, another sign that she was doing drugs. And she was. But not hallucinogens. Today she was doing cocaine, doing her best to be sharp and—

Focused.

Alma fished her cell phone from a coat pocket. Working through the fright, she flicked by applications, hunting for the camera function before this new message could disappear. They were all so quickly there and gone.

No good. Her hands were shaking. The phone dropped to the floor.

Idiot.

She wanted to run, but her legs had gone to noodles that could not carry her anywhere. She could only stare at the five chalk words on the slate.

IT WON'T HURT MUCH, ALMA.

"I'm sure if you only ask him," said Leonard Crippen, "Bugsy will tell you his full name is Willard Albright."

"That's the alias he gave us." Mallory leaned toward the drama critic. "Do you have binoculars for your seat in the *back row*?"

"His real name is Alan Rains . . . or maybe that's his stage name."

Riker looked up from his notebook. "Bugsy's an actor?"

"You no doubt see him as a cute little fellow with a Bronx accent. But he cut his teeth on Shakespeare at Yale Drama School."

"So you *do* know him well." Mallory made this sound like an accusation.

"Oh, yes," said Crippen. "I'm his biggest fan. Whenever he gets a new job as a gopher, he pays me a visit and pitches that company's play. And he acts out all the parts."

"The whole play?"

"No, only scenes from first acts. Bit of a tease. If I want the end of a story, I have to go to the theater like everyone else. Then I review the play—so Bugsy will come back to me with another one."

"You do it for laughs," said Riker.

The critic expelled a puff of air—incredulous. "I *do* it for the pleasure of his performance. Bugsy's brilliant. If he didn't pitch the plays, I'd never get to see him act. Writing a review is a small price for that experience—even a tiresome play by Peter Beck. Though I must say I was pleasantly surprised. This one's not at all Beck's style. He writes tedious melodramas about family relationships. But the current play seems to have a touch of Hitchcock. Of course, I only know the first act. I'm sure you read the whole thing." He turned from one detective to the other. "You *didn't*?"

It was perverse. Of course it was. But the ghostwriter had made her a better actress, and this idea had once fed Alma's theory that Dickie Wyatt had left her all those messages, pushing her into a state of terror, another country with a scream for an anthem. Who but Dickie would have cared enough to scare her?

Back in the safe cradle of her Ohio hometown, no one had ever been unkind to her. She had been loved—poor preparation for *this* town, for this role that required cold sweat and a skippy heart. But now she had the hang of fear; she lived inside of it, slept in it, woke to it. But today's threat was different. It promised pain. Alma read the words over and over. Where was the ghostwriter now? Coming for her? Right behind her? She had pills for moments like this, but trembling hands could not manage the childproof cap on her anti-anxiety meds, and the pharmacy bottle dropped to the floor. She willed herself to walk toward the alley door. Then she ran.

Behind her, she heard the sound of fingernails screeching on slate.

She stopped.

And turned.

No one there.

Against her will, her legs walked her back to the blackboard. *No-o-o!* She screamed, or thought she did. Her mouth opened wide, but nothing came out.

The five words were gone, replaced by so *many* words filling out the slate, a zillion letters printed in the seconds it had taken her to cut and run.

"I don't think they held out on you," said Leonard Crippen. "I'm sure the theater company has no idea that Bugsy is Alan Rains. He only had one role in a Broadway play, and only for six months. Well, that was *years* ago. He's very different now. His speech, the way he dresses—the way he *doesn't* comb his hair. And he smells like a clothing rack in a secondhand store. All of that fits the role he played on Broadway. He even took the character's name, Bugsy—a small, scared creature of desperate moves—a gopher. And now he's Bugsy all day, all night. I've never known him to step out of character."

"So he's crazy," said Riker.

"Aren't they all? The theater's a dicey way to make a living. No safety net. No guarantees that you'll pay the rent next month. You'd *have* to be insane to want that life. Now this is where it gets very cruel."

More detectives had straggled into the squad room. Some of them perched on nearby desks, and others formed a loose circle around the critic, listening to the story of a sorry little man who could not find his way out of a play.

Fingers fluttering, all in a panic, Alma Sutter fumbled with the key to open her dressing room door. One blind hand flicked on the light switch, as if that might save her. She slammed the door and locked it. Panting from her run up the stairs, she sank into the arms of a padded chair. Waves of hair fell down around her shoulders. Her top-knot had come undone and so had she.

The closet was wide open, and the bright red dress she wore onstage should have been the first thing to catch her eye. But it was gone, replaced with another costume.

So the ghostwriter had a key to this room. There were no safe places. Where was he? Right *now*—where?

A row of glowing bulbs lit the makeup mirror on the wall. And below it, pots of paint and sticks of more color, brushes and tubes had been swept to one side, making space for a pair of scissors laid out on the table like criss-crossed knives.

Very sharp.

The first cut was tentative, sloppy.

Alma cried.

"It's all about unacted desires." The squad room was now full of cops. His audience complete, the critic stood up, swept back his hair and addressed them. "Allow me to set the stage." He lowered his head as a modest bow. All eyes were on him when he raised his chin and said, "The curtains part, and you see a sparsely furnished bedroom in a New York high-rise. The back wall has a large window with a skyline view. There's a lamp on a table, but no chairs. Scores of matchboxes are glued to the wallpaper. The main character, Rollo, a rather corpulent fellow—"

As a concession to this particular crowd, he said, "A *very* heavy man languishes on a brass bed center stage.

"That role should've been played by a younger actor, but it's Axel Clayborne, so who cares? He plays an invalid. Stage left, a door opens, and you see a young woman, Susan. She enters walking backward. She won't take her eyes off two identical young men, who seem to be herding her into the room. The twins leave. She tries the doorknob. Useless. She's locked in. The woman turns to the invalid on the bed. She's timid, frightened. Susan tells Rollo she's come to help him. And, given her current predicament—he laughs.

"They develop an instant rapport based on mutual terror of the twins, who keep popping into the room. Rollo asks them to fetch a chair for their guest. They go to the closet and pull out a wheelchair. Rollo explains that he outgrew it years after the accident. He tells her that the twins stuff him with food day and night. 'One day,' he says, 'I won't be able to fit through the door.' Slowly he turns to the window, a wider exit. Then he tells her how his spine was damaged. This leads into the story of a family massacre, which his two brothers survived without a scratch. But other relatives? Not so fortunate.

"Now Rollo tells her about his dead dream. Before he was paralyzed, he had trained as a dancer. And that brings us to the Fat Man's Ballet. In the middle of Susan's line, the lights go out. She falls silent. Then a spotlight shines on Rollo, the only one not in shadow. Susan's frozen like a statue. You hear the opening strains of the *Firebird Suite*. The lights flick on and off as the invalid rises from his bed, and he begins to dance in his pajamas and bare feet. . . . And he is *beautiful*. You wouldn't expect that. There's no comedy here. No one laughs at the dancing fat man. The audience sees his dream play out. The heart melts. Then he makes one fabulous leap onto the bed. You want to applaud. But then . . . he leaps out the window, shattering the glass. The audience gasps. The lights go out. You hear the city sounds of traffic in the dark. Then dead silence. The stage lights come up. The window is unbroken, and the invalid is back in his bed. The actress moves again and speaks the rest of her interrupted line.

"That was the first fantasy sequence. The next one was so frightening, it gave a fatal heart attack to a woman in the audience. . . . But I can't bear to ruin it for you. You really *must* see the play."

It was a stage manager's job to assume responsibility for absolutely everything. All during the rehearsal period—which would not *end*—between changing lines and stage blocking, new lighting cues and a mountain of paperwork, Cyril Buckner also played the rabbi, doling out wisdom. Then, as the actors' priest, he heard confessions. He had also stepped in after Dickie Wyatt's contract had lapsed, and now he did that man's job, too, keeping faith with the director's vision—and the ghostwriter's play, which would not stop changing.

On the plus side, the increased rehearsal time was a luxury in Broadway economics. On the downside of high legal fees and stalled openings, he now had a skeleton

crew. Declining cuts in pay, most of his people had quit
before the first performance. And the unions were knocking on his door, banging it down, wanting to chat about
violations like replacing the doorman with a rent-a-cop,
and *not* replacing other people, and maybe the TWU had
discovered that the dresser, Nan Cooper, was working for
free. Add one more hassle to the mix, and Cyril was going
to *kill* somebody.

Anyone would do.

Today, he had begun with new bits of action for the
Rinaldi brothers, who played out their psychotic roles to
the nth degree, on and offstage. Typecasting had been
Dickie Wyatt's art, stumbling only when hiring Alma
Sutter, no one's first choice for the role of Susan. Now
the ghostwriter had given her *more* lines.

And where *was* that stupid bitch?

The stage manager cum director read Alma's part for
Axel Clayborne, who lounged on the brass bed, flanked
by the twins. This actor was always line perfect. And so,
when he missed the next cue, Cyril Buckner was startled,
and he looked up from the page to see all three of his
actors peering into the wings.

Alma Sutter stepped through the scenery door to stand
under the spotlight. She raked one hand through her
mutilated hair, and then, parading upstage and down in
her new costume, she asked, "What do you think?"

"Shoot me," said Cyril. "Just *shoot* me and get it over
with!"

The Rinaldi twins, as usual, were speechless.

Axel Clayborne clapped his hands. "The haircut

reminds me of a salon on the Lower East Side. Their idea of styling hair's a bit like rough sex in the Third World. But Nan Cooper's a wizard with scissors. She can fix that. Otherwise, it's wonderful. Edgy. Risky."

"Bullshit!" Cyril turned on Alma. "What the *fuck* have you done to yourself?"

She felt the punch of words more than most people, and now she backed away, her hands flying up to protect her ears. "It's the ghostwriter's change, not mine."

"*Screw* him!" The stage manager crumpled the change sheets in one hand. "You can't *do* this. We're already pushing our luck with the cops."

"Oh, I don't know," said Axel. "I suppose it depends on whether or not you think the ghostwriter murdered Peter. You believe it, don't you, Cyril? So who would you rather piss off—the cops or a psycho?"

SUSAN: What are they doing with
       that matchbox?
ROLLO: They're collecting the dead
       flies. Every boy needs a
       hobby.
                    —<u>The Brass Bed</u>, Act I

9

Out on the street, the line was long for the sold-out performance, and reporters interviewed ticket holders, asking if they liked their chances of living through this night.

Sidestepping the cameras and lights, a troop of detectives from Special Crimes entered by the alley door. More than half the squad had volunteered to do backstage reconnaissance off the books, only wanting the rest of the story that Leonard Crippen had begun at the station house. The motives of the civilian audience were less pure: blood and guts *and* a play for the price of admission.

Mallory led the way to the stage manager's desk in the wings, where they all stopped to read the latest message on the blackboard.

Cyril Buckner joined them to cock one thumb at the

words printed in white chalk. "Never mind that. He's screwing with you guys. But we're playing it safe. You saw the ambulance parked outside? We hired it for the night."

"Cheap publicity gimmick," said Detective Janos.

"No, we *also* gave complimentary tickets to three cardiologists. We don't *want* anyone to die tonight."

Riker was born with a face that said, *I know you're lying.* It was his best comeback line, and he never needed to say it aloud. The stage manager walked away—quickly. The detective stayed to stare at the ghostwriter's message for his partner. It could only be a continuation of the threat to take off her head: MALLORY, TONIGHT'S THE NIGHT. NOTHING PERSONAL.

He turned to the pair of wheelchairs parked in the wings. A mannikin sat in one of them, draped with a sheet—like a corpse.

Mallory walked toward the tiny camera hidden on a shelf overlooking the blackboard. It was still in place. She ran a wireless feed on the screen of her cell phone. "Bugsy, when did that message show up?"

"Maybe an hour before you guys walked in the door."

She sped up the film, rushing it toward that time stamp, and watched the jerky motion of foot traffic passing by the board. The screen went black on Bugsy's mark for the timing of the chalkboard threat. Had her perp covered the lens of this camera, too? She reached up to touch the small device. No tack to the surface, no evidence of tampering. "Did the lights go off tonight?"

"Yeah, a few times. On and off. A glitch in the system. Happens a lot. Gil ran through all the cues on his panel. Everything's workin' fine now."

So the ghostwriter had worked in the dark, and the missing pair of night-vision goggles would help with that. What else did he have in the way of technology? How had he known she was filming the board? There had been no one else in the theater when she had selected her hiding place.

Mallory looked up to the chaos of wiring, rope and cables overhead and considered Bugsy's theory that the ghostwriter had a camera of his own hidden somewhere up there. A movement caught her eye, and her gaze shifted to the high catwalk, where she saw the back of Gil Preston, who moved quickly toward the other side of his metal walkway in the air.

Her answer might not lie in technology; it might be as simple as a bird's-eye view. Or something else. She switched off the desk lamp and saw light leaks in the stage set's flimsy wall.

Peepholes?

The theater was humming with hundreds of conversations. Every velvet chair was occupied except for the four front-row seats reserved for the NYPD. Riker removed a gold, tasseled rope from the armrests of one, and he sat down as a gleeful Leonard Crippen settled into the dead playwright's seat.

The houselights dimmed. The curtains parted to a

round of applause for the famous movie star on the brass bed. And thirty seconds into the first act, this night began to slide downhill. Enter Alma Sutter, backing onto the stage, being herded through a door by the creepy twins. Her waist-long hair had been chopped back to blond curls that only grazed her shoulders, and she had changed her stage costume—radically. No red dress this time. She wore a blazer, jeans and a silk T-shirt.

Did she seem taller now?

The detective had to rise from his seat, enduring hisses from the people behind him, to see over the edge of the raised stage. He expected high heels, but the actress wore black running shoes like Mallory's. Alma was simply *acting* taller. Riker donned his bifocals for a better look at the bee-stung lips drawn on the woman's mouth in the same red shade of lipstick that his partner used, and Alma had even changed the color of her eyes to Mallory green.

Leonard Crippen whispered, "Marvelous likeness."

Riker shook his head. This was so wrong. He only heard bits of the actors' conversation. He was more aware of the weight of a gun in his shoulder holster. When the stage lights flickered, the gun weighed more.

Onstage, the actor in the fat suit raised his voice, and this time Riker heard each word as the man demanded a chair for his guest. One of the twins pulled a wheelchair from the closet, and the fake Mallory sat down. The actress's impression was not very good, even by Riker's low standards. He ceased to listen to her lines of dialogue. He only caught the tone. She spoke like a dime-store replica of Mallory, missing every subtlety and abusing the flat affect that his partner only trotted out when she wanted to make a scary point. But when Riker removed his eyeglasses, the physical likeness was good—too good.

While the spotlight was on Axel Clayborne during the Fat Man's Ballet, Riker was looking to the shadows where Mallory's doppelganger sat in the wheelchair, one hand lifted in a lifeless mannikin pose. He had no easy moments until the fantasy sequence ended with a crash of glass from Clayborne's leap through the window. And now a blackout. Ten seconds of darkness.

C'mon! C'mon!

Fifteen seconds. *Twenty.*

The stage lights came up. The broken window was mended. The invalid was lying on his brass bed, and the frozen woman came back to life. Riker could no longer look at her and see anyone but Mallory.

The actors resumed their conversation of sudden deaths in the family—lots of them.

By stage light, Riker checked his wristwatch. They were closing in on the time when Peter Beck had been murdered.

Onstage, the bedridden invalid was somehow offended by what the woman said, but Riker had not been paying attention to those lines. The lights flickered to cue another fantasy scene, and the actress froze into her statue pose again. The man rose from his bed, one hand clenched.

Riker's hand moved toward his gun.

But the actor did not strike her. He gently touched her hair, her face. He leaned in close and inhaled her perfume. The stage went dark for a count of five seconds, and when the lights came back on, Clayborne held a baseball bat in his hands. Flickering in and out of darkness, the actor slowly raised the bat for a swing. A spotlight was trained on him as the bat connected to the fake Mallory's face— and smashed it. Her bloody head went flying off her body to roll toward the footlights.

A fake head.

And now for Riker's next surprise, the crowd *cheered*. *Goddamn pack of ghouls.*

His gun was in his hand when the lights went out again.

The detective ticked off forty sweaty seconds of darkness, and when the stage lights brightened, the actor was in his bed once more, the actress's head was back on her shoulders, and they were talking, gesturing, all the signs of life ongoing. The curtain came down, the houselights came up, and—*Oh, Christ!*—Mallory was seated beside him, holding a pair of night-vision goggles.

Two heart attacks in one night.

"Lots of time to slit your throat," she said.

Leonard Crippen was clapping and shouting, "Brilliant! Just brilliant!" When the audience applause died down, he said, "An original scheme of unrequited love. He hates her, loves her, wants to bed her and behead her. On opening night, Clayborne got a bit carried away with that baseball bat—like he was going for a home run. And that poor woman who died in the audience? She was sitting front-row center when the rubber head flew into her lap."

Mallory leaned forward in her chair to see around her

partner and glare at the critic. "And you didn't think that was worth mentioning? . . . *Earlier*?"

"I *said* I didn't want to ruin it for you." Crippen sighed, clearly feeling unappreciated.

"So Dr. Slope was right about the lady's heart attack," said Riker.

There was no way to plan a thing like that. The opening-night fatality had been a natural death and not a rehearsal for the murder of Peter Beck.

"That head wasn't in the police report for the first death," said Mallory.

"Yeah." Riker faced the critic. "No flying heads. I would've remembered that. So a woman drops dead in the front row. And somebody thoughtfully removes the fake head from her lap *before* the cops show up?"

"No idea," said Crippen. "The audience was cleared out almost immediately. I don't know *when* the police arrived."

"Then it wasn't cops who shut down the play," said Riker.

And they had been lied to.

"Oh, no. The stage manager cleared out the theater that night. He didn't tell you? He begged the crowd— well, maybe twenty people on opening night. He *begged* them not to give up the finale for the first act. No doubt he was thinking of the lawsuit potential for killing a theater lover that way. For my part, I didn't mention the flying head in my review—so as not to ruin the first act for the next audience. . . . I have rules. Well, last night, when Peter Beck died, I had the same—"

"Trouble." Mallory stared at the floor in front of the last empty chair in this row, where trickles of blood flowed in thin streams.

The drama critic watched the paramedics load their patient onto a gurney, and he sighed, though not in sympathy with the young victim. He turned to the detectives, asking, "When will we *ever* move on to the second act?"

The teenager on the gurney was ashen, but still alive. The slashed wrists were bound in thick bandages. His companions for the evening, a girl and a boy, attended the same high school in the neighboring state of New Jersey. They were also members of the same suicide club, though tonight they had shown less resolve than their friend, and their own razor blades had been taken away from them.

Attracted by the recent death count for the play, they had hoped that a triple suicide would get their names in the newspapers. "And maybe we'd be on TV," said the schoolgirl.

Riker never flinched. He had heard every damned thing.

But the theater critic was not so blasé. "A suicide club? You're a bit young for such a dead-end idea."

The girl only lifted one slight shoulder in response, and her friend said, "We're from Jersey," as if that said it all.

"You two can go." Mallory waved them toward the aisle, where police officers waited to transport the youngsters to Bellevue's psych ward, thwarting any other plans they might have for ending this night.

Riker looked out over the audience. It was a real New York crowd—*pissed off.* They wanted to stay, regarding the latest victim as part of a show that was not over yet. And damn it—the kid wasn't even *dead.* Grudgingly, they filed out the doors to the lobby, prompted by police officers.

In the back row, people struggled to pass the inconvenient obstacle of a man who had not yet surrendered his seat. Much annoyed, a woman nudged him, and then, dropping her testy attitude, she bent down to lift the brim of his baseball cap for a close inspection of his pale face.

And a sniff.

She called out to the two detectives standing near the stage. "Hey! You missed one!"

ROLLO: They need me for my disability checks. But
also . . . they need an
audience.
—The Brass Bed, Act I

10 The strong cologne slathered on the corpse could not completely mask an odor of putrefied flesh. But going by appearances and not the smell, the man with pale skin and a stubble of beard might be only dozing. Decomposition had not yet grotesquely altered the features, though wrinkles would have smoothed out with the ultimate relaxation of death, and so he might be thirty or ten years older. And he had not died in that red velvet chair, not tonight.

Riker snapped on latex gloves and lifted the ball cap to see a good head of brown hair, no distinguishing bald spots. In life, the victim had been a sloppy eater—or maybe drunk when he had stained his shirt with food. And there was crusty vomit trapped in the laces and tongues of his shoes.

Just the kind of corpse that Riker could relate to.

He caught the eye of the man piloting the medical examiner's gurney. "Hold off till we get an ID." The detective jabbed one thumb back over his shoulder to point out the cast and crew lining up in the aisle to view the dead body. "Maybe another fifteen minutes, okay?"

Riker turned to the young man at his side, an on-call pathologist, who hoarded words as if they might be worth money, and whose name he had not bothered to remember. The pencil-line moustache alone had earned the detective's contempt. "Is there *anything* you can tell me?"

"Rigor passed off." The doctor lifted the corpse's left hand and let it fall. "But this is secondary laxity. The victim didn't die tonight," he said, telling the detective nothing that he had not already guessed the moment he saw the body—*smelled* the body.

"Great," said Riker, "just *great*." He elbowed the boy pathologist out of the way, and then leaned down to peel back the dead man's coat—a *nice* coat, *lots* of money. He freed the arms from the sleeves, and leaned the torso forward. Raising the shirttail high, he could see dark stains on the shoulder blades where contact was made with the ground and gravity had pooled the blood. He knelt down to lift one of the victim's pant legs and found more stain on the calf muscle. "And now we know the guy was laid out flat after death." Some winters they would find the bodies of street people dead of exposure, but those corpses were almost always curled on their sides, different blood pools. He rolled the shirtsleeves up past the dead man's elbows. "Okay, we got old track marks from a needle, but no new punctures. Good to know." And the detective left the on-call pathologist as he had found him, a man with nothing useful to do.

Riker strolled down the aisle, passing the line of people waiting to view the corpse. Joining his partner near the stage, he said, "I figure the guy's been dead at least two days."

Mallory resumed her conversation with the head usher. "And you can't remember a *dead* man handing you a ticket at the door?"

Tough one. The usher scratched his head.

"The smelly man," said Riker.

And now the usher smiled. "Oh, yeah—the guy in the wheelchair. His nurse gave me the tickets. Hers was standing room, his was handicap seating. That means we park 'em in the aisle. He wore a baseball cap, so I never saw his face. I told the nurse to wheel him down front. She said no, he wanted to sit in the back. Well, nobody *asks* for a bad seat." The usher looked toward the last row, where the ME's team obscured the body. "So . . . is he wearing a—"

"Yeah," said Riker, "that's our guy. Can you describe his nurse?"

"There were at least a *thousand* people here tonight." And now he realized that petulance would not fly with either cop. "She had a black coat. No, maybe brown. Yeah, could've been dark brown. . . . I remember the nurse's cap for sure."

"Short woman, tall woman? Hair color? *Anything?*"

"Her mouth was huge, or maybe that was just the

lipstick. Who knows? All I remember is this big splash of red on her face. Does that help?"

No. Red was the color of distraction. It was the stand-out memory of every eyewitness, and all other detail would fade alongside it.

"Go!" Mallory waited in silence until the usher had joined the line halfway up the aisle. "Backstage, they've got two wheelchairs, one for the actress, one for the man-nikin. I'm guessing a chair was missing for about ten minutes before the play started." She held up a ticket with a number for their corpse's theater seat. "This ticket was reserved for Leonard Crippen. The cashier was holding it for him. She didn't know we moved him to the front row."

"Well, somebody knew that seat was gonna be empty." Riker walked toward the line of people that was now moving slowly toward the corpse. He pulled Crippen aside, asking, "Who knew we gave you Peter Beck's seat?"

The critic smiled and spread his hands. *Silly question.* "I told *everybody*!"

Both men turned toward the sound of a woman's scream.

Nan Cooper, first in line to view the corpse, yelled, "*Dickie!* Oh, God, *no!*" The wardrobe lady's legs failed her, and she would have fallen, but Cyril Buckner caught her in his arms.

The stage manager stared at the dead man. "That's our director, Dickie Wyatt."

The line broke formation, and all of them gathered near the corpse. No one spoke. Nan Cooper buried her face in Buckner's breast. She could not stop crying. Alma Sutter was also tearing up. The rest of them only seemed surprised—except for Axel Clayborne. Riker could not read this man's face.

Cops, cast and crew were spaced out in separate rows of red velvet chairs. For this special occasion of a third death in as many nights, each suspect had a man from Special Crimes to take down a statement. Tomorrow these elite homicide cops would be lost to their own cases—unless Mallory could find a way to hold on to them.

Detective Gonzales stood by her side. He had the physique of a bodybuilder, though he was best known as the squad's Doubting Thomas. There was no one better at poking holes in statements, and he doubted every word out of Alma's mouth. "Nobody backs up the actress's story about the blackboard. They all think she's nuts. But me? I say she's lying."

Mallory agreed. She would not buy insanity. One certifiable lunatic like Bugsy was all that the odds would allow. She drifted down a row of tipped-up seats, stopping behind a conversation between Alma Sutter and Detective Janos. The actress was elaborating on her story: The ghostwriter was after her—*only* her—leaving secret messages and forcing her to *do* things.

This fairy tale was pushing the patience of Janos, not an easy feat. Despite his thuggish appearance, he was a very gentle man, and so it was almost an outburst of temper when he said, so softly, "I'm not buying it, lady. The ghostwriter? That's bull. He tells you to cut your hair, and you just *do* it? Gimme a break." He openly assessed her wardrobe, her newly shorn locks and the contact lenses of neon green. "It was *your* idea to impersonate a cop tonight."

So far, no one from Special Crimes was buying into any part of the ghostwriter story, nor could they believe that any grown-up would. All the detectives smelled collusion. As Mallory walked away, she heard Janos say to Alma, "Incidentally, the real-deal detective wears better threads than yours."

Stealing up on Axel Clayborne's blind side, Mallory sat down behind him to listen in on his interview with Rubin Washington, a detective with nearly as much seniority as her partner. Unlike Riker, Washington was no film buff, not the least bit awed by the movie star. And he had already taught this actor that charm only irritated him.

Clayborne was subdued when he said, "In hindsight, I suppose Dickie's death was predictable. Anyone can tell you he was getting high in rehearsals. Then his contract expired after the third week. That's when the stage manager took over for him. But the play's opening was always getting canceled by lawyers. And now we *still* meet for—"

"*Not* what I asked," said Detective Washington. "Where's Dickie Wyatt been for the past two weeks?" No one else had been able to fill that hole in the dead man's timeline.

"I thought he took a job out of town. He wasn't answering his phone or his—"

"The audience was let in a half hour before the play started. Where were you?"

"In my dressing room. It takes a while to do the makeup for the bulging cheeks and the—"

"Can anybody vouch for you? Just yes or no, okay?"

"No."

Mallory shot a hand signal to Washington, and then she leaned forward, very close to Axel Clayborne's ear, saying, "You and Dickie Wyatt were tight. He directed your films in Hollywood. He even got blacklisted with you."

The movie star twisted around in his seat to face her. "You Googled me. I'm flattered. Yes, Dickie and I were old friends."

"You're all smiles again!" said Washington, and he said it loud, as if this might be a beating offense. He leaned across the armrest to crowd the personal space of the actor. Nose to nose, faking anger, he said, "You weren't too broken up when you saw your buddy's corpse tonight. *No* tears. *Nothin'.* Your friend dies, and you don't give a rat's ass?"

Axel Clayborne was not *acting* surprised. He was stunned. Speechless. He had a lost look about him—an actor with no script.

Mallory rose from her seat and moved on down the row, pausing behind one of the Rinaldi brothers and his interrogator. The actor was saying nothing, only nodding or shaking his head, sometimes giving a shrug in response to a question. She turned around and watched the other twin being questioned four rows away. More shrugs and nods. Maybe these two had once shared a lawyer and taken advice to keep their mouths shut, to volunteer nothing. Had the background checks missed something?

And what else might have been missed for the lack of manpower? She had been crippled at the outset by CSI Clara Loman. And now Jack Coffey hobbled her case. The lieutenant had failed to do his damn job, refusing to stand up to the brass and decline homicides that any precinct could handle.

Rows and aisles away, Detective Sanger questioned Ted Randal, the stagehand her partner called Lollypop. Mallory watched the body language. Each time the boy threw up both hands, she knew he was giving responses like "I didn't see nothin', I don't know nothin'" and last came the one-hand finale of Talking-to-Teenagers, "So *what*?"

Elsewhere in the audience, other interviews were winding down when Riker walked out onstage. "I can't find Bugsy. Who cut him loose?"

A detective got up from his seat in the audience. Lonahan was remarkable for dogged persistence, hairy knuckles and a loud voice. He stood near the back row, yet he had no need to shout. "I finished the guy's statement, but I didn't say he could leave."

Riker's eyes fixed on the critic in the front row. He must have read guilt on Leonard Crippen's face. He walked to the edge of the stage and hunkered down to stare at the man. "Tell me where Bugsy is." Unspoken were the words, *or I'll shoot you.*

The critic heaved a sigh of *I give up* and said, "You'll find him in Times Square. He'd want to get a jump on the theater crowd tonight. It takes a while to teach home-less people to tap-dance."

"Bugsy has something of a cult following." In the company of two detectives, Leonard Crippen descended the stairs to the sallow lighting of the subway. "He'll only perform one scene this time. If you want to see the whole play, you have to catch his act in a different place every night."

Mallory waved her badge at the clerk in the token booth, and the turnstile opened for them. "He always does his act around Times Square?"

"Yes, and always underground," said the critic. "Better acoustics."

The three of them moved across the wide space of crisscrossing shift workers, partiers and tourists, all bound for platforms or exits. Through the soles of Riker's shoes, he could feel the rumble in the tunnels as trains pulled in and departed. And now he could hear a high-pitched screech as they came within sight of train brakes sparking off rails.

Crippen led the way down the platform. "After each performance, Bugsy tells his audience where the next scene will be. If they miss a night, they can find his loca-tion on a fan's webpage. Personally, I don't own a com-puter, can't abide them. I have an office boy keep track of him. And that's how I know he's—" The critic pointed to a cluster of people near one tiled wall. "*There*. Follow me." Crippen walked over to a long wooden bench that held the standing overflow of the audience, and some of these people gave him smiles of recognition as they made room for him. With a creak of old knees, he climbed up to join them.

Riker flashed his badge to make room for two more. Standing on the bench, the detectives could see over the heads of the gathering to the open space where the gopher stood in front of three ragged people, who smiled with less than full sets of teeth, and Bugsy spoke his line, "I'm so tired. I can't."

His chorus of homeless people performed a few competent soft-shoe steps, all yelling, "*Dance*, boy, *dance*!" And Bugsy did. He tapped out a nervous tattoo of leather, toe and heel, running in place, and he was good. He was *great*. The audience clapped and whistled. And then the little man said, "I'm doin' the best I can." The homeless trio did their own dance steps again, yelling their same line, as Bugsy made a deep bow, folding then to his knees and lowering his head. His act was over.

The clapping began with cheers and whistles from the crowd.

Riker was reminded of days when panhandlers were plentiful, and the subways were more entertaining, dance and song for coins in the hat or the hand. There were not so many ragged people in plain sight these days. He knew only one Bible verse by heart: *The poor we shall always have with us.* And so he suspected the mayor of easing the budget crunch for sheltering the poor by giving them one-way bus tickets to warmer climates. And that was *cold*.

Leonard Crippen waited for a lull in the wild applause,

and then, in an aside to Mallory, he said, "I call his chorus the tap-dancing Iagos. You see, their role in this particular scene is to torment Bugsy."

Riker read his partner's mind. By Mallory's lights, that
was *her* job.

Bugsy's audience was departing, some of them waving
at the drama critic and calling him by his first name as
they took their leave. "Well," said Mallory, "it looks like
you go to a *lot* of Bugsy's subway shows."

"Oh, yes," said Crippen. "*Years* of—" Perhaps it was
her *gotcha* smile that made the old man realize he had
been caught in a lie to the police.

"I'm a little confused," said Riker, not at all confused.
"You told *us* your only chance to see Bugsy act was when
he pitched you a new play." He nodded toward a departing couple who had bid the critic farewell and "*—see you
tomorrow night.*"

Mallory was still smiling. Big lies, small ones, she loved
them all, and she knew how to work them like crazy.

Crippen pursed his lips and pretended distraction,
watching the gopher pass a baseball cap among the
remainder of the crowd, filling it to an overflow of dollar
bills. And now the critic found his voice again. "That was
a scene from the play that won him a Tony Award. Too
bad we missed the beginning. His soliloquy opens with
'I'm just a little man, and I'm dancing as fast as I can.'"
By heart, Crippen recited lines of glowing reviews for the
Broadway play that had starred a young actor named Alan
Rains, alias Bugsy.

Mallory and Riker were not listening. They were

watching the gopher give all the bills in the hat to his ragged chorus line, every dollar. The detectives turned to the critic, wordlessly asking, *What the hell?*

"Well, Bugsy can't *keep* the money," said Crippen. "The character he plays doesn't have any."

They stared at him, willing him to make sense. When nothing came of that, Mallory dragged the old man off toward the wall, and Riker grabbed the gopher by the collar of his jacket.

SUSAN: Do they hate all women?
ROLLO: I think they rather enjoy
         spending time with
         women . . . so to speak.
                    —<u>The Brass Bed</u>, Act I

 Bugsy rode in the back, slouched low, shoulders hunched, doing his best to disappear into the car's upholstery.

The black Crown Victoria pulled up to the curb of a SoHo street two blocks from the station house, and Mallory let the engine idle as she turned around to face their passenger. "Your bedroll's still at the theater?"

Poor Bugsy. His night was not over yet.

Neither was Riker's. His coat pockets were filled with detectives' interview notes, and he stepped out on the sidewalk with plans to spend a few hours wearing his reading glasses. As the car sped away, he turned to face the saloon that he called home, though his apartment was up the stairs from this bar that catered to police.

When he moseyed inside, he was hailed by the barkeep,

his landlord. More hands went up, and other voices called out to him from tables all around the room. The place was toasty warm, and the lighting was low key, but no one would call it cozy. Even off duty, these men and women were packing guns, and the tension level would be in flux all through the night, rising with every sober cop to walk through the door, carrying a bad day on his back.

A mahogany bar ran the length of one wall, and the only civilian customer sat a head taller than everyone else on the barstools. Charles Butler was always the tallest man in every room, even while sitting down. And he was definitely the only three-piece suit allowed to drink here. The surrounding police knew how to make the public feel unwelcome, but shrinks like Charles were pariahs.

And rich guys? Forget about it.

Yet they all tolerated this man, whose passport to the cop bar was issued by Riker, and none would challenge it.

The psychologist had been a good friend to that late, great cop, Lou Markowitz, and that was enough to make him Riker's friend for life. He slapped the man on the back. "Hey, how's it goin'?" And when Charles turned to face him, the detective's first thought was trouble. Missing was the goofy hello smile, a fool's smile that belied a boxcar string of Ph.D.s.

From the neck down, Charles Butler was a well-made man, but north of that great body, his heavy-lidded eyes were the size of hens' eggs with small blue marbles floating in the whites, and his nose might attract pigeons looking for a likely perch. A comical face. High anxiety did not belong there.

Riker pulled out a barstool and sat down. "I saw you take a run at Mallory this morning." He had watched this poor bastard reach out to her, but then Charles had thought better of making physical contact. Very wise. Now the detective asked the man who loved Mallory, "What was that about?"

"She wouldn't take any phone calls or return them. I didn't know what else to do."

"Yeah, I see the problem." Actually, Riker did not.

Of course, Charles would never show up at Mallory's apartment unannounced. Nor would he make a social call to the squad room. The penalties for that kind of behavior were severe. But the man had seemed right with the world this morning, and blown-off phone calls would not account for the worry in his eyes right now. Charles Butler had the look of a man who should not go to sleep tonight, for he would surely wake up screaming.

Riker glanced at his watch. This was going to take a while.

Well, whatever this man's story might be, it could have been worse. At least Charles had not been sitting in the front row when Mallory's lookalike got her head knocked off. Riker could not get that image out of his mind. He flicked one hand at the busy bartender to ask, *What's up?* Where was his drink? He *needed* that drink.

"It's not just me," said Charles. "She's cut ties to everyone."

Except maybe, oh, thirty-five thousand cops.

The psychologist emptied his glass in one draught, not his usual manner of drinking goddamn expensive liquor, smooth, *sipping* whiskey. "David was so concerned, he called Lieutenant Coffey. . . . He probably shouldn't have done that."

"Probably not." But David Kaplan had been Lou Markowitz's rabbi, and that job title had high privileges at Special Crimes. Jack Coffey would have been sympathetic, making excuses for the bad behavior of Lou's kid—her heavy workload, the budget cuts, the jumped-up pressure on the job.

What *else* had Coffey volunteered?

And what had the rabbi passed along to Charles Butler?

Riker glanced at the tally of drinks listed on the bar tab. This was where he really shined at math. Counting the shots of liquor, he could roughly guess the hour when Charles had started drinking, and now he knew why his friend was so rattled.

The bartender laid out a cocktail napkin and the detective's customary drink, the cheapest bourbon in the house. Silently saying grace, *God, bless this booze*, Riker downed half his glass, and then he smiled at the man beside him. "So, Charles, how did you like the play?"

Only one light was left burning in the theater. A wire-caged bulb hung down from the catwalk and lit the brass bed on the stage. "That's the ghost light," said the gopher.

Mallory and Bugsy sat in front-row seats, eating slices of pizza and tipping back bottles of beer. She stretched out her long legs, and he perched on the edge of his own chair, ready to fly.

"It stays lit all night long," he said, "*every* night—even when the theater's got no show runnin'."

"Safety regulation?"

"Naw, that ain't it. We got a jillion built-in lights. But that one? Somebody's gotta set it up. Doesn't always hang down from a wire. Some places, it's a bulb that sits on a battery. But it's only got one job." Bugsy settled back in his chair, not so frightened anymore. Or maybe he was only tired. His head lolled back, and the solitary light was reflected in his blue eyes. "There's people who'll tell ya it keeps away ghosts, but that ain't right, neither. Theater ghosts don't hurt nobody. No, it stays lit so the ghosts won't ever be left alone in the dark. . . . Ya see those lights in theaters all over the world. They've always been there, even back in the days when all they had was candles."

"You believe in ghosts?"

"I dunno. It's more like tradition, I guess. It's good luck if ya see a ghost, an' every theater's got one. Ours is the old guy who built this place. A long time back, he drove an actress crazy, so the story goes, and that's why she stabbed him to death. . . . I know a lotta stories." Bugsy turned to her, and for the first time he smiled without a touch of fear, so open, unguarded now.

Done with her pizza slice, Mallory wiped her hands with a napkin, saying so casually, "The accent is perfect, but you never lived in the Bronx." This native son of Connecticut had grown up in a gated community—if she could believe in the fruit of her subway chat with the lying drama critic. "You come from money, but you live like a bum in flophouses with rats and roaches. And that's when you've got the price of a room. Half the time, you bed down in theaters. You went to Yale Drama School, but you took a job as an errand boy."

"An' I had to audition to get this crummy job," said Bugsy.

She paraphrased a review for Alan Rains, the real name of this Tony Award winner turned gopher. "You were a shooting star at twenty-one. Five years ago, the critics loved you. Then something happened. What was it?" When no answer was forthcoming, she leaned toward him. "How crazy are you, Alan?"

"Bugsy's the name," he said.

"No. That's the name of a character in a play. Bugsy isn't a real man."

The gopher only nodded in complete agreement, and then he shut his eyes—and he shut down. Still as a photograph. Still as death.

Mallory grabbed his arm and shook him hard. "Alan!" Was he breathing? "Bugsy?"

The gopher's nickname was the charm.

His eyes slow to open, his body squirming, he came back to life—back to her. Though he was not smiling anymore. Bugsy seemed nervous again. And fearful?

Yes, that, too.

Mallory stayed with him for a time, but now they only

spoke of ghost lights up and down Broadway. He *did* know a lot of stories.

The detective led the psychologist to an empty table in the back, not wanting to advertise his partner's business to the whole bar.

"Just tell Rabbi Kaplan she doesn't have time to socialize." Neither did Riker, not even time to dance with his niece at the wedding reception last night. But he always made time for friends in need, like this sorry man, who was so troubled by a headless Mallory. And now he discovered that Charles had left the theater after the bat-swinging scene and before the director's dead body was found.

As they settled into the chairs, Riker shot a glance at the cocktail waitress on the other side of the room, and he raised two fingers. Ruby gave him a thumbs-up to say that fresh drinks were on the way. And now it was time to take his favorite shrink to school on life in Copland. "Did Lou ever tell you about the bad old days when he set up our unit?"

Charles nodded. "The city needed a full-time task force for the—"

"The big messy murders that jam up every copshop. Back then, a busy precinct might handle four stiffs a day, two cops per kill and six minutes to close their cases. Lou took over their bottleneck cases."

The waitress had two drinks on a tray, and she was heading for their table.

Good girl.

"But our idiot mayor keeps cutting the budget. No new hires to replace guys who leave. Get the picture?" No, he could tell that Charles Butler was still seeing that other picture—Mallory getting hit in the face with a baseball bat and her bloody head rolling across the stage.

"Fewer cops in every precinct," said Riker, who played therapist tonight. "Now *every* homicide in town's a bottleneck, and Special Crimes is feelin' the squeeze."

"You should call Major Case," said the waitress, as she set down their drinks.

Riker did not shoot her. He liked redheads. "Kid, you've been watchin' television. You know that can't be good for you. Major Case doesn't handle homicides. They never did." He could see that the girl from the TV planet had it in mind to argue with him, but Ruby left the table without a fight.

The detective turned his tired eyes to Charles Butler, a quasi Luddite who owned a television but never watched it. "So Mallory's got no spare time, and the rabbi should cut her some slack."

"You *know* why Louis started that poker game."

Yeah, he did. Lou had founded the weekly game of close friends so that his Kathy would never be alone, not even when she was all grown up—when she carried a gun, a big one. But Lou's poker cronies with their stupid rules and small stakes *still* tailored to a little girl's allowance money—they played cards like old ladies. *Hell with that.* Riker had played with them one time. Never again.

Charles did not have his heart in this argument—Rabbi Kaplan's argument. He sat well back in his chair and finished his drink before he said, "It's not like she's surrounded by friends at work. She's got you. . . . Anyone else?"

And did the man actually need an answer for that question?

No, Kathy Mallory made no effort to make friends, and Riker could not count himself as one, either. They never hung out together off the job, no drinking, no ball games or movies. Sure as hell no girl talk. She would be the last one to bring him her problems. Mallory had barely tolerated Lou Markowitz. In the early days of foster care, her pet name for him had been "Hey, cop." And the only clue that she had fiercely loved the old man was the grudge she held against him for dying.

"That poker game is her safety net," said Charles.

"Oh, sure." Oh, *crap*! There was no such thing in a police world, where life was simplified: Lay down and die or muscle up. But the man across the table was an alien in cop culture.

This was an interspecies communication problem.

A dicey problem. Whatever he said, he knew that Charles would carry it back to the rabbi. On this account, Riker sipped his bourbon, stalling till he found the right words to politely make the case for leaving Mallory in peace. "Why not just poke her in the eye with a sharp stick?"

Half the woman's face was covered by a woolen scarf, which could not kill the stench of gasoline, but frosty clouds of breath did not hang in the air to give away her position.

The underground parking garage was cold enough to

freeze meat, every finger and toe, though Clara Loman had not waited long. Officially on sick leave—no doubt thanks to Mallory—the CSI supervisor had returned to her office on the sly to download codes for the tracking device installed in every NYPD vehicle. The rest of her night had been spent following the young detective's movements on a glowing laptop map. And so she had managed to arrive at this underground parking garage ahead of her prey.

From her hiding place behind a cement pillar, the gray-haired woman watched the tall blonde hand over keys to an unmarked police car. Clara pulled back as Detective Mallory turned around to fetch her personal vehicle.

Pressed up against the cold cement, Clara listened to the soft footsteps, which ended at the parking space for a small, silver convertible some three yards distant.

And now it was time—before the car door could open—before the detective was safely inside.

Longing for the pleasure of heart-attack shock when she stole up behind the young cop to catch her by surprise, Clara stepped out from behind the pillar—

To see the barrel end of a revolver—

Only inches from her head.

Surprise!

Mallory lowered her weapon and holstered it. And then, as if they did this sort of thing every night of the week, she said, "So you've got something that couldn't wait till morning?"

That was too civil. Clara awaited the derision, the sarcasm that must surely follow, but none came her way. "I gave you a copy of the play. Did you bother to read it?"

She already knew the answer, given the lack of a follow-up phone call. "Did you even turn one page?"

"Not yet."

"Then you *missed* something." Clara Loman took some satisfaction in the slight widening of those strange green eyes, only a flicker, but still gratifying. Stifling a smile, she said—no, she *commanded*, "*Read* it! I highlighted all the passages of interest, elements of a family massacre that *I* found interesting . . . ten years ago."

```
SUSAN:   They slaughtered the women
         and children . . . but
         not you.
ROLLO:   I think they were tired,
         poor tykes.
                      —The Brass Bed, Act II
```

12 Clara Loman's apartment was a sunny disappointment for Riker, nothing like a bat cave. It was a spare and orderly place that might house an Amish woman—except for the grisly photographs framed on every wall, some of them bloody, all of them pictures of crime-scene crews and their changing personnel over the years. Apart from the dead bodies included in a few candid shots, this was clearly a display of Loman's only family.

One picture showed a very young Heller posed in conversation with his mentor, dwarfing her in size and respecting her with a bow of his head, the better to listen to what she was saying. Though there was no tie of blood between them, Riker captioned this one *The Good Son*.

"Your partner's already here," said Loman, dryly making the point that he was late.

The lady held a frying pan, and should he be worried about that? He had never seen her in street clothes before. Today, in jeans and a sweatshirt, she was dressed in solid gray right down to her boots, and he wondered if this was Loman's idea of fashion, matching the color of her clothes to her hair.

He followed her into a small dining room, where he sat down with Mallory, who was eating breakfast and leafing through a copy of the play. Like the rest of the furnishings, the table and chairs were plain and serviceable. And so were the scrambled eggs. Loman dished them out with nothing fancy like salt and pepper to make them less bland. While Riker shoveled his food and inhaled orange juice, his partner laid out the gist of this meeting.

"The ghostwriter ripped off a real massacre." Mallory paged through the manuscript, showing him lines high-lighted with a yellow marker, all the details of a killing spree. "Descriptions of victims. Their ages. Relationships to the survivors. Only one thing doesn't match up."

Clara Loman sat down at the head of the table. "There were only *two* survivors from the actual massacre. No older brother, dead or alive. Otherwise, it's too close to the real thing for coincidence. Even the line about lapsed insurance pans out. I found the company that sold policies to the grandmother. And that's not public knowl-edge."

Now Riker was reminded that, like other CSIs, Clara Loman had once been a precinct detective, a good one.

While the partners finished breakfast, their hostess lectured them on the importance of maintaining a good blood-splatter catalog. "Cities get the high crime rates, but small towns have the most grisly murders. And, contrary to mythology, their police departments don't enter all those cases into ViCAP."

Mallory, on best behavior, listened politely, as if she knew nothing about the flaw of the FBI's national database for violent offenders. And she was respectful when the older woman hammered on the detectives' grave oversight, their failure to read the play. Clara Loman was getting even with them for the insult to her pride. But, if Riker understood his *partner's* game, and he was pretty sure he did, she was recruiting this CSI for their case.

And so he followed Mallory's lead, nodding and smiling, playing the penitent dolt sorely in need of help.

"Years ago," said Loman, "when I had a larger budget, I employed a clipping service." She slid her plate to one side and opened a scrapbook to turn pages of pasted-in Xeroxes until she found the one she wanted. "This is it." She pushed the album across the table to Riker, and he pulled out his spectacles to read the front-page story of a Nebraska massacre.

"Oh, the things you can learn from newspapers," said Loman. "Especially the ones in isolated places. Whenever I found a murder I liked—lots of blood-splatter potential—I'd contact the local police and request crime-scene photos. In this case, a county sheriff handled the investigation. You'll find a few more articles in there, but don't waste your time. The reporters never got any more information. Statewide, the story dried up fast."

How could that be? A family massacre was the kind of

case that would not die. It was the stuff of media wet dreams. Riker turned a page of the scrapbook to read one more detail. "So the two boys were hiding in an attic bedroom. Maybe the killer didn't know they were up there. Sounds like a whacko off the street."

"Or the kids did it," said Mallory.

Riker stared at the grainy newsprint picture of a wood-frame house on a street lined with tall trees and police cars. "You got the crime-scene photos?"

"No," said Loman. "The county sheriff wouldn't share with me or anyone else, not even the feds. He never made a single plea for public assistance. No press conferences, no tip lines. And the murders were never solved."

"Then the sheriff knows who did it," said Riker, "but he can't prove it."

Mallory nodded. "And maybe he's writing a book. He wouldn't be the first cop to make a profit on withholding evidence."

Clara Loman held up a yellowed index card. "These telephone numbers are old ones, but they might be useful. James Harper is still the sheriff. That last number is for his home. He might have changed it since then. Ten years ago, I terrorized a civilian clerk to get it."

Mallory smiled in approval.

"Maybe the sheriff is your ghostwriter," said Loman. "The play has a slew of forensic details, right down to the order of each victim's death. And blood on the ceiling—that's cast-off splatter. It fits with the axe mentioned in the play—blood flying off the blade on the rise before the next cut. There's nothing about that in the newspapers, no mention of weapons. But the body count is right, the ages of the victims, all female, and the survivors—twelve-year-old twin boys."

Riker closed the album. "How old is Sheriff Harper?"

"He must be near sixty by now," said Loman.

Too old to fit anyone on their suspect list, but Riker did wonder if folks in Nebraska wore pointy-toed boots like Cyril Buckner's.

Jack Coffey leaned back in his desk chair. Mallory and Riker remained standing, waiting—*quietly*. They only showed this kind of respect when they wanted something.

The lieutenant perused his newspaper. "This time, the play got reviewed on the front page of the *Daily News*." He held up his copy to show them the headline: *Play Slays Audience*. He read the smaller bold type aloud. " 'Three down and one treading water.' Your suicidal Jersey kid's gonna make it. So scratch that one off the list. And scratch Dickie Wyatt, too. I called the ME's Office for a prelim. The guy was a junkie. Simple drug overdose."

"Simple?" said Mallory. "He's the third death in—"

"In three nights." Now, on a prescient roll, Coffey voiced her next complaint. "And the corpse was moved *after* death. *Yeah, yeah.* You know what this tells me? That theater crowd's playing you. So they used a dead body to milk publicity. I don't care. We don't handle crap offenses like interference with a corpse." And what did *she* care about the death of Dickie Wyatt? Junkies were at the bottom of Mallory's food chain.

"It's murder," she said.

"Your dead playwright—*maybe*, but the junkie director was dead days before you found him. *No* connection."

"You're kiddin' me," said Riker.

"Am I laughing?" The lieutenant idly turned the page of his newspaper. "One of 'em—maybe *all* those bastards knew their director OD'd. And why waste a perfectly good corpse? How could they know the suicide kids from Jersey would give the play a headline?" He folded his paper. "So now you're down to one murder. Oh, *excuse* me. The ME calls Peter Beck a *suspicious* death. Wrap it fast. We got other cases in the house."

Riker held up an old scrapbook. "We got a new angle to work. We need another man on the—"

"Give us Sanger," said Mallory. "Him and his partner, they're only chasing down loose ends and babysitting a witness. One man can do that solo. How *hard* can it be?"

"Don't wanna hear it." Jack Coffey handed her a pink message slip with the name and phone number of Commissioner Beale's favorite city councilman, a pest who had already racked up three calls today. "This moron should not piss me off one more time." And neither should she. "You get that theater manager on the phone, *right now*! You tell him the councilman gets to see the rest of the damn play tonight . . . if that's not too *hard*."

"No curtain tonight," said Cyril Buckner. "Detective Mallory just called. She shut down the play." The stage manager handed fresh change sheets to the actors gathered onstage. One day soon, he would rip that damn blackboard off the wall.

Axel Clayborne scanned his new lines. "Did she say why?"

"Bad behavior," said Cyril. "Too many dead bodies in the audience."

The actor nodded. "I suppose last night *was* overkill."

The stage manager faced his cast and crew. "All right, people, you're on salary. Show or no show, you're here every day. Everybody stays up on their lines. Nobody gets stale."

"You don't need stagehands," said Joe Garnet. And Ted Randal seconded this opinion with a nod.

"Yeah, we do. We'll use some of the time for an understudy rehearsal. We've had lots of changes since the last one." He turned to Bugsy. "They're all here, right?"

The gopher nodded and jabbed one thumb toward the wings, where the four understudies were waiting.

"Good." And now Cyril remembered to look up, and he called to the lighting man, "No changes for you." Gil Preston was so easily forgotten, so often out of sight.

When Clara Loman walked through the stairwell door, she drew a hard look from the lieutenant. Jack Coffey was probably wondering why this woman was haunting the squad room of Special Crimes.

Riker nodded toward their visitor. "You think her boss knows she's still working our case?"

Mallory turned her head to see the CSI marching toward them. "She's using sick days. Heller won't know unless Coffey rats her out."

Clara Loman stepped up to Mallory's desk and laid down a sheaf of papers. "Results on the alley debris." She turned a cold eye on Riker. "And the *DNA* tests? The ones you thought were a waste of time? Nan Cooper's swab matched up with two half-smoked filter cigarettes, but not this." She held up a photograph of the butt-end remains of one hand-rolled smoke lying in the snow. "The saliva on this reefer belongs to the security guard, Bernie Sales."

"More than just weed." Mallory was reading the toxicology report. "It's laced with opiates."

"Oh, shit," said Riker in lieu of a thank-you.

"Nice job," said his partner.

But Loman had not waited for this commendation. She was already walking away.

When the stairwell door had closed behind the CSI, Riker said, "At least the security guard's in the clear. Stoned, he couldn't do a murder in forty seconds. But it looks real bad for Nan Cooper."

"Either she needed an alibi," said Mallory, "or she gave Bernie that little gift to keep his mouth shut. Maybe he recognized her." Turning her laptop around, she showed him her updated background check on the wardrobe lady, including an alias.

"That can't be right," he said. "That *can't* be her. No way."

Bugsy fetched a cup of tea for Alma and then printed out a new diagram for Cyril, his boss. Oh, but who was *not* the boss of him? The gopher looked about him, swaying from side to side, not knowing who next would pull his strings. And now he ran to catch the second ring of the telephone on the stage manager's desk.

It was Mallory calling.

Though she could not see him do this, he stood up straight, smoothed back his uncombed hair and said, "Yeah, Detective Riker just took her away. . . . No, I never seen her get high. . . . Yeah, her and Dickie Wyatt were best buds."

And now, behind him, he heard his other master's voice as Cyril Buckner yelled, "Bugsy! Where's Nan Cooper?"

Jack Coffey was reading his latest message from the irate Councilman Perry when he looked up to see Mallory standing in his doorway. "You *shut down* the damn play? Was I not real clear about—"

"It ties into a cold case . . . and a killer who did five murders before that play was even written."

Jesus Christ! Was she lying? He could make her prove it, but he sensed a new game in the works, one that might wreck his day. Easier to give in and confound her and say, "Okay, no show tonight. Your case—your call."

That should have annoyed her, but she never missed a beat in saying, "If you won't give us Sanger, give us Janos. He's got his only suspect in custody. His partner can wrap the paperwork."

A reasonable request, assuming that she had not just padded her body count—and even if she had. He would have sympathized with any other cop on the squad, but never with her. Sympathy was a sign of weakness in Malloryworld, and it would cost him points in their ongoing boxing match of feint and jab, duck or lose your teeth.

What she asked of him was fair, but he said, "You're not all that shorthanded. I couldn't help but notice—you guys got your own personal CSI." He wondered if she was extorting Clara Loman. And his next thought? This was something he would not want to know. "Did you call the ME to check on your junkie director?"

"No, I didn't need to." She was all sarcasm now. *Not a graceful loser.* "Your cut-rate prelim on Dickie Wyatt— that didn't come from Dr. Slope. He would've set you straight. So I know you talked to the on-call pathologist, the moron who rode with the meat wagon last night."

True. And interesting. She might be holding out on him, always an easy guess, or maybe she wanted him to run her errands, work her damn case. Either way, Mallory was daring him to make a follow-up call to Dr. Slope, who—no doubt about it—would deliver her sucker punch. Did she really believe he could not see that one coming?

Not gonna play.

And the prelim for Dickie Wyatt would nag at him all through this day—until he realized *that* was the first jab of a one-*two* punch.

Nan Cooper sat down at the table in the interrogation room. The overhead fluorescent lights made her red hair look even thinner today. The bald patches glowed. At the center of the table was a thick folder with her name on it, but the wardrobe lady had only glanced at it. "What's up with you guys? I got an alibi."

"Bernie Sales, the security guard?" Riker shook his head. "We got a few problems with his statement. You were smokin' cigarettes in the alley the night Beck died, but Bernie was smokin' dope."

Mallory pulled the toxicology report from the folder, laid it on the table and used one long, red fingernail to underscore the critical line, " 'Cannabis cured in opiates.' . . . We know he got that reefer from you."

"That bastard gave me up?"

"Yeah," said Riker. "Bernie isn't all that swift even when he's *not* stoned. The guy has no idea where he was during that forty-second blackout. You *reminded* him . . . before the first cop showed up."

"And now I'm a suspect?" Far from indignant, the lady smiled, but her eyes traveled back to the folder—so thick with information.

Mallory plucked out another sheet of paper and slid it across the table. "That's a copy of your brand-new union card in the name of Nan Cooper."

"Yeah? So? Cooper's what it says on my birth certificate, and I go by plain ol' Nan. The fancy version is—"

"Nanette," said Riker. "We know. But when's the last time anybody called you plain old *Cooper*?" He laid down a photocopy of a Screen Actors Guild card in the name of Nanette Darby. He had seen all her old movies, shown in the late-night hours after closing time for his favorite bar. Curiously, this comedy star had not aged, not from the balding hairline down. "I never would've guessed—"

"Nanette Darby's my stage name." The woman folded her arms. "So . . . not a federal crime."

"You gave us a phony address," he said. "So we gotta wonder—"

"It's legit. I sublet that apartment. That's where I get my mail."

"Yeah," said Riker. "But Nanette Darby's mail goes to a much nicer address on Central Park South."

"And your *very* nice stock portfolio lives at Morgan Stanley." Mallory opened the folder and spread a stack of financial documents across the table.

"It's incredible what those guys can do with a chunk of cash." The bark of a New Yorker was gone. The woman's speech smoothed out to homogenized American, the accent from nowhere. "I did pretty well for myself—back when I was somebody."

"So you're filthy rich," said Riker, "but you're doin' grunt work? . . . You can see why that might bug us."

"And the disguise," said Mallory. "Your wigmaker's very good."

Nan Cooper lifted one shoulder in resignation and then removed the wig of sparse strands to reveal thick raven hair in a short, stylish cut. "You're sharp, kid. Nobody else ever caught on."

Riker could believe that. Why would anyone but Mallory take a second look? Who would buy a wig with bald spots? He tapped a photograph clipped to the inside of the folder. "But you still don't look like your passport photo."

"Oh, that's an old picture." The actress squinted at the small portrait of a more mature movie star whose sagging eyes and mouth were upstaged by a bulbous nose that was once America's favorite honker. "I was pushing forty when the work dried up in Hollywood. Time for a face-lift. The surgeon took off fifteen years, and he lopped off half the nose. But then I couldn't get any decent parts. You know why? Without that fabulous beak, I just wasn't Nanette Darby anymore. . . . What a kick in the head."

"So you took a job as the wardrobe lady," said Riker. "You—a rich woman."

"A *dresser.* That's my job title. Hey, it's still show business, right?" Realizing that neither detective was buying into this, she said, "All right, I wanted back in—but not as a dresser—as an *actor.* I worked out a deal with Dickie Wyatt."

Was she lying? Riker had met all the actors' understudies when he had taken this woman from the theater. "So . . . Alma's got *two* understudies?"

"No, babe. I was a *star.* He'd never insult me with an offer like that."

"Of course not," said Riker. "So he gave you a *crummier* job."

"There's more to it. I've known Dickie forever. I knew him before he got his first job in Hollywood. He was the best. Biggest heart in the business."

"He was a junkie," said Mallory, who always made

distinctions between drug addicts and humans. "I've seen his track marks."

"*Old* ones from the early days in La-La Land. In the movie game, if you can survive without booze or drugs, you're not really *in* the game. No offense, kid. I can see you're competitive. But Hollywood's a meaner killing ground than New York City."

"Okay," said Riker. "So Wyatt moved to New York, and you followed him."

"No, I got here years ahead of Dickie, but I had no luck with auditions. I was down to doing cattle calls. You know what that's like? They trot the actors past this kid casting director. He doesn't even ask your name. He inspects you like meat. If you make it past that cut, then you get to open your mouth, maybe say a line or two. And they only do that so they can check your teeth."

"What about Wyatt?"

"Dickie got work right away, no problem. Stage or screen, he was a great director. And he looked out for me—got me some small but really choice roles. He wanted to give me a part in this play, but that prick Peter Beck insisted on hiring his girlfriend. Well, Dickie asked me to stick around. So I got a wig and a union card for a dresser. You know the rest."

"Oh, yeah," said Riker. "If poor Alma should drop dead one night—"

"I step over her corpse, whip out my guild card and take over the role. I've got a replacement contract as Nanette Darby. Dickie's idea. He said Alma's lousy contract didn't make her bulletproof. The agent who drew it up was in diapers."

"So Alma could be fired," said Mallory, "once Peter Beck was out of the way."

"You know . . . I *like* where this is going." Nan Cooper thrust out both hands in the prisoner's posture. "Go ahead. Put the cuffs on. I'd *kill* for that kind of publicity. Most people think I've been dead for the past ten years. Arrest me. I'm *begging* you."

The lady was disappointed when the detectives escorted her to the stairwell. No arrest, no handcuffs. "Not my lucky day," she said as the door closed behind her.

"She's in on it," said Mallory.

And Riker agreed. Maybe a long bitter decade was time enough to write a play.

Frank, the liveried doorman, pocketed the money as smoothly as a maître d', and he craned his neck to look up at his very tall benefactor. "Okay, she *was* home a couple of times when the rabbi came by. But the rest of the time? No. She's been working real long hours."

"Thank you," said Charles Butler. He had a theory that his own bribe could not compete with what Mallory paid for her doorman's discretion. And, in good conscience, no gentleman would outbid a lady.

He held up another fifty-dollar offering. "Anything else you can tell me?"

There was real love in Frank's eyes when he looked at the crisp new bill hanging in the air between them, just waiting to be snatched up. But he slipped both hands into his pockets and away from temptation. He shook his head. No deal. Sorry—*so* sorry.

Mallory's tips must be lavish. *That* or she really scared the doorman.

Charles walked up the street and turned a corner onto Central Park West. Southbound cabs were plentiful here, but he had yet to raise his hand to hail one, and ten of them sailed by. He was stalled. A little movie theater in his brain replayed the stage beheading in an endless loop.

Last night's performance had not done justice to Mallory. The actress's impersonation had been badly flawed, leaning too heavily on the most disturbing standout traits. Yet the caricature had rung true enough to cost him sleep—and to make him just a touch stupid.

Fool.

What could he have hoped to learn from a doorman?

And neither could Riker throw him any scraps. That detective could divulge nothing to a civilian who was not yet in the game, though that status was subject to change via a formal invitation from the NYPD. His telephone might be ringing with just such an offer at this very moment.

Riker *had* promised to call.

On the strength of that promise, Charles had unboxed an answering machine that had been state-of-the-art years ago when Mallory had given it to him for Christmas. All her gifts were computerized. She was so determined to yank him out of a past century, where he lived among antiques that required no owner's manual to operate. Oh, but now he could imagine Detective Riker's shock if the man should call and hear the electronically recorded message of a confirmed Luddite.

Charles was aware of less flattering designations. In his occasional role as a consulting psychologist, he had once or twice heard himself referred to as a witch doctor. This remark had been muttered by the more cynical detectives, though all of them probably saw him that way. Indeed, in his current sorry state, he could almost see himself reduced to casting chicken bones by the light of the moon. He looked up at the daytime sky. In this moment, he might be taken for a man seeking omens in the shapes of passing clouds.

Facts gleaned from newspapers and personal experience were few, but only two of them mattered: Mallory had been written into a play, and the writer's intentions were clear.

Off with her head.

```
SUSAN:   An axe . . . and a
         baseball bat.
ROLLO:   The bat was mine when I was
         a boy. The twins never
         played. Well, not until
         that night. They played
         with the women and the
         girls all night long.
                    —The Brass Bed, Act II
```

13 Detective Janos walked down the hall between Mallory and Riker, outsizing them gorilla fashion, but he was kindly and tender when he spoke of his own case and the recently booked suspect, a homeless man who had molested and murdered a schoolboy.

Only *one* dead schoolboy.

Mallory was keeping score. That case should have been worked out of an East Side precinct. And there were others that did not belong in this copshop.

"The skin around the perp's ankles is turning black," said Janos. "You know what *that* means."

"Yeah," said Riker, "gangrene and goodbye, feet. It means there *is* a God."

"So the lieutenant says I'm all yours." Janos inclined his head to Mallory. "*Now* do I get to read the play?"

"I made a copy just for you." She led the way into the incident room.

Cork lined every wall from the baseboard to the ceiling molding, and it held paper trails of bloody morgue photos, crime-scene diagrams and text—for too many murders. The wall space allotted to the theater homicides was attracting the attention of other men, including one she coveted for his background in Narcotics.

Though Detective Sanger had joined the elite murder squad years ago, he still wore the long hair of a narc and a diamond pinky ring, the bling of an undercover drug dealer. He was staring at her posted wish list; it begged for details that required more time than she and Riker had between them.

"This reads like a weird bridal registry." Sanger reached out to the evidence table, where telephone records for the theater company were stacked, and he lifted two sheets off the top. "This just came in. Cell phone calls for Dickie Wyatt, your junkie director. He canceled his landline weeks ago. I bet you couldn't find a recent address, am I right?"

"Yeah," said Riker. "When Wyatt left the play, he sublet his apartment. The new tenant's clueless."

"Take a look at this." Sanger pinned the cell phone history to the cork wall and pointed to a date. "That's the end of a two-week period with no activity. Your guy ordered blockers for voice mail and texting. So he's got no stacked-up messages for the downtime." His finger moved on to a line near the bottom of the sheet. "Then here—a few days before Wyatt turns up dead—he takes a call. I checked. It came from a deli pay phone."

The detective smiled as he stepped back from the wall. "And that's how I know your guy was in lockdown rehab. Wyatt sublet his apartment so he wouldn't go home to triggers for his drug habit. You look cross-eyed at the chair you sat in the last time you got stoned—that's a trigger. He would've surrendered his cell phone when he went into treatment. So I know he was fresh out of rehab when he took that last call. That means he's got another place out there. A hotel or a sublet. He didn't stay with a friend. He would've avoided every old tie to his dope days. Find out where he got rehabbed, and you might get a current address."

Janos raised his eyebrows. "How do you—"

"Magic." Sanger shot both his cuffs to show that he had nothing up his sleeves. "Or maybe I'm just fuckin' good at this." He turned to Mallory with an afterthought. "Oh, and two weeks of rehab? That says minor relapse, not heavy using. You get a hair-strand drug test on that guy—you'll see I'm right."

And now she had lost the man. He was walking toward his own wall, his own case, on the other side of the room. And she was already scheming ways to get him back.

"Hey," said Riker. "Wanna take a ride down to the ME's Office?" Getting no response, he added, "You can have another tox-screen war with Dr. Slope. C'mon. It'll be fun."

"No need," said Mallory. "He loves dead junkies."

Dead or alive, drug addicts were the doctor's hobby, and this had always mystified her. Edward Slope was so enamored with this brand of scum, he had even formed a charity clinic so that he could work on the live ones in his spare time. On Dickie Wyatt's account, the chief medical examiner would run every test in his arsenal—the deluxe autopsy.

Charles Butler was snagged the moment he entered the station house, and now he crossed the squad room alongside the commander of Special Crimes. He was looking down at the bald spot on Jack Coffey's head when the man said, "Hell, no. You don't need an invitation. Mallory's bitching about getting shortchanged on manpower. She's gonna *love* this."

Judging by the lieutenant's tone, Charles knew this was far from true.

He was a dead man.

Yes, Mallory would definitely kill him. Or maybe Riker would get to him first.

Oh, this had been a grave mistake. He had only stopped by to offer a few thoughts on the pathology of a playwright with fantasies of decapitation—perhaps not terribly useful thoughts. And maybe this excuse for a visit was a bit too contrived. He should have called ahead—or followed Riker's simple instruction to wait by the telephone.

As they entered the incident room, the lieutenant announced, "Look who I found downstairs!"

Mallory glanced at Charles and then, with no further

interest in him, turned back to her chore of pinning papers on the cork wall. Riker was not smiling, not loving this, either. While these two detectives were pleading a case for needing more help from their squad—help should not walk in the door with their boss.

Well, could this be more awkward?

Charles was a man treading water, waiting for a lifeboat to sail by. And it did, in the form of Jack Coffey, who placed one hand on the psychologist's arm and led him away.

Out in the hall, the lieutenant said, "Suppose we sit in on a few interviews?" Two doors down, he fitted a key into a lock, and they entered a familiar room with three tiered rows of tip-up theater seats, and a window of one-way glass the length of a wall. Years ago, Coffey's predecessor, Louis Markowitz, had bragged that this was the Cadillac of watchers' rooms, coveted by every other police station, including One Police Plaza.

The two men sat down in darkness, facing the window on the lighted interrogation room and its occupants: a very patient Detective Janos and a sulky teenager.

Janos's first case assignment had ended five minutes ago, when the stagehand, Ted Randal, had stalked out of the room with the flippant excuse of "Places to go, man."

Now the detective sat across the table from the other boy, Joe Garnet, who ignored him to take a cell phone call and say, "Yeah, I'll be there in ten."

And Janos smiled, not the least bit annoyed by this rudeness. Oh, perish the thought. He was making a note on the exact time of Garnet's call when he heard the second ringtone from the boy's cell. After the last interview, he had many such notes to match with telephone company records—to confirm a theory that no match would be found, not to the phones listed in the names of the stagehands. The nonstop action on the throwaways would be a clue to a sideline, most likely drugs, but Janos called it leverage for another day and another conversation.

Kids were just too easy.

After only a few minutes of talk and another ringtone, Joe Garnet left the interrogation room, not bothering to ask permission and offering nothing so polite as a goodbye. But Janos was not dejected by this lack of respect. All teenagers were Heaven-sent to test his faith in the sanctity of human life. He would never dream of popping one of them in the nose—*really* hard, several times.

The rap on the door signaled the arrival of the Rinaldi brothers, Hollis and Ferris.

Janos sang out, "Gimme a minute!" He scanned statements given to other detectives following the discovery of Dickie Wyatt's corpse, and all that was missing was an actual statement of anything. There were notes on gestures only. The brothers had kept silent.

So much for his mission to trip them up on a lie.

Previously, they had been interviewed separately. Today he planned a different strategy. The twins entered the room together and sat down on the other side of the table. Both young men were deep into their weirdo routine: slouched like rag dolls, eyes wandering, mouths open, as if to catch the odd fly passing by.

Janos read a few lines of their identical résumés. "You're a long way from Hollywood." That was where they had started out as child actors in films he had never heard of, though there was one respectable movie that anyone might recall. Then, well into their teens, they had worked in a few horror flicks. Well, *that* fit. "There's gaps here, years between acting jobs. What were you guys up to all that time?"

The twins shrugged in unison, still acting the roles of mute dullards.

"I have great respect for artists." It occurred to Janos that he could grab their scrawny necks and cut off their oxygen for a while—but that was not his way. "A police station can be a jarring environment for sensitive, creative types." *Big* smile. "Relax, boys. Take all the time you need . . . I got all day." He rose from his chair and walked up to the wide one-way glass, a mirror on this side, and he straightened his tie. "All damn day." He was watching their reflections when the metamorphosis began.

Without a word or a glance between them, they sat up straight in perfect unison and folded their arms. When Janos turned around, he was looking at two young men who were neither witless nor unfocused. And they *still* creeped him out.

"We lived on residuals between acting gigs," said one Rinaldi, who might be either Hollis or Ferris. "Every rerun on TV, we get a check."

"It was harder to find roles when we got past the cute stage," said the other twin.

Ah, lie number one. They had never been *cute*. Even

now when they had shed their stage characters, they set off alarms in the crawl of his skin. Janos sat down at the table and glanced at their résumés. "So you did a real blockbuster when you were just kids. An Axel Clayborne movie. Is that how you got hired for the play? He liked you?" No way. Scratch that. "He *remembered* you from that old flick?"

"No, we auditioned for the director."

"Wyatt hired us."

Their speech was flatline. A voice-stress analysis would be no help with the likes of them. Janos knew he could stab them with his pencil *right now*—if he were the sort to do that—and they would never show pain, so *much* pain—though they *would* bleed.

The detective looked down at his notebook and scribbled one more connection of crisscrossing paths with another player. He was beginning to see patterns of multiple alliances—and not the broad collusion that Riker and Mallory were looking for. The Rinaldi twins reminded him of the stagehands, whose bonding extended to no one else. The wardrobe lady had been in league with the late Dickie Wyatt. And then there was last night's interview with Alma Sutter, a woman who had impressed him as a nation unto herself, and so he doubted the quality of her relationship with the dead playwright—but they *had* been paired up.

He turned from one twin to the other. Were they playing him? Oh, yeah. Their eyes were locked on him. Eyes of glass—no clue. What now? They leaned forward, tensing, set to spring across the table. Their expressions were eerie, more like an idea of smiles, and he wondered if they knew how Halloween this was to him.

"Did you kill Peter Beck and Dickie Wyatt?"

They slowly moved their heads side to side, smiling all the while.

"Just for the record," said Jack Coffey, "that second guy, Dickie Wyatt? He wasn't murdered. He OD'd on heroin." But apparently Mallory had another believer in Janos. The lieutenant turned to the psychologist, who sat beside him in the dark. "So what do you make of those scary little bastards?"

"They're impossible to read for deception," said Charles Butler. "No inadvertent mannerisms to indicate anything reactive. . . . Very cold, those two. . . . Do you know if they lived in an abusive home? Maybe a stint in foster care? It would help if you could find someone who knew them as children."

"We could look into that." Actually—they could not. There was still information in the world that Mallory could not steal by robbing data banks. Even with Janos on board, the workload left no time for a background check that required knocking on doors and prolonged games of telephone tag. "You think the Rinaldi brothers could do a murder?" And now Jack Coffey waited on the man's standard disclaimer, a disdain for the snap diagnosis.

"They *could*," said Charles, with no hesitation. "And afterward . . . no feeling of remorse. You can read a lot into the detective's reactions, his comfort level. At the top of the interview, Janos knew they were playacting, but he also knew there was something wrong with them at core. Maybe just a twinge in his gut. Sometimes that's the only warning you ever get. . . . But look at them now. These two like to advertise the naked truth of what they are. That's their idea of sport."

In search of a misplaced visitor from the Midtown North Precinct, Riker returned to the incident room to see that Charles Butler had found the missing man. Now the psychologist, a devout pacifist, lifted Harry Deberman off the ground by six inches, gripping the smaller man's coat lapels in his fists.

And four detectives stood idly by, watching a civilian manhandle a cop. *That* was interesting.

Riker moseyed across the room, very laid back, his best form for breaking up fights in the making. "Hey, Charles. How's it goin'?" The psychologist was startled, as if waking from a trance, and surprised to see a man in his hands, hanging there, feet pedaling the air. Wits now collected, Charles's face colored with an embarrassed flush, probably wondering what to do next—while the cop from Midtown North continued to dangle. And Riker said to the dangling detective, "You got no business back here."

"Christ! You gonna *do* somethin' about this guy?"

"Maybe. . . . What's the beef, Harry?"

"I just asked if anybody was bangin' the ice queen."

And now it all made sense. The other men in this room

might not find Mallory all that friendly or likeable, but she was *their* damn ice queen.

Riker smiled at Charles. "You mind? She's my partner. I got dibs."

The man in hand was slowly lowered to the floor, and Riker leaned in to ask, "Harry, you like your nose the way it is? So pretty and straight?"

Deberman did his best trick. He ran for the door.

But that exit was blocked by the entrance of Jack Coffey, who now grabbed both sides of the door frame—no way out—and he said, "Okay, Deberman, let me guess. Your captain's an Axel Clayborne fan, right? We'll get him an autograph. Don't let me catch you sneaking back here one more time."

"I'm on loan. I got the transfer sheet." Deberman fished through his pockets, muttering, "Where the hell is it? The captain said you'd need a man with experience in the Theater District."

"Go back and tell him I said thanks."

Riker could finish that thought for the lieutenant: *Thanks for sending a worthless sack of garbage, hardly a man, and not a very good spy.*

"But I don't need you," said Coffey, a man with standards. He was short on manpower and at the point of dragging toddlers off the street to fill out the ranks, but not yet desperate enough to make use of a notorious screwup cop like Harry Deberman.

The drama was done. Deberman was escorted out by four detectives and their boss, leaving Riker alone with a contrite Charles Butler, a rational citizen, who had run amuck today in protective overdrive. The detective had long ago tired of explaining to this man that Mallory was the one with the gun.

And she needed no help from civilians to defend her honor. The entire squad had speculated on her sex life and arrived at a general consensus: If Mallory *did* have sex, she would never leave any survivors to verify it. And so this was a dead issue among the detectives of Special Crimes.

Riker sent the psychologist home with a strong suggestion. "*Stay* home till we call you." Charles's display of gallantry would certainly get back to Mallory—maybe six seconds from now. She would not like being the object of a squad-room joke, and it was doubtful that she would find use for a consulting shrink anytime soon. She could hold on to a grudge for years.

SUSAN: Why don't they <u>say</u> some-
       thing? (One twin takes a
       practice swing with the
       baseball bat. Susan
       screams.)

ROLLO: I told you they didn't need
       words.

                    —<u>The Brass Bed</u>, Act II

Riker and Mallory had parted company in SoHo, and now they were meeting up again on Avenue A in the East Village, each of them following their own stagehand. The pimpled boy, Garnet, and Randal, the lollypop kid, were dressed in clean parkas and jeans. When the wind was blowing his way, Riker noticed that they smelled better, a likely sign that the duo was looking for female companionship. At their age, every night was date night in New York City.

But no, they took their shadow cops for a stroll through Tompkins Square Park.

Behind the cover of the band shell, the detectives watched them scoring dope out in the open, sitting on a bench with another amateur at the drug trade, a youngster who toted a book bag that gave him up as a student from NYU.

"Janos was right about those two," said Riker. The stagehands *were* stupid kids. "They're making this way too easy." He used his cell phone to photograph the stage-hands' drug buy. The student had even accommodated these shots in the dark by waiting for his customers under a lamppost, and this did not speak well for higher education. Was that kid stoned? Yes, he was. In the old days, a drug dealer never sampled his product. Oh, where were the pros of yesteryear?

The buy was done. The stagehands and their shadow cops were off again. The next stop was a saloon with an older clientele, a place that would not cater to teenagers with fake IDs to jack up their ages. The bartender's suspicious eyes were on Garnet and Randal, but they never bothered to take off their parkas. The detectives watched them through the window, and the stagehands watched the door. Now one boy nudged the other when a customer Riker's age entered the bar, a rich man judging by the cut of his coat and the pretty woman at his side. The teenagers walked up to him with no hustle, no sales pitch or haggle on price. By handshakes all around, Garnet's hand palming cash, and Randal's shake slipping contraband to the buyer, the deal was concluded, and the boys were out the door and down the street, followed by Mallory and Riker. Neither one of the stagehands ever looked back. They did not possess one iota of the paranoia issued to every New Yorker at birth.

Onto the next block, they were into the next bar, where customers were a blend of ages, twenties to forties, and the teenagers were not even carded. Garnet slapped hands in a high five with the bouncer at the door, and Riker knew more money had traveled from pocket to pocket. Everything could be bought in this town. Given enough cash, ten-year-olds could get stinking drunk in this dive. The detectives watched the stagehands spend their proceeds, trying their luck with the ladies, but they always approached the prettiest girls. Pimples and Lollypop had no shot with Pretty.

Past ten and into the nightclub hours, Riker bowed out of the shadow detail as the teens descended steps to a basement club on Houston. The place was jumping with live music that shut off like a radio when the door closed behind Garnet and Randal.

Riker had aged out of his garage-band days when he had played a wicked electric guitar, though damned if he could say how he had gotten from then to now. A middle-aged man could not follow the boys down into that young scene below the sidewalk.

But Mallory could.

Age bowed to Beauty. He left her standing there and headed south for the station house and a long night of cold calls to drug-rehab centers, hunting the one that might have sheltered Dickie Wyatt. Riker favored night-shift workers for these interviews. Bored witless, they were the ones most likely to welcome conversation in the small hours.

As he strolled past the desk sergeant, the man pointed to the visitors' bench on the other side of the room, and Riker turned to see Axel Clayborne rising from his seat.

"I never told him you'd be back tonight," said the

sergeant, an unabashed Clayborne fan, who had certainly done just that. "He's been parked here for an hour."

Riker watched the smiling movie star cross the floor, one hand extended for a shake. The detective kept both hands in his coat pockets, saying, "It's late. Try me tomorrow."

Clayborne's smile never faltered with this slight. "Thought you might have time for a drink. I'm buying."

"Oh, yeah?" Any suspect walking into a copshop of his own volition had Riker's attention, especially at this time of night. Some perps, the bold ones, the sickest kind, loved to insinuate themselves into an investigation.

"I'll be right with you." The detective opened his notebook and scribbled instructions for the desk sergeant to fetch him some backup, while telling the civilian, "I know just the place."

Clayborne followed him back outside, into the wind and through the slush as they crossed two streets and turned a corner, heading toward the neon light of a cop bar.

When they walked in the door, Riker saw two men from Special Crimes ending a long day into night at one of the tables, and he spotted another man from his squad at the bar, but they were here by luck. Detectives Sanger and Washington had come in behind him by design, donating free time to the cause. With only brief eye contact and a nod toward the movie star, Riker snagged the other three men into the action as he led the way to an empty table and took the chair that put his back to the wall. The actor sat down with no view of the room, unaware of men drifting toward him from all quarters.

"Save me some time," said Riker. "Give me the name of Dickie Wyatt's rehab clinic."

"So that's where he was." Clayborne shrugged off his coat.

"Like you didn't know."

"Dickie never told me where he was going."

"He was an old friend," said Rubin Washington, who stood behind the actor's chair. "But not a *good* friend. You didn't miss him much when he died."

Riker caught a wince of pain on the actor's face that put a lie to that.

Washington sat down and humped his chair closer to the actor, bumping up against him now to make the angry point that he was not a man to be screwed with. "Where's that rehab clinic?"

Gonzales wore a mean scowl as he pulled out a chair and sat down on the other side of Clayborne, completing the squeeze.

"You'll have to excuse them," said Riker. "They didn't like the play. Dressing that actress up like a cop? That didn't win you any love. Now gimme a name."

"I didn't *know* Dickie was in rehab," said Clayborne. "When his contract was up, he left the play. The next day, his phone was disconnected, and he was just . . . *gone.*"

"Then you must be one of his dope buddies." Detective Sanger settled into a chair beside Riker's. "You'd be like poison to an addict in recovery."

"We used to get high, okay? *Dickie* was the addict. I only kept him company."

"Shooting heroin with your best bud," said Sanger. "What a pal. So who supplied the dope that killed him?"

"Not *me*." Clayborne was close to indignant. "And I only did recreational drugs. A few lines of coke, some reefer now and then. Dickie used to shoot up, but he got clean years ago. He was—"

"You're *lying*," said Washington, leaning close to the man's ear, but not to whisper. He shouted, "Wyatt was getting high during rehearsals! *You* told me that!" The detective *radiated* intimidation.

The waitress held her tray to her breast like a shield, and she backed away from their table.

"That was a relapse," said Clayborne, "a bit of back-sliding on Dickie's part. So rehab makes perfect sense. He was vigilant about staying clean. And valiant. Every day was a fight to beat his habit. Heroic, I'd say."

Two more detectives joined the party to flank Riker's chair when he said, "You know who you sound like? . . . The ghostwriter."

"Yeah," said Gonzales, removing his topcoat. "Flowery, kind of fruity for my taste." And now he also shed his suit jacket for a public display of muscle—and a gun in his shoulder holster. "So it was *your* idea to knock off Mallory's head in that play."

In a breach of cop etiquette for public places, more guns were exposed all around the table as detectives continued this striptease—off with the coats, rolling up shirt-sleeves, a signal that things were about to get physical. And this was a lie. The saloon had one rule—no blood-letting. But Clayborne believed his eyes, and he turned them to Riker, the only man still fully dressed and close to civil.

The game was Good Cop—*Gang* of Bad Cops.

Lonahan walked up behind the actor's chair and placed his beefy hands on the man's shoulders. He spoke in his normal tone of voice, loud enough to be heard in the outer boroughs. "So you got a little fantasy goin' here— killin' women. Ain't that what your play's about? And now Mallory's the—"

"It's *not* my play! And I don't wish *any* harm to Detective Mallory. I *like* her."

And every cop at the table took *that* for a lie.

Except for Riker. He believed the actor, but only because of the man's short acquaintance with Mallory. Anybody under eighty would be attracted to her—then disturbed by her—and last would come the back-away dance that begged distance from her. Clayborne might have a high tolerance for strange, but it was a rare man who could truly care for that little sociopath—a man like Charles Butler—who had just walked in the door.

The tall psychologist spotted Riker from across the room. Then he smiled and raised both hands in a show of surrender as he approached the table. The comical face that could not hide a thought announced that he was here to make peace.

The detective turned to the actor. "I want you to meet a friend of mine."

Mallory's first dancing partner had been Louis Markowitz. He had taught her the fox-trot, the waltz and the tango, but he had truly been a fool for rock 'n' roll. So said his wife, Helen, the dancing queen, on nights when the two of them rolled back the living room rug to twirl and shake it up and down the floorboards, stepping to the beat of vintage tunes from the sixties and seventies.

The whole house had rocked throughout her childhood in their care.

Early into her teens, she had learned to dance with partners her own age, to touch classmates without hurting them. However, Helen's talking-to-boys lesson had been something of a failure. Her foster father had explained the flaw one spring night in Brooklyn while they sat outside on the front porch. A date had escorted her to a school dance, and she had come home alone. "It's not your fault, kid," the old man had said to her then. "You were born with gunslinger eyes. Forget that boy. One day you'll meet a guy you can't scare." He had laughed. Like that was a joke. "But, seriously, kid, how did you like the band?"

Tonight, Mallory stood inside a crowd of bodies pressed up against hers in smells of perfume and cologne, sweat and booze. They all swayed and stomped to the worst of rock music from a live band, and every one of the musicians should be shot dead. Yet there *was* a beat, and she danced to it, danced with every comer, never losing sight of the stagehands, who sat out every song at the bar with their backs to the room, having given up on being turned down by women.

Joe Garnet took a call on his cell phone. Mallory noted the exact time as she grabbed her jacket off the back of a chair with an idea that the three of them would be moving on soon. *Yes.* The boys pulled on their parkas, and

Ted Randal made a call as they all walked out the door, the two stagehands and their blond shadow.

She followed them back to the park, where they stood by the same bench, looking around, and an angry Garnet said to his cell phone, "Where the hell are you, man?" The night was too bitter cold for their dealer to run an open drugstore, and he had yet to show.

Now they all had time to kill.

It was one o'clock. *Perfect*. She searched her pockets and found the index card that Clara Loman had given her this morning. She read the contact numbers for the Nebraska sheriff who had refused to share details of an old family massacre. Mallory figured the man for an early riser who would have gone to bed hours ago. Her call was picked up on one ring—had to be a bedside phone—and a sleepy voice said, "Yeah?" And when she had given him her name and rank, he asked, "Do you know what the hell time it is, Detective Mallory?"

She heard the sound of a lamp switched on. There would be no warm-up for the sheriff. She planned to knock him off his stride, knock him right off the edge of his nice warm bed. "About that old massacre," she said. "Did the twins know any forensic details? Or did they really stay in the attic the whole time their family was being slaughtered?"

Silence.

She needed better bait. "Why weren't those boys registered for school? Both of the girls were."

"I'd have to say I'm definitely cozying up to you, ma'am. Call me back if you can tell me something *useful*."

Click. His lamp switched off. *Click.* The connection went dead.

Bastard.

The stagehands had hooked up with their dealer. Cash and drugs changed hands, and they were on the move again, crossing wide Houston. The teenagers stopped after four more blocks into SoHo, and Garnet pressed the buzzer for an apartment building. This Greene Street address was familiar. The detective flicked through the contact information on her phone. Alma Sutter lived on the fourth floor. Mallory counted up four windows high to see a light. Then a second light came on, and a woman's shadow moved across a drawn curtain, and the stagehands were buzzed in. A dope delivery? Yes, it was. Moments later, the teenagers were outside again and hustling down the sidewalk, counting cash.

So they were only dial-a-dealers. That explained why those bone-stupid amateurs had no arrest records. Little fish. Detectives from Narcotics would waste no time on them. The stagehands bought their supply on the fly and marked it up for customers. Chump change—only enough money for nightclubbing. If she picked them up on their next run, she would only net a possession charge, not enough drugs to scare them with trafficking. If they were the source for Nan Cooper's weed or Dickie Wyatt's fatal dose, she had no leverage to make them talk.

Mallory raised her eyes to Alma Sutter's lighted windows. The usual customer base for home delivery was rich. The actress was not. But some addicts were too paranoid to risk a drug deal on the street, and that category might fit. Did Alma need something to help her sleep tonight— or maybe to calm her nerves for the next go-round with the police?

Sheriff James Harper lay on his bed in the dark of a Nebraska night, waiting for that damn cop to call back.

When an hour had passed, he gave her up as a waste of time and lost sleep. There had been many such calls over the years, though other cops had shown the decency to phone his office number in the daylight hours. In his conversations with police and FBI agents around the country, he had learned many things, like how to read a blood-splattered wall, and they had taught him the range of sickness that could lead to a family massacre. But he had never given his tutors anything in return, other than telling them that their own bloodbaths were not related to his old cold case.

Mallory's call was a standout. Why had she bothered to check out the children's school records?

And why didn't she call back? All the other cops did, persistent cusses, calling again and again. But not her. Maybe she was afraid to make him angry by disturbing him again so late at night.

Well, that was the trouble with females.

No balls.

The sheriff closed his eyes and fell asleep.

Acting out an old cliché about drunks, Axel Clayborne slid off his chair and disappeared beneath the table.

Thump.

Charles Butler had matched everyone's drinks, shot for shot, and *he* was not inebriated—not so it showed—unlike his companions from Special Crimes. Consequently, the detectives all voted him the best candidate for body disposal. And now, with only two fingers hooked round the edge of the heavy oak table, he easily moved it to one side.

"Cool," said the waitress.

"He's just showing off," said Riker.

After picking up the unconscious actor, Charles slung him over one shoulder, as if the man weighed no more than his topcoat, and Clayborne was carried up the stairs to Riker's apartment, thus tidying up the floor of the saloon to the barkeeper's satisfaction.

Mallory never touched the wall switch by the front door of her apartment. Lights in her windows tended to attract the attention of Rabbi Kaplan, as if he could see them all the way from Brooklyn across the river.

More likely, the rabbi had a spy in Frank the doorman.

In darkness, she skirted furnishings of black leather, hard wood and sharp edges of glass. Upon entering the bedroom, Mallory undressed by the digital glow of a bedside clock. She set the alarm and dropped off to sleep. When the buzzer sounded, it was four o'clock in the morning of a Nebraska time zone.

The voice that answered her call was testy, saying, "What the—"

"The five-year-old was the first one to die," said Mallory. "That's where your blood trail starts. . . . Then her sister. . . . Then the women."

"Well now, that's more like it. So tell me something I *don't* know. What have you—"

Click. Mallory hung up on him, rolled over and went back to sleep.

The sheriff lay in the dark—just a tad slack-jawed. He had actually confirmed case details for that cop. God *damn.* He blamed this screwup on his interrupted sleep. And maybe, pushing sixty now, he was getting too old for this job. Or the girl from New York City just knew how to pick her moments—and ran a better game.

Was she that smart?

For what remained of the predawn hours, he replayed the worst night of his life in another house, a dead-quiet one on a tree-lined street. The youngest child had indeed been the first to die, and hers was the first body found, all curled up under the quilt. In search of her missing head, he had found the older girl on the floor between the beds—also hacked by an axe and all her bones broken by a baseball bat.

Then the mother.

Sarah Louise Chalmers, a widow at the young age of thirty-two, had been slaughtered close to the door of the master bedroom. So he knew she had risen in the night, responding to screams of one child or both. Sarah's divorced sister had her blood splattered all over another bedroom. That woman had also been running to meet her killers at the door, where the first drops of her blood had hit the floor, elongating backward as the fight spilled into the room, chasing round the bed. The wet, red hallway tracks had split off, one pair to each of these women, and then they had crisscrossed during the attacks. The grandmother had not a mark on her, but that death, once he understood it, had been a little horror show unto itself.

Tonight, he walked barefoot through the rooms of his own house, a lonely place for half the past decade. He entered the den, which was littered with old crime-scene photos. His ex-wife had objected to the amount of time he had spent holed up in here behind a locked door, hiding what he could never share with her. She should have thanked him for that, for sparing her bad dreams of bloodied corpses.

He had called out for survivors on that long-ago night. It had been a hell of a trick skirting slicks of blood in the hall to search the fourth bedroom for Sarah's nephew, who lived in that big old house of blended, fatherless families. The red footprints had shown no sign of even pausing by the older boy's door.

James Harper looked at the wall clock. He had no chance of getting a cop's personal phone number, but someone in that city would tell him where Mallory worked.

Minutes later, when he heard a voice on the telephone say, "One Police Plaza," the sheriff stated his business, and the man on the other end of the line explained that the NYPD was one of the largest employers in the nation, second only to the military. "We got close to forty thousand cops!" And Mallory was not exactly a rare surname on his personnel directory. "So help me out here, pal. You got her rank? Maybe you know what borough she's in?"

The sheriff ran one hand through his graying hair. What had she said the first time he had been awakened from deep sleep? "She's a detective, if that helps."

"Naw, that only narrows it down to—"

"She called me about an old homicide case at four in the damn morning. And she sounded real young. Voice like silk, and no scruples about waking a—"

"Oh, yeah," said the voice on the phone, running over the sheriff's words from the mention of lacking scruples—apparently a good clue. And evidently, among young homicide detectives, females named Mallory were not so common. "I used to work in her precinct," said the cop from New York City. "She's a real pisser."

For the second time that night, the sheriff said, "Tell me something I *don't* know."

As he wrote down the telephone number for the Special Crimes Unit, he was staring at the photograph of a narrow back staircase in the house of murdered women and children.

There had been no blood on the steps leading up to the attic bedroom, where the twins were hidden—still hiding under the same bed when he found them. As he recalled, their pajamas were blue, their eyes were wide, and the boys were small for their age, weighing next to nothing when he had carried them down the stairs, bundled in a blanket to shield them from the sight of blood.

No one had heard either one of them say a single word from that night on.

ROLLO: The kitchen smelled like
fresh-baked cookies. The
rest of the house smelled
of blood.

—The Brass Bed, Act II

15

Mornings at the Riker residence could be ugly.

And so the drapes were closed and all the shades pulled down when the detective fumbled for slippers to protect his feet from stray bottle caps and bits of broken glass. Slippers were easier to operate than a vacuum cleaner. Not yet ready for sunshine, his eyes were scrunched shut as he opened the bedroom window for a blast of cold air—and slammed it once his heart was started.

When Riker emerged from the bathroom, there were bloody bits of toilet paper to mark the places where he had cut himself shaving. He slowly made his way through the obstacle course of the living room, where the floor was layered with newspapers and junk mail, take-out cartons, a discarded sock—and one movie star.

Last night, Charles Butler had considerately dropped the drunken Axel Clayborne on the cleanest patch of carpet.

Though a *good* host would check for a pulse, Riker only glanced at the body on the floor. Somewhere in this mess, his cell phone was chiming with Mallory's ring tone, the opening bars from an old Eagles tune, *Desperado*. He lifted an empty beer carton and there was his phone. He answered her call, saying, "Hey, kid. . . . Oh, not much. Charles says Axel Clayborne's a flaming narcissist."

And the actor lying on his floor said, "You need to replace the bulb in your plastic Jesus night-light."

The high tin ceiling had a fanciful curlicue pattern from the early 1900s, and the ochre walls were racked with cooking utensils that had no wires or batteries. There was no tick of a clock, not here; he would not allow it. The only sound was the gurgle of a percolator brewing in the old-fashioned way. In this age of instant everything, time moved slowly in Charles Butler's kitchen. Everyone who came knocking on his door gravitated toward this room, this place of laid-back comfort and perfect peace. Just now, it was flooded with sunlight, the heady aroma of coffee—and exquisite tension.

This morning, there had been no knock to announce a visitor, no footsteps in the hall behind him, but he knew she was there. He could tell by a change in the air, something akin to electricity:

This prickling of the flesh.

The fine hairs standing upright.

Years ago on another winter's day, the late Louis Markowitz had sat at this same table, drinking coffee and explaining rules for the Heart Attack Express, a game he had devised for a very young Kathy Mallory in the early days of her foster care, a time when she had distrusted Louis, and building bridges to her had required extreme craftiness on his part. A feral street child was not in the jump-rope set, nor a cuddler of teddy bears. And so the policeman and the little girl had terrorized each other, creeping up on each other in the dark or in the daylight, surprise attack from behind with the jab of a finger and the tagline, "You're *dead*."

Targeting the back of the neck had been the child's idea. The lack of sensitivity there had made it hard for Louis to instantly distinguish between fingertips and lethal weapons.

Upon entering her teens, she had surpassed the master, killing her foster father with ease and evading all his attempts to kill her. "At my age, it's like getting hit by a train," the old man had said to him on that day—hence the name of the game. And then, with great pride, he had added, "That's my baby. And the game never ends. She *still* kills me."

Louis Markowitz had met a death all too real in the line of duty, leaving his Kathy no one to play with—for a time. This morning, she had come to play with Charles, to kill him with a touch, and he was insanely flattered.

He would judge her to be no less than four feet behind his chair. Though her perfume was discreet, the perk of his large nose was the gift of great sensitivity. Had she come any closer, he would have detected the scent of some alien flower that never bloomed in nature. And, by trial and error, she knew this. So Mallory would have to make it a quick kill, crossing that gap in a rush to touch him. With great effort, he kept his muscles from tensing in anticipation. And now, to foil her, he said, "You're just in time for coffee." Without a backward glance, he rose from his chair and reached out to a wall rack to pull down another cup. When he turned to greet her properly and perhaps to gloat a bit—he sucked in his breath.

He would never expect footsteps, but there had been no scrape of chair legs, nor a rustle of paper. Mallory had closed the distance, and then some, to take a seat on the far side of the table. By all appearances, she might have been sitting there, leisurely perusing his newspaper for hours—though she had materialized in the space of his skipped heartbeat.

Scary? Truly.

And the Heart Attack Express rolled over him.

Charles took a deep, slow breath as he lifted the percolator from the stove burner and poured coffee into her cup. "Last night, I met one of your suspects, the film star."

"The narcissist." She laid the *New York Times* to one side as he handed her the steaming cup. "Isn't that what you called him? Is that like a cousin to a psycho?"

"No, it's hardly an exclusive club." He sat down at the table, unable to repress his smile, though he knew it made him look foolish. Sadly, in moments of extreme happiness, like this one, he must always play the clown in the room. "You *will* find narcissism in sociopaths. As they see it, the universe revolves around *them*. However, neither trait will constitute mental defect. In the wide spectrum of—"

"I've got one lunatic in the mix. His name is Bugsy. He used to be an actor, but now he thinks he's a character from a play. How credible is that?"

Not terribly, not in *her* view. That much was obvious. In Mallory's world every form of insanity was the fabrication of a suspect or a defense lawyer.

"Well, I'd need more to go on," he said. "There's role-playing, fantasy, delusion, psychosis." And, of course, her personal favorite—fakery. "Narrowing that down would take some—"

"You'll find all of Bugsy's info on the wall in the incident room, but this'll get you started." She laid down a notebook opened to a page of lettering so neat a machine might have printed it. At the top was the Connecticut address for a Mrs. Rains. "That's his mother. She'll see you this afternoon." Mallory peeled off the center sheet of the *Times* and opened it wide to hide behind it.

Charles lifted his cup for a sip. "Has this man ever been institutionalized?" He was talking to the air. In the time it had taken him to turn the notebook page, the spread sheet of newsprint softly wafted to the table.

Her chair was empty.

He felt a cold touch at the back of his neck as she whispered, "You're *dead*."

His coffee cup crashed to the floor.

Surprise.

And endgame.

A month might pass before they played again. He would never know the moment of her next attempt to kill him. And Louis's old poker crony, Rabbi Kaplan, still persisted in the belief that a penny-ante card game might be *fun* for her.

Charles did not hear the door close, yet he knew that he was alone. Though he might not see her coming, he could always tell when he had been left behind. So simple really. He kept getting hit by the same damn train.

The detectives stood side by side, pinning new sheets to the cork in the incident room, while Riker filled his partner in on the best parts of Boys' Night Out. "Totally hammered, Clayborne never changed his story. And Charles couldn't catch him in a lie. The guy's got no idea where Wyatt did his time in rehab. Maybe there wasn't any rehab."

"There *was*," said Mallory. "Sanger doesn't blow smoke."

True enough. That was one reason why Lou Markowitz had recruited the man from Narcotics. Sanger's expertise always panned out.

The messy data of other cases was splashed across the other walls, but Riker noticed that every time a detective wandered through the door, that man's eyes would go first to *this* patch of cork. Mallory had made it the most inviting, tacking up plastic bags with night-vision goggles that she had purchased just for them.

She had finally learned to share her toys.

And *all* the detectives played with the goggles, periodically turning out the lights, and then—lights on again—staying awhile to check out the rest of the wall, lingering by the photos of the blackboard's changing messages. Here and there, these men had pinned up notes of phone calls made and free-time speculation.

This morning, the unwieldy stack of telephone company records had been neatly sorted into piles on the table and summarized. This was Janos's contribution, and now he drew a small crowd of three detectives who had strayed from their own wall space.

The big man stood before the cork wall, arranging notes in a wide circle, and saying to his audience, "It'd take days to backtrack every damn number, but here's the gist." Janos tacked up the last sheet at the hub of his paper circle. "Cyril Buckner's cell phone is the only one that connects to the whole theater company. He calls them. They check in with him. Nothin' odd about that. He runs the show." The clockwise wave of his arm encompassed the outlying sheets. "The rest of 'em pair off—at least on the phone records."

Only Mallory showed no interest in Janos's notes. She sat down at the evidence table, pushing her laptop to one side to scan pages of telephone calls in the way another cop might read a newspaper. She had an affinity for figures, finding patterns where other people only saw columns of random numbers. Her foster parents had mortgaged their house for private-school tuition to nurture that talent and watch it blossom into a child's play of breaking into other people's data banks. Now their baby was all grown up and *still* robbing banks. Her laptop was opened, and she summoned up more numbers—and a telephone company logo.

Riker drew closer. What the hell was she doing?

Every single phone company would have cheerfully *given* her all the records she could carry—but protocols were time-consuming. Hacking was easier. Faster.

In a room full of witnesses?

Did she take all these cops for fools?

Riker saw the gamboling puppy icon for a computer virus she called Good Dog. He reached out to close the lid of her laptop—and not gently. They began a small war of the eyes, and he won—or so he thought. At the other end of the table, columns of numbers and text scrolled out of a printer's mouth. Good Dog had brought home a slew of bones.

Ten paces down the wall, Detective Janos was working his pattern for an audience that had grown to five detectives. He stepped back from his spread of players laid out two by two, and he pointed to a set of pages at the top of his circle. "The stagehands have real light phone histories. They were both makin' calls from the station house, but that day shows zero connections on their records. They gotta have other phones."

"Prepaid burners," said Sanger. And of course the man from Narcotics would find that interesting. What honest citizen paid for a legitimate cell phone and then shelled out more money for a prepaid cell before using up the free minutes?

Riker glanced at his partner. She was blending her new

sheets with the sorted stacks of phone records and making new configurations on the table.

Janos's pointing finger moved on to his next set of notes. "Alma Sutter and Peter Beck called each other two and three times a day. Lovers, right? But on the opening night of the play, her only call is less than a minute. That says hang-up to me, and the honeymoon's over for those two. In the last few weeks of Beck's life, he makes lots of calls to the theater people, but nothing stands out except— well, they never call *him*." He reached out to a pair on one side. "The Rinaldi twins only call the stage manager and their agent in L.A. That's it. They got no friends. But they're creepy little guys, so that makes sense."

In sidelong vision, Riker saw his partner pinning sheets of paper to another patch of wall space. The heads of other detectives were turning her way.

But Janos had their attention again as he pointed to another pair of notes in his circle. "Axel Clayborne and the dead director, Dickie Wyatt. These guys called each other every night till Wyatt's phone went quiet." His finger moved to the bottom of the circle, where Dickie Wyatt appeared again in a pairing with Nan Cooper. "The wardrobe lady used to call him a lot. So these two make another pair. If there's collusion, I say it doesn't go beyond two people." Janos stepped back from the wall. "That's it. Nothin' else stands out."

All eyes turned to Mallory. She had created a large square of sheets, each one running seamlessly into the other. And now, with great concentration, she drew lines in black and some in red ink.

Janos and the other detectives drifted down the wall to watch Mallory do her spooky act, marking up her square with perfectly straight lines that normal humans could only make with a ruler. A new category had been added to the stagehands' phone records, and the hand-printed sheet was marked in giant letters: THROWAWAY CELLS. Everyone moved closer to admire this page. It was impressive. The great appeal of prepaid phones was that they could not be traced back to purchasers.

With this single piece of paper, she had won the heart of Detective Sanger. "Mallory, how'd you *do* that?"

"Last night, I made notes on every call the stagehands got." She reached up to tap a sheet for Alma Sutter. "For the past month, a lot of her calls went to prepaid cell phones." One long fingernail touched a single number underlined in red. "The time on this one matches my notes on Joe Garnet's cell. I watched them score the drugs and make a delivery to Alma's place. Her phone records logged a month of burners, probably every phone the stagehands used." She circled numbers on the wardrobe lady's sheet. "Nan Cooper made a few calls to burners with matches on Alma's records." She drew a straight line to the pages for Garnet and Randal. "Now we know where Cooper got that reefer, the one she gave the security guard."

Detective Sanger finished reading her pinned-up notes on last night's surveillance of the stagehands. "Dial-a-dealers. Good call." He turned to Mallory. "They got no rap sheets, right?"

"Both clean."

"Figures," said Sanger. "Small buys, penny-ante profits on the markup." He removed the list of throwaway cell
numbers from the wall and also pulled down the stagehands' photographs. "I'll reach out to my old squad—see
what they've got on that park. They might have a few
buys on film. They lean on a dealer—and maybe you can
nail your boys for trafficking." He left the room as the
other four men drifted away to their own cases and places
on other walls.

The show was over.

And now Riker understood his partner's reckless need
for hacking. She had to lay her trap for that detective
before the man lost interest and walked away. And it had
to be Sanger's idea to help. Mallory was no good at begging favors.

Janos stared at a center page in Mallory's spread. He
pointed to Peter Beck's call sheet. "What's this about?"

Mallory had underscored the flurry of seemingly random calls that the playwright had made during the last
week of his life. "It looks like he's losing it here. Angry
man. Lots of money. He did most of his venting in a
lawyer's office. The firm—"

"Loyd, Hatchman and Croft," said Janos. "I'm already
on it." He checked his watch. "I plan to interrupt their
lunch hour." He did the best lawyer interviews. He had
no peer on the squad.

Alma Sutter passed by the blackboard. No messages
for her today, thank God. When the actress climbed

the stairs and unlocked the door to her dressing room, she found two lines of cocaine laid out on her makeup table.

A gift? Maybe a threat?

If the police should search this room—

There were no safe places for her anymore.

Got to get rid of this coke.

And she did. She rolled a dollar bill into a straw to inhale the lines of white powder and hide them in her nose. Just a few lines of cocaine would make her shine in rehearsal today. That was the law in New York City: Shine, baby, shine, or get back on the bus and go home.

The silence dragged out, but the policeman failed to catch every polite signal to end the interview at Loyd, Hatchman and Croft, PLC, a tony Park Avenue law firm.

Securing a copy of Peter Beck's will had been no problem. Detective Janos was waiting for better information, and he waited peacefully. No loud demands, no threats. He was a gentle soul by nature, and he would never grab that mealymouthed little prick behind the desk and break his fingers—one by one—*both* hands.

No. Unthinkable.

Instead, he settled into a chair just large enough to contain his gorilla frame, and he sat there, deadpan—with a badge—with a gun. Now and then, he shifted his weight, and the chair's joints made tiny wooden screams of distress. Smaller men—and they were always smaller—

often felt the need to rush in and fill these awkward gaps with useful information.

But not this man.

The attorney in the beautiful suit only faked a smile. Tight-lipped. Pissed off. He looked down at his gold wristwatch that told the time around the planet. And all the while, money was ticking by with missed phone calls and letters and meetings to bill at exorbitant rates per minute—judging by the lush digs of deep carpet and wood paneling. And so it was money that finally made the lawyer crack when he said, "What you're asking for is gossip. I don't do that." He rose from his chair, a stronger suggestion of *That's it. We're done. Get out!*

"I can see this might take a while." Janos held up a brown paper bag. "Since we're just sittin' here." He slowly opened the bag to pull out a soda, and he set it on the lawyer's desk. While the other man hastily placed a coaster under the sweating aluminum can, Janos pulled out a sandwich tightly wrapped in tinfoil, and set it down beside his cola, saying, "I guess I don't get a lunch break today. But a man's gotta eat, right?"

This opening gambit only startled the lawyer. The best was yet to come.

"We know about the ghostwriter." Janos tucked a deli napkin under his chin. "And we figure Peter Beck wanted out, but his name's still on the contract for the play." He popped the tab on the soda can, inserted the straw, slurped loudly—and spilled a little. Now, best for last, he unwrapped the sandwich so its foul perfume could be fully appreciated. For this interview, the detective had selected the smelliest combination of meats and gross cheeses to be found in all of New York City.

Talking to lawyers was truly an art form.

Janos lifted the sandwich, threatening to eat it, and then he paused. "God, I love this stuff." He smiled. "Even if it *does* make me gassy."

Understood.

The lawyer could hardly wait to say, "Most clients come in with practical requests. But sometimes they want blood. Peter fell into the latter category."

The detective lowered his sandwich. "Who did Beck wanna bleed?"

"Eventually, the entire theater company. He said they were all plotting against him. But the first time he came in, he wanted me to find something in his contract that would let him fire a member of the crew, an insignificant little man named Bugsy."

Another connection for the cork wall.

"Did he say why?" To prompt the lawyer, Janos raised his smelly sandwich to his gaping mouth.

"Apparently, having this man on the crew was a guarantee that Leonard Crippen would review the play. Peter hated Crippen, loathed him with a passion."

First the reward—Janos sealed the sandwich in its tinfoil wrapping, and then he asked, "Why?"

"Crippen and Peter had . . . *artistic* differences," said the lawyer.

"You mean the critic hated his plays."

"Crippen only panned the early work. He never bothered to show up for the later plays, and I'm sure he would've avoided this one—"

"If not for Bugsy."

"But then the ghostwriter distracted Peter. So Bugsy got to keep his job."

"Peter Beck walked out on the play," said Janos. "So why didn't he kill his contract with the theater company?"

"I don't know. We messengered the legal work to his apartment, but Peter never returned the signed papers. And I thought that was odd. Without his name on the contract, the financial backers would've pulled out immediately. No funds—no play. Peter also wanted to change his will, but he never got around to that, either."

"So . . . when Beck died, he owned the rights to the ghostwriter's play?"

"As I understand it, none of the lines from Peter's play survive in the new version. So it all hangs on copyright. If the other playwright has one, he owns the rights to his own work. Here's the snag. You can't find a copyright without the name of the author—or at least the title. If the copyright was deliberately hidden, and I assume it was, it might be listed as an untitled work. A date is also helpful. I explained all of this to Peter when he asked me to run a trace."

So Peter Beck had not bought into the ghostwriter nonsense—the idea that his play was being altered line by line.

Janos handed the man a card. "Don't tell anybody

what's in the will. Let me know who shows an interest in rights to the play."

"Alma Sutter called the day after Peter died. I haven't gotten back to her yet."

"Don't."

Alma got down on hands and knees to look for stray grains of cocaine. All she found was a dust-covered pill that *might* be speed, and she popped it into her mouth.

The others would be assembled downstairs in another twenty minutes. She composed herself and tweezed her brows in a magnifying mirror.

Oh, shit. There were white grains around her nostrils.

What if she had walked out onstage that way?

A distant screech of nails on a blackboard made her drop the hand mirror. It hit the floor and cracked. She bent down to pick up the shards with the mad idea that, if she could only glue them back together, the gods would never know this had happened.

Oh, now her fingers were bleeding.

And all around her were tiny reflections, bits of her face in broken glass—Alma in a hundred pieces.

Lieutenant Coffey stood in the doorway of the incident room. The facing wall had accumulated reams of data on the theater homicides, more material than his detectives could wade through in a month. And there was Charles Butler, the man with perfect recall, reading all of it at the speed of light. Tactfully, Coffey walked away without making his presence known. Every freak trait embarrassed Charles; the man was even apologetic about his height. Best to give him privacy until he was done. And then Mallory and Riker would have the perfect case file, one that could walk and talk.

Shorthanded, my ass!

The hallway opened onto the squad room. Jack Coffey turned toward Mallory's desk and aimed his body at her like a cannonball. *Oh, too bad.* She saw him coming. Could she tell he was angry? He hoped so. But just to be sure, halfway across the room, he yelled, "Your calls are stacking up—on *my* phone!"

To make the point that she had been shortchanged on help, the detective had selectively transferred her incoming calls to him. And because she always played games within games, she only rerouted the ones that were guaranteed to suck him into her case—or go nuts. And she was probably wondering if he had finally broken down and placed a call to the chief medical examiner on the matter of Dickie Wyatt's death.

Ain't gonna happen. Ain't gonna play.

"You're the only cop in New York City who's got a lieutenant for a secretary." He stepped up to her desk and laid down a message from the CSI supervisor, Clara Loman. "Heller took her off this case. So why is she updating you on Broadway chili joints?"

"Well, she's got free time. And you won't give us enough warm bodies to work our homicides."

"I count one *maybe* homicide."

"So you never called Dr. Slope," she said. "Did Loman find a match for Dickie Wyatt's stomach contents?"

What? Why chase down a dead junkie's last meal? "Loman didn't say, and I didn't ask." Coffey slammed two more messages on her desk, both from a sheriff in the Midwest. "Are you *ever* gonna call this guy?"

"Did he tell you anything helpful?"

"No, Mallory. The bastard only wants to talk to *you*."

"He'll call back."

And of course his gun was locked in a desk drawer, a squad-room policy created for moments like this. *So* tempting. Coffey pointed to the ringing phone on her desk. "I don't like to *bother* you . . . you being shorthanded and all, but . . . could you take that damn call *yourself*!"

Mallory picked up the receiver, listened a moment and then said, "*Both* of them?" She slammed down the phone and unlocked a drawer to get at her weapon. Holstering her gun on the fly, she ran for the coatracks.

Jack Coffey yelled at her back, "Both *what*?" And his next thought was *No!* He was *not* getting sucked into this. Yet he sat down at her desk to punch in the number for a redial.

And Dr. Slope answered the telephone.

Alma Sutter crept across the stage, slow-stepping, though her brain was racing on a combo of cocaine and mystery pills found on the floor. She *had* to see that blackboard. This was a test from the gods of broken mirrors. Oh, there it was, her message in chalk: ALMA! ANY MINUTE NOW!

She dropped to her knees and felt the pain of bone hitting wood. *No, no, no!* Oh, but she had pills for occasions like this, a pharmacy bottle stitched into the lining of her purse—her rainy-day stash. She turned her body round and crawled across the floorboards on all fours, jazzed on drugs and moving with the speed of a trotting dog.

ROLLO: After my little sister's
head was hacked off, and
while it was falling to the
floor, do you think she
could see the carpet coming
up to meet her? Was there
time for the head to say
goodbye to the body?
                   —<u>The Brass Bed</u>, Act II

16 Wall plaques and framed certificates attested to the chief medical examiner's importance in the world of forensic medicine. Dr. Edward Slope's hectic schedule was also in evidence with files stacked on his desk, awaiting review, and a tally sheet of dead bodies that were forming ugly gangs in the morgue. It was a logjam of a day that would never end. Yet he toyed with a pencil and stared at the ceiling—waiting for his visitor to finish leafing through an uncommonly thick autopsy report.

The doctor anticipated questions. He had one of his own: How was Kathy doing this?

The day's first surprise had come hours earlier with the appearance of a CSU supervisor. That gray harpy had demanded tox screens and other test results. At the time, he had thought it odd for a woman of Clara Loman's stature to perform a menial's task—well *beyond* odd to fetch reports for a homicide detective; Clara ranked such cops among roaches and vermin. So, just this moment, he was a bit more blasé about the commander of Special Crimes running errands for Kathy Mallory.

Jack Coffey looked up from his reading to ask, "Who *eats* heroin?"

"*And* barbiturates—served up with chili. Now *that's* a first."

"I thought stomach contents would've been soup after—"

"New York chili *is* formidable, even after days of stewing in gastric juices. But one of my samples was congealed around the buttons of his shirt. Another one came from the vomit in his shoes. Nicely preserved vomit. Mr. Wyatt's body was stored someplace cold."

The lieutenant's head rolled back. It was his turn to stare at the ceiling, squinting a bit, as if he might have lost something up there. "So the guy with the slashed throat, he's only a *suspicious* death . . . but the junkie's a *homicide*?"

"Both men were murdered. I just upgraded the playwright." And apparently Kathy had failed to mention this to her boss. "You see, we had a problem with what *might* be the dragline of a fingernail running parallel to the wound. That wouldn't square with the suicide of a nail biter. But the only prints on the weapon were Mr. Beck's. So your slasher *had* to be wearing gloves, right? Back to the problem of a naked fingernail. It only works if the glove was torn. So then I examined the abrasion for microscopic traces of—"

"*Okay*, I'll buy it." Coffey closed his eyes a moment. "Tell me about the other one, the damn junkie."

"I can tell you Mr. Wyatt's chili didn't come from a can—no preservatives. And there's no red dye in the meat. Not a grocery store item. So I ruled out a home-cooked meal. And that leaves—"

"A restaurant." Coffey rippled the pages of the preliminary report. "You got a time of death in here?"

"At least two days before you found him."

"Can you—"

"Yes, I can narrow it down. Mr. Wyatt didn't even have time to digest his dinner. Ingested with chili, the heroin wouldn't have taken effect right away, but if you find out when he had his last meal, I'll swear in court that he was dead within the hour."

"Good enough," said Jack Coffey.

Faint praise.

This was a tighter time frame than any cop had a right to hope for. And now, before his visitor could ask the next predictable question, Edward said, "Zero possibility of suicide for Mr. Wyatt." The doctor laid down an autopsy photograph, a close-up of ugly blue bulges in veins once abused by hypodermic needles. "These track marks are old ones. No new punctures. But he obviously knew *how* to shoot up. Ergo, his chili was dosed by someone else. *You* know it. *I* know it." Done with that, he nodded at the report in Coffey's hands. "Page fifteen, you'll find his hair-strand test. It's good for a ninety-day drug history. He was clean up till last month. There's a range of a few weeks with markers for heroin—the trace amounts of an occasional user. Then nothing leading up to his death. And I'd call *that* suspicious, too. It won't fit the relapse pattern of a heroin addict. But it *might* suggest a few weeks of rehearsal for your killer. Say he spiked Mr. Wyatt's food a few times before the fatal dose, just to—" No need to finish. He could see that suggestion was clearly a stretch for the man from Special Crimes.

Jack Coffey was wearing his best political smile, so insincere, a bit of condescension that the police reserved for pathologists who liked to play detective. Kathy Mallory had a smile rather like that one in her toolbox, though hers was more expressive, closer to actual spite.

The lieutenant laid the report on the desk. "Sit on this for a while, okay? We'll let our perp think he got away with murder." He stood up, jingling car keys in one hand, but he made no move toward the door. "One question. Mallory *never* called you, never pushed you for results on Dickie Wyatt?"

"Why would she bother? She knew I'd pull out all the stops for a drug overdose." Edward Slope took loving care with every dead addict, indulging both his vocation and avocation. Much of his free time was devoted to keeping these hapless souls alive, and every autopsy furthered that end. Kathy had counted on that. "This was her lucky corpse."

The detectives had first tried Alma's dressing room, but there had been no response to a knock, and Riker trusted his partner's instinct for live bodies behind closed doors.

Downstairs, Mallory opened a metal locker—and slammed it.

Midstride, Bugsy heard that bang and jumped—a short hop—and then completed his run to flick another wall switch.

The backstage area was now daylight bright and still no sign of Alma Sutter. Onstage, the assembled theater company had no clue to her whereabouts, only volunteering that she was late for rehearsal—though her name was on the sign-in sheet at the stage door.

Riker opened a trunk, a small one that would only work with the theory of a dead actress chopped up in pieces. But what the hell. Disappointed with the contents, only clothing, he turned to his partner. "Loman figures our perp mixed the heroin with chili to buy himself alibi time to get clear of the body. She thinks we're looking for an idiot. Wyatt could've lived for thirty minutes to an hour. Lots of time to name his killer."

"She's wrong," said Mallory. "Our perp only wanted Wyatt to walk out the door before the drugs kicked in, and that's smart. If a customer drops dead in a restaurant, the staff's going to remember who he had dinner with that night. So the poisoner commits a murder in plain sight—and buys himself anonymity."

"Or *her*self." Riker believed that women made the best poisoners. Sexist? Maybe, but true. "Alma had motive. Wyatt wanted her out of the play." Then again, if it was the killer who moved the corpse to the theater, they were still looking for a man with the upper-body strength to lift a hundred and eighty pounds from a wheelchair and into a theater seat. Or two women acting in concert? One woman and a gopher?

Every hideyhole on this floor had been checked, except for one more trunk, and it was padlocked. Before he could call out to Bugsy, the little man appeared at his side with a key ring in hand, and he unlocked it. Riker lifted the lid to see more costumes. Then his exploring hand touched something hard—and sharp. He tipped the trunk to empty the contents onto the floor, and now an axe lay on top of the clothing. This was nothing from a woodpile, but large and long in the blade—a fireman's axe made to chop down doors. "That's no prop."

"I know. It just turned up one day." Bugsy raised his eyes to the dressing-room doors along the walkway above. "Up there. Joe Garnet's dad found it. He was our prop master. Nice old guy. Well, there *was* an axe in the dialogue, but nothin' like that on his prop list. So he figured the twins left it there—a joke on Alma."

"Scaring the *shit* out of her? That's a *joke*?"

"Yeah. *No.*" Bugsy back-stepped, startled, as if this reprimand had been meant for him. "The prop master told me to hide it, lock it up—and don't tell nobody."

Mallory left off rummaging through lockers and joined them to stare at the axe on the floor. Turning now, she ran up the stairs to the warren of small rooms. Riker caught up to her on the walkway as she bent down to a few seconds' work on a keyhole. The door to Alma's dressing room swung open.

The actress lay on the floor, eyes closed, one arm twisted under her body, and her legs were sprawled at odd angles.

Not hiding. Not napping.

———

Jack Coffey answered his desk phone to pick up another one of Mallory's rerouted calls. It was the Midwest sheriff again, and the man still refused to state his business, only insisting that it was "mighty important." The lieutenant looked up to see Detective Sanger hanging in the doorway. Coffey tapped the glowing phone number on his caller ID. With no words between them, but enough said, Sanger returned to the squad room on the run.

And now Coffey said to the man on the phone, "Obviously, Detective Mallory doesn't give a shit about your little problem out there in the sticks."

This lure was met with dead silence on the other man's end of the telephone line.

"Sheriff? I might be the only friend you got in this town. If you can't give me—"

"It's about the massacre," said the man from Nebraska.

The massacre.

Multiple murders were stock and trade, but *massacre* implied a spree killer with a high body count. No such case in the house. And did he plan to share that information with the lawman from the boonies?

No, he had a better idea.

"The next time you call Mallory—don't use your own phone. Oh, and reroute your call through a different area code. Hang on a minute, okay?" He covered the receiver.

Detective Sanger leaned into his office. "Couldn't be more legit, boss. The sheriff's calling from his office phone." Sanger held up his cell. "I got a deputy here who says he's eyeballing the man right now."

Coffey smiled and said to the sheriff, "Gotta pencil? I'm gonna give you Mallory's cell phone number . . . and her home phone, too."

The snows of Nebraska were two feet deep across a flat plane that stretched all the way to the horizon line, and the brightness would have blinded him without dark glasses. But the endless expanse of sky was clear and blue as the sheriff rumbled down plowed road, trusting the wheel to his deputy, who put on more speed as they got closer to the airport.

The sheriff held a cell phone to his ear and smiled at the man in the driver's seat. "Jilly's outdone herself." Jillian was his communications expert, a glorified dispatcher who also kept his small fleet of jeeps in good running order. "She routed me through Canada."

And it worked. The young voice at the other end of this convoluted connection said, "Mallory."

"I propose a trade," he said to the girl from New York City. "I give you something, and you—"

"Sheriff, I'm busy right now. Maybe later I can spare six minutes to solve your—"

"Oh, I solved it," he said, and—*click*—he cut her off.

Damn jerkwater cop.

Mallory pocketed her phone as she walked through the emergency room, returning to Alma Sutter's bedside, where Riker was carrying on the questioning under circumstances far from private. Crying and screaming from other quarters penetrated the curtains drawn around the bed of the quick-recovery artist.

The actress was awake and neither drowsy nor spacey. She was hyper, jazzed on something, but what? All hospital treatment for a drug overdose had been refused.

"You might wanna give the ER doc a sporting chance to help you," said Riker. "He identified a few pills we found on the floor. Anything else he should know about?"

Alma shook her head. "Just sedatives." Hardly sedated, the jangled actress fumbled with her compact and dropped it before she could finish repairing her makeup. "I have a prescription."

"Sure you do," he said.

"You can ask my doctor. He's treating me for anxiety. I have *lots* of anxiety." Her compact was retrieved from the tangle of bedsheets, and now its mirror reflected a smiling face out of sync with that ailment. Alma put on a touch of angst in the way another woman would put on lipstick.

"Tell you what," said Riker. "Forget the drugs, okay? Just tell us about your inheritance from Peter Beck."

"Peter mentioned me in his will?"

"Yeah. Sweet, huh? We know you called Beck's attorney before rigor mortis set in on the corpse."

"So you've *seen* the will." Alma smiled at him.

The implied murder motive had failed to register with her. Too difficult to follow? How dumb could she be? Mallory crept up on the woman's blind side. "You *knew* he planned to leave you the rights to his play."

"Of course I did." Alma's words came out in a rush. "That poor, *dear* little man. Peter spent a solid year writing that role for me. He said it was like giving a woman flowers from his own garden." She bit her lip to slow down her runaway mouth. "Then the play changed. And *I* changed."

"Because Dickie Wyatt was riding you every minute," said Mallory, "making life hell for you, driving you nuts."

"*Yes*! And he made me a better actress. I was *grateful*!"

"And the ghostwriter was—"

"That *spook*—he gave me the inside track on cold, creepy *fear*." She clutched the bedsheet and raised it to cover her face. When the sheet dropped away, the detectives were looking at a face of abject terror, the genuine article, and then—Alma grinned. "You see? I didn't lie when I told you the ghostwriter tortured me, but he helped me, too." Now a dab of sarcasm. "He made me so freaking *good* at acting scared." And for the finale, she folded her arms and stared Mallory down with an implied So *there*. Take *that*.

Riker gave her an approving nod. "Not bad." Alma *was* a good actress—and so she was not to be believed, not by him. "You're talkin' to grown-ups now. We *never* bought that story."

"But it's true!"

"Naw, the ghostwriter's your buddy." Riker leaned over her. "You just stood back and watched all the damage he did to your boyfriend."

"You went along with it," said Mallory, working the other side of the bed. "Like all the rest of them. You chose up sides against Peter Beck and—"

"No!" Alma turned from one detective to the other.

"You've got it all wrong. After Peter walked out, I was his spy in the company." One hand went to her mouth, perhaps overplaying the gesture that said, *I've said too much*. "You can't tell anybody about that, okay? . . . Peter asked *me* to walk out, too. He wanted me to do it on opening night—just walk off stage in the first act. Well that's *crazy*. I'd never work again after a stunt like that. The theater, this role—it's all I care about, all I've ever wanted since I was *ten years old*! So I turned him down. I said no."

She fell back on her pillow, tired from running her mouth a hundred miles an hour and punctuating sentences with sniffles—both markers for cocaine, an expensive habit for a woman with an overdrawn bank account.

"Well, Peter was furious," said Alma. "He didn't even show up on opening night, and I'm *damn* sure he spent that day cutting me out of the will. He made it a promise."

"And after he died," said Mallory, "you *still* called the lawyer . . . to check on your inheritance."

"Detective, if you had a lottery ticket, wouldn't you check the numbers? The odds are a million to one . . . but you'd check."

Good answer. And one mystery was solved. Alma was not dumb.

Sheriff Harper was definitely flying over another state's area code by now, though he could not see the ground for clouds. He thought of using the airplane phone lodged over his tray-table meal of stale potato chips, but then his cell phone vibrated in his breast pocket.

And now Mallory was saying, "You *think* you know who did it. But your case is still on the books. You don't have the evidence to—"

"Little lady, I got bundles of evidence. I got blood-work, weapons, every damn thing. I got shoe prints in the blood. I can even tell you who owned those shoes. Hell, I *got* the damn shoes."

That should have piqued her interest, but she hung up on him.

No matter. A satisfied man, he was getting into the rhythm of this long-distance relationship. His mood changed when he felt the buck and roll of the aircraft. He looked out the window to see clouds boiling up to touch the plane's icy wing. No! The clouds were *not* rising—the plane was going *down*. The captain's piped-in voice called for the attention of the passengers, and now came the pilot's giveaway words for impending havoc and sudden death, *"Remain calm!"*

SUSAN:	There was no warning? When the boys were younger—
ROLLO:	Everyone knew what they were. A neighbor woman once came to the house. Timid soul, afraid to come inside. Said she didn't want any trouble. She only wanted to know if her cat had died quickly . . . or did it suffer. My mother screamed and slammed the door.

—<u>The Brass Bed</u>, Act II

17

Shoes?

Did the sheriff have two shoes or two pairs?

Mallory's thoughts were interrupted when Leonard Crippen opened his door, startled to see her standing there.

She favored surprise attack.

Not quite the impresario today, the drama critic had been caught in baggy old knock-around pants and a cardigan. Even the yappy little dog at his feet wore a casual sweater. "Hush, Kiki," he said, but the tiny poodle yapped on till it mustered a bark, so brave while hiding behind its master's legs.

The detective held up her copy of the play. "Peter Beck didn't write this. . . . Can you at least *pretend* to be surprised?"

No, he only eyed the manuscript with a greedy look. "When I talk to Bugsy, is he—"

"Oh, no," said Crippen. "Please leave Bugsy alone. He's a complete innocent." The old man stood back, inviting her in with the grandiose wave of one hand. And the dog took cover behind a chair.

A log burned in the fireplace, and every other creature comfort that could be smashed into one room was here. A woolen lap rug lay on a well-padded recliner, and by the window, a bistro table had chairs for two. Books lined his walls, the music on the old-fashioned record player was soothing, and every surface held a bowl of hard candy. An open door to the kitchen gave her a view of shelves lined with glass jars of tea bags and cinnamon sticks, and upon the counter was a spread of toast and jam.

Her suspect was a hobbit.

Crippen held out one hand to receive her shrugged-off jacket, and he hung it in a closet, smashing her new shearling into a jumble of old winter wear with visible lint and an odor of mothballs—but she did nothing to harm him.

"No one had to tell me that play wasn't Peter's work." He turned to the small table by the window and pulled out a chair for her. When they were both seated, he said, "That fool never had an original idea in his life. And no sense of humor, either." Crippen reached out to lightly touch the manuscript, asking, "May I?"

Mallory shifted it from hand to hand, as if she might be considering his request. "Bugsy didn't give you a copy?"

"No, he'd never do that. He only acted out a few scenes for me. Never even hinted at what came next. That's why—"

"Peter Beck always got good reviews from other critics. Why not you?"

"Higher standards, my dear. It's not enough to string lovely words together. There should be . . . *more*."

"You *knew* about the ghostwriter."

He sighed. *Caught.* "Yes, but I heard that from Donna Loo, the very chatty cashier. You'll forgive me for not mentioning it. When she told me, it was strictly *entre nous*." He rose from his chair, turning his back on the detective. "I'm going to put a kettle on and make us some cocoa. Just the thing for a winter day."

While Mallory waited for Leonard Crippen to emerge from his kitchen, she leafed through the play with Loman's yellow highlights on every other page. She was looking for the sheriff's shoes, but there were none—only mentions of footprints. She reread the lines on bloody tracks from room to room.

How did the sheriff get the killer's shoes without making an arrest?

Shoes. Her foster mother, Helen, had left a lot of shoes behind when she died, and her husband had not been able to part with a single pair. Mallory remembered the day when the rabbi's wife had come to help Lou Markowitz with this chore of finding new homes for Helen's old things. And when Rachael Kaplan, with the kindest intention, had tried to make off with the shoes, the old man had wept—and kept them. After his own death, Mallory had preserved all of Lou and Helen's clothing in their closets and drawers—and locked the house against the kindness of others.

In the next room, a teakettle screamed.

She scrolled down the contact list on her cell phone, clicking on Sheriff Harper's number. And when he answered, she said, "Not a typical rage killing. It was premeditated. A lot of thought went into your massacre, including the footprints . . . from borrowed shoes. One of the murdered women was a widow. You've got the bloody shoes of her dead husband, right?"

All she heard in response was "Crap!" And a click.

Was Detective Mallory that smart?

The sheriff sat with other displaced passengers in an airport far from home. He stared at the glass wall overlooking the tarmac, and he took this view on faith because all he could see was a massive curtain of dense falling snow. Due to zero visibility, no planes were taking off today.

Why had he run his mouth that way?

For ten years, he had said not one word to any cop outside his own tight circle of jurisdiction. And one word—*shoes*—that was all she required to extrapolate a whole lot more. His fear was that she had no need of that tip. Over the past decade, other lawmen had tried to draw him out, speculating on some insane drifter, a rage killing, or maybe a crime of opportunity—but Mallory *knew* things.

Maybe the girl didn't need him anymore. Could she be close to an arrest?

He rose from his seat, gathering up his coat and bag to wait in the line for car rentals. It was a short wait. Everyone ahead of him was turned away. Each prospective customer was told the same thing: Many planes had been brought to ground before theirs had limped into the airport on one working engine. Oh, and congratulations for cheating death so narrowly, but there were no more cars to be had.

Could he afford to wait? No. This was a race. He could almost hear Mallory's footsteps coming up behind him.

The sheriff showed his badge to the young man behind the rent-a-car counter, saying, "Son, I don't care *what* you told those other folks." Any kid who smiled like that, showing every tooth in his head, just *had* to be lying. "Get me a damn car with four-wheel drive."

While Leonard Crippen set out mugs of hot cocoa, Mallory was following a line of thought from an offhand remark by Charles Butler: *Scratch a critic, you find a failed author.* And now she pursued this idea, approaching it sideways, asking, "Do *actors* ever write plays?"

"Oh, yes. Cross disciplines are very common in the theater."

"Bugsy was nicely educated. Yale Drama School. Do you think he could—"

"No, he couldn't." The critic smiled and waved both hands to say this was ridiculous. "When he was Alan Rains, *maybe*. As Bugsy? No, it's not in his character." He laid one hand upon the manuscript at the center of the table. "*Now* may I—"

Mallory picked it up and held it out of reach. "He's *still* Alan Rains."

"Wishful thinking, my dear." The old man heaved another sigh.

The detective wished he would stop doing that, though she had now developed a lexicon of his sighs, and some of them lied—like this one, the expression of deep regret.

"There's no one home but Bugsy anymore," he said.

"Then who's been acting out those scenes in the subway—entertaining you for *years*? A gopher?"

He flashed her a quick smile of touché. "Talent will out, I suppose. The ghost of a talent in Bugsy's case. But it's not his nature to *murder* anyone."

"He'd need a strong motive," said Mallory. "Bugsy doesn't give a damn about money. It would have to be something like hate . . . or *jealousy*. You can get into that, can't you? Maybe that's why you panned all of Peter Beck's plays."

"No, my dear, only his early work. I never saw the rest of them. Why waste an evening sitting through a tired, hackneyed—"

"I suppose you could've written a *better* play?"

Crippen's understanding came in a slowly widening grin as he pressed one hand to his breast. "*I'm* a suspect?" He laughed. "Oh, that's *marvelous*. Bless you, child. To answer your question, no, I couldn't. Peter had a slender talent at best, but I have none at all, not in that vein. I'm only a humble critic."

"Leonard Crippen is a *vile* man," said Mrs. Rains, a resident of Connecticut.

The woman was in her mid-forties, though she appeared to be ten years older. Charles Butler had seen this kind of damage before, the common fallout of losing a child. And her son Alan Rains, alias Bugsy, might be best described as lost.

Only the mention of the drama critic had set her hands to trembling when she attempted to fill their cups. Charles gently relieved her of the heavy pot and completed the tea service for both of them. Such a lovely teapot, and a rare one. The maker's stamp in the silver dated it back to the days of the American Revolution. The lady shared his love of all things antique, and there were many other fine pieces in the shadows all around him. What would the room be like if she would just open the draperies?

This was a house in mourning—no other way to read it. The mantelpiece was only missing the black funeral bunting. It was a memorial for her son, lined with photographs of him in a march from infancy to manhood. And the centerpiece was a Tony Award. The handsome young actor was very much at home in his skin, his grin radiating confidence in every portrait.

Back in Manhattan, on Mallory's cork wall, a candid shot of Bugsy had the gopher smiling the way a dog might smile—out of fear, so eager to please. That person was not pictured here.

White lilies adorned a small table that held two more photographs in ornate frames. Here, Alan Rains posed with a teenage girl, who wore a corsage on her gown—America's quintessential picture of a school prom night.

In the second frame, the same girl wore a wedding dress. Another shrine? "Your daughter-in-law?"

"Margret," said Mrs. Rains. "Mags . . . that's what we called her. Still a child when we buried her, only twenty-one years old. Alan was destroyed. He had to be sedated . . . so he couldn't attend her funeral service. He never saw Mags in her coffin. After the burial, Alan would leave the house every day—and I'd sit by the phone. I knew a waiting room would call . . . the one in the hospital where she died . . . or a waiting room in a doctor's office. There were three of those. You see, he wouldn't believe she was dead. How could that be? How was it possible that he'd never see his wife walk through another door? And so, every day, he'd find his way to one of those waiting rooms . . . the perfect places to wait for Mags. And then, after an hour or so . . . a receptionist would call me . . . and—"

The lady's voice broke. "He stopped doing that after about a month. Then he never left the house at all. Hardly ever left his bed." She fell silent for a few moments. "When I tried to help my son, Leonard Crippen hired an attorney to stop me."

And that lawyer had won the motion to release Alan Rains from a psychiatric facility, thereby revoking the mother's guardianship of her adult son, her only child. Charles had this much from Mallory's notes on the old sanity hearing. "I'm told it was a civil rights attorney."

"Yes, and he beat me in court. As long as my boy doesn't pose a danger to himself or to others, it seems Alan has the legal right to go insane. And Mr. Crippen does his best to keep him that way." Her hands tightened around the fragile china cup.

Charles feared she might break it.

He knew he should go, but he could not leave her, not after bringing on all this fresh anger and pain. Was she about to cry?

"Sometimes I visit Alan's subway performances. . . . My son still recognizes me. . . . I wonder how long that will last." She set down her teacup, and now her hands were tightly clenched, fingernails digging into her palms.

Fists and tears.

ROLLO: When our neighbors were
interviewed after the massacre, those who still had
surviving cats and dogs,
they only had the nicest
things to say about the
twins.

—The Brass Bed, Act II

18

While Leonard Crippen turned the first few pages of the ghostwriter's play, Mallory wore a cell phone earpiece, a connection to Charles Butler in the nearby state of Connecticut, and she listened to the highlights of his interview with Bugsy's mother. When Charles was done, the detective reached across the table and snatched the play from the critic's hands.

Startled, the old man opened his mouth, but the only sound heard was the yapping of the lapdog, the first to take umbrage. Mallory rolled the manuscript in one tight fist, the universal sign language for *Bad dog! I'll beat the crap out of you!* And the poodle fled the room.

The drama critic raised his eyebrows to ask, *But what have I done?*

Now she could believe that this man had not written

the play. He had never even read it, and he desperately wanted to. Or maybe he had been an actor in his younger days. "Let's talk about Bugsy—your *other* pet—and what you did to his mother."

"So you've spoken to her." Crippen slowly released a stream of air in imitation of a man deflating. "I imagine she thinks the worst of me."

"Understatement," said Charles Butler's voice in Mallory's earpiece.

The drama critic rose from the table and picked up a pink watering can in the shape of a tin flamingo. Nervous and in need of props, some suspects played with pencils or cigarettes during an interview. This one watered flowers.

"Well, I can't have you believing that I let Bugsy go on this way for my own amusement." He paused to wet the soil of an African violet. "Years ago, I went to visit him at a hospital in Connecticut. That's where I met his mother. Mrs. Rains was having him evaluated so she could put him away. I gather he'd become something of an embarrassment to her."

"She *loved* her son," said Charles's disembodied voice. "Still loves him."

The critic bent over to stream water into another ceramic pot. "His mother thought the madness began *years* before she had him hospitalized."

"He's lying," said Charles.

Crippen moved on to the last potted plant. "I suppose young people in love are psychotic. When Alan Rains seventeen, he gave his girlfriend a kidney. That's not y love, Detective. That's a case of I-can't-live-without-the-girl love. The boy colluded with her parents, and they told the doctors that Alan was her brother. The surgery was over and done with before Mrs. Rains could step in and stop it."

"She never tried to stop it," said the eavesdropper in Connecticut. "She was proud of him."

"They were married when he was nineteen," said Crippen. "And he left Yale for New York. They had a few hardscrabble years in the city. The girl was on transplant medication, very expensive. Imagine the pressure on poor Alan to succeed."

"The mother sent them money every week," said Charles. "She loved them both."

And the critic prattled on. "Four months into Alan's starring role on Broadway, the girl became very ill. She was rejecting the kidney. Alan quit the play to take care of his wife. Walking out on a hit play is endgame for a young actor's career. He gave up everything for her—and the girl died anyway. A true American tragedy."

"More like Shakespeare," said Charles. "That's the way the mother sees it. When our Romeo became Bugsy—that was just the next best thing to being dead."

Mallory heard a woman's voice in the background, then a crash of dishes, and now the click of a disconnected telephone.

"Well, you know the rest," said Leonard Crippen. "His mother tried to have him committed to a loony bin."

"That's when you got a lawyer to bust him out of that hospital."

"Guilty. However, in my defense, Bugsy has a constitutional right to be whomever he likes, crazy or no. My attorney only laid down the law. . . . But you don't approve. Let's see if I can guess why. Perhaps it's because Alan Rains was a young hero, offering up his body parts to save the girl he loved. He was a passionate soul, and he—"

"He was a better man than Bugsy. But *you* decided that Alan Rains wasn't worth saving . . . and now the law says no one can save him."

The old man set down his watering can and heaved a long sigh, one that conveyed great sorrow. Over the passing years, had he second-guessed his act of meddling? Or was he only sorry to be caught?

Mallory dropped the manuscript on the table, but the critic would not touch it until he had her nod of approval. His dog hovered on the threshold of the room, also waiting for a nod from her.

The aftermath of the snowstorm trumped murder in the headlines today, but there was treasure buried on the inside pages, and all the daily newspapers were spread out on the detectives' facing desks.

"Here's another link." Mallory circled a paragraph in half-page obituary for Peter Beck. "The playwright and director were roommates in college—years before er one of them met up with Axel Clayborne."

iker parried with his own find. "But Clayborne and were joined at the hip. It says here, those guys did everything together—plays, movies. And then, things fell apart when they were working in Europe." In the next line of type, Riker found a mention of a film made in Italy, one that he had really liked, though he would never admit to seeing a movie with anything as classy as subtitles. "After a few years, Dickie shows up in New York—without his buddy, Axel. You figure they had a fight, a big one? Maybe one of them carried a grudge?"

Naw, that was too lame to get her attention. No, wait. She *was* listening. Mallory pushed a folded newspaper across the dividing line of desks, and he read the circled article on the late director of stage and screen. Years ago, on a movie lot in Rome, Dickie Wyatt had been arrested on a charge of drug possession. But Axel Clayborne had stepped up to claim the heroin as his own property. So the actor, an innocent man, went to jail, and his friend, the addict, went free.

> Spared the ordeal of sudden withdrawal in a prison cell, Dickie Wyatt escaped the night sweats and cramps, violent shakes and nausea chased by a river of vomit.

Riker read that last line again. Hell, it was almost poetry.

Mallory had moved on to a gossip column. She drew a perfect circle around another paragraph. "Hollywood's calling. The film rights are worth millions."

Murder for profit would always be her personal favorite.

Around the squad room, heads were turning toward the stairwell door. Leonard Crippen stood on the threshold, dressed in funeral black and sporting a fedora. He doffed his hat with a flourish, and then his damn calling card, an opening sigh, was heard by one and all. Now that he had everyone's attention, the old man slowly moved down the aisle of desks to stand beside Mallory's— awaiting her invitation to sit down in the visitor's chair. And with her nod, he did.

"I can tell you this play wasn't a spontaneous rewrite during rehearsals." Crippen handed her the manuscript. "The foreshadowing is too intricate, too well thought out."

"So the ghostwriter read Beck's play *before* he wrote—"

"Oh, I doubt that," said the critic. "Forgive the cliché, but Peter *does* knock them out like sausages. There's more work, more time invested in what the ghostwriter's done—so his play came first. Imagine, if you will, that it's a sleeve tailored to fit neatly over any old play by Peter Beck."

Other men were listening in, drifting closer to the conversation, and Detective Gonzales spoke for them all, asking, "So you know how the play ends?" He stood behind Mallory's chair, pointing down at the crown of her head. "She won't tell us. And Riker can't read."

"I'm sworn to secrecy." The critic looked to Mallory, ntly asking if he should continue.

he locked the manuscript in her desk drawer. "So the writer's play was written first?" Riker smiled when she fed the critic a lead for her next ploy to sucker a room full of cops. "How is that *possible*?"

Gonzales and the others stayed to hear the answer.

"Peter Beck always wrote the same play, over and over. It's always a family drama. They all have four characters, the standard cast size to fit every financial backer's wallet. You can count on one dominant father figure. Apparently Peter had daddy issues. And there's never more than one female role, always an ingénue, and that cut down on the complexity. Peter had trouble with women. Rumor has it, this was true on several levels. Well, you've seen him. Funny-looking man. A good enough wordsmith, I suppose, but nothing new to say. So he throws in bits of wisdom culled from *Bartlett's Quotations*. This passes for meat in literary circles."

Crippen paused, no doubt to heave one more heavy sigh, but apparently, he read something in Mallory's face that said, *Don't*.

And he continued his lecture. "Well, the lesser critics come away with the sense that they're somehow increased for attending these hack performances. Oh, and Peter always uses the three-act format. Did you know that the ancient Greeks wrote plays for a single ninety-minute act?"

Riker made a rolling motion with one hand to tell the man that his monologue was dragging, and they mig lose their audience of cops.

The critic ignored Riker and rose from his chair to to the whole crowd. "Peter was raised on television gramming. He liked the idea of ratcheting up the te just before the commercial breaks. But tension was not his forte, and some—"

"Hey!" Mallory curled a newspaper in her hands, rolling it tight. *Tighter.*

"Long story short," said Leonard Crippen, speaking faster now, "if you want to hijack a Broadway play, say—substitute one of your own—you'd choose any old thing by Peter Beck. Then your financing is guaranteed. Oh, and the element of the ghostwriter? Well, that was pure genius." He picked up the gossip column that Mallory had circled in ink. "You *know* what the publicity is worth . . . even without corpses in the audience. Though I must say that *was* a nice touch. This was all planned out well in advance. *And*, if the ghostwriter can keep his anonymity, that show will run for years." He spread his arms wide. "Everyone loves a mystery."

The critic's arms dropped to his sides. What? No applause?

"I don't buy it," said Gonzales, and the skeptical faces of other men echoed this complaint. "The ghostwriter ~rap—that idea only works on paper. No cop would ever ~ieve this guy could get people to follow orders on a board."

~e'd only need the support of the director," said ~n. "The director is God to the cast. And, in this ~ also the play's producer. Dickie Wyatt would've ~ everybody."

~es shook his head, unconvinced. "But the

~one overrides a playwright," said Crippen. ~nked one rung below the stagehands. No,

I take that back. Even Bugsy was more essential to the performance."

Riker had been fetched from the squad room, and Jack Coffey swiveled his chair to face the television set in the corner of his private office.

"I taped a press conference . . . just for you." The lieutenant pressed the play button on his remote, and the screen came to life with the wide-angle picture of a city hospital. The camera lens closed in on the face of a young man, who answered reporters' questions about Alma Sutter's near-death experience, painting her as yet another victim of the cursed Broadway play.

Coffey paused the film. "You told me she was fine."

"She *was*!" Riker stared at the frozen screen image. "This is bullshit. Who *is* that little prick?"

"That's Alma Sutter's agent. You guys got zero containment on this story. And I got six minutes before that phone rings. Who's gonna get a piece of me first? The chief of detectives? Some clown from the mayor's office? It's a crapshoot. But you better give me *something*!"

"Tell 'em it's the agent's scam. Alma's not even *at* the hospital. Cyril Buckner called and told her to get her ass back to the theater."

"After she OD'd? Did this guy somehow miss the fac' that she was taken away in an ambulance?"

"I don't think Buckner misses much," said Riker. " I was there when Alma took his call. I heard her s only fainted—just a case of malnutrition and stress. S him the docs gave her a vitamin booster. That was a lie, but she's not about to tell him she OD'd on drugs. I *know* she went back to the theater. I flagged down the lady's cab."

"How close are you to—"

"Give us more men, and we'll wrap it up faster."

Jack Coffey's desk phone rang. And now the cell phone in his pocket was ringing, too.

Bugsy carried bags of deli sandwiches to the Rinaldi brothers, who had stopped taking meals with the rest of the theater company. Today they used a footlocker for their table as they squatted on the floor in the wings.

He set down their lunch orders. They never thanked him for anything.

The twins had seemed halfway normal when he had first met them. Then they had stepped into their roles and stayed there, never speaking anymore, only making needs known by grunts and giggles, true to their roles in the play. These days, they even attacked their food in a dim-witted way, dribbling here, spilling there. He watched them rip open the bags, sending french fries flying and dropping bits of coleslaw on the floor.

Another mess to clean up. Animals. *Chimps!*

The gopher shifted from foot to foot, looking this way and that, waiting for the next dustup. Alma Sutter sat at the stage manager's desk, swilling coffee and reading one of her many dog-eared books on acting, as if she could learn her craft that way. She popped something into her mouth. Not a candy. Not a vitamin.

If not for the drug habit, she could afford an acting coach. Though just now, she acted scared, one hand rising to cover her mouth.

Not bad. Was she practicing some new piece of stage business—or maybe an acting exercise from her book?

Her head snapped to attention, and then her whole body trembled.

Bugsy approved. Those new moves would work nicely with a role that was wall-to-wall terror.

Bring it on, girl.

Now came the slow turn of her head, and she stared at the blackboard behind her chair. Though there was nothing written there, she quickly turned away, convincingly horrified.

Very convincing. This was *good.* She was playing off her own paranoia, using it, *working* it. Bugsy could almost hear the scrabble of ghost chalk on the board.

Alma had attracted the attention of the Rinaldi brothers, who quick-stepped out of character, no longer slack-jawed, dull-eyed boys. As her head lifted again, so did theirs, and they copied her act, move for move, tremble and fear. And then they locked eyes with the actress.

She yelled at them, "You hear it, too!"

The Rinaldi twins snapped back into their stage r[...] and grunted in unison, a dialect of chimpanzee [...] meant *What? Are you nuts?*

Riker and Mallory were last in line, and Janos w[...] head of this parade as eight detectives marched [...]

hall to the incident room. And, all the while, their leader played up the Midwestern slaughter with a houseful of blood and a headless girl.

When they had all gathered before the cork wall, the story hour began with Janos reading aloud from recently posted newspaper articles on an old family massacre in Nebraska. And when he was done, he turned to his audience. "It all pans out with the play. The mother and her sister, a grandmother, the little girls and twin boys in the attic."

And Gonzales said, "But nothin' about a murder weapon."

"Two weapons." Mallory opened her copy of the play to a page of highlighted lines. "A baseball bat and an axe."

Gonzales shook his head. "That's not—"

"Okay," said Janos, before Gonzales could poke a new hole in his pattern. "Those are details the sheriff held back. So if the ghostwriter got that part right, we can nail him."

"A bat and an axe?" This was news to Washington, ⸻ had no idea how the play would end, and Janos, his ⸻artner, would not tell him. "Okay, that says crime ⸻ortunity. The women and kids were killed with ⸻ found at the scene."

⸻" said Riker, not wanting to douse this contri-⸻ the prevailing theory of a premeditated mass ⸻braska's woodpile country. Half those people ⸻ around. And a baseball bat fits with kids

⸻uy that," said Gonzales the Spoiler. "But ⸻uy in the brass bed? In the play, he's a ⸻ newspapers only count the two boys.

You *know* the reporters interviewed neighbors up and down that street. Hard to screw up the body count."

"Unless the third kid was a shut-in," said Lonahan. "The guy in the play's a cripple."

"Nice point," said Riker. "If we had more time, we'd canvass the neighborhood by phone, maybe turn up someone else livin' in that house."

"Then," said Janos, "there's court records, tax records and—"

"So," said Gonzales, "you figure this sheriff keeps a material witness in the closet—for *ten years*? Too bad we can't just ask him."

Mallory smiled at his mention of the word *we*.

Though the sheriff's rented jeep was the only vehicle on the highway in this storm, he had managed to run it into a ditch hundreds of miles short of New York City.

His head ached something fierce, and it took some time to focus his eyes.

He stared at the blood on the steering wheel. A minute crawled by before he looked at the rearview mirror and made the connection to the bleeding wound on his forehead. And now he realized why this vehicle had not been snapped up from the airport rental lot: The airbag had not been replaced after some previous wreck. What else might be wrong with this damn jeep? And how long had he been unconscious?

God *damn*, it was cold.

He closed his tired eyes for a moment, allowing reason

to make inroads through the wad of cotton that passed for his brain, and then he did the logical thing, making repeated attempts to call for help—while sitting in a cell phone dead zone.

If his runaway wife were here, assuming that she still cared if he lived or died, she would look at the bright side: All this fucking snow would surely melt in the spring. *Foulmouthed woman*. And then, with the lightest sarcasm, she would suggest that he might want to hole up someplace warm—since the car was dead *and* the heater. But, stupid man who never listened to her, he should on no account close his eyes one more time or he would surely die.

Before his ex-wife, who wasn't there, could kick his ass out of the jeep, he opened the door, putting all his weight behind a mighty shove against the imprisoning snow. It was past knee deep when he left the vehicle. Every step was struggle and strain before wife-sense kicked in again, and he swung his suitcase like a hammer, tamping down snow to make the steep incline climbable, though it was slow going.

His back ached, and his arms were sore before both feet were finally planted on the roadbed. While following a hazy glow that might be a sign for a motel, he fell on his face to roll the rest of the way down an off-ramp.

He could hear his ex-wife laughing all the way from Nebraska.

Flat on his back, he longed to close his eyes, to sleep a little. But he picked himself up and batted off the caked snow. As he slogged across a motel parking lot of cars buried under white mounds, in his thoughts, he composed a postcard to the laughing woman who was always stepping lightly around his mind—making promises to her that he might keep this time—this hundredth time.

When he was past the glass doors and standing in the lobby, he had no feeling in his hands or feet, but he had apparently passed through the dead zone. His cell phone was ringing, Mallory calling. The postcard to his wife was forgotten when the young detective asked, "Which boy owned the baseball bat? Or did it belong to one of the girls?"

Did she know about the axe, too?

The sheriff hesitated just a hair of a second too long. And he knew he would not be believed when he said, "I know their dad played ball in his younger days."

"You won't tell me the truth, but you won't lie. Is that it?"

"Neither one of those boys ever played—"

"What about the *third* boy . . . the older one you've got stashed away? Odd that the neighbors never mentioned him to reporters. But they never saw that kid, did they? He never left the house. Maybe that was *his* bat . . . before he was bedridden. . . . I guess that's your cue to hang up on me, Sheriff."

And he did.

ROLLO: The window glass was made
to ward off pigeons, bul-
lets and small aircraft.
How could you possibly
expect to break it with
your shoe?
—<u>The Brass Bed</u>, Act II

 Axel Clayborne danced the Fat Man's
Ballet, completing a twirl on the ball of
one foot, arms and legs flung wide as
the points of a star, and then a short
run of steps ending in a leap onto the brass bed. But there
was no second leap through the wide window. He was
staring at it when the stage manager appeared beside the
bed. "Cyril, do we want crashing glass for a rehearsal?"

Cyril Buckner shouted at the stagehands in the wings,
"Forget something?"

Joe Garnet and Ted Randal appeared behind the window in the scenery, and they pulled out the pane of break-
away stunt glass. That took five seconds by Riker's count.

The detective and his partner sat with Gil Preston in
the dark of the back row for another five wasted minutes.
Mallory could not get one complete sentence from the

young man, who sweated and stammered and could not get past "—l-l-let—"

And Mallory said, "Let go? The understudy was fired? When did that happen?"

Yes-or-no answers were easy, but this one might take a few days. Before Gil could soil his pants, Riker shot a glance at Mallory, and then he tapped the face of his wristwatch, shorthand for *Time's a wasting*.

With her knapsack slung over one shoulder, she stepped into the aisle and walked toward the stage.

Riker resumed the interview. "So tell me about the ghost-writer's line changes. That must've pissed off the actors."

"The twins didn't care," said the suddenly stammer-free Gil. "They don't have any lines. And Axel Clayborne's word perfect in six seconds. In the beginning, it wasn't a problem for Alma, either. But these days, she's not all that good with changes. Kind of spacey—when she isn't hyper."

"What about the stage manager?"

"Oh, Cyril just went along with the director. They all did. Except Peter. He was always getting angry and walking out."

"What about you?"

"It drove me *nuts*! And that was *before* I took over the lighting director's job." Gil faced the stage, where Clayborne had begun his dance again. "I was just an assistant when the ghostwriter came up with that ballet scene, but *I* did all the work. And those damn blackout scenes—new light cues every time they changed the blocking. Well, you can't do Axel's follow lights from a booth. I had to drag my light panel up to the—"

"Okay, I get it." Riker opened his newspaper to the sports page, as if this interview might be over. It was not. "Ever play baseball?"

"Sure, who didn't?"

"I didn't," said Riker. "I was a city kid. Stickball's my game. But you were born on the Texas Panhandle. Geography ain't my strong point, kid. Is that anywhere near Nebraska?"

Inside a locked drawer, Cyril Buckner's small computer awakened from sleep mode, wirelessly stretching, reaching up through layers of wood and surrendering to the remote keyboard on Mallory's open laptop.

She sat at Buckner's desk in the wings, and he remained standing, surly as a schoolboy in detention. He had no regional accent, but that was the way of Army brats; they grew up here and there and everywhere, never stopping long enough to acquire a local dialect.

While aiming for a look of boredom, she tapped the keys of her laptop, her window on the computer in the drawer, and covertly opened his personal files, hunting for family ties to Nebraska. "So they all bring you their little problems. Alma seems edgy to me. Did she ever come to you with anything interesting?"

"Like a murder confession?" Could the detective have found a dumber way to waste his time? By the look on his face, he thought not. And he never noticed the theft in plain sight, the download of his private journal.

Mallory opened more of his files and stole copies of them, one by one. "I was thinking about her drug habit."

The man's bad attitude vanished, and she caught him in a smile. For her next trick, she read his mind. "You know she's jazzed on something, but you can't ask her to pee in a cup—that's not in Alma's contract. So now you're thinking maybe I can prove it for you. Then you can fire her for cause." Yes, it was all panning out. His nod was so slight. Was he even aware of doing it? "You like Alma's understudy that much?"

Buckner turned smug, too secure in that last wrong-track question. He was hiding something—not for long, though. More files sailed from drawer to desktop, streaming faster than a judge could deny a search warrant.

"But that understudy won't get the job," said Mallory. "You fired her. . . . I know about Nan Cooper's replacement contract. Don't lie. One warning is all you ever get from me." As she spoke, Buckner's copy of that contract was downloading from his laptop to hers, followed by all of the other contracts.

"Dickie mentioned it before he left. He asked me to look after Nan."

"And sabotage Alma?" No, that was a dead end. The man was only annoyed. Before he could respond, she asked, "Who else knew about Nan Cooper's replacement deal?"

The stage manager shrugged. "Nobody."

This *might* be the truth—if everyone else in this theater had the same simple faith in locked drawers. She put his laptop back to sleep and closed the lid on her own machine, signaling the end of the interview—before she got to the only question she cared about. And now she phrased it as a parting thought. "I hear Clayborne never played baseball in his life. Bugsy tells me the man was clumsy when he swung the bat in rehearsals. But Leonard Crippen said he did pretty well on opening night. So who stepped up and taught him how to swing that bat like a pro?"

"I did."

As the stage manager walked away, Axel Clayborne strolled into the wings and stood beside the young cop seated at the desk. She opened her laptop to stare at the screen, and he recycled a line from an old movie script. "You have the eyes of a stone killer."

Apparently, Detective Mallory had heard this one before. She never looked up from her computer. A passing bug on the wing would have elicited a stronger response. And so, playing a fly on the wall, he casually perused her glowing screen as she sifted through files. The young cop was reading the cost sheet of a canceled marketing campaign for a play that was hemorrhaging money. He watched her open another file to study a history of stage diagrams for blocking the fantasy sequence.

He leaned down to say, "I heard you casting aspersions on my bat-swinging technique."

"But *not* your dancing. I know you were trained in ballet—*years* of training." Only Mallory could make that sound like a history of child molestation.

"I can tap-dance, too. That was my entrée to Broadway. I was a chorus boy my first time out. This is the same theater where I—"

"So the ghostwriter wrote the Fat Man's Ballet just for you. That was a piece of luck, finding a classically trained ballet dancer who could act."

"Luck? Hardly. More like inspiration. The ghostwriter's changes began after we were in rehearsals and—"

"That'll work for the media, but not the police. I don't think Peter Beck believed it, either. His work wasn't being changed. It was being replaced with a full-blown play." She scrolled back a few pages and stopped at a photograph. "Here. This is where the ballet scene showed up on the blackboard."

He looked down at the complex scheme of dance notations made in chalk.

"I could e-mail this to the SSDC. That union handles choreographers, right?"

"No, don't do that." No one from that union had been involved in the ballet scene, and now he had a vision of marchers with picket signs outside the theater. "Why would you—"

"A choreographer might tell me it takes lots of time to work out a dance routine like this one. But these diagrams date back to the second day of rehearsals." She had yet to look up from her laptop screen. "That must've put you at the top of Beck's shortlist. Did he call you out?"

"Gunfight parlance? I *love* it." But the young gunslinger beside him was not amused. "In fact, Peter did accuse me of being the ghostwriter. I told him I'd never even *thought* of trying my hand at writing."

"Then you lied," said a man's rough voice behind him.

Axel turned around to see that Mallory's partner had quietly joined them.

Riker slouched against the wall. "I know why you got blacklisted in Hollywood. You thought a screenplay sucked—so you rewrote it. That movie went over budget. *Big* time. The studio shut down production. And they *canned* your ass."

Axel turned his smile on the prettier detective, his preferred source of abuse. "Film studios are run by morons."

"Pissed-off morons," said Riker. "They had to eat the losses."

"They had no vision, no faith," said Axel, appealing to Mallory.

Whoa, no mercy there.

He spoke to the neutral zone between the detectives. "My director did the rewrites on that film. I always give credit where it's due, and Dickie Wyatt was a freaking genius."

Cyril Buckner stood in the center of the lobby, warding off reporters, shouting, "She only fainted, damn it!" In response to another question hollered from the back of the crowd, he said, "I don't care *what* Alma's agent said. She was back at work an hour later!"

One reporter directed a cameraman to change his angle, and then he yelled, "Miss Sutter!"

Buckner turned to see Detective Mallory in dark

glasses. She had just passed through the lobby doors, and now she was surrounded by cameras and lights as reporters called out "Alma" this and "Miss Sutter" that.

Idiots.

He glanced at the theater poster on the wall, a rush job, a brand-new shot of Alma Sutter in stage makeup and the detective's haircut. But the two women were hardly identical. Yet the reporters were mobbing the young cop, mistaking her for the actress, who was the paler version of Mallory.

And now he understood their error.

Outside the context of a stage, Alma was only a face in the crowd, not all that special in New York City, home to a million pretty girls, most of them not so well dressed as Mallory. Buckner coveted her shearling jacket, and he could even name the pricey designer. But there was more to her draw than wardrobe. Though her eyes were hidden by the aviator sunglasses, another designer item with *real* gold rims, Mallory had star quality, attracting these satellites and pulling them toward her, commanding attention without a hand lifted, without a word spoken.

And another reporter called out, "Miss Sutter?"

Mallory smiled with more perfect teeth than Alma's, saying, "Yes?"

"Is it true you only fainted?"

"That's right. I just needed a vitamin shot. Good as new. But I'd like to take this opportunity to thank the police for doing a wonderful job—even though they're so *shorthanded* on this case."

The reporters and cameramen followed her out to the street, where she signed an autograph for an excited passerby, who had no idea who she might be, but she was so obviously *somebody*.

"Shorthanded?" With a flick of his remote, Jack Coffey killed the broadcast on his office television set. It was only a local cable show, but that clip might make the network news tonight.

He *could* commend Mallory for undoing the damage of the agent's press conference at the hospital. Or he could shoot her for that public reprimand on his allocation of manpower. What to do? The lieutenant was leaning toward the bullet remedy when he turned to the man standing before his desk.

"She's right," said Detective Sanger. "Mallory and Riker need more backup."

Traitor.

"I gave them Janos. How'd they snag *you*?"

"I took a look at their drug angle." Sanger handed him a sheet of Alma Sutter's phone records and pointed to an underscored number. "If this throwaway cell links back to the stagehands, and I'm *real* sure it does, that ties them to a dealer. And I *don't* mean their dweeb connection in Tompkins Square Park. That kid's a lightweight, a joke. *This* guy peddles heroin with one street name. Let's say the ME can match it to Wyatt's last fix. The connection's still dicey. It all hangs on phone records. The stagehands would have to roll on a customer . . . like Alma Sutter. Her records are the bible for the burner phones. She's the cast junkie."

It would also help to know where Dickie Wyatt ate his last bowl of chili.

"But Mallory and Riker have too many leads to chase down," said Sanger. "They got ties to an old massacre in Nebraska. There's a profit motive in Beck's will. And then there's a copyright angle, the drugs—"

"Okay! Enough. You're the new man on the theater homicides. Hook up with Clara Loman. She's working a chili angle for Mallory." And when Sanger's eyes got a little wider, the lieutenant said, "I don't want that getting back to Loman's boss." If Heller found out that Mallory was co-opting CSU staff, there would be war. "When you hit the chili joints, flash pictures of Wyatt and Sutter."

Long after his detective had been dismissed, Jack Coffey remained to replay the TV clip of Mallory impersonating the actress. He played it again and again.

Shorthanded? *Yeah, she was.*

The NYPD was always making pitches to the public, begging for tips and leads on a case. This was the first time in the history of the department that a cop had made a public plea for help from her own boss.

Damn *right* she was angry.

"I checked with the lieutenant! He *okayed* it!" The desk sergeant was not about to lose face in front of his officers, those who had gathered nearby to watch this fight. "*Not* my fault," he said to the detective, though he *had* given Mallory's package to the wrong man.

The thick manila envelope, *clearly* marked, should have been picked up by Robin Duffy, a retired lawyer from Brooklyn. He had lived across the street from the Markowitz house during all the years of her foster care. She trusted Robin because he had no agenda other than to make her smile, and, toward that end, the old man would gladly swallow cyanide for her.

But the man who had made off with her evidence tonight was not so amenable.

Mallory stared at the sergeant's logbook of signatures. Thanks to Jack Coffey—*bastard*—those documents were now in the hands of a poker fanatic on a mission from God.

She turned her head to look through the glass doors of the station house. There he was, a slender, bearded man standing on the sidewalk, holding her package in his hands—call it bait—and the rabbi had an air of false innocence about him, given that the name of his game was *Ransom*.

He only had to wave at her, and she nodded her understanding of his terms; she had known him that long—most of her life. Though he had come for her unarmed, Mallory would have no recourse but to follow him into an evening of slow torture among men who played cards like demented nursing-home escapees.

She turned away from the desk sergeant and walked toward the doors to meet up with David Kaplan, her foster parents' oldest friend and spiritual adviser. He was already smiling like a winner, and *that* she could fix.

Behind her, the sergeant called out, "Hey, if you can't trust a rabbi, who *can* you trust?"

Yeah, *right*.

The walls of Charles Butler's library were fifteen feet high and colored with book bindings from floor to ceiling. Below a tall arched window, a Queen Anne desk was laid out with platters of meats, cheeses, sliced-and-diced vegetables, and there was mustard in three different shades from bright yellow to spicy brown for spreads on whole wheat, rye or pumpernickel—all the makings of triple-decker sandwiches.

And the air was richly flavored with whiskey and cigar smoke.

The poker table dated back to a gambling era of legend, bright lights and tommy guns—the birth of Las Vegas. However inspiring, it had not improved Charles's odds of winning, not by one whit. His blush conceded to Kathy Mallory that he was holding a worthless hand, and with only the tilt of her head, she asked, *Why drag out the humiliation?*

So he folded his cards.

Edward Slope was still in the game, and he would be until the last nickel chip was lost. Stubborn man, his jutting jaw indicated that he could not beat two pair, but he would not fold. And, "No," he said to Mallory, "I'm not going to run a hair-strand test on the playwright.

You've already got a perfectly good tox screen and a rather obvious call on cause of death."

"Which one?" Mallory smiled. "Did you make two or three obvious calls? I've lost count."

The doctor streamed cigar smoke over her head. He was stoic, giving her no satisfaction, unless Charles counted that small throbbing vein in the man's forehead and the tight grip on his whiskey glass.

"I need that hair-strand test," she said. "I want a longer drug history for—"

"Tough. There's no reason to suspect a drug habit. The man was a damn vegetarian."

"*And* a drunk."

"*I* can't justify it—so *you* can't have it."

This exchange of sniper shots across the table was as close as the two of them could ever come to civil discourse.

Seated in the club chair to her left, David Kaplan wore the faint smile he reserved for the happy occasion of holding good cards. Thus Charles, the most luckless player of the lot, could see that the rabbi was entertaining a notion that he might have a fair shot at winning this hand.

Fair? What a dreamer.

No doubt, it was Mallory's very lack of fairness that had allowed the rabbi to win a previous hand, building his confidence and his contributions to the pot. Poor David was done for, though no such intention was writ on Mallory's face. It was more a matter of her style. Soon the players would be all in—every chip. The faster they lost to her, the sooner she could leave them. And that was thanks to an unbreakable bylaw of this game begun in her childhood: The players could not buy more poker chips to extend the pain of being beaten by a little girl with a big talent for fleecing them. The late Louis Markowitz had once referred to this old rule as a cap on his foster daughter's weekly allowance money.

On the other side of the room, Robin Duffy sat in an armchair by the light of a Tiffany lamp. It was odd to see this small bulldog of a man with a somber expression. He was rarely without a smile and always joyful in Mallory's company. But now, in her service, the retired lawyer sat out the game to sift through her evidence of legal documents. And to compensate him for this, she had taken over the old man's seat at the table and played in his stead. Thus, Robin could not fail to be the night's big winner by proxy.

Edward Slope stared at the backs of Mallory's cards, as if she might have marked them with a clue to what she was holding. The doctor prided himself on his inscrutable granite façade, but Charles found it rather easy to read the man's thoughts. Just now, the doctor would be wondering why Mallory would want more forensic tests on a man who had clearly died of a slashed throat. Might that be a ploy to distract him from a bluff? What the *hell* was she up to? As if seeking guidance from the founder of the Louis Markowitz Floating Poker Game, Edward's eyes wandered to the empty chair, where Louis's ghost was undoubtedly laughing his ass off.

Mallory further confused the doctor by losing interest in the hair-strand test. Now she only concentrated on getting at the remains of his stash, saying, "Don't embarrass yourself."

Magic words. Edward met her bet and raised it. Daring man. Chips worth many nickels and dimes were pushed into the pot. And David was right behind him in lockstep. Seeing the doctor's raise, the rabbi also stepped off Mallory's cliff, every chip wagered.

They would never learn.

How could they *not* be suspicious of her tonight?

With *no* argument, she had politely dealt the cards counterclockwise in deference to a crescent moon. She had even credited the proper wild card for an even calendar date coinciding with curbside trash collection. And she had also allowed for other cards that were wild for reasons related to weather.

Robin Duffy preempted the wholesale slaughter that was surely coming. He returned to their company with Mallory's stack of papers in hand. The lawyer's jowls lifted in a broad smile when he noticed how his pile of chips had grown in his absence. And he said to her, "I know how they did it, but there's a snag in the plan."

The old man had everyone's ear as he slid into the dead man's chair before the only space on the table not cluttered with plates and glasses, chips and cards, and he laid down the documents. "Peter Beck had no legal recourse, not in regard to line changes. He traded away all his rights for a casting veto." Robin held up a clipped sheaf of paper. "This is his contract. It grants the director absolute creative control. Dickie Wyatt could alter the play in any way he saw fit."

"He didn't *change* Beck's play," said Mallory. "It was *erased*."

"But there was no breach of contract." Robin rippled the pages of the next document, a court transcript. "Now here's where it gets interesting. When the play became unrecognizable as Peter Beck's work, he won the right to void his contract . . . but he never did. And that's peculiar. Evidently, Beck hated the new play. He calls it drivel in this transcript. So why would he want to keep his name on it?" Robin turned to the expert in all things psychologically inexplicable.

But Charles did not plan to psychoanalyze a corpse. Only hacks would do that. Relying solely on logic, he said, "My guess? Not one of his original lines survived. That's newsworthy. Perhaps he wanted to avoid public humiliation on a grand scale."

"No, that's not it," said Mallory. "Beck's lawyers were behind a slew of court appearances. That's like begging for the story to get out. Why would he make it a bigger story? Why drag out the fight?"

"A costly fight." Robin turned the pages of another transcript. "This is the last court hearing. The playwright stalled the play's opening with injunctions while his contract was in dispute. He was in control on that front— until a judge sided against him." Finding the sheet he wanted, the lawyer pointed to a paragraph. "The play was undercapitalized and over budget. They'd laid out enormous funds for marketing, and Beck's lawyers killed the ads." He tapped one line of text. "Here's where the judge accuses the playwright of using financial-starvation tactics for extortion."

"He wanted them to restore his own play," said Mallory.

"That would've made sense, but—" Robin turned the page. "Here it is." He traced the lines of a closing paragraph with one finger. "The judge reminds Beck that he can sever the contract at will, and he tells the man to fish or cut bait. But Beck won't do it." The lawyer closed the document. "And that's why the play was finally allowed to open with certain provisos. The theater couldn't use the playwright's name or his title on their marquee, and the—"

Correctly guessing that he was losing Mallory's interest, the old man leaned across the table to catch her eye for a wink and a promise that, "It gets better. You'll like *this* part. Dickie Wyatt was also the producer. His financial backing came from a Chicago investment group. This play was just another line on their company spreadsheet— oversight by bookkeepers. But they had a solid interest in all this litigation. I'm damn sure they were paying for it. The legal fees were gigantic." He opened another document that began with a list of attorneys and their clients. "The investors were never represented in court."

And, *yes*, she did like that part. "*Better* leverage. Beck could've nailed them."

"Right you are," said Robin. "If the backers were never told that their funds were used to finance litigation—and for the *wrong* play—Dickie Wyatt could've faced criminal charges. And I'm sure the attorneys pointed this out to Peter Beck."

"And that was his hole card," said Edward Slope. "He could've shut that play down anytime he liked." The doctor turned to Mallory. "So he was going to make that

announcement on the night he died. There's your motive
for murdering him."

"But that's insane . . . isn't it?" The rabbi turned to
Charles. "Mr. Beck fought so hard to have his own words
restored. Why would he use his only leverage *after* the
play opened? Doesn't that defeat the objective of a hole
card? You'd play that card to win a game—not to send
the other players home and walk away with nothing."

And now *all* eyes turned to Charles, who only spread
his hands to say, *Who knows?*

But they were patient. They waited him out. Edward
pulled the sandwich plate beyond his reach, and David
confiscated his glass, leaving the psychologist to cast about
for some honest loophole in his high standards that pro-
hibited channeling the thoughts of the dead. Ah, and now
he had it! A rough profile might pass for the witchcraft
they wanted from him.

"Well, given only the facts at hand . . . his play was
being erased slowly. Pieces of it getting lost every day."
Whiskey and sandwich were restored. "Over time, frus-
tration would be building. Anger. Humiliation. Beck was
a celebrated playwright. That stature usually comes with
a substantial ego. And that works nicely with a need for
ultimate control right up to the end. He might've been
in a volatile state of mind and—"

"Going crazy," said Mallory, lover of brevity. "And
then he snapped. That's why he went to the play the night
he died. He wanted a public showdown."

David Kaplan turned to Mallory. "This murder was
planned in advance?"

"It was."

"Then . . . the murderer knew what was going to happen. So Mr. Beck must've played his hole card *before* he got to the theater."

"Right." Mallory nodded homage to the rabbi's logic. "But obviously it didn't work. So all he had left that night was revenge. Beck was there to get even with all of them. He was going to kill that play—loud and public."

There were nods from the others in deference to this reasoning, for she was the recognized Queen of Get Even.

"Dickie Wyatt had the best murder motive—the most to lose," said Charles. "But he died *days* before Peter Beck. In fact, I'm wondering now if that heroin overdose was an accident. It might have been a suicide if he—" Charles pressed up against the back of his chair, as if Mallory had pinned him there with an angry look, or, more precisely, ocular evisceration. The documents on the table were fair game, but how *dare* he disclose information found on the cork wall—*her* wall?

David Kaplan rested one hand on her arm, calling her attention away from Charles.

Thank you. Thank you.

"So Mr. Wyatt is off your list," said the rabbi. "Who else was likely to be aware of Mr. Beck's intentions that night?"

Mallory was not inclined to give up more details—or waste any more of her time. She opened her pocket watch, a pointed reminder that she had business elsewhere. Facing the rabbi, she sweetly called him on his cards, and then destroyed him by beating his three kings—though her own hand could only be read as a straight flush in a world where grown men had previously agreed that deuces were wild cards on a night with a waxing moon.

Charles turned to the window. The moon was indeed lit like the slanted grin of a vanishing Cheshire cat.

Edward Slope killed all her joy in his own slaughter by simply laying his cards facedown in surrender. In a deviation from their personal war games, he failed to make the usual allusion to her childhood habit of dealing from the bottom of the deck. "I know what's bothering you, Kathy. It's all about style and odds. Am I right? Dickie Wyatt was the victim of a poisoner—not a slasher."

What? Three surprised men turned to the doctor, and Charles spoke for the lot of them, saying, "That was *murder?*"

Mallory glared at the chief medical examiner, who correctly interpreted her expression—her intention to gut him—and he smiled.

"Your secret's safe." After a glance around the table, Edward said, "They won't tell anybody. . . . So first, Wyatt was poisoned. It would've been more logical to kill Peter Beck the same way. Why fool with success? And the two victims were on opposing sides. The motive for Beck's murder won't work for Wyatt. That's also a problem, right?"

"But you've got it all figured out." She tapped her long, red fingernails on the deck of cards, a clear warning that he was annoying her—and that should *stop*.

Delighted, the doctor continued. "Your suspect pool is a small one—all theater people. Not a street gang, not a drug cartel. So you've got zero odds of *two* killers with unrelated motives. Fair enough? . . . Well, *I* say the director was poisoned in a failed attempt on the playwright. Now you're down to only *one* killer, one motive for murdering Beck. And Wyatt's death gets written off as collateral damage. Neat, isn't it?" He puffed on his cigar and taunted her with a smile. "You *like* neat."

In unison, the other three players, who comprised the gallery for this new game, turned to Mallory's side of the table, awaiting her counter shot.

And she said, "You *know* Wyatt's last bowl of chili was heavy on meat. But Beck only ate rabbit food. So, even if we make the stretch, and *assuming* those two would ever sit down at the same table—it's not like they could've eaten the wrong meals by mistake. . . . I thought you *liked* logic."

The three spectators turned back to Edward Slope for the next slam.

"That's what *saved* the playwright," said the medical examiner. "If the poisoner didn't know—"

Mallory put up one hand to prevent him from finishing that thought. "The cast and crew ate lunch together. Everyone knew Beck was a vegetarian—everyone who might want him dead. Does that *simplify* things for you?"

The gallery nodded in unison, all three of them silently awarding her the game point. Ah, but wait. The doctor was showing signs of a rally.

"There *is* such a thing as vegetarian chili," said Edward. "In any case, my logic still holds. You can't argue with indisputable odds."

Now it occurred to Charles that Mallory may have

wanted that hair-strand test to look for evidence of a previous attempt on the playwright's life—by a poisoner, lately
turned slasher. Had this occurred to Edward? No, the
doctor showed no poker tells for a trump card yet to play.

Edward Slope expelled cigar smoke, and now came the
barely repressed smile that always accompanied a winning
streak. "The odds are what they are, Kathy. You only get
one motive to cover both victims." His smile changed to
the one that advertised his intention to needle her. "No
other scenario is plausible . . . because you've only got *one*
killer."

"Sounds like a bet." And perhaps just to drive the doctor
insane, she said, "What are the odds I've got *four* killers?"

Edward's smile was cagey. "You mean . . . conspiracy?
That might only indicate guilty knowledge." He had
clearly seen that one coming, and now he dismissed it
with a wave of his cigar. "Every conspirator faces a murder
charge—even if they don't do the hands-on killing." He
shook his head, feigning sadness, a suggestion that Mallory was off her game tonight.

Wrong. That much was evident at a glance.

Working around the bylaws of the game, rules designed
so that no player could lose more than ten dollars in one
sitting, she held up a hundred-dollar bill, stating no bet,
only saying, "I say what I mean. I don't need conspiracy
charges. *Four killers.*"

Judging by his rare air of confusion, Edward Slope
knew nothing of the Rinaldi twins and their possible link
to an old massacre. Yet now, for all the world and every
poker chip thrown in, this esteemed forensic pathologist—

who would have cheerfully bet against *two* killers—could not tell if Mallory was running a bluff with *four* of them.

It was a stellar moment in the annals of poker night. Charles knew that Robin and the rabbi shared this thought with him, and they were all somewhat humbled by it.

Poor Edward *had* to wonder. A poisoning and a slit throat were solo acts, were they not? And his morgue was short a few victims to fit her four-killers scenario. Or was there a cheat of words he had missed, some verbal variation on palmed aces and marked cards? The doctor had only to nod and the bet would be made—such easy money—but he just sat there, considering her angles, *paralyzed* with his wondering.

What was she up to? Even Charles, a master of poker tells, could not tell.

Mallory's *gotcha* smile was in place as she rose from her chair and left the table on that maddening note of impossible odds for a game that was not rigged—or even a game that was. And of *course* it was, though damned if the doctor knew how.

Ah, but making people crazy was her favorite sport and the only possible objective in this gambit. Or was it?

Well, *no.*

Charles now recognized Mallory's sideways you'll-never-see-this-one-coming maneuver. And it was foreseeable that Edward Slope would lose a night's sleep. Come morning, the man would still lack a resolution for her wildly illogical count of killers. And then there was the wager. By habit, she only made sucker bets that she *could not lose.* And so, *starved* for logic, Edward would do the hair-strand test that she wanted for Peter Beck. Oh, yes. That seed planted, the doctor would first look there for something, *anything* that might have gotten past him, rather than face the humiliation of her *explaining* it to him.

How predictable.

Mallory had won, even though Edward, a most decisive man, was still stuck in wager limbo when she walked out the door.

> **ROLLO:** Granny was the last one. I remember the soles of her feet. Wet. Red. She'd walked through the blood of her daughters and her granddaughters.
>
> —<u>The Brass Bed</u>, Act II

20

This stretch of Broadway had seen an era of elegant dining dissemble into honky-tonk days of performing fleas and whorehouses that later gave way to peep shows and then a drug trade, which in turn was replaced by giant cartoon characters, Jumbotrons—and a pizza parlor.

Charles Butler was accustomed to white linen laid with fine china and crystal—a far cry from the bare Formica tables and paper plates of this hole-in-the-wall establishment. It was smashed into the grand-scale circus of Times Square, where electronic animation and dazzle laid down a carbon footprint to shock the world—and *no* shame. He rather liked it.

The Theater District was the neighborhood of electricity. It was in the very air and also wired into one of his companions. There was a tempo to the gopher's nervous energy. Feet tapping the floor, hands lightly slapping the tabletop, he was waiting—*waiting*—anticipating the psychologist's first taste.

"This pizza crust is superb." Charles smiled at the little man who had led them here. "Excellent choice."

Bugsy ducked his head under the weight of this praise. The little man obviously lived to please, and now he continued his conversation with Mallory, she who *must* be pleased at all cost. "No, it was nothin' personal, but Dickie never wanted Alma for that part, not from day one."

After wolfing down his slice of pizza, the gopher elaborated on this for Charles's benefit. "Ya see, the playwright rammed this girl down the director's throat. That didn't help. An' we're talkin' Broadway here. Alma just wasn't good enough to make the cut. . . . But, ya know? At the beginning, she wasn't that bad. There were times when she made Dickie's eyes light up. The talent was always there, but her boyfriend didn't believe in acting classes. Peter didn't have no use for directors, neither."

Charles could tell that this was old news to Mallory. Nevertheless, she pushed her untouched paper plate toward the gopher—a reward that said, *Good dog*—and he grabbed up the pizza slice. She leaned back to watch him demolish his food. And when he was done chewing, she asked, "So how did Alma feel about the director?"

"She worshipped Dickie," said the gopher. "He was God to her."

This was clearly not what Mallory had expected. Her

eyes narrowed as she leaned toward the gopher. "You told me he was riding her all the time."

"He *was*. And Alma worked her tail off—just to get one payoff smile from him. That always put her over the moon. After Dickie left, her acting went down the tubes."

"Something happened," said Mallory, prompting him.

"Blame the drugs," said Bugsy. "They make people crazy."

The detective's mouth was a grim line, a sign that her patience was frayed. She had been seeking an event, not a diagnosis.

Bugsy turned to Charles's friendlier face. "Alma's a little squirrelly. She thinks the ghostwriter's after her. The poor kid." The gopher's sympathy was there to read in the simple lift of one thin shoulder. "She works so hard. But it's hard to be good when she's scared all the time . . . stoned all the time." The little man looked down at his watch. "I gotta go. I can't be late. This job's all I got." His anxiety was palpable, and yet he sat there waiting on the detective to release him. She nodded and, that quick, he was out the door and gone.

Mallory turned to Charles. "*Don't* tell me he has a split personality. I don't want to hear that."

"Oh, no, nothing of the kind. Multiple personalities begin with early childhood trauma. Bugsy's personality was fully formed long before his wife died. Based on what his mother told me, this current behavior was triggered by grief and—"

"Behavior? He's *delusional*."

Well, of course. So simple. Why had he ever bothered with all those years of schooling and training? "According to Mrs. Rains, her son was clinically depressed after the death of his wife. Now *that's* a documented mental illness. I promise you Alan Rains did *not* wake up one morning as Bugsy the gopher. But it takes more than twenty minutes to do a proper evaluation. I'd need a few sessions alone with him."

He was losing Mallory. She preferred speedy bullet replies over considered, thoughtful ones. Patience exhausted, she pushed back her chair and rose from the table. Raising one hand in goodbye, she walked toward the door.

"Oh, one more thing," said Charles. "About that old sanity hearing years back. The court document might be useful if you can get me a copy."

Well, *that* stopped her. Mallory turned around to face him. Was that surprise or suspicion in her eyes? Either way, this could not be a good thing.

"You've already *seen* it," she said. Not asking. *Insisting.*

Charles shook his head.

The detective sat down at the table. "You've seen everything, the *whole wall.*"

"But no court transcript." And it was not as if eidetic memory would allow him to forget a document like that one—or even a fly speck on her cork wall of papers, photographs and diagrams. "If it had been there, I would've—"

"No!" Mallory slapped the flat of her hand on the Formica. The table rocked on its uneven legs. And then she spat out, "Deberman!" At the mention of that name, Charles felt the heat of a blush coloring his face. She leaned toward him. "I believe you *met* him." And, with more sarcasm, she said, "You *remember* that day."

He was unlikely to forget grabbing a detective by the lapels of his coat and lifting the man off the floor—in defense of her honor. When word of that foolish altercation had gotten back to Mallory, had she laughed? The others did. Or had he merely annoyed her?

"*Think!* You were in the incident room. Where was Deberman standing when you went after him?"

"He was in front of your case wall. But I didn't read any material that day. I was just waiting for—"

"After Deberman left, was there a blank space on that wall?"

Recently, her wall had become a bit jumbled with paperwork tacked up in the haphazard way of normal people who did not possess her mania for neatness. Though, he must say she had done her best to right many a wrong-hanging sheet. But on *that* day, the wall had been different; he had only taken notice of it because the paper display had been so obviously shaped by Mallory's pathology—machinelike precision.

He looked down at a napkin and, upon that clean white field, re-created the earlier cork wall. Going back a bit in time, his job was made easier by Mallory's meticulous pinning style, her creation of geometrical perfection. He saw it now, a square comprised of paper, each piece equidistant from the others to within the smallest increment of an inch.

And one hole in her pattern.

Yes, it was now very clear. The empty space was inches longer than the standard format for typing paper. He looked up to meet her eyes. "There was a blank spot in the upper left-hand quarter. . . . And it *was* the length of a legal document."

"That was the transcript for the sanity hearing. . . . Now *Deberman* has it. And that bastard has my margin notes. He knows Alan Rains is Bugsy . . . and Bugsy is *crazy*."

Guilt set in. Riker surely would have noticed the theft of the transcript that day—if not for the diversion of the thief dangling above the floor, shouting as he hung there, his feet kicking out in midair. Following that distracting scene, the hole must have been filled in by another piece of paper, someone else's contribution to the wall.

"Delusional or not, I need Bugsy to be *legally* sane," said Mallory, as if that would make it so. And now she tacked on her deadline. *"Today!"*

Backstage, the actress reached out to grab Bugsy by the arm while he was on the run. He stumbled and stopped.

Oh, shit! Alma was high—eyes like shooting marbles. Cocaine again? And maybe some speed? Yeah. The girl was twitchy and quick, blocking his only exit, her hands slicing air fast as blades on a fan, locking him in between the stage manager's desk and a wardrobe rack. Had the twins been at her again? The gopher looked at his watch, though the battery had died years ago. He must hurry.

Hurry where? Just now, he could not say.

Alma pressed both hands to her ears. "I *hear* things—

nails scratching on the blackboard. And I hear footsteps behind me, but there's no one there. Nobody believes me, not even the cops. The ghostwriter wants to hurt me, maybe *kill* me!"

Oh, Alma, come down from the ceiling. It's not safe up there.

Poor kid, she'd get the boot from Cyril Buckner if he saw her this way.

"Hey, it's not like you're the only one to get spooked in this place." Bugsy perched on the edge of the desk and nodded to the chair behind it. "Sit down. I'll tell ya the story."

Alma did take a seat, but she could not sit still. Her legs moved up and down like pistons, like she could run somewhere in a chair.

Bugsy told her the tale of another actress driven insane by a haunt. While he talked to her softly, she popped two pills, tiny white ones. Valium? Yeah. *Good.* And when his story was done, he said, "But here's the kicker. That old bastard was *alive* when he drove that poor woman nuts. He wasn't no ghost—not *then.* Ya get it? Nobody's gonna get hurt. Theater ghosts don't *do* shit like that. I'll show ya."

He hopped off the desk and unlocked a drawer to pull out the stage manager's laptop. "There's maybe forty theaters in this town, and they all got ghost stories." He powered up the machine and tapped in the words *Haunted Theaters* to call up a website. "It's all there. All the ghosts that never hurt nobody. You're gonna be fine . . . just fine."

She looked down at the lighted screen. And Bugsy ran away. He had nowhere else to be, but he could not be late.

More pills had gone down her throat to balance out the Valium, too much of it. She had crashed too fast, and nausea came on in a wave as she continued to scroll down the glowing pages of hauntings, though the words hardly registered anymore.

But her faith was strong.

Alma believed in the power of lucky shoes, broken mirrors, the jinx of the Scottish king—and the ghostwriter. Now the actress knew she was not going to find him on the Internet.

He was behind her.

Though there was not much space between the wall and her chair, she sensed a presence within touching distance. She could *feel* eyes on her. She was deaf to Cyril Buckner calling her name from the stage.

"Alma?" Gil Preston touched her shoulder, stepping back a pace when she raised her arms to protect herself. "Alma, they need you onstage." She stared at the beanpole boy, uncomprehending, and he had to say it again. "Cyril needs you *now*."

The actress upset the chair in her rush to stand, and it crashed to the floor as she ran through the scenery door to find her mark on the floorboards, and she stood there to face the actor on the brass bed.

Axel Clayborne spoke his line, her cue, and—she—said—*nothing*.

The new words were lost, and scary seconds were ticking by. Her mouth was dry. Her mind was blank. She turned to see Cyril Buckner's angry face. *Panic time.* She fled the stage to collide with the stagehands in the wings. They followed her up the stairs to her dressing room. And when they were all locked inside, she looked down at her hands. Tremors! Christ! "I need something to—"

"We know what you need," said Joe Garnet.

"I'm screwing up so bad. I'll get canned if Cyril thinks I'm high, but my nerves—" And now her whole body quaked.

"It's okay, we got a pill for that." Ted Randal dropped a yellow tablet into her open hand.

"What's this?"

"It's what you need," said the stagehand. "It'll kill the shakes—*real* fast." Ted produced another pill, a red one. "Give it a minute. Then take this chaser."

With absolute trust in a doctor-patient relationship with her drug dealers, Alma put the teenager's pill into her mouth. The panic dissipated. And so quickly. She raised one spread hand. Rock steady. But her mind was still blank.

Ted gave her the red pill. "This'll get you up to speed."

And it seemed like the pill was no sooner down her throat than—speed indeed—she was zooming. Her opening line popped back into her brain, and then the next line and the next. *Absolute focus.* Moving quickly through the door, she descended the stairs, three at a time—she could *fly*—stumbling only once in her hurry. She ran toward the stage—then stopped.

The actress shied back into the wings.

The others had not waited for her. The dresser, Nan Cooper, was playing the scene with Axel Clayborne, speaking Alma's words as an overhead light bounced off a balding patch on the woman's scalp.

Even that wardrobe hag was line perfect.

Alma came down from her high. Shrinking now, sinking to her knees, she fell to earth, all the air sucked out of her.

The players went on with the scene. No one looked her way. She was invisible to them—as good as gone. Alma pressed both hands to her mouth so no one would hear her crying.

Bugsy scrambled up the aisle, silently saying his new lines.

Pastrami on whole wheat, orange soda.

Really hoofing it now, he sped through the lobby.

Ham and Swiss cheese on rye, coffee light.

Out the street door, onto the sidewalk, into the sunlight. *What?* Two cops in uniform—*watching* him.

Burger, fries and a Coke.

Turning left now, heading for the deli—one cop on either side of him.

Four-bean salad and coffee black.

"Alan Rains," said the cop on his right, and he said it like a command to stop.

Cheese Danish and Perrier.

Their hands were on him. They dragged him away.

He was going to be late.

Mothers are fierce. They
fight just as hard when
their arms are broken. They
fight to the death.

—<u>The Brass Bed</u>, Act III

21

This was all wrong—like reading another man's diary.

Carpetbagger.

Captain Halston had entered the incident room uninvited and unannounced. Playing prince of the city today, the new commander of Midtown North—*smarmy twit*—had explained his plan to cut the legs out from under Special Crimes. *Prick.* And then, in a show of no hard feelings—*Oh, yeah*—the captain had extended his soft manicured hand, maybe expecting the lieutenant to kiss it. This interloper was leaning way too heavy on his higher rank.

In response, Jack Coffey had taken a seat in a metal folding chair—*no* handshake—and finished eating his sandwich. *Screw* Halston.

Now, done with his lunch, the lieutenant crumpled his

empty deli bag into a wad the size of a walnut—while the captain from the Theater District strutted up and down the length of the cork wall. Another man from that precinct, paunchy Harry Deberman, trotted at his master's heels.

Riker walked in the door and turned to his boss. "What're they—"

"The deputy inspector from Midtown North retired. Halston's filling his slot for a while. The captain tells me we now have a joint task force." There was no need to add that placing a captain in charge of a busy precinct could only mean that man's career was on the rise; it was an elaborate job interview for the next rung.

Riker nodded his understanding. "So Halston's out to grab headlines—from *us*."

Mallory entered the room in time to see the Midtown poachers ripping sheets from the wall. Jack Coffey disliked repeating himself, and so he said to her, "The chief of *D*s saw your ad on TV. He figured you could use a little help." This was a lie, but he had no doubt that, by now, the chief of detectives *had* seen her impersonation of the actress on the local-news channel.

Mallory shook her head to say, *That's not possible.*

Coffey smiled. This was her blind spot in life: She truly believed that dark glasses rendered her unrecognizable— not so pretty—all but invisible. That queer flaw of hers fueled a running squad-room joke that, like a vampire, she could not see herself in mirrors.

Harry Deberman hitched up his pants and waddled toward her, gloating as he held out a photograph of Bugsy.

"You screwed up on the guy's flophouse address. He hasn't been there for months."

"Very sloppy work." Captain Halston tore another sheet from the cork, ripping it and scattering pins on the floor. "I had Alan Rains picked up outside the theater." The man stepped back to survey the whole wall. "Well, I think we've got what we need for his interview." When the captain turned around, he was quick to drop the smug attitude and startled to see Riker—one very pissed-off detective—standing on the far side of the room.

Back in the days of Riker's legendary drinking binges, before falling down through the ranks, he had been *Halston's* captain. Drunk or sober, few cops in the NYPD commanded more respect, and so, in many ways, Riker still outranked this man. And now the detective issued an order to the captain. "Bugsy is Mallory's informant. She'll do the interview."

Halston's eyes darted toward the door. He had a history of retreating from every showdown, but that was not an option today. "My shop," he said. "One hour."

Riker nodded and the deal was done.

The captain summoned enough bravado to swagger out the door, followed closely by his dog, Deberman.

"An hour." Jack Coffey caught Mallory by the arm. "That gives you time to go home and change. Don't let me see you wearing that shearling jacket to Midtown. There'll be reporters crawling all over that station house. We don't want them confusing you with Alma Sutter again, *do* we?"

She looked down at his grip on her cashmere blazer,

probably checking his fingernails to see if his hands were clean where they touched her. And where did he get off *touching* her? But this was a conversation of the eyes. Aloud, she said, "You *know* why they grabbed Bugsy."

The lieutenant let go of her arm and shrugged. "Halston wants to put on a show for the media, and the gopher doesn't have a pricey lawyer. He was the easy choice."

Riker shook his head. "That's not it. When they charge Bugsy with murder—"

"Ain't gonna happen," said Coffey. "We got a deal. Midtown's only charge is a misdemeanor. And that's just to make the arrest look solid. Halston's real happy to let Special Crimes do the real work. But his squad delivers the first break in the case—Bugsy. Then the captain gets his headline and goes away."

"Naw," said Riker. "You can't trust that prick. Halston's planning to kill our case *today*. He's gonna hang it all on Bugsy."

"No way," said Coffey. "He *can't*. He's got nothing to back it up. The *last* thing Halston wants is a murder charge."

"You're right, but he doesn't need to go that far." Mallory stared at her ravaged wall. "It all fits. The day you caught Deberman sneaking around back here? He stole the transcript for Bugsy's sanity hearing. Now Halston knows Bugsy was institutionalized. So he's got a patsy too crazy to stand trial. At the press conference, he only has to say the magic words—*a person of interest*. The reporters fill in the rest. . . . Case closed."

"Yeah," said Riker. "We're dead the minute Halston trots that little guy out in front of the cameras."

Mallory stood before a blank space on the cork wall. "They ripped off the interview notes for Beck's lawyer. He can give Halston a motive. His client tried to get Bugsy fired. Not a great motive—but Bugsy's crazy, isn't he? And this won't ever go to trial."

The lieutenant raised both hands. "Enough." He knew they were right. It was a case with no forensics—*thank you, Clara Loman*—and all they would ever get was circumstantial evidence. When the real killer stood trial, his defense counsel would only need to point a finger at the certified lunatic in custody—reasonable doubt for any jury. "Nothing I can do to stop it. But with Mallory doing the interview, maybe we got a shot at damage control."

"Okay," said Riker. "So what's Halston's bogus misdemeanor?"

"Interference with a corpse. If the little guy wasn't totally nuts, that would be a six-hundred-dollar fine." But custom dictated that lunatics undergo evaluation on a psychiatric ward. And there Bugsy would stay.

As Mallory turned to leave, Coffey said, "Hold it! You *will* lose that new jacket. And then you find something in your closet that does *not* say you rob banks on the side. You *got* that?"

Riker waited in the car, watching a skinny guy in gold braided livery usher his favorite tenant out to the sidewalk. Mallory must be a big tipper. Frank the doorman stopped just short of carrying the train of her coat.

And *what* a coat. This was no concession to Lieutenant Coffey.

Her long black duster was cut like something from an old western movie, but with miles more style and made of leather. The silk T-shirt had been replaced with a black cashmere turtleneck, and she had swapped out her pricey running shoes for a pair of wildly expensive high-heeled boots.

When she slid behind the wheel, Riker reached out to touch a leather sleeve. *So* soft. Calfskin. And he would bet that the sacrificial calves were so tender they had never made it out of their mothers' wombs alive. "Coffey's gonna shit a brick."

And they were off.

As the car peeled away from the curb, Riker reached out to drape a Saint Christopher medal on her rearview mirror. This talisman for the patron saint of travelers was just to remind her that he very much wanted to live through this ride.

Mallory crawled up the rear end of her first victim's car. "If the day goes sour, take the subway back to SoHo." And the car up ahead sped out of her way.

"Okay by me," said Riker, "but why?"

She turned to face him, taking her eyes off the road as she sailed through a red light and away from the sound of screeching brakes in the wake of terror left behind them. "Don't *mosey* out the door. Get out of there as fast as you can."

And the words *plausible deniability* came to mind.

———

This watchers' room was missing the amenities of Special Crimes. Here, the one-way glass was not so wide, and Midtown North had nothing as fancy as rows of tip-up seats. A stack of folded metal chairs leaned against the rear wall, but every man remained standing.

The lieutenant stood beside a young assistant district attorney. Ten paces away, gunfight distance, Captain Halston had surrounded himself with four unnecessary detectives selected only for a show of force, a reminder to Jack Coffey that he was outnumbered. They all faced the glass and its view of the little man seated alone at the table in the brightly lit interrogation room.

Hunched over, Bugsy worried one hand around the other. All the way crazy and very scared, he was the most helpless creature God ever made. Every two seconds he looked up at the door, awaiting his interrogator.

"Detective Mallory's late," said Captain Halston.

Mallory was on the floor below, shopping in the Midtown North locker room, and she picked one lock after another to ransack the gym bags of cops who liked to work out at the end of a shift. She found what she wanted in a woman's locker. After hiding the stolen goods under her duster, she passed down a hallway, unchallenged by uniforms and clerical personnel, though she wore no visitor's name tag, and there was no gold shield on display.

In this cophouse that catered to celebrities and other VIPs, she was only wearing money today.

The detective climbed the stairs to the next floor and joined her partner outside the watchers' room, where he stood in company with a bald man, who was unshaven and lumpy in a loud, checkered suit. He made Riker look well dressed.

"Mallory, you remember Eddy Monroe. He's Bugsy's lawyer."

Who could forget the laziest hack in the Public Defender's Office? Monroe favored quick resolutions, sometimes dirty ones, and this character flaw carried into his personal hygiene. He smelled, and his fingernails were grimy.

"Bugsy waived his right to counsel during questioning," said Riker. "What a surprise, huh? Poor Eddy had to hoof it over here for nothin'."

Mallory turned on the lawyer. "Did you actually *talk* to your client this time?"

"Well, no." Monroe spread his hands to ask, *What the hell for?* "Interference with a corpse—a penny-ante charge, and they're not even gonna fine my guy. I got him a deal." The lawyer raised one fat thumb. "First, you get his confession." Next he held up his index finger. "Then I plead him out." And last came the middle finger for the fuck-you finish. "And we all go home early."

"*So* classy." Riker turned to his partner. "The arraignment's already on the docket, and Bugsy hasn't even been charged yet."

"Yeah," said Monroe. "It was timed for the press conference. You got an hour, Mallory. Shouldn't take that long. I hear my client's bug-shit crazy."

And the gopher could not be in worse hands.

Mallory was wearing her shades when she entered the watchers' room, dressed like visiting royalty.

Late. No apology. No excuse.

Every cop turned her way, and the tension ratcheted up a notch. Only Lieutenant Coffey was smiling, far from pissed off with her new-and-improved wardrobe selection. He stared at her high-heeled boots. His detective was now two inches taller than the captain and half his men.

The young assistant district attorney rushed to the stack of metal folding chairs. Lifting one, he carried it to Mallory so the *lady* could sit down.

"What the fuck?" Captain Halston snatched the chair from the ADA and flung it back to the wall. "She won't be staying!" He turned his anger on Mallory as he pointed at the glass window on the adjoining room. "Get in there. *Now!*"

Not so fast.

She only looked *down* at the captain. And then she made a show of *slowly* turning to her boss, deferring to Coffey, a man of lesser rank. She stood there, motionless, a woman with all the time in the world.

And when Jack Coffey thought he could drag out the fun no longer, he gave her a nod and said, "Go."

She turned on one heel and marched out like a good

soldier. Later in the day, he would recall this moment as the one that should have set off warning bells.

Detective Riker had the public defender in tow, more like in custody. His hand was on the lawyer's back as he propelled him through the door of the watchers' room.

Surprised and then angry, Captain Halston glared at Eddy Monroe. Was he silently reminding the man that this was not their deal? Riker caught the captain's eye and managed to convey that Monroe would *stay*—that this was the *new* deal.

The more witnesses for a lynching, the better.

There could be no argument, not with an assistant district attorney in the room. That youngster looked to be fresh out of law school, no doubt handpicked for this assignment because he lacked experience and guile—a boy still in love with all things legal.

Riker faced the one-way glass as his partner entered the next room and sat down across the table from Bugsy. She held out a pen and a pad of lined, yellow paper. The writing pad fell to the table when Bugsy grabbed both her hands and held on tight, so happy to see her, too afraid to let go of her.

She spoke to him softly. Too softly. Captain Halston reached out to the control panel and jacked up the volume to hear her say, "Trust me."

Bugsy's head bobbed up and down in the affirmation of a dumb animal. He released her hands to pick up the pen. Following instructions, he turned his eyes down to the yellow pad, and he wrote out his real name, Alan Rains. When she dictated his bogus flophouse address, he looked up for one quizzical moment, and then he scribbled another line for her.

"In your own words," she said, "write down how you stole a wheelchair from backstage—how you used it to transport Dickie Wyatt's corpse to the theater seat."

He raised his eyes to hers and shook his head.

"Do what I tell you." She said this in the same soft vein as *Trust me*.

And Bugsy, true to the character he played in life, did as he was told. He bent down to his work, confessing to pushing a two-day-old corpse around in a wheelchair.

On the other side of the glass, the youngster from the DA's Office said, "She's not eliciting a confession—she's *dictating* it."

Captain Halston placed an avuncular arm around the young lawyer's shoulders. "Kid, we're not taping this. Don't worry about it. Your boss can tell you cops do this kind of thing all the time."

The worried ADA glanced at the public defender, who showed no interest in this debate. Eddy Monroe leaned back against the rear wall and read the sports pages of his newspaper, unconcerned. And this seemed to mollify the DA's man—the DA's *boy*.

Finished with his writing, Bugsy looked to Mallory for more instructions.

"Now we have to mention how you got that corpse," she said.

Bugsy's only sign of rebellion was to mouth the words, *Please no.*

"Do what I tell you, and I promise they'll let you go. I'll take you out of here myself. We'll go get some pizza and beer."

"This isn't right," said the ADA.

"Yeah," said Captain Halston, "it *is*." He placed both hands on the younger man's shoulders and squeezed— *hard*. "Mallory can lie to him all day long. She can be a lying bitch on wheels." The captain raised his voice to bully volume. "The Supreme Court *fucking said so!*"

"Amen," said Eddy Monroe, looking up from his newspaper. He gave the ADA a thumbs-up. "Relax, kid. It's all good."

In the other room, Mallory was saying, "Look, Bugsy." She pointed to the one-way glass. "There's an audience behind that mirror. They all turned out to see you." In a lower voice, she said, "Today you play the part of the man who killed Dickie Wyatt."

"What's she *doing*?" Halston looked back over one shoulder to see if this had gotten the public defender's attention. It had not. In a hoarse angry whisper, he said to Jack Coffey, "We're going for a light charge here. She *knows* that. Wyatt wasn't even a homicide."

Riker smiled. Apparently no one from Midtown North had bothered to check with the Medical Examiner's Office. And Dr. Slope was still sitting on Dickie Wyatt's autopsy report.

"Gimme the lieutenant's personal notes." The captain snapped his fingers, and Harry Deberman handed him a small notebook page filled with lines of Jack Coffey's handwriting, the spoils of Halston's raid on Special Crimes. "Jack, you talked to the ME's Office right after your guys found the junkie's body. Am I right? It says here, the pathologist's call was a drug overdose."

"I *told* her you only wanted a half-assed job," said Coffey, "but I guess she just can't help herself." His eyes were on Bugsy in the next room, where the little man was still writing out the details of his imaginary crime. "Mallory's bringing it home, wrapping the case. A murder confession—just in time for your big press conference."

"Murder?" Eddy Monroe dropped his newspaper and stepped up to the glass. "This ain't the deal I cleared with my boss. Halston, what're you tryin' to pull? You *tryin'* to get me fired? The deal's off! Gimme back my paperwork!"

"I got better paperwork." The captain turned to Harry Deberman. "Give him the transcript."

Detective Deberman handed a thick wad of paper to the defense lawyer. "Here. This says your client's already done time on a psych ward."

Once the papers were unfolded, Riker recognized the stolen transcript of Bugsy's old sanity hearing.

"And Dickie Wyatt OD'd," said Halston. "He killed *himself.* Monroe, you *know* we're not gonna charge a lunatic with a murder that never happened." Halston turned to the younger lawyer. "*You* tell him!"

"Mr. Rains can confess to a murder," said the ADA, "but the police aren't obligated to charge him. I personally guarantee they'll go with the lesser offense—interference with a corpse. But if he's certifia—"

"Good enough." Eddy Monroe stuffed the transcript into his briefcase.

The ADA jabbed a thumb at the one-way glass and asked the captain, "How crazy *is* that man?" As Eddy Monroe beat it out of the room, the younger lawyer called out to his back, "Could I *see* those papers?"

Too late. The door closed.

"No, you don't." Captain Halston gripped the ADA's arm, restraining him when he tried to follow Monroe. "There was a sanity hearing *years* ago. Our guy walked free. So he might be nuts, but he's *legally* sane. *Not* your problem, kid."

Riker knew Eddy Monroe would never read through that transcript—not before the arraignment. Too much like work. If only he had been a better lawyer, he could have quashed the confession and walked his client out the door. Even less work.

And how carefully had the captain read that transcript of mind-numbing legal jargon? Had he even scanned the summary page? The old sanity hearing had damn little to do with sanity. Five years ago, only Bugsy's freedom had been at stake.

Still at stake—thanks to Eddy Monroe.

And now Riker had to get himself and his boss out of here fast, before Mallory's fallback plan began. As the others filed out through the door, he glanced at the window on the interrogation room. Where had she gone?

Did he really want to know?

———————

Where was she?

Bugsy sat alone, staring at his broken watch and waiting out Mallory's promised return in ten minutes. He heard the click of the lock. The door opened, and she entered the room, but with no key in her hand, only two bits of metal that were quickly pocketed.

"Time to go." The detective leaned over the table to set down a shallow box of brown bags and paper cups. "I hijacked it from a delivery boy." She pointed to a customer's name on a deli order. "This one's for Detective Kay. Remember—his lunch comes last." Next, she opened her coat and pulled out a plastic bag with the protruding brim of a pink baseball cap. "Just a few things I borrowed for a wardrobe adjustment. And you'll need these." She handed him her sunglasses.

He nodded as she gave him the rest of his instructions, and when she quit the room, the door was left ajar.

Bugsy pulled a bright pink T-shirt from the plastic bag. It matched the borrowed cap, and this color decided him on a persona of campy effeminate. He donned Mallory's sunglasses as he carried the box of food and drink down a hallway that opened onto a room of desks, where men and women talked on phones and tapped the keyboards of laptops. Affecting a high falsetto voice, he sang out the names of two detectives. As hands went up, he carried deli bags and cups to each of them.

And now for the last one. "Detective Kay?"

"Over here."

Bugsy danced up to the man's desk, the one closest to the stairs, and he set down a brown sack. "Ham on rye." Now the paper cup. "And a coffee light. That's seven-fifty." He held out one hand for payment.

The detective gave him a ten-dollar bill. "Keep the change, kid." The man gave Bugsy a long appraising look. "*Nice* shades. Are those rims real gold?"

Bugsy giggled like a shy girl and sashayed out of the room and down into the stairwell, where Mallory snatched the pink cap and stripped off his T-shirt. She handed him his coat and a set of keys. When they reached the ground floor, he trailed ten feet behind her, invisible in her wake.

Mallory stood at the rear of the crowd in the briefing room. Riker was long gone, back at the SoHo station house by now. And apparently the lieutenant had also left Midtown North, wanting no part of the upcoming perp walk, the cameras and lights and the lies to come.

Captain Halston stood behind the lectern. Following his announcement that a person of interest was being detained, he responded to rapid-fire questions from reporters by raising both hands for silence. "No," he told them, "I'm not going to name this individual just now." But, if they were patient, he assured them, they could catch a glimpse of the man being escorted from the building.

An alarm sounded in a jarring metallic scream as a uniformed officer sprinted toward the lectern. Another uniform closed the door and stood before it, arms folded.

All through the building, officers would now be blocking stairwells and fire escapes.

Mallory looked out over the crowd of media. The cophouse reporters in this mix knew that sound. It was not a fire alarm, but the steady siren of lockdown mode. One newsman turned her way, and his was a face she knew well. Lou Markowitz had made good use of this reporter from time to time—this memorable man named after his left leg.

Woody limped toward her on one prosthetic limb. "Hey, Mallory. What's going on? Who got away?"

"No idea."

Sardonic to the bone, he said, "Okay, next question. Who's the captain's person of interest?"

"As far as I know, there isn't one."

"You mean—not *anymore*," said Woody Merrill.

The reporter's photographer joined them, and he pointed to the commander of Midtown North. "I was three feet from Halston when this cop runs up and tells him the guy's gone—just *walked* out."

"He didn't say *what* guy? No name? No—too easy." Woody turned back to Mallory. "Okay, so now I know the person of interest is on the run. He's the killer, right?"

"Special Crimes has nothing to do with this circus," said Mallory. "The man Halston detained was nobody I'd call a person of interest. It's still my case. I should know."

"So the captain's blowing smoke? Can I—"

"Don't." Mallory smiled at this veteran, once revered by her foster father for his wartime service and sacrifice, and she repeated Lou Markowitz's terms, word for word: "You quote me—and I blow out the kneecap on your *good* leg."

Mallory stood beside a reeking alley Dumpster that hid her parked car from view of the sidewalk. She held a flat carton in one hand and a six-pack in the other.

Bugsy fitted his key in the lock and opened the theater's rear door. After relieving her of the pizza and beer, he stood to one side and said, "Ladies first."

Before she flipped the wall switch, she knew the place was empty. Dead space. "All clear," she said, and Bugsy followed her inside. They passed behind the stage set, where the ghost light glowed through the backdrop of the scenery window, and they climbed the stairs leading up to the dressing rooms.

"I sleep in the one at the end." The gopher led her down the railed loft platform to stand before the last door, where he pulled out his key ring. "This room was locked up for goin' on twenty years. It's cursed. Nobody ever goes in here but me. I got a toilet and a sink." He whispered, "Don't tell nobody," as he unlocked the door and turned on the light. "The others got renovated, but this one's still a dump. So don't expect much, okay?"

When Mallory entered the dressing room, the first thing she saw was a cracked mirror with missing shards. It was ringed with small lightbulbs, only two of them working, and it hung above a skirted table, where lipsticks and makeup brushes were layered in dust like every other surface. A tangle of wires plugged into the only electrical socket.

The gopher set the pizza carton and six-pack down on a bedroll of threadbare blankets, a small pillow and stacks of newspapers for his mattress. A past flood of leaky pipes had peeled the green paint and warped the baseboards around a rusted radiator. A hot plate sat on the floor beside it.

All the conveniences of home for the homeless.

Bugsy pointed to the armchair that held his duffel bag. "Don't sit there. Ya might choke on the dust." He used a rag to polish the seat of a wooden chair for her, and then he sat down on his makeshift bed on the floor, where he drew up his legs, hugged his knees and rocked his body, rocking away the day's anxieties. "I wish I could stay here forever. These are the best digs I ever had."

But she knew he had grown up in a house expensively furnished with antiques that met Charles Butler's high standards. "I hear your mother's place is really nice."

"I got no mother," said Bugsy. "When I was born, it tore her up so bad she died."

Was that a line from a play?

Maybe the drama critic was right, and Alan Rains was gone. No one home but Bugsy anymore. "I'm sorry for your loss," said Mallory, one motherless child to another. "So what've you got for me? Any new messages on the blackboard?"

"Alma says yeah, but I don't think so. She's always seein' things that ain't there. Hearin' things sometimes." The gopher looked up at her, his eyes less fearful now. He turned to the makeup table. "I'll tell ya how that mirror got cracked. See where that one big piece is missin'? They found it buried in the heart of the old guy who used to own this place. Did I tell ya this story? The actress who killed him was nuts—thought she was stabbin' a ghost." He popped the top off a beer bottle and handed it to Mallory. "They say the old man haunts this room, but I ain't never seen him. I showed Alma where to find the story on the Net. I thought it might help. She thinks the ghostwriter's the haunt."

"But not you. *You* don't believe in ghosts." Not much.

Bugsy took her meaning. His smile was sheepish. "Hey, this place is where we *make* the stuff that isn't real." He bowed his head. "Ghosts. I dunno. Late at night, *I* hear things, too. Midnight, a security guard does his rounds, but sometimes there's footsteps that ain't his. More footsteps in the mornin'. That's been goin' on since the play opened. Ya know what's *really* creepy? What I *don't* hear. Listen." He held up one finger to ask for her silence. "Nothin'—no mice crumbles in the walls. Old theater like this one, that's weird. If ya got no mice, that means ya got rats. And that's a fact. But I never seen any. No sound, no sign of 'em. . . . Ya get my drift?"

Yes, she did. What was so scary it scared away rats?

ROLLO: Why? What possessed you to
       go anywhere with those two?
SUSAN: They gave me this note. It
       says you need help.
       (She hands him the piece of
       paper. He stares at it.
       Shakes his head.)
ROLLO: I had no idea they could
       write.

                          —<u>The Brass Bed</u>, Act III

22

Charles Butler flipped through the pages of the play. "Seriously? You've never read it?"

"Just the highlighted parts," said Riker, "the lines that match up with the massacre." The detective faced the cork wall, where more layers of paper had been added, more data than ten cops could read. And so it was catch-up time for Charles, the human wall that could talk to them. "Lots of updates. Only one for Axel Clayborne." Riker tapped a line of Mallory's personal notes.

"Money problems?" The psychologist pointed to an old newspaper article that he had committed to eidetic memory days ago. "According to this, he was one of the highest paid Hollywood stars. Even if he hasn't made a recent film—"

"Well, he doesn't have *my* money problems." Riker's bank account was chronically overdrawn. "Mallory says he's good for a million in liquid assets. Maybe a little more." In New York City, home to billionaires, that would not make the actor a wealthy man, not even a rich one by this town's standards. "The guy lost most of his money in the meltdown. Too many risky ventures—like his condo. If he sold it in this market, he'd still owe a seven-figure bundle on the mortgage." And so, though a stretch it might be, a man with a million dollars in his pocket had turned up on Mallory's radar for her best-loved motive—money.

"But Clayborne must be making a fortune on Broadway."

"That's where the million came from," said Riker. "That's what they paid him up front. I'll tell you what's not on this wall—Dickie Wyatt's autopsy." And damn the chief medical examiner for spilling his results at the poker game. "I'll show you a copy, but you can't tell anybody you saw it—sure as hell *not* Dr. Slope." Mallory's version of the autopsy was an early draft, hacker's goods, and Slope should never find out that she had been illicitly looking over his shoulder.

Riker left Charles to his work on the cork wall. When the detective entered the squad room, he found that his desk chair was occupied. The lieutenant sat there, arms folded, patiently waiting in ambush.

"I'm getting calls from the media," said Jack Coffey. "They tell me Midtown North's got a runner, a person of interest in our case." He raised his eyebrows to ask, *What a surprise, huh?* "They got no name, no description. No idea how the guy skipped out. So . . . just in *case* they call back, you got any thoughts on that?"

"Nope." And did the boss believe that? *Nope.*

"Good enough." Coffey stood up and walked away, probably wondering where Mallory was when the lockdown alarm had sounded. And where had she stashed Bugsy? But answers to those questions could only make him sorry for asking. Over one shoulder, the lieutenant said, "The press calls were forwarded to *your* phone."

What foresight—a punishment detail for a predictable lie.

Every button on the desk telephone was blinking red with calls on hold. Once upon a time in New York City, the NYPD had employed twenty-eight people to deal with the media, and they had done a first-rate job, supplying actual news. But a previous mayor had gutted that department and turned it into a PR machine with sanitized press releases. Now reporters, the best of them, banged on station-house doors and choked the phone lines with the idea that if they badgered the cops long enough, they might get to the truth.

Like that ever worked.

Riker sat down to field questions from broadcast news and print reporters, expressing surprise that there *was* a person of interest in their case. "First I've heard of it," he said to the guy from the *New York Times*, "and I'm *workin'* that case." Four calls down the line, "Naw," he said to the CNN lady, "no idea. You'd have to ask Captain

Halston. It's *his* precinct." And now he learned that the captain was unavailable for comment. And to a network newsman, he said, "Seriously? An escape from Midtown North?" What a shock. He yawned and glanced at the clock on the wall.

Time's up. Ready or not.

Riker rose from his chair, leaving half a bank of blinking lights for reporters left on hold as he walked down the hall to the incident room. There he found Charles Butler standing before pinned-up photographs of the theater chalkboard, riveted by the ghostwriter's messages to Mallory. The psychologist held the tightly rolled play manuscript, and he slammed it into the palm of one hand, over and over—just a hint that he had found it disturbing.

The detective joined him at the wall and asked, "So . . . how's it goin'?" Though he could see for himself. Charles had peeled back three layers of paper to find the blackboard photo with the threat to decapitate Mallory. He had obviously never seen this one before, and the clue was in his frog eyes; they popped and then shut tight.

"I *knew* it! It fits with the—"

"Never mind that," said Riker. "The bastard's only messin' with her."

"What? He wrote her into his play so he could knock off her *head*." He ripped the photo of the blackboard from the wall. "Between this message and the actual performance, I count *two* threats on her life!"

"The play doesn't count. That was a mannikin head. You were *there*. You *saw* it." Riker took the photograph from his hand. "Forget this. Just a bad joke."

Charles held up the manuscript. "You should *read* this play."

"I told you. I *did*. The body count, the crime-scene details—"

"But the play's backstory, the massacre—it's all about killing women. The *love* of killing women. And now the playwright has his sights on Mallory."

"I got twenty bucks that says she gets him first."

Apparently Charles saw no humor in that, and more's the pity, nor did he care to place a bet. To placate the man, Riker pulled out his cell phone to check in with his partner.

The detective laid her cell phone on the makeup table and pulled out her gun.

She must have heard it, too.

Bugsy turned to the open doorway, listening to the sound of someone crying out there. He was quick to get out of the cop's way as she moved through the door. Zap, she was gone.

What now?

Well, the beer was getting warm, and the pizza was getting cold. He was about to chomp down on a slice when her abandoned cell phone rang. He answered it. He *had* to answer it. This was one of his jobs in life. "Hello?"

And a man's deep voice said, "Where *is* she?"

"Detective Mallory? She just stepped out. Can I take a message?" Bugsy rummaged in the drawer of the makeup table and pulled out an ancient lipstick tube.

When he uncapped it, the red stick was dry and crumbly.
He made a test mark on the cracked mirror. Good to go.
"Who's callin'?"

"One word," said the voice with a Midwest twang.
"*Massacre*. She'll know what that's—"

"Oh, the massacre? *I* know that story."

Damn boots.

The high heels made too much noise. Mallory slipped
them off and walked the stage in stocking feet.

Animals could make sounds that were almost human.
Had to be a cat. And cats scared rats. Two mysteries were
solved—the sound of crying and the silent walls that were
curiously vermin free. She holstered her gun and, boots in
hand, climbed the stairs to the warren of dressing rooms.
Near the end of the loft platform, she could hear Bugsy
talking. There was no fear in his voice, but she pulled out
her weapon, tread lightly to the door and cracked it open
by an inch.

The little man was sitting on the floor, holding her cell
phone to his ear and saying, "No the twins don't have no
jughandle ears. . . . Yeah, the ears are the only thing about
those guys that *is* normal."

Mallory shot into the room to snatch the phone from
the gopher's hand, and he jumped, badly frightened. With
the click of a button, she killed the connection and stared
at the word printed on the mirror in thick red lines,
MASSACRE. She clicked through her phone menu for

the list of recent calls, and there was Sheriff Harper's cell phone number.

"Did I do wrong?" Bugsy had gotten over his fright, but now he looked worried.

"No, you did good." She looked down at the crumbling lipstick in his hand. "You told the sheriff about the play?"

"I never said nothin' about a play." Bugsy pointed to the word on the mirror. "That was the message he left. So I tell him I know that story."

"And you *told* him the story," she said. "And then?"

"I was just a little bit into the massacre when he gets real excited. Well, excited for *him*. The guy's about as low key as it gets. But when I mention the twins—real quick, he asks if I seen 'em. And I say, yeah, sure, every day. Then he asks about their ears."

"Jughandle ears." Mallory's phone was ringing in her hand. The sheriff's number was on the small screen, and she let it ring through to voice mail. "Does this theater have a mouser?"

"A cat? No, I never seen one. No litter box, nothin' like that." He turned toward the door. "Oh, the cryin'? Sometimes I hear Alma cryin' in her dressin' room, but that don't sound nothin' like what we just heard." And now he cried like a woman, muffling the sound with one hand, as Alma must have done.

Mallory sat down on the bedroll beside her informant, her all-access pass to the backstage lives of crew and cast. He was the best of observers, providing the tone and tenor of their words—even tears. "Exactly *when* did Alma start crying?"

———

Hot damn! He *knew* the twins had to surface one of these days.

The sheriff's jeep crawled down the Indiana road behind a snowplow. He could make better time running barefoot. At least the snow had stopped. And according to the radio, it was real sunny in New York City.

Miles to go. States to cross. Better roads ahead.

Last night, holed up in a motel, he had used the time to assign a special ring tone just for Detective Mallory, and now his cell phone played the opening bars to "Cry Me a River." He held the phone to his ear and a silky voice said, "How old were your prime suspects when you lost them, Sheriff? Those boys with the jughandle ears."

"*Witnesses*—not suspects. They were twelve when they went into foster care."

"No family left to take them in? They killed them *all*?"

Oh, what the hell. Why not prime the pump a bit. Yeah, keep her talking. "A family member did come to get 'em after a week or so. An aunt or a cousin, I forget which. That gal kept the boys long enough to sell their mother's house and clean out the family bank account. Then I figure she dumped the kids somewhere out of state. I tracked her down to Memphis, and she told me they'd run off."

"But you knew she was lying," said Mallory. "Maybe they weirded her out—or they tried to kill her, too. What about the older boy, the invalid?"

That fella, Bugsy, had also known about the third survivor.

"What happened to him, Sheriff? You didn't say."

And he would not say now. *Click*.

If the boss was pissed off about snatching Bugsy from Midtown North, he had an odd way of showing it. The squeeze was over. Riker and his partner were no longer shorthanded. Every man on the squad had been allocated hours to track down leads, and the early contributions were branching out to a second cork wall.

But their human data receptacle, Charles Butler, was leaving them, buttoning his overcoat as Mallory handed him a key. She caught Riker following this transaction and shot him a look and a shake of the head to say he would not want to know what this was about.

So it had to be about Bugsy, and it would be ungracious to stomp on her gift of deniability. Riker turned back to the wall as the door closed behind the departing psychologist.

"Nobody ever saw a wheelchair." Detective Gonzales spoke with pins in his mouth as he tacked up notes. "I vote for bedridden." By telephone, he and his partner had canvassed a stretch of road in a small Nebraska town, running traces in three states to locate people who had moved away over the past ten years. "The morning of the massacre, somebody left that house in an ambulance. No siren. So that was no emergency run."

Mallory stared at the wall, and Riker watched her struggle with the haphazard pinning style of Gonzales and Lonahan. God help them, their sheets of paper were not fixed to the cork at perfect right angles in ruler-straight rows. But she did not take their pins and papers away from them to do it up right. The little neat freak was tense but hanging tough.

"No siren," she said. "So the ambulance was only for transport."

"Yeah, that's what I figure." Detective Lonahan pinned up his last sheet.

Only *one* pin—not one at each top corner. And the paper hung crooked enough to distract Mallory. Riker willed her not to touch it. He *loved* what these slobs had done, all the hours that had gone into this canvass.

"So it looks like we got an invalid," said Lonahan. "Just like the guy in the play, but he was no heavyweight, nothin' like Axel Clayborne in that fat suit."

"You got a witness description?" Mallory turned away from the messy paperwork. All was forgiven.

"Yeah," said Gonzales. "The lady across the street saw the ambulance guys take him outta the house. But she's got no idea who he was. A shut-in could've been livin' there for years. Who'd know? The neighbors never set foot in that house. But the year before the massacre, they all heard the gunshot when Mrs. Chalmers's husband offed himself. Everybody on that block figured the twins drove him to suicide. The two little girls seemed normal enough, but their brothers were really strange kids."

"That fits the Rinaldi brothers." Though Riker could never see them writing a play. Judging by the first act, the author had a sense of humor, and dark it might be, but the twins had none at all.

"And then," said Gonzales, "after the dad's death, the grandmother came to live with the widow and her four kids. Later on, a sister moved in."

"And there was one more," said Lonahan. "I talked to the lady who saw the ambulance pick up the invalid, an older kid. She didn't recognize him."

"A *kid*," said Mallory. "Did she say how old he was?"

"She didn't get a real good look at him. Took him for a teenager. But here's the best part. The lady remembers a gym bag ridin' with him on the gurney when they wheeled him out of the house. So she figures he wasn't a visitor on his way home. He lived there."

"Because he packed a gym bag," said Mallory. "Not a suitcase."

"A *small* bag for an overnight stay," said Riker. "The invalid's got the all-time perfect alibi. It's so perfect, I'm startin' to think maybe the twins didn't do it."

SUSAN: A brass bed with wheels?
ROLLO: As if a bed could take me
anywhere. I'll never leave
this room. Neither will you.
—The Brass Bed, Act III

23

Jack Coffey clicked his remote control to surf the television channels. The local news on the escape from Midtown North was light, and the publicity-hungry commander of that precinct was not responding to calls from reporters. This was code for a man in hiding.

And then the picture changed. There on camera was an NYPD media liaison hosting a press conference, and the room was packed. The woman smiled as she recited a lame story of faulty wiring that had *accidentally* set off the lockdown alarm. In response to a query on an escapee, she laughed. Oh, what a good joke *that* was. And *so* sorry, no, she had zero information on any person of interest to Captain Halston. Leaving her audience now, the lady turned her back on frustrated reporters and their shouted questions. Unsaid, but taken for granted, were her good-bye words, *Thanks for playing.*

This could only mean that the new commander of Midtown North was downtown at One Police Plaza, explaining how he had botched this day. And so ended the meteoric rise of that thieving twit, Captain Halston.

And where was Bugsy now? He did *not* want to know.

Who the hell was Bugsy? Another cop? A *friendly* New York cop?

The sheriff put aside thoughts of the man who had answered Mallory's cell phone. A state trooper, walking down the lineup of cars, was approaching the jeep. The officer knocked on the glass, and James Harper rolled down his window to hear that all vehicles were being turned back. A six-car pileup on the bridge ahead had made this road impassable.

The turnaround of traffic got off to a sluggish start, and an hour passed before he was heading in the wrong direction, traveling slow on ice-slick road. By the time he drove into the next town, he had lost twelve miles of ground.

Though it was hours before dark, he found a motel room for the oncoming night, and there he spread his old crime-scene photographs across the quilt in a bloody patchwork of red shoe prints and human remains.

The sheriff had decided that Bugsy was definitely not a detective. That man had sounded more like an overgrown kid with a campfire yarn.

Good storyteller, though.

And Bugsy's story had fit in most particulars, though, here and there, the tale had gone awry. But, for damn sure, that man knew details that could only be gotten from a witness—or pieced together from shoes tracked through blood and the barefoot steps of the grandmother, who had been hustled from room to room, forced to visit the hacked and bludgeoned corpses of her nearest and dearest.

No bloody footprints had gone near the room of the older youngster, the bedridden boy. Did Mallory know that? Did Bugsy? And who the hell *was* that guy?

"Oh, no, I couldn't take your last slice," said Charles Butler.

And Bugsy, somewhat relieved, closed the lid of the pizza carton.

The psychologist had finished both his beer and an evaluation of the theater company's gopher. Now he experimentally stretched out one long leg. The other had gone to sleep while sitting cross-legged on the bedroll.

When would Mallory arrive?

His eyes kept drifting back to the cracked mirror, a perfect metaphor, even down to the missing pieces. He had found his host absolutely charming and positively insane, though the gopher would not fit the legal definition of insanity. The Bugsy persona was functional and in possession of a conscience, a clear understanding of right and wrong.

The doorknob turned, and Mallory walked in, allowing Charles another opportunity to watch her interact with the little man beside him on the floor.

Bugsy gave her a tail-wagging smile. "I got some beer left."

"No thanks," said the detective. "Charles and I have to leave. But I brought you some dessert." She opened a napkin to show him a large brownie. "You said you loved them."

How kind—how *oddly* considerate.

She hunkered down beside the gopher, affording Charles a closer inspection of the brownie, and he noticed a pattern of holes in the crust, perhaps a baker's signature design. Very *neat* holes. Perfect symmetry . . . perfectly Mallory. He stared at her. *Oh, you wouldn't!*

Bugsy pointed to the pizza carton. "I'm kind of full right now."

"That's too bad." Mallory feigned deep disappointment.

Charles *knew* she was faking it.

"I made this brownie myself," she said.

In a pig's eye. Oh, *no!*

And before Charles could say, *Don't do it!* Bugsy had crammed the whole thing into his mouth.

Mallory turned the car south toward SoHo, admitting to "just a few ground-up pills to help him sleep," as if she drugged people's brownies every day. "I need him to stay put for a while."

Either her driving had improved, or she did not want to distract him.

Buckled in on the passenger side, Charles quickly finished reading the transcript for a sanity hearing, though that was a bit of a misnomer. It was more like a tutorial on a Supreme Court decision. On to the second document, he flipped through the pages of an old psychiatric evaluation of Alan Rains. This had not been court-ordered but paid for by family. "This is *privileged* information. You can't—"

"We got the report from his mother," said Mallory. "It's fair game."

Could he believe that? She lied with such ease.

Going on groundless faith, chomping the brownie as it were, he read the evaluation nearly as fast as he could turn the pages. It took less time to consider the findings. "I agree with Bugsy's psychiatrist. Profound depression. It's all here—every sign. It's a pity the hospital stay was cut short by Crippen's lawyer. Even grief counseling would've been better than nothing. Based on current behavior—" Oh, there was that word again, the one she so disliked. "I'd say he's role-playing. Though it's an extreme case—and more complex than delusion. Bugsy *works* at it to the point of exhaustion. That's why he shut down when you challenged the false persona. I wouldn't try that again if I were you."

"So he's crazy, right?"

Succinctly put.

"Yes, he's ill. Has been for a long time. Mrs. Rains comes into town once a week to see his subway performance. She says he still recognizes her. I'd expect facial recognition. That fits. But I doubt that he calls her *Mother*."

"No, he wouldn't," said Mallory. "Bugsy's mom died in childbirth."

"His *fictional* mom. He won't tell me about the first

time he rode a bike, kissed a girl, any schools he attended as a child. He'll only relate what Bugsy knows. So every day, all day long, he exhausts himself, constricting his whole life to the confines of a character on the pages of an old play." Because Charles knew that Mallory loved brevity—hated it when he took the long way round—he cast about for summary lines that were not clinical. "Alan Rains was grieving. Profoundly depressed. Unbearable pain. *Years* of it before he made a conscious choice of hells. He picked the one where he had no wife . . . she never died." Charles glanced at the other document, the one that spoke mostly to law, the one that said, with greater authority, Bugsy's fate was fixed in stone.

"*Years?*" Mallory pulled over to the curb at a bus stop, her favored parking space, and she switched off the engine. "No, he was already Bugsy when Crippen's lawyer got him released from the hospital. That was only *months* after his wife died."

"That's not what his mother said." Charles held up the documents. "And there's no mention of Bugsy in either one of—" Oh, wait! Context was *everything*. "You seriously thought that Alan Rains became Bugsy overnight? Is that what Leonard Crippen led you to believe?"

"He flat out lied about it."

"Then maybe we should also look at the critic's pathology. I know the Bugsy persona didn't exist when Alan Rains left the hospital. That's when Crippen brought him back to New York and got him the first gopher job. Menial work was probably all that Alan could handle. Depression is crippling. It would've been hard to hold down any job. So the critic must've used his influence to keep Alan employed . . . and that was the beginning of a very unhealthy dependency."

"But Crippen was his biggest fan."

"Hardly. Mrs. Rains showed me all the reviews of her son's Broadway debut. Crippen's was the standout, the only one that didn't shout the actor's praises. He acknowledged Alan's talent, but the whole column was peppered with sniper shots—some of them rather cruel."

"*Not* a fan," said Mallory. "*Another* lie." Her hands curled around the rim of the steering wheel in a tight squeeze. "So Alan Rains was working as a gopher—just like the character he played on Broadway."

"Years go by," said Charles. "And over all that time, a mentally ill man, a *gifted* actor, reclaimed his old stage role—with the encouragement of Leonard Crippen. Didn't you wonder *why* the critic had Bugsy visit him to pitch those plays?"

"We already caught him in *that* one." She banged the wheel with one closed fist. "He told us it was his only chance to see Bugsy act. But he could've seen a performance any night of the week in the subway."

"Bugsy was *Crippen's* masterpiece," said Charles. "That monster could never get enough of him."

The gopher yawned as he laid out tattered pages long ago ripped from the binding of a play. He never carried more than one scene into the subway, and he would need only one beggar to read the other part for this one. Cold reads were never very good, but, in his experience, drunks and stoned junkies did not improve with rehearsals.

What now? All his work was done.

Bugsy looked down at his wristwatch, which had been frozen at four o'clock for the past three years. It was early yet, and he had no fear of being late for tonight's performance. Well, now he had nothing to do but wait.

He could not stop yawning.

A nap might be a good idea.

He smoothed out his bedroll, fluffed the pillow and slid the girl's photograph underneath it. She had no face. That part of the picture had been kissed away, though Bugsy had no memory of doing this. And no memories of her. She was Alan's girl.

The gopher laid his body down and went to sleep—and dreamed he was a man.

ROLLO: Begging has no effect on
them. My grandmother tried
to trade her life for
chocolate-chip cookies. She
baked them at two in the
morning. I'm sure they were
delicious. She died anyway.
                —*The Brass Bed*, Act III

 They made an odd pair.

CSI Clara Loman wore winter boots to match her clothes. She was head-to-toe gray, so drab alongside Detective Sanger, who loved all things flash—loud-colored shirts, louder ties and the sparkle of his diamond pinky ring. They stood together at the cork wall, pinning up their notes and talking chili. They had not yet found the restaurant for Dickie Wyatt's last meal.

Sanger laid out the crux of the problem for Riker and his partner. "Wyatt *loved* chili. The guy was on a quest for perfection from Harlem to Battery Park. If chili's on the menu, he's been there. I heard that from a waiter in Times Square. But there's only a few places near the theater that remember the guy as a regular."

"And nobody remembers seeing the actress," said Clara Loman.

"Pretty girls like that get noticed," said Riker. "The Alma connection might be a dead end." And they had their boss to thank for that chunk of wasted time. So he picked his next words carefully to keep peace in the house. "Alma's got the drug connection—but why poison Wyatt *after* he quit the play? He's not buggin' her anymore. So what's the point? Where's her—"

"We could have two killers," said Loman. "That would solve the problem of no common motive for both murders. If the perps worked together—"

"*Strangers on a Train?*" That was one really fine old Hitchcock flick, and the plot worked for two murders in a swap of kills. But it would *only* work in the movies. Yet Riker pretended to give this some consideration before he said, "Naw. Too much of a stretch."

And apparently, that had not been diplomatic *enough*.

Clara Loman had pinned up her last sheet, and now she turned on him. Before the CSI could get in his face, Mallory, everyone's last choice for diplomacy, said, "Collusion works for me. But, right now, we need leverage on the stagehands. Alma wasn't their only customer."

"A possession charge won't scare 'em," said Sanger. "Let's see where they go tonight. We might get lucky."

"Good night, Nan Cooper, old girl." The balding red hag wig and cut-rate dress were tossed on the bed, and Nanette Darby, a woman of means, sat down at the vanity table, wearing her own black hair and clothing selected from the bedroom closet. She had chosen a cashmere blazer and designer jeans like Mallory's. The last item of the young cop's wardrobe had been purchased this afternoon, the very same brand of black running shoes—with a shocking price tag.

The former film star faced the oval mirror ringed by small bright bulbs, and she pressed a button at the base to ramp up the luminosity for stage lighting.

The wigmaker stood behind her chair, proudly holding the accessory that would complete her ensemble. Adolpho had truly outdone himself this time. And so that his client could fully appreciate his art, the man explained the difficulties of matching the strands of varying shades found in the natural blonde. "The styling was difficult, too. The detective certainly has her hair done on Fifty-seventh Street. This is a four-hundred-dollar cut." And so ended his pitch for a huge tip in addition to a rush-time payment.

The actress already knew that the detective had taste exceeding her paycheck. And she liked this element of the role—a cop who *might* be dirty.

Adolpho settled the wig on her head. With a change of hair, Nanette had daily moved back and forth through time, from a hag aged by bald spots to a woman in her forties, made thirtyish by surgery. And now, she lost more years as the blond curls softened wrinkles that lotions could not fix. She put on the finishing touch, green contact lenses.

"Wonderful," said Adolpho. "You could be that cop's younger sister."

"Liar." But it was a lie well told, and worth a bit of cash on top of his promised tip of cocaine. Now where were those nasty boys with her dope delivery?

The maid appeared at the bedroom door. "They're here, ma'am. The doorman's sending them up. Should I let them in?"

"Oh, *hell*, no!" The stagehands had never been allowed inside. There were too many expensive objects in the foyer, pricey, pocketable, hockable things. And the teenagers would be surprised if they saw a maid. On their previous visits, Nanette had always responded to the doorbell herself. Well, not quite herself. The boys only knew her in the guise of the redheaded dresser, Nan Cooper.

And tonight those two young morons would provide the acid test of wig and wardrobe. As Nanette Darby strolled through the rooms of her lavish apartment, her face became a mask, and her eyes were green ice when the bell rang. She opened the door to Joe Garnet and Ted Randal. Their frozen, frightened poses were delicious. The boys with the bag of dope in hand took her for a cop they had come to know all too well.

Good job.

A woman her age could not pass for twenty-something much beyond their immediate reactions, but she was well satisfied.

When their cash-for-cocaine transaction was done, she lingered at the door to hear the latest news about Alma Sutter. Poor—dear—*cra-a-a-zy* Alma. "Oh, she's coming unglued? Well, that's tragic." But not fast enough.

Nanette thought she might have to push the bitch down a flight of stairs.

Getting good roles used to be so easy.

The stagehands must be flush with cash. They were hailing a cab.

Clara Loman had followed them on the B train uptown to Columbus Circle, and then she had called in their position on Central Park South. Now Detective Sanger's car pulled to the curb alongside her. He had acquired a passenger since they had parted ways at the subway station. Detective Riker stepped out and held the door open for her, gallantly giving up his shotgun seat to ride in the back.

Up ahead, the teenagers climbed into an eastbound cab, and the unmarked police car rolled after them.

It could not be said that Clara was warming up to homicide detectives as a species, no one would dare say that in her presence, but she was enjoying herself for the first time in years. Sanger had complained that shadow details were ninety percent tedium. The CSI thought otherwise, even after spending hours outside of nightclubs, waiting for the stagehands to spend their drug profits. She had sorely missed her days in the field, gathering her own evidence.

Clara turned around to face the man in the backseat. "It's late. They'll probably spend what's left of the night in the clubs." The teenagers seemed to have no ambition beyond a good time.

"Nope," said Riker. "We picked up a ping on Garnet's cell phone."

"All we got is a pay-phone location." Sanger turned south on Fifth Avenue. "The call was under a minute. That's enough time to—"

"To phone in a drug buy." Clara, in her early days as a street cop, had the hang of drug deals when Sanger was only a know-it-all embryo. "So where to? Alma Sutter's place?"

"Naw," said Riker. "Garnet's pay-phone call came from TriBeCa. Mallory's headed down there now."

"But the kids are pansy dealers," said Sanger, "and they always travel light. So first they have to score some dope. *That's* the next stop."

But they did *not* stop. The stagehands' cab never even slowed down. The detectives and the CSI traveled past every turn for the places where Garnet and Randal shopped for their drugs. And now they were heading west.

"Something's wrong," said Sanger. "These kids got a routine. I *know* they're not holding."

They were deep into TriBeCa when Clara Loman recognized Mallory's personal car, a small silver convertible, pulling up beside a pay phone. The origin of the buyer's call? Yes. The cab slowed down, and Sanger's car sailed on by in the seamless switch of shadowers.

While Sanger rounded the corner and parked at the curb, Riker was on the phone with his partner, saying, "Up the block, that's Axel Clayborne's address, right? . . . No, Mallory, here's the hitch. He's not a customer. . . . No, the kids didn't score any drugs on the way."

And the stagehands outstayed their normal transaction time in Clayborne's apartment building—another break in their routine. Sanger characterized it as "Beer-drinking time," and later as "Shooting-the-shit time." Turning to the other detective in the backseat, he asked, "You see these guys as buddies? A movie star and two dumb-ass kids?"

"No theories," said Riker, and then his phone rang. "That's Mallory."

"Finally." Sanger started the engine. "They're on the move again."

Riker held his cell phone to one ear as the car rolled away from the curb. "Mallory says when they left the building, the kids were divvying up cash—lots of it."

Mallory let herself in through the alley door to the theater. She pocketed her pouch of lock picks and made her way toward the wings by the glow of the ghost light shining through the scenery doorway. Stopping by the blackboard, she read another change printed there, a few words to better phrase a line of dialogue.

She ran one finger across the bottom of the slate's wooden frame. Dust. The chalk on the board was going to powder, falling away. Heller had said that it was old chalk, no modern binding.

Old chalk. Old theater.

Flicking on a wall switch, she descended a flight of stairs to the basement and a score of small rooms. She opened doors to see shelves of wigs and racks of wardrobe in one room, a sewing machine and bolts of fabric in another.

The last door opened onto a workshop with carpentry tools. The area directly under the stage was an open space, where cartons were stacked and their contents labeled. *No chalk.* Scenery flats leaned against the walls in the form of painted trees. She saw rolls of sky blue silk and black canvas dotted with lights for a starry night. But not one stick of chalk.

Mallory could also see that the cleaning crew rarely bothered to come down here. She stood between two rows of stacked boxes, where there were no signs of foot traffic, no shoe tracks but her own in a layer of dust, none to say that the CSIs had searched this area. *Lazy pricks.* So much for all that overtime spent hunting chalk.

But she was not the only recent visitor.

She was looking at paw prints, lots of them. That would explain last night's crying, but there were no signs of a cat living in this theater. How did it come in and go out? Could Clara Loman's crew have missed something else?

Though she was reluctant to let go of any odd thing, the cat's passageway might be only a rat hole, and she was not inclined to search for it tonight. Bone tired, Mallory climbed the steps leading up to the stage and then one more staircase to the row of dressing rooms. She walked down the loft platform to the last door. With a few seconds' work, the lock was undone.

Bugsy was still asleep. She checked his breathing by penlight, watching the rise and fall of his chest, though she had been careful in doping his brownie, just enough sedation to see him through till morning.

No subway performance tonight.

His pillow was bunched, and half a photograph pro-truded from the bedroll. She knelt down to pick it up and stare at the picture of a girl with a worn-away face. The dead wife? The detective slid the picture back under the pillow of the sleeping gopher, a made-up man with no past, apart from that ghost of a girl, faceless now, almost gone.

Mallory envied his gift of playacting. She would like to pretend that there were no gaping holes in her life, no hollows in the shapes of those who had died and left her all alone in—

Why would he keep that old photograph?

She trained the thin beam of her light on his face.

Are you in there, Alan Rains? Still there?

Riker answered his cell phone just inside the door of his apartment.

More trouble.

After listening awhile, he said to the West Side patrol-man, "Yeah, I know the guy. Let me talk to him." And now that the phone had been handed over, Riker heard out the officer's prisoner, and then he said, "Charles, it's okay. . . . Naw. She's a big girl, packs a big gun. . . . So you just *happened* to spot her at the theater?"

The detective could read much into the silence. The theater would be a good place to stash Bugsy. Charles But-ler must have gone there to check on the little man. And then, along came Mallory. The situation worsened as Riker listened to the man's next words.

Oh, crap.

"You followed her *home*." Riker said this in the tone of *Say it ain't so.* "And you thought maybe she wouldn't notice you tailing her?" Charles's car, the most expensive Mercedes-Benz that God ever made, tended to stand out in traffic. "Oh, I guarantee she's pissed off. . . . Yeah, yeah."

And now Charles was sitting in the backseat of a police car. Riker never had to ask why the West Side cop had taken an interest in the tall man standing outside of Mallory's building on a bitter-cold night—keeping watch. If Charles had flashed his goofy smile, that would have completed the officer's profile for a lunatic.

Of course Charles felt protective, but the man had not thought this through. So the detective spelled it out in words that a civilian could understand, words that had never sunk in before, but he was game to make one more try, yelling, "*She's* the one with the damn *gun*!"

No luck this time, either.

The man on the other end of the line had a plan to stand guard all through the night—if Riker would only square this with the nice patrolman, who had handcuffed him.

"No, Charles. *Real* bad idea. Get away from Mallory's building before she shoots you. She can do that from a high window. The kid's a great shot."

And her anger would be righteous. Tomorrow her name would figure in a patrolman's report—and not in any flattering way, more like a very bad joke on her.

"Put the cop on the phone." When he was done talking with the patrolman, done vouching for Charles's sanity and good intentions, Riker lacked the energy to turn on a lamp. He sat down in the dim glow of streetlight shining through a slit in a window curtain. The dead cell phone fell from his hand.

In the kitchen, only steps away, a cold beer was calling his name. Dead tired, he rose from the chair and dropped his coat on the rug before entering the next room, where the sticky linoleum floor was not half as clean—and this passed for wardrobe maintenance. The bulb in the refrigerator made a bright slice in the open door, and he shut it quickly.

He did his best thinking with the lights out.

A bottle cap pinged off the countertop in the dark.

Maybe Charles had been right to worry. Mallory never would. She seemed not to care about the all too personal attentions of the ghostwriter. Would she see a kill strike coming—by a razor, an axe or a bat? It would happen in the dark—the only way to get her.

Charles had said that the play was about the love of killing women. Riker bolted down his beer as he considered the snag in that theory: Both murder victims were males.

Crimes of expediency instead of fun?

Was Charles afraid that the sick-fun part was yet to come?

Tired, so tired, Riker moved from room to room, skirting obstacles of trash by memory. Passing by the pitch-black bathroom doorway, he recalled Axel Clayborne's complaint: The bulb of his plastic Jesus night-light had burned out.

If only a hot shower could wash away idiocy.

A bit damp, but wiser now, Charles Butler turned off the bedside lamp and burrowed into pillow and quilt, weary but too distracted for sleep.

Riker had been correct to upbraid him. Of course Mallory would have seen the Mercedes headlights following her home tonight. He could quite easily buy into the myth that she could even see in the dark. So beautifully equipped to survive was she—and with no help from him.

Fool! He would *never* get that part right.

But perhaps he could also blame his recent foolishness on nights without much rest. So disturbing was the image of Mallory's lost head rolling across a stage, he had been forced to consider a world without her. Could he live in such a place?

He *had* found some measure of peace by simply standing outside of her apartment building, standing guard against every comer—except for the patrolman, the one who had pulled up alongside him, finding his behavior more than old-world odd, not quite so gallant—stalking a woman.

Fool. Clown.

Could he picture Mallory laughing at that scene? No, not on this planet.

Sanity and clarity restored, he knew there would be payback. But was it so wrong, this need to keep her safe from monsters?

In her opinion? Oh, yes. Very wrong. And how would she react tomorrow? How angry might she be?

For an hour more in the black of night, these thoughts crept around his mind, gnawing at him like vermin, raising his anxiety, and then—

An ice-cold jab at the back of his neck.

Eyes shocked wide and stuck that way, he was paralyzed, apart from the racing pulse, the galloping heart. And now—the endgame line for the Heart Attack Express.

"You're *dead*!" said Mallory.

Fine! Fair enough.

SUSAN: If you die, the disability
checks will stop.
ROLLO: Oh, dead or alive, I have
my uses. A corpse can
attract more flies for
their collection.
                    —<u>The Brass Bed</u>, Act III

25

Here on Fifth Avenue, God's house spanned a city block, but it always took the tourists by surprise. The majestic spires gave them no advance warning. That grandeur was hidden and dwarfed in a neighborhood of skyscrapers, and the entry was only a short flight of steps from street level. Riker saw it as the in-your-face kind of Gothic cathedral.

The great doors were flanked by two other entrances, all of them built to the scale of giants, and so the steady stream of mourners was not impeded by five detectives gathered on the sidewalk out front.

"The Rinaldi twins got no life." Janos pulled out a bagel and passed the deli sack to his partner. "Every night, they eat dinner in a crummy hole on Lexington. I talked to their regular waitress. She said they grew into scary little weirdos gradually. Before they started rehearsals, they just made her squirm a little."

Detective Washington flipped the pages of his note-book. "They didn't lie about their residuals. They're not rich, but when they're outta work, there's enough income to pay the rent and then some." He flipped another page. "Either they got no medical coverage or they're insured under another name."

"It doesn't matter," said Mallory. "Plastic surgery won't show up on insurance records."

Why the interest in plastic surgery? Riker was not the only one to wonder. There were quizzical looks from the other men.

Mallory faced Janos, their expert on the Rinaldi broth-ers. "Did the agent give you their headshots?"

"Yeah, and the twins had surgery for sure." Janos held up his phone. Onscreen was an image of the twins as children. "No pug noses in this one." He clicked to the next portrait. "Now this is a later shot, but see? They look a lot younger. The agent wouldn't say, but I figure their noses got clipped to keep 'em from aging out of kiddie roles."

Mallory took the camera from his hand. As she clicked through all of the actors' photographs, Riker squinted to watch the Rinaldi brothers age from boys to men.

"No jughandle ears," she said. "Ask the agent if they ever had—"

"Just curious." And mildly pissed off. Riker leaned toward her. *Jughandle ears?*

Before he could ask what she was holding out on him,

Mallory volunteered that "The boys from the Nebraska massacre had—"

"No way," said Janos. "You like these guys for the ghostwriter? Dead wrong. They're not imbeciles, but they're not all that smart. They got one trick. They're flesh-crawlin' scary. That's *it*."

"Nobody took a hard look at Gil Preston," said Gonzales. "He got high grades at Columbia. Maybe lightin' up stages isn't his dream job. I bet *he* could—"

"No," said Mallory, "he's harmless."

And four men deferred to a woman's radar for any poor bastard so labeled as lame.

Janos handed Riker a copied magazine article dating back to the sitcom days of the Rinaldi twins. "It's a press agent's bio. Two kids growing up in an ideal American family and a picture-postcard town. Check out the shot of Mom and Dad."

Riker did not need his eyeglasses to make out Janos's margin note: *No such people, no such place.*

Charles Butler unlocked the theater's alley door with a newly minted key. Mallory had stolen the one used for a template, though Bugsy would have given her a hundred copies if she had only asked.

Before the end of this morning's session, the purloined original must be restored to the gopher's key ring—*surreptitiously*—per the thief's instruction. And *then* Charles would be forgiven for last night's unfortunate stalking incident.

A small price.

All he had to do was deceive the little man whose trust he had earned, and Charles said to himself, as Mallory would say, "Yeah, *right*."

He carried his bag of pastries and coffee up the stairs and down the railed walkway to knock on the door of the last dressing room.

"Come in." There was no wariness in Bugsy's voice, no curiosity about who might be out here.

Perhaps the effects of the drug had not yet worn off. Charles opened the door to see the gopher crawling about on the floor, sorting through the tattered pages of his old play, the one he had starred in on Broadway. "Good morning, Bugsy."

"I missed my performance last night. I only figured on takin' a nap, but I slept like the dead."

"There'll be other nights," said Charles. But there should be no more brownies from Mallory. And now for her chore of subterfuge, his penance, he pulled the stolen key from his pocket and handed it to Bugsy. "I believe this is yours."

"Yeah, thanks." And the key was pocketed with no suspicion, no questions asked. Though it could hardly have fallen off the gopher's formidable key ring, theft would not occur to him. Since it was returned in a straightforward manner, he would assume that the key had been borrowed, not stolen.

So simple. Charles knew it would be.

Bugsy lacked guile, and his heart was generous. In previous conversation, he had voiced empathy with Alma

Sutter, and he clearly felt protective of her. That fit so well with his gift of a kidney to another young woman. A more facile psychologist would have labeled him with a rescue complex and called it a defect. But Charles saw the gopher as a noble, albeit improbable, knight, sans shield and sword and armor. Vulnerable. Fragile to the core.

When they were seated side by side on the bedroll, sipping coffee and eating bakery goods, Charles learned that the gopher had a perfectly normal response to the Rinaldi brothers. They made him uncomfortable.

"And they drive Alma nuts. That's their idea of fun."

"Only her? They single her out for abuse?" Charles turned toward the door. "Did you hear that? Sounds like someone crying."

"Yeah," said Bugsy. "That's Alma. I never get used to it."

"But there's no rehearsal today." Charles glanced at his watch. Right about now, the actors and the crew would be assembling for the funeral service. As yet, he had no idea why Bugsy had been excluded. "Why would she—"

"Sometimes Alma drops in just to check out the blackboard."

"And now it's upset her." Charles got up from the bedroll and walked to the open door. This would certainly bear investigation.

"Don't bother. There's nothin' on the board to make Alma cry. There never is. She's just seein' things again." With one finger, the gopher made a spinning motion at his temple. "Not quite right in the head. . . . Poor kid."

Poor Alma. Poor Bugsy.

Charles stepped over the threshold to stand by the

railing. He looked down to see a doll-size Alma Sutter backing out of the wings and covering her mouth to stifle the crying. She turned around, dabbed at her eyes with a tissue and then shredded it, leaving a trail of wet confetti as she tottered across the backstage area. This actress was the true ingénue, not yet a woman, but practicing—a girl on the verge of toppling from the great height of her mother's high heels.

He knew that everyone she met today would share the same thought: *Don't fall.*

Alma was late, though most people had not been seated yet.

The funeral service for Peter Beck had filled the cathedral with mourners, and the procession up the center aisle was moving slowly. It was an easy guess that most of them had come for a glimpse of the rich and famous, and everyone with a press agent had come to be seen.

The actress scanned the crowd, counting the house by habit, as she took another step, making little progress toward the pew reserved for the theater company. She recognized the back of every head in that front row. Even a few of the understudies had come.

Oh, *no.* One ankle twisted outward, and she almost tripped in her stilettos. *Damn it all!* She had stupidly reversed her wardrobe mantra: High heels for cocaine—*flats* for Vicodin.

Was she weaving?

Alma glanced at the theater's cashier, the slim brunette who walked alongside her, and she thought of asking

Donna Loo for a supporting arm. Before she could speak, the other woman was roughly pushed out of the way.

And now the Rinaldi brothers appeared on each side of Alma, walking in lockstep, pressing up against her, shoulder and thigh. It was like cuddling with worms. Nowhere to go but forward, and her ankles wobbled. One of the twins stroked her arm in a mockery of offering comfort, and they both stared at her with that look of dead flies for eyeballs, and, oh, those stereo halfwit smiles.

They giggled.

Her stomach was queasy, her palms were wet.

The organ music was loud, and her voice could not rise above it when she screamed, "Get *away* from me! Leave me *alone*!" She turned and tried to push her way through the people who blocked her escape, begging, "Let me get *out*!" No use, the aisle was packed with bodies. And then—*inspiration*—she yelled, "I'm gonna throw up!"

A path was opened for her, and the grinning twins trotted along close behind her—giggling.

While detectives snapped photographs of mourners mounting the stairs to the cathedral, Riker noticed that it was a very cheerful crowd.

A limousine pulled over to the curb, not the first one to stop here this morning, but it was the longest car. The chauffeur had a bit of a hike to let his passenger out by the rear door. The first cry went up, and a flock of funeral-goers turned like birds in formation. They flew down the steps to converge on the movie star, whipping out auto-graph books on the run. Axel Clayborne signed for his fans and smiled for photographers.

Riker was still preoccupied with the stretch limousine. How did that thing turn corners?

"Captain Halston hasn't backed off." Mallory pointed to a lone figure standing on the sidewalk at the corner. The man was bareheaded, hands in his pockets and stomping his feet to keep warm. "That guy's from Mid-town North."

"Ron Bowman," said Riker.

"Didn't he used to be one of *your* men?"

"Yeah. In another life." That was back when he had rank and a squad under his command—good times—when he had rolled into work still drunk from the night before, stayed that way all day long, and *still* racked up commendations. A screwup Judas cop had done some damage to hasten the end of Riker's captaincy. And then, in the tradition of weasels, Halston had made his way up through the ranks, and now, with command of Midtown North, he also had Ron Bowman, Riker's favorite blue-eyed boy. The final insult.

How did Bowman like his new commander?

Riker walked to the edge of the stairs, and waited until the other detective's searching eyes had found him. He made a curt wave to Bowman, signaling, *Come here.* And then he jabbed the air twice to say, *Now! Right now!*

The cop from the Midtown precinct did come, but in his own time, time enough to remember his roots and find a smile for the first man who gave him a chance to shine. Bowman was fourteen years older now. How fast these rookie dicks grew up.

When they stood facing each other, Detective Bowman recited his standard snatch of poetry. "O' Captain, my captain."

"You're still an affected little snot," said Riker.

And then they fell into the natural patter of "How's it goin'?" and "What's new?" gradually winding down to "Yeah, Halston's still a real shit." However, that man was Bowman's shit, Bowman's captain now. "So, if I find Alan Rains first, I'm gonna bring him in."

Right or wrong, orders were followed in Copland.

"Well, the guy's in the wind," said Riker. "No chance he'd turn up here. Makes me wonder how hard you guys are workin' this case."

"The whole squad's hunting down Alan Rains, or Bugsy, whatever the hell you call him. Halston thinks that little guy's all he needs to blow Special Crimes out of the water—hopefully before he gets demoted and shipped out to the South Bronx."

Riker smiled. He could dream. "Got any leads?"

"I found a website posted by one of Bugsy's fans. Last night, we made a sweep of the subway under Times Square . . . and we'll make another one tonight."

A nod from Riker thanked him for the heads-up.

Both men turned to see Alma Sutter running out of the cathedral—full throttle in four-inch heels, an accident in the making. She lurched in a stumble of one shoe off and one shoe on.

Any second—

Holy *shit*! Who knew Janos could move so fast? He broke her fall when she tumbled.

The Rinaldi twins stood on the top step, their backs to the cathedral doors.

Smiling.

Freaks.

SUSAN: What happens after—
ROLLO: First the funeral, then the
       worms.

                    —The Brass Bed, Act III

26

When Alma Sutter had *not* broken her neck, the Rinaldi brothers lost interest in services for the playwright, and Mallory watched them descend the steps to pass by Sanger on the sidewalk below.

The detective was wearing his dark suit for funeral surveillance, but flash persisted in the bright splash of his purple shirt and tie. Grinning, he climbed the steps to join her in front of the cathedral doors. "I found Wyatt's sublet!"

And *when* had this man decided to blow off her search for Wyatt's last bowl of chili? How much time had been lost?

"I tossed the place," said Sanger. "He left his cell phone behind, but no laptop or personal papers. The guy who lives in his old apartment tells me Wyatt had a ton of books, and there's none in the new place. So I figure he rented a storage locker. I'll keep—"

"Or you could stick with the chili angle," said Mallory, dialing back anger, tempering it to the helpful suggestion, "that might be a better lead." There was no protest, no pissing contest. He simply nodded an acknowledgment that she *might* be right.

Her partner had climbed the stairs to stand behind Sanger, and now Riker wore his damned nanny smile—so proud of her for playing nicely with the other kids. She glared at him. His smile persisted. *Bastard*.

Riker slapped the younger man on the back. "Nice job. So now we know where Wyatt's been for the—"

"No, he spent those two weeks in a private hospital uptown." And now Sanger had redeemed himself. "Very pricey rehab, but the guys in Narcotics got moles everywhere. Get this. Wyatt admitted to a relapse, but he couldn't remember taking any drugs. He stuck with that story all through group therapy. So the mole figured it must be true."

"And blackouts won't square with his ninety-day tox screen," said Mallory.

"Nope. When Wyatt went into rehab, he tested for trace amounts of drugs. Not my idea of a relapse for a heroin addict. This only works for me if somebody was dosing the guy."

Mallory could think of six ways to do that with food items other than brownies.

In the line of duty, homicide detectives attended many services for the dead, and this one had all the hallmarks of a preplanned funeral guided only by undertakers. The priest's homily had been spare, here and there, dropping in phrases culled from the *Times* obituary, and not one personal touch volunteered by anyone who might have known Peter Beck.

The last hymn was sung, and the organ music died down. The priest called for a loved one to say brief words of remembrance. Stone-quiet seconds dragged by. No one came forward. Uneasy, he riffled the papers on his pulpit, perhaps late to realize that no such speech had been planned. A mistake? Yes, a notable one. And what was he to do now? He could not abide the empty silence. The service could not end this way. The priest searched the faces in the first pew, looking there for rescue among those seated in the place reserved for the most bereaved. But those people were staring at the ceiling or checking watches and otherwise ducking his eyes. There were no takers for the pulpit, and the ongoing silence was the real eulogy for the playwright.

The only sympathy for Peter Beck lay with a detective, Riker, who rarely got personal with the dead. He took umbrage at that miserable slight to a man whose work and life had been ripped away. And now this final cut. So public.

At the center of the gathering, a woman rose from her seat to stand alone in a plain woolen coat among the cashmeres, camel hairs and furs. No designer purse. No pearls. The priest smiled and beckoned to her. The crowd was dead quiet, and her small voice carried as she made her way out of the pew, passing seated people with her murmured sorries for treading on toes.

When she had climbed the steps to the pulpit and turned to face the crowd, Riker recognized her. This was the woman who had given him one of the playwright's lost gloves, and now she introduced herself as Sally Ryan.

"I was his bartender," she said. "I didn't know him long, maybe three or four weeks. He was a real nice guy. Never said a mean word to me, and he tipped big. . . . Peter was a sad man. . . . He didn't used to drink. Never touched the stuff, he said. But he learned how. At the end, he could hold his liquor, but he'd lost his play, lost his girl, and everyone he knew was against him. He was *crazy* sad. I seen him cry that last night. Like every night, Peter came in alone, drank alone. And I read in the papers . . . he died in the company of strangers." She looked out over the assembled mourners and then narrowed her focus to those in the first pew. "Who knew he had so many friends?"

Riker whispered, "Bring it home, Sally."

And she yelled, "You fucking *bastards*!"

Charles Butler was startled to see Janos filling out the open doorway of the dressing room. Was Bugsy's location now the open secret of Special Crimes?

"Change of plans. Mallory's not coming." The detective, with one pinky ring delicately extended, held up a white sack that bore the name of a midtown restaurant. "Brunch." His feet were rather small for a policeman the size of a great ape, and he stepped lightly around the bedroll to clear a space on the dusty makeup table, where he laid out an assortment of sweetmeats in small pastry shells. Then he set down two paper cups, precariously close to the edge. "Cream for you, Charles. And, Bugsy, you take it black, right?"

"Right," said Bugsy. "How was the funeral?"

"Best I ever went to." The detective backed out of the room, motioning for the psychologist to follow him. When they stood on the walkway before the closed door, Janos explained that no fugitive warrant had been issued for Bugsy. "So you don't need to worry anymore. No jail time for aiding a—" And now, because Charles's thoughts were advertised on his surprised face, Janos said, "Mallory never ran that past you, did she?"

And though this was obviously a rhetorical question, Charles said, "It must've slipped her mind."

"That funeral was crawling with dicks from Midtown North. They're out to arrest Bugsy again."

Again? Oh, so much had slipped Mallory's mind. "You think they'll come here?"

"No, they figure he's gone underground. So Mallory wants you to keep an eye on Bugsy for a few hours." Janos scribbled a TriBeCa address on the back of a card. "Then meet us here tonight."

When Charles returned to the dressing room, he found his paper cup on the floor, lying in a river of spilled coffee, and the gopher was on his knees, mopping it up with paper napkins.

"Jeez, I'm sorry." Bugsy handed him the remaining coffee cup. "Really sorry. Here, you take mine."

"Oh, I couldn't."

"Sure you can. I got instant." He pointed to a hot plate in the corner. Then he reached into his duffel bag to pull out a tin of coffee. "I insist. . . . Is that okay by you . . . if I insist?"

The watering hole on Lexington Avenue had zero ambience. Afternoon light streamed through an unwashed window. Drinks were cheap and the sparse clientele was scruffy. Riker had selected this place to make their witness feel more at ease. Saloons were his venue, *his* church, but he had bowed out of the interview with Peter Beck's favorite bartender. He would not say why.

Mallory suspected him of making a point—pointing out a flaw of hers. Did he blame her for the poor result their first time out with this woman?

Sally Ryan had confessed more in the cathedral than she had given up on the night of the playwright's death, and Mallory *might* allow some fault of her own. She had no patience with the sacred code of confidentiality between bartenders and drunks. This time, it was an effort to go slowly, Riker style, as she sat on a barstool beside Sally Ryan, matching the woman's shots of bourbon with tea-colored water.

"So he broke up with his girl," said Mallory. "You're sure about that?"

"Peter was in tears. He told me Alma was the last one on his side, but not anymore."

"*When* did he tell you that?"

"The night he died. I didn't see him the night before.

I asked if he went to the play's opening. Peter said no, he slept through it."

"So you figure he started drinking early that day and passed out, right?"

"Yeah, but that's not like him. Peter was the loyal type . . . did all his drinking in *my* bar. . . . Well, that's what I used to think."

All those empty bottles in Beck's apartment said otherwise. Customer loyalty had broken down—and the man as well. On Beck's last walk to the theater, he had stopped at least twice to drink himself senseless. "You were the first one to serve him that night. What kind of shape was he in?"

"He had a load on when he walked in the door," said Sally Ryan. "First time that ever happened. I made a joke about it. Asked him if he was cheating on me, getting smashed with somebody else. Then he looked around, like he lost somebody on the way in the door. Then he cried."

He had lost his girl.

The police had come calling, knocking on the door, *banging* with closed fists. She recognized the voices when Riker and Mallory took turns shouting her name.

Alma Sutter sat on the floor of her bathroom, squeezed between the tub and the toilet, where the water in the bowl swirled round and round. And down went her pills and powders, every last grain of coke and X, Valium and Oxy. All her highs and lows.

Goodbye.

But she could never lose all of it, could she?

No, there would always be *something* left for the cops to find. Reefer between the couch cushions? Vicodin in a cupboard? A drawer she had missed?

The police would arrest her. Another actress would take over the role—and never, *never* understand fear the way Alma could play it.

Christ! When would they stop the damn banging?

Shaky and sick, she leaned over the bowl to chase the drugs with vomit. And now her hair was stringy with slime as she reached up to pull the silver lever on the toilet tank. And she froze. Dead still.

Oh, no, please no.

The banging and yelling had stopped—no noise to mask the flush. Aw, the *stink*! So cold, she shivered, queasy, wanting to retch again, one hand jammed into her mouth.

Were they gone?

An hour crawled by.

Were they gone yet?

Axel Clayborne's lament was a rare one in New York City—too *many* closets, tall ones built into the walls. And the thousands of square feet also accommodated free-standing armoires that could hide a multitude of ponies.

The view from his wide windows sparkled with the first city lights.

Night was coming on.

Time was running out.

Where the *hell* had he put them?

He opened one last closet, though he suspected that he had already searched this one twice. Ah, *success*. One by one, he pulled out the boards that had been hiding in the back behind his luggage. He carried them to the center of the room, where he inserted them into an opening between the halves of a dinner table, elongating it by these added leaves until it was the length of a laid-out body.

The doorman buzzed him on the intercom to announce a visitor.

And that must be the centerpiece for his table—right on time.

Six unmarked cars were double-parked in front of Axel Clayborne's high-rise, and the penthouse was brightly lit. "There," said Mallory, pointing to a delivery van from a liquor store. "They're restocking the booze."

"I'd say that crowd's loose enough." Riker stepped out on the sidewalk, a signal to the rest of the squad, and now they were all on the move, crossing the street to stun the doorman, who had never seen so many badges at one time, and the wave of cops carried him backward through the glass doors and into a lobby of shining steel pillars and deep-pile carpet. They crossed a half acre of wasted space to stand before the private elevator for the penthouse. There was no button to summon it, only a slot for a keycard.

And Riker yelled, "Open the damn doors!"

A man behind the lobby desk depressed a button to

open the elevator, and he was reaching for a phone, when Mallory said, "Don't! It's a surprise."

To ensure that surprise, Detective Lonahan remained at the desk while the rest of the squad rode up to the penthouse floor, where the doors opened onto a wide vestibule of sofas, chairs and clothing racks holding everything from ratty old parkas to high-end furs. A young man asked if he could check their coats.

He could not.

One more door to go. Mallory turned the knob and led the way into a space the size of a gymnasium with a wall-to-wall view of the skyline, a crowd of dancing people—and one corpse. The casket was laid out on a long table and surrounded by bottles of whiskey and wine.

The room was revved up with music from a live band, and the floorboards thrummed as hundreds of shoes stomped to the beat. Riker spotted the wardrobe lady, alias the Hollywood comedy star. Nan Cooper's mascara was runny with tears while she grinned and danced to rock 'n' roll. And more detectives poured in to mingle with the bereaved laughing crowd. Wakes were always prized above backroom interrogations—lots of drunks in the storytelling mode.

Axel Clayborne yelled, "Hey, everybody! It's a raid!" And to his uninvited guests, he said, "How cool is that? But everything's in order—quite legal. No one stole Dickie's body this time." He handed his paperwork to Mallory, who let it drop to the floor. Turning his smile on her partner, he said, "So . . . you came to make an arrest?"

"Naw," said Riker. "We came to *dance*."

And the first dancing interview began when he grabbed the wardrobe lady's hand. Nan Cooper wore her own hair tonight. She was all decked out in her best dress and her best face—apart from the teary tracks of mascara. The lady laughed, surprised that a cop could dance to a rocking beat. He twirled her up and down the floor, then raised his gold badge to the bandstand and shouted the title of theme music for an old William Holden movie, "'Moonglow'!" And they glided into a soft tempo for slow moves.

"Very romantic," she said. "*Very* smooth." And before they parted, Nan reminisced about Wyatt's blacklist years in Hollywood. "No, Dickie wasn't the one who rewrote that old script, but he tried to take the fall so Axel could get away with it. And they *both* got run out of town."

The corpse might be the best-dressed man in the room.

Mallory reached into the casket and drew back one lapel of the dead man's suit. Next she checked the sleeves and the cuffs of his pants.

"Enough of that!" Axel Clayborne appeared at her side, grabbed her by the hand and led her into the midst of the slow-dancing mourners. He held her close and they stepped to the strains of "Moonglow."

She pulled back to ask, "When do the reporters show up?"

"You overestimate me," he said, drawing her close again. "I didn't want a media circus for this."

"You're going to waste a perfectly good corpse? . . . That's not like you."

The song ended, but he did not let go of her. Arms

around her, he said, "Every one of Dickie Wyatt's relatives went out with wakes like this one. They're all gone. He was the last of his line." The sweep of one hand encompassed the whole crowd. "All theater folk. We're his only family now, and we take care of our own."

The band played another slow tune, one she could name from the shortlist of Riker's favorite black-and-white movies, "As Time Goes By." And they danced.

"I hear Beck had a *family* fight with Wyatt," she said.

"No bloodshed. Only a shouting match. Peter thought Dickie betrayed him, and of course that was true." He whispered in her ear, "*Everybody* went along with the ghostwriter."

All around them detectives swirled with dancing partners. One would cut in on a woman, and another would threaten to dance with the man left solo. Janos, the least reticent about this, zeroed in on his favorite couple, the Rinaldi brothers, who sat on a couch by a wall. He ripped one twin away and danced the startled actor all over the floor. Done with that one, he chased down the other, and he had to climb over the couch to get at him.

Clayborne held Mallory close as the tempo ramped up a notch. Closer. Tighter. Almost like sex. And she said, "You told us you didn't know Wyatt's current address."

And now there was a telling fault in his rhythm—like a polygraph blip. "I remember saying that."

She turned her head to look at the coffin. "Your friend is wearing a very nice suit. And no pins. It was tailored to fit him. Very fine work. But funeral homes never get quite that fancy."

Back in step, he pressed his cheek to hers, saying, "I paid top dollar."

"For a *used* suit? I don't think so. You got it from Wyatt's closet. You lied to us. You *knew* where—"

Axel Clayborne laughed. "Do you realize that you're leading?"

Detective Gonzales danced with Dickie Wyatt's agent, a stout woman twenty years his senior, and she flirted like a drunken cheerleader as they made slow turns around the floor.

"Oh, yeah," she said, "they had a history. Back when they were kids, my guy helped Peter Beck get his first play produced. It was a little theater down in the Village."

"So Wyatt worked with him before the—"

"No, Dickie *should've* gotten a job out of that. Fair's fair, right? But Peter said he didn't *need* a director. Can you beat that?"

Dancing on in slow revolves, cheek to cheek, with one of her hands on his ass, Gonzales learned that the playwright had no use for set designers or lighting directors, either. And Peter Beck had truly *despised* acting schools and coaches. In a nonunion venue, he had gotten away with refusing to audition any formally trained actors for his first play.

"Sounds like amateur night," said Gonzales.

"You got *that* right, sweetie." The agent rewarded him with a big smile and a squeeze to his buttocks—*both* hands now. "Peter thought his precious words would carry the whole play. Well, the play *bombed*. His second time out, he got a shot at Broadway—but he had to give up creative control. He won his first Pulitzer for that one. All Peter had to do was get out of his own way."

"So the guy had talent," said Gonzales.

"Oh, *hell*, yes. That big ego of his? Peter could back it up. He was *brilliant*."

"So why did Leonard Crippen give the guy so many rotten reviews?"

The lady stopped dancing, and she was not smiling anymore. "Crippen's a sadistic troll. He's only kind to mediocre playwrights—*vicious* with the great ones. As critics go, he's a pervert. . . . Crippen *hates* talent."

Riker held a cell phone to his ear. "Just checkin' on Bugsy."

Mallory nodded and drifted back to Axel Clayborne, who was keeping company with the dead man on the table. She looked over the crowd. "Where's Alma?"

"Probably too stoned to find the place." The actor mixed whiskey with water and placed the glass in her hand. "The girl's got a habit."

"I can see why you'd want to get rid of her. But what did *Bugsy* ever do to you?" And now for her first lie of the night, she said, "The day before Peter Beck died, Bugsy went to his apartment to check on him, and I *know* you put that idea in his head. Were you laying groundwork for a patsy?"

He stared at her, baffled—or acting that way.

"You set him up," she said. "The perfect scapegoat. Another squad is hunting him down tonight. If they catch him, he goes to a psych ward. You know what that's like? Crazy people banging their heads on the walls, shitting on the floor, pissing on *everything*. Droolers and screamers. I don't think Bugsy can stand up to that, do you? Is that the plan? He disappears into that hole, and everybody figures he's guilty. But the insane don't stand trial. So after a while, the media gets bored and goes away. My case is dead . . . and you get away with murder."

"I'd never hurt Bugsy. You have to believe me. I like that little man. I've got no reason to cause him any—"

"You hurt Peter Beck. *He* never did you any harm."

"I never—"

"You *did*. . . . You *all* did." She turned to the casket. "And then there's Dickie Wyatt. Did you help your junkie friend along? Maybe you dosed his food? Just enough to get his habit rolling again?" Ah, finally, the words she needed to cut him and bleed him—if only she could believe the pain in his eyes.

"I loved Dickie."

"Yeah, *right*." She looked down at the corpse. "Dragging his body into the theater to milk cheap publicity for—"

"Mallory, don't get the wrong idea. I'm a devout heterosexual—but I *loved* him. Of all the people in this world, I loved Dickie Wyatt best." He leaned into the casket and kissed the dead man's mouth.

Detective Janos danced with a skinny brunette, the theater's cashier. Donna Loo's speech still had a trace of her

Brooklyn roots, a vestige of dropped consonants that her acting coach had failed to beat out of her. "But I'm workin' on it," she said.

"I hear you're the one who told Crippen about the ghostwriter."

"Just followin' orders. He would've panned any play by Peter Beck."

"Whose orders?" And her next words were so predictable that he said them in unison with her. "The ghostwriter."

They danced by Riker, and Janos called out to him, "Hey, where's Charles Butler? He should've been here by now."

Riker shouted back, "Why would *he* be coming?"

"Mallory invited him."

"Then who's babysitting our little friend?"

"Nobody told *me*." Janos and Donna Loo danced away.

Riker stood by a window, looking down at toy cars in TriBeCa traffic. Holding the cell phone to his ear, he waited out five rings, long enough for Bugsy to beat it down the stairs to the telephone on the stage manager's desk. The little guy was quick. But not this time—or last time. The theater's answering machine kicked in once again. The recorded message advised all callers to ask the police when they could see the end of the play that was stalled in the first act, and the number for Special Crimes had been thoughtfully provided.

Something to look forward to—an angry theater-going public choking the squad's phone lines tomorrow.

He placed the call again to give Bugsy more ring time to run for the phone.

The detective turned toward the front door, though dancing couples blocked his line of sight. No problem. Charles Butler would stand a head taller than most people in this crowd. That man could not go unnoticed anywhere, and he was not here. Why had Mallory invited him? Who was watching Bugsy? And should he be worried? There was no way to know until his favorite Luddite showed up.

Riker was only a believer on religious holidays or any day when a gun was pointing his way, but tonight he abandoned custom, raised his eyes skyward and said, "Please, God, give Charles Butler a cell phone for Christmas."

Mallory appeared beside him and put a fresh drink in his hand. "So . . . no answer yet." Her tone was flat, missing the lilt of a question mark. No curiosity.

If he were only as paranoid as his partner, he might think she had not expected anyone to pick up a ringing telephone at the theater.

"Don't worry about it," she said. "I sent Lonahan to check on Bugsy."

"Something's wrong. Bugsy always picks up backstage calls." And when she showed no concern at all, Riker said, "Oh, not again. Tell me you didn't drug the little guy."

Before she could come up with a suitable lie, his cell phone rang, and he checked the small screen. "It's Lonahan." Holding the phone to his ear, he said, "Yeah?" After a moment, he turned to Mallory. "So . . . how heavy *was* that dose? Lonahan says Charles's out cold. . . . Bugsy's gone."

And Mallory sang out for all to hear, *"Runner!"*

ROLLO: You know what they've
done . . . what they are.
Of course it's going to
hurt.

—<u>The Brass Bed</u>, Act III

27 The squad of detectives swarmed into the street. Their cars were abandoned for a run to the subway station a block away. A train would drop them off at the last scheduled site for Bugsy's underground performance.

Gonzales was startled to see Axel Clayborne running with the pack. The man sprinted ahead, trying to put the make on Mallory. *Pure suicide.* The detective heard the actor yell at her, "You've got me all wrong!" This was the line Gonzales had used on Wyatt's grab-ass agent, but the woman had slapped him anyway—*again*—yelling, "Dickie was a stand-up guy! He'd never do that to Peter Beck!"

The detective could still feel the sting to his twice-slapped face as they ran down the sidewalk, then down underground, where a gang of cops and one movie star rode the rails to Times Square.

A drunk was vomiting close to the tracks in the location posted on a fan's website. So Bugsy and his audience would have decamped for someplace where the air was marginally sweeter. He could be anywhere in this maze of tunnels and train platforms, twenty feet, forty and seventy feet underground.

"I'll get him a lawyer," said Axel Clayborne. "A good one, whatever it takes."

For the second time in as many minutes, Mallory said, "Shut up!"

"Okay, everybody," yelled Riker. "Spread out!"

The squad broke up into solo runners—except for Mallory, who could not lose the movie star. And Clayborne was attracting way too much attention, collecting an entourage of people, staring at him, pointing, following him. He ran alongside her, winded when he asked, "So, this other squad—why do they think Bugsy moved the body?" And this was met with silence from the running woman. The actor and his little band of fans were falling behind as he called out to Mallory, "I can swear in court—he never *touched* Dickie's body! It's the truth!"

She headed into a pedestrian tunnel, easily gaining speed and leaving him behind, calling back over one shoulder, "I have to wonder how you know that!"

Mallory stopped at the tunnel's end. *Damn.* The Midtown North detectives must have begun their sweep of the subway. Harry Deberman was standing on the platform by the tracks with his back to her. The moron was looking left and right, hoping to spot one man when he should be looking for a crowd—Bugsy's audience.

When Clayborne and his admirers had caught up to her, she said, "Make yourself useful. Go downstairs and check the lower platform."

He did as he was told and disappeared on the way down to the next level, taking his fans with him and gaining a new one on the stairs.

Eyes on Harry Deberman's back, Mallory made her way across the platform to a cluster of people. When she heard the first note of a violin, she knew it was the wrong performance, and she looked back at Deberman. The detective was still oblivious. He had the look of a man killing time—while collecting overtime pay for no work.

It might be worth a minute's conversation to find out how many of Midtown's cops were working this detail tonight. Mallory circled around to another staircase, walked half the way down, then turned and started up again. *Now* Deberman spotted her. He trotted toward her, saying, "Thanks for savin' me some time, kid." He looked down the stairwell behind her. "So he wasn't down there, huh?"

"Yes, he was. I shot him dead."

"No need to get bitchy, kid."

Axel Clayborne stood on a wooden bench, the better to see over the heads of the impromptu gathering. Beside him, a bum held a battery-powered stage lamp, but the halogen bulb was dark.

Curious.

Beyond the crowd, on a patch of cement that stood for a stage, an old woman in dirty clothes held a page of script and read her lines, drunk and stumbling over the words, all but the last three, "Why, why, why?"

The watchers were silent, tense, *waiting*.

Bugsy's head slowly turned to take in every face in his audience, and then his arms spread wide to beg their understanding. "I was scared shitless *all* the time. . . . But life was large. It's like I was there for the big bang." He looked up. "Let there be light!" Upon this cue, the bum beside Axel clicked on the stage lamp. And now Bugsy stood in a bright spotlight. "A *big* bang, balls of fire . . . and me . . . and my cosmic rock 'n' roll band." He looked down at his shoes. "After that, what's a guy gonna do for a second act? . . . I'll tell ya. . . . I shrank myself down to fit in a tiny world. I'm alive, but try an' find me. Ya *can't*. I'm that *small*. Ya think I loved that girl? *No!*" he yelled, and then his voice dropped low. "I'd have to be life size, *man* size to love her. . . . I'm a bug." He raised his eyes to the bum with the lamp, and, on this cue, the spotlight winked out.

Axel applauded madly with the rest of the crowd, enthusiastically joining in with their whoops and whistles.

"You were supposed to *find* him for me, not—"

"*Jesus!*" Axel turned to see that Mallory had materialized on the bench beside him, where the bum used to be. She could stop a man's heart with a trick like that. And now

they both watched Bugsy passing the hat among the crowd.
When it came his turn, Axel emptied his wallet into it.

What?

He saw the gopher give all the money to his delighted,
toothless costar and the bum with the stage lamp.

"He can't keep it," said Mallory. "His character never
has that much cash."

"His *what?*" And now Axel recalled the day he had
gone to the police station to pick up a box of goggles—and
stayed awhile to chat about the gopher. "You're saying I
was right? Bugsy was a character in a play?" He turned to
stare at the gopher. "A *play* was based on *his* life?"

"It's the other way around," she said.

He found it surprisingly easy to believe her totally mad
explanation for why the gopher was bound for a psych
ward if he was caught tonight: A former stage actor, once
critically acclaimed, Bugsy was now a playwright's character, a little man who had lost his mind—a man who did
not exist outside the context of a play.

"You know what that means," said Axel. "Every waking moment of his life is a performance, and he's absolutely *stunning.*" But the gopher was so much more than
that. He was living testament to the world's greatest the-
orist on acting. "Bugsy is an idea come to life. He's Stan-
islavski's Magic If. The actor projects himself into the
imaginary realm of the play, inhabiting it . . . *as if* it were
real. We all aim for that, but no one ever *gets* there." He
stared at the gopher. "Only him."

Ah, but the police were heretics in the actor's church,
and Axel could see that the young infidel beside him

found this miracle—*boring*. How to sum it up before he lost her entirely? "Only a truly gifted actor could be *that* kind of crazy."

Mallory nodded her agreement, and now he realized that he had been telling her something she already knew—and *that* bored her. He would not underestimate her one more time.

"So all these weeks, I've been watching the best performance on Broadway, and I never knew it." But Axel knew why Mallory now scrutinized his face with such distrust, for he had been the first one to characterize Bugsy as a fictional man.

She folded her arms, disbelieving him even before she asked, "You didn't know he was Alan Rains?"

"Not a clue. I've never seen Rains act onstage." He turned to the other side of the platform, where men in suits were marching toward them. Resolute. Grim. They were cops, certainly, but no face he could recognize as one of Mallory's people. "Might that be trouble?"

Ron Bowman was in the lead. The other detectives from Midtown North were close behind him, and Harry Deberman was huffing and dragging in the rear. More men and women were coming down the stairs. Mallory stood between them and Bugsy, her jacket and blazer drawn back, her holstered gun on display.

Surprised, Bowman slowed his steps at the sight of her exposed weapon, a neon billboard sign that advertised *Cop War*. "I've got a warrant, Mallory."

"My collar," she said, "my prisoner."

"There's twelve of us . . . one of you." He gave her the easygoing shrug of a reasonable man who believed in the logic of numbers and—

"You miscounted," said Riker, moving through the ranks of the Midtown squad.

And they all stood aside for him.

The game had changed.

Riker could not lose their respect, not even if he were falling down drunk and puking. Standing upright and sober, he was a contender, and Ron Bowman, the pack leader, was stalled. But that could not last long.

"The prisoner belongs to us." Riker walked past Bowman to make a stand with Mallory. He made eye contact with every detective in the lineup, assured that not one of them would lay a hand on him to get to Bugsy.

Stalemate.

Last, Riker faced down his friend, the man he had raised from a kiddie cop.

One by one, the men from Special Crimes came stealing down the stairs to fall into place behind Bowman's squad. The detectives from Midtown North now turned around to stand toe-to-toe with the newcomers.

And the game had changed again.

"Cops squaring off against cops." Riker's tone was even and calm. "That's the kind of shit move I'd expect from Halston. But he's not here tonight. It's all on you, Ron. Your call."

Heads were turning among the men and women from Midtown North, and Bowman put his hands in his pockets to say the war was over. Nicely done. Without the need of a spoken command, his people backed off a step to stand easy. To Riker, he said, "You guys got no problem delivering the prisoner for arraignment?"

"First thing in the morning." Riker's word was golden. The deal was sealed.

The detectives from Special Crimes had won—and they had lost.

Charles Butler's kitchen was lit by a century-old fixture in the high tin ceiling. Hidden away in a cupboard was a modern coffeemaker that could not be operated without a degree in computer programming. That was last year's Christmas gift from Mallory. The antique lover wondered what kind of technological gadget she would give him this year, assuming that they were still friends when that holiday rolled around.

He was wide awake now—no thanks to her—and he lit a gas burner underneath his old percolator to make a pot of drug-free brew. He *knew* she had put the sedatives in the deli coffee. He turned to the man behind him, saying, *venting*, "Oh, and having Janos deliver it? Pure genius." Who could suspect that gentle gorilla of drugging innocent people?

Riker pulled out a chair at the kitchen table. "I know she's sorry about that." But this was said without much conviction.

"Sorry?" Mallory had yet to *allude* to the drugging incident, much less apologize, though Charles realized he had not been her target. Oh, no, he had recovered too quickly. Obviously, she had weighted the dose toward the much smaller man, intending the gopher to sleep through the night. And was that a comfort? *Hardly.*

"Charles, can you prep the little guy for the arraignment tomorrow?"

"I'll try, but there's no way that can end well. A few days back, Mallory challenged the Bugsy persona, and he couldn't handle it. The way she described it, I wouldn't say he was catatonic, but close enough. When a judge challenges him tomorrow in a public venue, Bugsy won't be responsive. If he has a meltdown in open court, that's reason enough to ship him off to a psych ward for evaluation. And *that's* going to be a disaster."

"The lawyers do all the talking in court," said Riker. "It might work out."

"I don't think so. His mind is very fragile." Charles kept an ear to the hallway that led to his guest room. Perhaps it had been a bad idea to leave Bugsy alone with Mallory, who had so little patience with make-believe.

He turned off the stove and left the kitchen. Riker followed him to the spare room, where the belongings of the houseguest were spread out on a four-poster bed. It was all rather humble attire. Apparently, the ratty old sneakers on Bugsy's feet were his only shoes.

"*No* socks." Mallory inspected this meager wardrobe of rolled-up T-shirts and jeans. "This won't do. He needs a suit for court."

"I don't wear 'em," said Bugsy. "I'm not the kind of guy to have a—"

"Yeah, *right*," she said. "Does *Alan Rains* have a suit?"

Charles stood on the threshold, eyes wide, hands waving, miming, *No! Don't!*

"Oh, sure he does," said Bugsy. "At his mother's house in Connecticut. She keeps Alan's old room just the way he left it—all his clothes, his shoes. And she has his Tony Award up on the mantelpiece."

Yes, that little gold statue was the first thing Charles had noticed when he paid a call on Mrs. Rains. And now he leaned against the door frame, finding need of some support.

Mallory, of all people, had made the breakthrough into verbalized memories, *real* ones, of home and family. The psychologist held his tongue as the young detective conducted a rather original, quite ruthless therapy session lasting precisely four minutes, and it was agreed that Bugsy would play the role of Alan Rains for his court appearance tomorrow.

Well, perhaps a Ph.D. in the mental-health field was overrated, but amateurs should not be allowed to tinker with the psyches of madmen. Oh, and Mallory's idea? *Totally* mad.

After Riker had completed a telephone call to Mrs. Rains in Connecticut, he made it clear to the gopher that he would see his mother in the morning when she brought his clothes to town. "You treat her with respect—like a good son."

"Got it," said Bugsy. "Alan *loved* his mother." He smiled, showing no resistance to this ludicrous plan.

On the contrary, he seemed to be looking forward to it.

No, this was all wrong.

It came too easily to Bugsy, this idea of stepping out of the gopher character to act like his true self in court; it was nothing forced, not something he need grapple with. But then, Mallory was not challenging the false persona. She had only given him another part to play—the role of the man he used to be.

Something had changed.

And Charles died a little. Bugsy was not role-playing tonight. Metamorphosis complete, he *was* the gopher. Truly lost. And it seemed that Alan Rains had met a death of sorts.

So much for hope. Stomp *that*.

ROLLO: Everything will be all
right. . . . And now it's
your turn to lie.
—<u>The Brass Bed</u>, Act III

28 Sunlight flooded this public room of century-old wainscoting and decorative molding. The large space was divided by a gated rail to keep the gallery visitors in their place, apart from the tables reserved for lawyers and clients. All faced the judge's vacant bench. Affixed to the wall behind it was an emblem that bore the words *In God we trust*, a phrase akin to *God, help us all*, and Charles Butler thought it lent the judicial system the air of a dice roll.

A clean-shaven Bugsy entered the courtroom, his hair no longer a bird's nest but cut and combed. The black suit and red silk tie helped him to blend well in the company of lawyers, though he was much better dressed than his public defender. And there were other changes in him. He exuded the confidence of a privileged life—as he played the role of a madman playing sane.

He was quite as handsome as the young man he used to be. This was the opinion of his mother, who had come to town early this morning with a selection of clothing and shoes from the closet of Alan Rains. She would have outfitted her son with a better attorney as well, but Mallory's advice had prevailed. The detective had insisted that, if she could find Bugsy a worse attorney for this proceeding, she would do it.

Mrs. Rains sat beside Charles Butler in the gallery. She smiled. She *glowed*. "Alan doesn't want me to stay for the arraignment. And I don't want to make him anxious. I promised I'd go straight home. . . . He called me *Mom*. I suppose that's enough excitement for one day." With a goodbye and a handshake, she rose from her seat and left to catch the next train back to Connecticut.

Mallory took the mother's place on the gallery bench and whispered to him, "We won't need you unless this goes sour. If that happens, you give the judge your assessment of Bugsy, and that should kill a trip to the psych ward. You only have to say he's crazy but harmless."

"That's true enough," said Charles. "So . . . why did he confess to a murder?"

"I told him to."

"What? . . . What did you say?"

At the bailiff's command, everyone stood up as the Honorable Judge Margo Wicker entered the courtroom in her long black robe. Her dark hair was pulled back in a severe bun, and she wore no makeup, no nail polish or any other sign of artifice. By the depth of the frown lines in her face, and particularly that angry furrow between her eyes, Charles pegged her for a no-nonsense type, and the term *hanging judge* came to mind. In a hushed voice, he said, "I don't see Bugsy getting much sympathy from her."

"It doesn't hang on sympathy," said Mallory. "It hangs on law. We lucked out with the judge. Nothing gets past Wicker. She doesn't do thirty-second arraignments." When the gallery was seated again, the young detective turned to search the faces in the back row.

Following the track of her eyes, Charles caught a nod from a prominent civil rights attorney, James Todd, a well-dressed man with a boyish face at odds with hair gone to gray. But he was better described by reporters as a cannon among hired guns—just Mallory's style.

At the front of the courtroom, Bugsy's public defender, Eddy Monroe, was an altogether different character, a slovenly impatient man in a checkered clown suit, who tapped one scuffed shoe, so bored as he listened to charges leveled by the assistant district attorney, a young man who might have graduated from law school only the previous day.

"On the first charge," said the judge, "flight to avoid prosecution. How do you plead?"

"Guilty," said the public defender.

"Not guilty," said Bugsy.

The opposing lawyer, the young one, had the look of a child shortchanged at the candy store. In the spirit of *I'm telling Mom*, he said, "Your Honor, the facts are indisputable. Mr. Rains was under arrest when he ran from the police station." He handed her a sheet of yellow paper. "And that's his confession."

The room was silent as the judge read every line. She

raised her eyes to glare at the young man from the DA's Office. "Mr. Rains confessed to interference with a corpse *and* murder . . . but you decided to let the murder slide? Now *I* call that interesting. But we'll get to that later." This sounded somewhat like a threat. She turned her frown on the older man in the checkered suit. "Mr. Monroe, apparently you didn't take your usual two minutes to meet with the client and get your stories straight."

"I didn't run away," said Bugsy.

"Mr. Rains," said Judge Wicker, "your attorney will speak for you."

After a glance at the public defender, Bugsy turned back to her. "But I've never even *seen* this guy before."

"How *do* I know these things?" The lady picked up her gavel and spun it by the stem. "I must be psychic."

Bugsy pulled crumpled bits of paper from a pants pocket and reached up to lay them before the judge. "Those are my receipts. I delivered lunches to detectives in the squad room. If you look at the order for the ham on rye, that one was for Detective Kay. Oh yeah, and a coffee light, extra sugar. He liked my shades." The gopher pulled a pair of aviator sunglasses from his breast pocket and waved them for the entire courtroom to see.

Very distinctive—and expensive. Charles turned to Mallory. "Aren't those *your*—"

To quiet him, she only needed to raise one finger, and he noted that it was her trigger finger.

Bugsy held the dark glasses high for the judge's inspection. "Detective Kay asked me if the rims were real gold.

I know he'll remember me. Well, after I got paid, I didn't know what else to do . . . so I left."

"You just walked out the door . . . of a police station?"

"Yes, ma'am. I *walked* out. I didn't run."

The judge smiled, though this was far from a happy expression—more on the maniacal side. "So . . . *while* you were in custody, you ran errands for the detectives of Midtown North."

"Yes, ma'am. That was *after* my confession."

"I could check that out with one phone call," said the judge, handing the receipts to the assistant district attorney. "And then, if you like, we can enter this embarrassment into the public record." This was phrased not as a question, but more like a dare.

"The people withdraw the charge of flight to avoid prosecution."

"Good choice," said Judge Wicker. "Next charge. Interference with a corpse. How does the defendant plead?"

"Guilty, Your Honor," said the public defender.

The judge looked at Bugsy, who shook his head in denial. Her eyes moved on to the man in the checkered suit. "Shot in the dark, Mr. Monroe. I'm guessing you didn't have time to—"

"I was *there*, Judge. My client waived his right to an attorney during questioning. But I *still* got 'em to drop the murder charge."

"That's right, Your Honor," said the younger lawyer. "Since his client has a history of mental illness, the people ask for two weeks' psychiatric observation."

Charles noted a subtle shift in Bugsy's posture, a slight sag of the shoulders, perhaps signaling the intrusion of a memory from that other life—real life.

"You have some proof of the mental history?" The judge sifted through the paperwork in her hands. "Am I missing something here?"

"I never saw the document," said the ADA. "Well, I saw Captain Halston hand it to the public defender, Mr. Monroe."

Eddy Monroe wore a look of confusion, something forgotten—and then an *aha* of remembrance. He retreated to the defense table for a search of his briefcase. "One sec, Judge." And now he rushed back to the bench with a fistful of wadded papers, and he handed them up to her.

Feet were shifting in the gallery, and whispers were heard among the restless visitors while the document was silently read, *every word*. Done reading, the judge stared at the man in the checkered suit.

Oh, if only a look could gut the lawyer like a fish knife.

"You never read this document," said Judge Wicker. "I bet you wonder how I know that." She turned to the ADA. "And you never even *touched* it? Well, that's all that saves *your* hide, young man. So . . . when Mr. Rains was taken into custody, the police had this document in their possession. It lists the attorney of record as James Todd. Did anyone call Mr. Todd to—"

"Hell, no!" yelled a voice from the back of the gallery.

"Mr. Todd, always a pleasure," said the judge, clearly lying, not welcoming one more complication. "Approach the bench."

The civil rights attorney had chosen his corner position well. The court waited in silence as he moved *slowly* past the seated visitors in the back row, building anticipation and tension on his leisurely stroll toward the judge. "The ADA got *one* thing right," he said as he passed through the gate in the railing. "My client has a history of mental illness. He wasn't competent to waive his right to an attorney during questioning." Turning to the little man beside him, Todd said, "Hello, kid. How've you been?"

Charles noted a wince before Bugsy forced a smile. Another indicator of unwanted recall? Yes. The little man waved one hand, waving memory away.

"Mr. Rains," said Judge Wicker, "would you prefer Mr. Todd as your attorney?"

Bugsy looked back at the gallery, searching faces until he found Mallory's, and, with her nod, he turned back to the judge to say, "Yes, ma'am."

"Done." The judge turned to the assistant district attorney. "And the confession is out. Would you like to beat a tactical retreat? . . . You want three seconds to think that over? *One, two*—"

"The people would be satisfied with a psych evaluation," said the young ADA.

"Defense counsel would *not*." James Todd glanced at his watch, then looked back over one shoulder as the doors opened, and Axel Clayborne strode into the courtroom. All heads turned toward the celebrity. And the judge slammed down her gavel three times to still the *ooh*s and *ah*s.

"Your Honor, *I* stole the body." The actor raised both arms in a crucifixion stance. "I'm at your mercy."

Very stagy.

Charles turned to Mallory, who had undoubtedly orchestrated this event. But why? In view of the lack of evidence, a tossed confession *and* a prosecutor perched precariously on his last leg, Axel Clayborne's appearance was over the top. Overkill.

"These people will only remember the movie star," said Mallory. "They'll forget that Bugsy was ever here."

But Charles sensed that was not quite *it*—not *all* of it.

The gavel banged on until the crowd was hushed.

"Mr. Clayborne," said the unhappy judge, "I don't tolerate theatrics in my courtroom. If you want to confess to a crime, your local police station is the proper venue. There *is* a procedure to be followed—even for celebrities."

One hand to his breast, the actor overplayed a wounded affect. "Well, I didn't *plan* to cut corners. Last night, I tried to confess to Captain Halston, but he wouldn't listen." Clayborne rested both hands on Bugsy's shoulders. "The captain seems determined to condemn my young friend to a psych ward. No idea why. He's innocent. And Captain Halston *knows* it."

To Charles's ear, this had the sound of a rehearsed speech, and Mallory's smile completed the case for conspiracy. Evidently, she disliked this Captain Halston.

"I'm going to regret it," said the deadpan judge, "but I have to ask. . . . *Why* would you steal a body, Mr. Clayborne?"

"Dickie Wyatt was the director of a play, but he died before opening night. He never got to hear one round of applause. A travesty. Well, he'd been dead for a few days.

Getting a bit ripe. So I figured, now or never, it was Dickie's last chance to—"

A bang of the gavel ended this speech, and Clayborne's smile faltered, perhaps correctly guessing that the judge was not a fan.

Mallory folded her arms, and this was Charles's first indication that the actor had gone off script.

Judge Wicker pointed her gavel at the assistant district attorney. "Do we have a cause of death for Mr. Wyatt?"

"Yes, Your Honor." The young lawyer handed up a small sheaf of notebook pages. "Personal notes acquired from Lieutenant Coffey, commander of Special Crimes. The lieutenant called the Medical Examiner's Office the morning after the body was found. He was told that the cause of death was a heroin overdose. The formal autopsy won't be released for a few more days, but it's—"

"*Not* murder," said Judge Wicker. "And that neatly explains why you agreed to discount that part of Mr. Rains's confession. But now it seems that Captain Halston suppressed an exculpatory confession." The judge looked out over the courtroom. "Would anyone else like to pile on? Maybe add to the confusion?"

Charles leaned close to Mallory's ear. "But Edward ruled that death as a—"

"Don't make me hurt you."

Fine. Enough said.

At the front of the courtroom, Axel Clayborne was performing again. "Your Honor, it's only confusing if you know the facts." The actor waited out the laughter from the visitors' gallery. "Dickie Wyatt was the first to die, but his body was the *third* one found. And the woman's death on opening night? That was a heart attack. The following night, the playwright appeared to have slit his own throat. And the reviews? *Fabulous.* So, on the *third* night—*just* to keep the ball rolling, I wheeled Dickie's corpse into the theater and sat him down in the back row. How was I supposed to know there was a suicidal teenager in the audience?"

"Six hundred dollars for interference with a corpse," said the judge, as if she had heard his excuse before and found it boring. Apparently, she had been on the bench *that* long. "Pay the bailiff."

The civil rights attorney said to her, "I move for a dismissal of—"

"*Hold* that thought." Judge Wicker fixed her eyes on the young prosecutor. "*Before* the confession—why did the police take Mr. Rains into custody? Did they have some cause for suspicion? Maybe a witness? Any old thing at all?"

"*I* had a witness." Axel Clayborne stood before the bailiff's table, counting out hundred-dollar bills. "I brought the head usher with me when I confessed to Captain Halston. You see, I was dressed as a nurse when I wheeled Dickie's body into the theater. So I stooped a bit—didn't want to seem too tall for a woman. But the usher recalled looking up at someone larger than he was. And he's taller than Alan Rains."

"Your Honor, that's hearsay," said the ADA.

"Oh, shut the hell up." Judge Wicker laid down her gavel and covered her eyes with both hands for a moment.

Then she crooked one come-hither finger at the uniformed guard by the door. When the officer stood before the bench, the judge's voice was low, but Charles thought he heard her say, "Bring me the head of Captain Halston."

Bugsy and the lawyers were still gathered before the bench when Axel Clayborne signed his final autograph, and the last of the gallery visitors were ushered out of the courtroom. The actor joined Mallory and Charles near the door, asking, "How'd I do?"

"You're a bad liar," she said. "You embellish too much."

"But it was all true."

"So?"

Riker entered from the hall. "There's reporters and cameras all over the place. We gotta take Bugsy out the back."

Angry, Mallory turned on Axel Clayborne. "You just *had* to milk the publicity one more time."

"Paparazzi tend to follow me around. You can't blame me for being famous. But this time, they're not here for *me*. On the way in, I saw Captain Halston holding a press conference out on the courthouse steps."

"It's true," said Riker. "I was there. Halston told the reporters a person of interest was being arraigned. This time, he named Alan Rains. Then a uniform showed up to bring Halston inside. The reporters followed them. They're all coming this way."

Mallory moved toward the door, and Clayborne said, "Bad idea. There's an army of jackals out there, and you're *so* photogenic."

She heard the rabble in the hallway and then turned to look at the gathering by the bench. Bugsy's act was degrading, feet tapping, hands fidgeting, sliding back into the role of the gopher.

Charles Butler was also watching—and worried. "I don't think Bugsy's holding up all that well. The reporters couldn't get at him if we took him to Edward's clinic. A good place to—"

"A clinic? Worst thing for him," said Clayborne. "No doctor would ever understand the—"

"*I'm* a doctor. You're an *actor*. Clear? Good." Charles turned back to Mallory. "Bugsy is in a vulnerable mental state. He needs—"

"Oh, please," said Clayborne. "*Spare* me. It's not some run-of-the-mill delusion, nothing so cliché. One night, a character in a play passed through the fourth wall, came down from the stage and walked into the world—a living, breathing work of art. Bugsy's alive, but what doctor could understand that he's not real—he's fictional."

Not *real*? Mallory turned to see that Bugsy had wandered away from the conversation of the judge and the lawyers. He was near the door when she sang out, "No, don't go out there!"

She lunged for him.

She clutched air.

He was swept away in a fast river of screamers and bright lights.

Alongside Mallory, Charles moved through the doors and into the running crowd, using arms and shoulders to help her plow the field, but Riker was more effective as he body-slammed a photographer and tripped a reporter.

The crowd of media set upon Bugsy in a frenzy, microphones thrust toward the back of his head and shouts of "Hey, Alan!" and "Mr. Rains" and "Stop!" followed by a barrage of "Did you do it?" and "How crazy *are* you?"

The gopher ran down the hall with barking reporters on all sides, photographers, pole lights and cameras engulfing him in the dog pack. Mallory elbowed her way into the thick of the fray, fighting a path through the mob to see Bugsy brought to bay, cornered at the end of the corridor.

Center stage in the world and frightened by it, lost in it, his head was bowed, and, apropos of no question asked of him, he said a line from a long-ago performance. "I'm just a *little* man." And then, head lolled back, eyes focused on nothing, he tap-danced for the jackals.

> **ROLLO:** Don't scream. Don't cry.
> Disappoint them.
>
> —<u>The Brass Bed</u>, Act III

 Words of a wise man: *Don't ever let me catch you punching out a reporter.* And the late Louis Markowitz had also told her, *It's unsanitary, kid. You don't know* where *that scum has been.*

Mallory washed off the blood of a reporter's split lip, and then she washed her hands again. And *again.* She would never get clean.

What a hell of a backfire day.

While splashing water on her face, she caught the movement in the glass above the row of sinks. There was no instant recognition of her reflection when she came upon it unawares, an effect of distortion from her early years on city streets, the residue of every bad thing she had seen or smelled or touched before the age of ten—and what had reached out to touch her. All the mirrors in the world had been cracked in childhood.

What did Bugsy see in *his* broken mirror?

She lowered her eyes and washed her hands again.

Captain Halston was crushed. He would not recover from today's carnage, but her case was in ruins. The media would cloud the landscape of suspects with Bugsy's taint of crazy. The detective banged her fist on the countertop, bringing on the pain, the only remedy she knew for rage.

And then she was calm.

Mallory picked up a bag of pharmacy bottles, the donations from station-house personnel, and she carried it to the crib, a bunkroom, where cops could catch a nap on the double-decker cots during all-nighters. There, Charles Butler had taken on the chore of getting the gopher out of his Alan Rains suit. And now Bugsy lay on a lower berth, dressed in his underwear, deep in shock.

"He's better off here." Mallory would tolerate no more argument about this. "It's quiet. Safe."

"I suppose you're right." Charles hunkered down to cover Bugsy with a blanket. "The bedlam of a hospital emergency room would've been a nightmare for him. But he still needs a medical doctor to write a prescription for—"

"Got it covered." She handed over the bag. "We took up a collection."

While the psychologist pored through the pharmacy containers, reading the labels, a uniformed officer entered the room with one more bottle of pills for the cause.

Bugsy turned on his side. The blanket was flung off,

and his T-shirt rode up to expose the old track of a surgeon's scalpel bisecting his body.

"That thing must be a foot long." The patrolman leaned down for a closer look at this wicked scar from a plucked-out kidney that a teenage boy had given to his girl. "What happened to him?"

"He fell in love," said Charles.

Riker had been real friendly on the way up the stairs to Special Crimes, but then the detective had gone off to scare up some coffee to take the chill off the day, leaving the sheriff to stand alone at the center of the squad room, a suitcase at his feet.

A visitor's name tag was strung around James Harper's neck, and he had just this minute removed his parka to display a gold star pinned on his Sunday-go-to-meeting sports coat. The other cops of this outfit paid him no mind, some of them crisscrossing the room and others shuffling paperwork and talking on phones.

And then he saw her, the only female on this murder squad—so said the desk sergeant downstairs. She was younger than he expected. His other bias was that the girl was too pretty, so pretty she was hard on a man's eyes. And cold? *Damn* cold. She looked right through him. The young cop had a real determined walk, and he could see that she was fixing to pass him by. He stepped into her path and flagged her down like she was a New York City taxicab. "Detective Mallory!"

She stopped to look him up and down. Sizing him up for a hick? Oh, yeah.

"Sheriff Harper, did you come empty-handed? If you did, you wasted a trip."

He picked up his suitcase and smiled. "I'll show you mine. You show me yours."

Detective Mallory walked around him—and away from him.

He followed her, saying to her back, "I got the whole damn case file." And this was true, though he might have implied that he had brought all of it in his suitcase. He had not.

The girl kept walking, and now they were turning down a hallway.

Right behind her, he said, "So when can we start to get reciprocal?"

"Just the minute you turn out your pockets and show me what's in that suitcase." She passed through an open doorway. "If I don't find an extradition order for *my* killer, I might throw you a bone."

He followed her into a room lined with cork and papered with diagrams, bloody photographs and such. He shot a quick look at an autopsy report—and another one. These walls held a ton of evidence. Reaching into his breast pocket, he pulled out the John Doe extradition papers. "You can hold on to 'em for a while. I don't mind." He had copies.

As she folded his warrants away in the back pocket of her jeans, other cops began to straggle into the room by twos and threes, and then the door finally closed behind the last detective. The sheriff was no longer being ignored. He stood at the center of a crowd, and none of these folks seemed real happy to make his acquaintance.

Riker moseyed down the hall, heading for the lynching party in the incident room, when he was waylaid by his favorite shrink, who carried Bugsy's duffel bag. "Hey, Charles. How's the little guy doin'?"

"Hard to say. An officer asked him about the kidney scar, and Bugsy said it wasn't *his* scar . . . it belonged to someone else."

"So he's totally lost it?"

"Well, that might be the medication talking. He's sleeping now, but when he wakes up, I'd like to move him to familiar surroundings. Is it safe to take him back to the theater?"

"Yeah, we got damage control. Reporters only call us to ask about Alan Rains. None of 'em made the Bugsy connection. And the cameras didn't get any good shots of his face—mostly Mallory's hand and mine." Riker checked his watch.

It was time to beat the living crap out of the sheriff from Nebraska.

"So, Charles . . . wanna go to a party?"

Detective Janos's hands described slow circles of confusion when he asked, "How could you just *lose* two twelve-year-old kids?"

All around Sheriff Harper, the other detectives took one step closer to prompt his reply, and he said, "No way to hold on to 'em. Like I told Detective Mallory, a relative took the twins out of state. I don't know which state she dumped 'em in, but you *know* they wound up in foster care. Once kids get lost in that system, they don't leave tracks." He turned to face Mallory. "How much luck did *you* have with that?"

"So you've been waiting all these years," she said, "for some other cop to find them for you."

"I figured they'd surface sooner or later."

"After they *killed* somebody!" This shot had come from an angry man behind him.

The sheriff's suitcase lay open at the base of one cork wall, and Mallory stood beside it, pinning up photographs, his candid shots of the Chalmers twins, nothing as grand as little mug shots. The boys in pajamas had lowered their heads, and strands of long hair covered their eyes—and their *ears*. He had to smile. He would bet his house and car that Mallory was still working on the bogus lead of jughandle ears. *Thank you, Bugsy, whoever the hell you are.*

She looked at the pictures on the wall, her arms folded, disapproving. "These are the best you've got?"

Oh, hell, no. He had left all the *good* pictures back in Nebraska. "No class photos," said the sheriff, and that part was true enough. "The boys were home-schooled."

"But not their sisters," said Mallory.

"Only the twins," said a pissed-off man on his right, the one with a loud voice like a damned foghorn.

"So the mother knew there was something wrong with those two." Detective Gonzales moved in on the sheriff's left flank. "That's why she kept them out of school."

"You always knew the boys did it," said Mallory.

"I got no evidence of that. No blood on 'em when—"

"But there *was* blood. Lots of it." Down the wall, a gray-haired woman—Clara something—was pinning up copies of his crime-scene photos and the personal notes robbed from his suitcase. "The sheriff found moisture in the shower stall and more blood in the drain trap. The killer apparently showered." The older woman shot a nasty look in his direction as she pointed to his picture of blood-red shoe prints on a hallway carpet. "Seriously? You've *got* the shoes, but you don't know who made these tracks?"

Since Mallory had already guessed this part, the sheriff saw no harm in telling the truth on this score. "Mr. Chalmers died the year before. A suicide. His wife never got up the steam to toss out his clothes. We found her husband's bloody shoes put back in the bedroom closet."

"How *many* shoes?" asked Mallory. "One pair? Two?"

The sheriff ignored her and stepped up to the wall, pretending interest in headshots of the Rinaldi brothers. "I can't tell much from these. The noses don't look right, and I never saw the Chalmers kids smile."

Riker ambled into the room. His was the only friendly face James Harper had seen all day, and now the man handed him the promised cup of coffee. The two of them stood before the cork wall, side by side in companionable silence for a minute or so. Then the detective reached out to tap the old photo of the twins in their pajamas. "They creeped you out, didn't they?"

"From the get-go."

And break time was over.

Detective Gonzales emptied the sheriff's suitcase out on the floor.

Now, among the remaining file holders and sundry items, James Harper was looking down at his soiled underpants and smelly socks with holes in the toes. These New York boys knew how to throw a party and do it up right. They might as well have stripped him naked.

And he had to admire that.

Gonzales had opened the last of the folders, and he looked up at Mallory, shaking his head. The loud cop, Lonahan, turned to face the sheriff. "We *know* a teenage boy lived in that house. But there's nothin' here, no pictures of him, no witness statement. It's like a big hole in your case. So this older kid—what was his name?"

The sheriff shrugged this off as a forgotten detail, and that was a mistake, a big one. Words or shrugs—lies were lies. He looked from one face to another, knowing he would not be believed when he said, "I think the older boy's name was Gerry. Somethin' like that." It went against his nature to lie to cops, and so he gave them one true thing: "The kid wasn't in the house when it happened. He had a solid alibi for that night."

"So you just lost track of him," said Mallory. "*And* the twins. That was careless."

"Hey," said Riker, the one decent man in the room.

"Give the sheriff a break. The kid wasn't even there that night. Who wastes resources on a dead end?"

James Harper had earlier bonded with this man in four minutes flat, discovering that Riker was also divorced, a common hazard of the cop's trade.

"We know this kid . . . Gerry? That's his name? He left the house by ambulance." Riker's tone was civil, not accusing. Just asking is all. "What was wrong with him anyway?"

"A car accident laid him up for a few years."

"Sounds like a bad wreck," said Mallory. "Was the boy driving the car? . . . Was he old enough to have a license?"

"I guess I wasn't too concerned with that," said the sheriff. "I had a lot on my plate. Three murdered women—two little girls in *pieces*."

Detective Sanger had found a file he liked. He scanned the papers as he spoke. "Mrs. Chalmers only had four kids, the girls and the twins." He looked up at the sheriff. "What about the lady's sister? We know she lived in that house. You got a married name for her? . . . She was divorced, right? . . . Was she Gerry's mother?" When no answers were forthcoming, he asked, "Was that woman divorced in Nebraska?"

The sheriff held up both hands in a gesture of helpless ignorance.

Mallory turned to a man with an eagle's beak and a real nice suit. This was the frog-eyed giant who had walked in behind Riker. And when the man spoke, he sounded nothing like a cop; he sounded like a walking, talking lie detector when he said to Mallory, "The boy *was* driving the car. At the time of the accident, he wasn't old enough to have a license. His mother *was* Mrs. Chalmers's sister, and she *did* divorce her husband out of state. I *think* she kept her married name, but I'd be guessing on that one."

While Janos typed in police protocols to enter a Nebraska website for birth records, detectives at other desks were hunting vehicular accidents racked up by unlicensed teenagers at the wheel. "So the older kid's name isn't Gerry, right?"

"Right you are." Charles Butler stood over the printer. He had been given the chore of reading likely accident reports as they rolled out of the machine. "That was the deception that set my baseline." And it was the only one he had failed to mention until now.

That false name had been the big lie that everyone had tipped to back in the incident room. The detective suspected that Charles had simply been too polite to tell them what they so obviously already knew.

What a gentleman.

"Rats!" Janos had just discovered that birth records were not cross-indexed under mothers' maiden names, and none of the neighbors had been able to supply a married name for the mother of the bedridden boy. It would have been so easy to stick pins beneath the sheriff's fingernails, but Janos was not inclined to do such things. Or he might have bent the man's arm back till he heard that stunning sound of a snapping bone—almost music—but the torture of another human being was unthinkable. Or, if not unthinkable—

"Forget Mrs. Chalmers's sister." Mallory sat down in the chair beside his desk. "That woman's a dead end." She laid a birth certificate on the blotter, though not the one he was looking for. It belonged to the invalid's mother. "If she'd ever applied for a Social Security card, the feds would've had this on file—and they don't."

He would never ask how she knew that. His old boss, Lou Markowitz, had set the rule by example, never questioning why giant government bureaucracies were so helpful to the squad's computer witch. "So . . . she couldn't have filed a tax return or a joint return with her husband. No tracks." Now he could see the mother and her exhusband as the cash-and-carry type, who had lived off the grid with their son, the bad driver.

It was still possible to get lost in America.

Rats.

Mallory gave Charles Butler a smile. "Nice catch with the sheriff's lies."

Very nice catch, since the sheriff had kept silent for much of the questioning. This man had caught lies untold.

"How'd you do it?" asked Janos. "Micro expressions? That kind of thing?"

"Oh, no. Waste of time." Charles laid down his stack of accident reports. "There *are* involuntary expressions of core emotions, but you'd have to catch the cues flying by in a fifteenth of a second. And there's no universal Pinocchio expression. Micro expressions won't catch lies. That's a fairy tale."

"So how—"

"I do it with poker tells. The sheriff was easy to read because he doesn't *like* deceiving you. That was obvious in the first big lie, the one everybody caught. The man hesitated. Next, he inhaled a puff of air. Then pursed lips. And then he gave you that made-up name. So that's three tells for one deception. The giveaway for his nonverbal lies is pursed lips and an upturn at one corner of his mouth. Micro-expression data lists that one as a sign of contempt. But he showed no contempt for any of you, not even when you dumped his dirty laundry on the floor." Charles turned to face Mallory—who was not there anymore. His lecture had gone on too long for the likes of her, and she had slipped away.

Janos rolled one hand as encouragement to continue. And Charles did. "So when you asked questions that got *no* verbal response, in *his* case, in *that* situation, the expression meant he was holding four aces while trying to convey that he couldn't beat a pair. I know people who have other poker tells for the exact same thing. Twitchy fingers, a tilt of the head. Different tells for all of them. . . . So much for the myth of one-size-fits-all science."

Janos gave him a broad smile and hoped that Charles could not read the thought behind it. This lecture on poker tells would be interesting to everyone on the squad who knew that Charles Butler stank at poker—and that was everyone. This man could read another man's hand, no doubt about it, but never hide cards of his own. Charles could not win with deception, and yet he *loved* the liar's game.

The detective turned his eyes to the wide window on

the lieutenant's private office, where Riker sat drinking coffee with the enemy.

And the games went on.

Sheriff Harper had a second cup of brew while waiting for the boss of this outfit to show his face again.

Riker passed the time with him, commiserating on divorce lawyers and the misery that women left behind them—when they left. This smiling, laid-back cop was right when he said he *knew* things about women. Now he knew the first name of the sheriff's ex-wife and even her maiden name. He also knew what she did for a living these days, as well as the fact that she had not left her hometown after the divorce.

But, thankfully, the man from Nebraska had not been asked one question about the family massacre, for he would deeply regret a lie told to this very decent man.

James Harper looked out through the window on the squad room, and he saw Mallory with a duffel bag slung over one shoulder as she walked alongside a small, scruffy man in baggy jeans. Her free hand was on the little fella's arm, as if he might need help walking to the stairwell door. "A person of interest?"

Riker glanced at the window. "Naw." The detective sipped his coffee and smiled. "So your ex-wife moved back in with her dad."

"Yup. Only six blocks away."

Lieutenant Coffey entered the private office.

About time.

The lieutenant was definitely one angry man as he faced his detective, saying, "The play goes on tonight."

What play?

"Bad move." Riker rose to his feet, not liking this news one bit. "You *know* what's gonna—"

"Tell it to Councilman Perry. That twit leaned on Beale again."

"So what? The commissioner can't interfere with an ongoing—"

"Yeah," said Coffey, "I've heard that joke, too. Since when did regulations ever stop that old fart? And now he's got the mayor onboard. God forbid one closed theater should interfere with tourism. We got nine hours before—" The lieutenant turned around to face James Harper. "Oh, you're invited, Sheriff. We got front-row seats for the hottest show in town."

Well, *finally*. Some hospitality.

Mallory entered the dressing room and dropped the gopher's duffel bag on the padded armchair. A small dust cloud rose up from the cushion.

Bugsy's sedation had worn off, but he had been silent during the ride from the station house. Now he sat down on his bedroll. So very still. This was not his twitchy nature, and neither was the sadness. Mallory had brought a bottle of pills to help him sleep—to forget this day. That would be the easy way out.

For him.

And for her.

Instead, she turned to the makeup table and stared at the broken mirror. "That story you told me? The one about the old murder? I looked it up." Two decades ago, that case had been neatly wrapped within an hour. She reached out to touch the glass and run one finger around the outline of a missing shard. "There was no murder weapon at the crime scene. A hunk of glass might match up with the ME's report, but the theater owner's corpse wasn't found up here."

"I know," said Bugsy. "The way the real story goes, it was the family's idea to move his body outta the lady's dressin' room." With some effort, he rose to his feet. "I told ya about the renovations, right? The theater let us use the stage at night—saved a bundle on rentin' rehearsal space." He pulled down a decades-old calendar, exposing a clean square of green wall. At its center was a small, round spot of raw plaster. "Before the contractors fixed up the other dressin' rooms, I found plugs like this one in all of 'em. . . . Filled-in peepholes."

Mallory nodded her understanding: Twenty years ago, the victim's family had not wanted this room searched by the police. The hole in the wall might have exposed the murdered relative as a sexual deviant—a peeper.

"See this?" Bugsy pointed to a patch of the mirror where a second shard was missing, a smaller one. "The way I heard it, while they were cartin' the old guy's body downstairs, the actress was up here, slittin' her wrists." He pulled back a scatter rug to reveal a bleached-out section of floor—blood evidence destroyed. "The lady was still alive when the family dragged her outta here. The cops found her bleedin' to death in the alley."

"Did you tell that story to Alma Sutter?"

"Yeah, I tried to tell her she wasn't the only one to—" His head snapped toward the open door.

Mallory had also heard it—the sound of an object hitting the floor below them, something dropped or knocked over. Other people had keys to this theater and reason to be here, but it was the absence of any more sound that made her slide the revolver from its holster. This was the guilty silence of someone frozen in waiting—another listener downstairs.

ROLLO: There is one thing that I
can do if you allow it.
                    —The Brass Bed, Act III

"Lock up after me," she whispered. "No noise." Gun in hand, Mallory stepped over the threshold of the dressing room.

Along the railed walkway, she stopped at every door beyond Bugsy's. No need to pick the locks. She had a good ear for a dead room. She descended the stairs, treading lightly, and crossed the floor behind the stage set for a look at the blackboard.

The slate was wiped clean.

Mallory walked to the alley door and tried the knob. Still locked. There was no noise, and she could not say why reflex kicked in, why she spun around to point her gun at a ginger cat—*with chalk-dusted fur.*

The cat arched its back, tail high, and hissed with a show of sharp teeth. Then, conceding victory, it fled, followed closely by the detective holstering her revolver on the run. Mallory crashed through the clothes on the wardrobe racks in time to see the animal disappear through a rubber pet flap in a door—an undersized door with an old-fashioned keyhole lock.

Another damn screwup!

This exit had not been marked on the crime-scene diagram. But this time, Clara Loman could not be faulted; before her late arrival that night, the floor plan had been sketched out by her CSIs. And not one of those bastards had thought to search behind the wardrobe racks. *No, too much work.*

The ancient lock was easily picked with tools from her pouch, though she could have opened it with any small bits of metal that came to hand. The lock undone, she opened the door.

Not a building exit.

Mallory stepped through the opening in the brick wall and onto a small, square landing. One narrow flight of stairs led upward, and this would be the long-dead peeper's passageway to the dressing rooms. The other one, a down-staircase, faded to black after six steps. Smells of piss, feces and wood rot rose from below. She flicked a wall switch, and a bare bulb came to light at the foot of the stairs. Though she stepped softly, the ancient wood creaked underfoot. Half the way down, she stopped.

Another creak of the wood.

She turned to see Bugsy four steps above—armed with a baseball bat. Her own noise on the stairs had masked his steps coming down behind her. Surprise number two:

Her gun was pointed at his head, an act of reflex, but he showed no sign of fear, though that was his normal state in every waking minute.

He lowered the bat.

She lowered the gun.

By hand signals, Mallory pointed the way back up the stairs, mouthing the words, *Get out! Now!*

Shoulders back, he stood up straight, and his feet were firmly planted in a very unBugsy way. *Acting* brave?

No, that wasn't it.

Hello, Alan Rains.

What a hell of a time to go sane.

All her gesturing was of no use. He meant to make a stand with her. He was her wingman now. In sign language, they agreed that he would remain here to guard the stairs leading up to the door. *No* noise.

When Mallory touched down on the last step, she saw crisscrossing tracks, paw prints of chalk dust, each trail fading to nothing. Nearby was a Kitty Litter box overflowing with turds. Beyond that, she saw a bone-dry pet bowl with the word *water* printed on the side. Only the one empty bowl. There was no sign that the cat was ever fed. And this told her it was a working animal, catching its own supper of mice or rats.

The ceiling was a patchwork of tin squares stained with rust, and the floor was stacked with dusty cartons, trunks and crates. Alongside a mop covered with mold, a workman's ladder with a broken step was propped against one wall. And cat turds littered the floor. This space had gone unused for so long, even the existence of the theater's mouse catcher had been forgotten.

On the far side of the room, the ginger cat crouched beneath a pipe joint that leaked occasional drops of water into the patient animal's open mouth. His perch was a drip-stained carton. One side of the cardboard had collapsed and spilled out a cache of small, soggy boxes that were falling to pieces, releasing sticks of white chalk, some of them degraded by water leaking from the pipe above. Mallory rounded the crate to surprise the cat.

Yellow eyes big with fear, it ran for cover behind a steamer trunk, leaving a chalk-dust trail on the floor.

Other trails, faint ones, repeatedly led to a door with scratches on it as high as a cat could reach. There was no lock, but the knob would not turn under her hand. It was stuck—fused shut with rusted works. Mallory applied more force until she heard a click and a metallic snap of something broken inside the mechanism. And still the door would not open. One foot wedged against the wall, hand to the knob, she pulled.

The cat reappeared. It was at her heels, then brushing past her legs. Frantic now, it clawed the wood, mad to get inside. Whatever was in there, it outweighed the animal's fear of humans. The door was giving, and now it opened— to show her a grimy toilet and nothing more.

The cat smelled water.

The animal was on its hind legs, pawing the closed toilet seat, crying—*so* thirsty.

Mallory snapped on a latex glove. After flushing the

toilet, she opened the filthy seat cover as fresh water swirled into the bowl. Then a quick flash of flying ginger fur—and now the cat artfully balanced on the porcelain rim, head dipping low, drinking its fill. Above the light noise of the lapping cat, Mallory heard a sound upstairs, a subtle movement of shoes—stealthy. The detective stood motionless, listening, her ears stripping away the ceiling, to hear the sound of nails scratching slate.

An invitation?

The cat stopped lapping. The detective drew her gun.

On the run, Mallory took the stairs three at a time, hissing to the little man with the baseball bat, "Stay here."

But he would *not* stay. He was right behind her when she passed through the open door. She held up the flat of one hand to tell him to stop, and then used her gun to point him back down the stairs. The gopher would not go, but his expression was not defiance. What was it?

Resolve.

Alan Rains had resolved to stand by her.

Defeated, she moved toward the blackboard, where she read the line: GOOD MORNING, DETECTIVE MALLORY.

She turned her back on the slate to face the rectangle of ghost light shining through the open door in the scenery. There was no one on the stage. Another scratching sound called her attention back to the board, where the message had changed to say, I MISSED YOU.

Impossible.

Only seconds had passed, not time enough for the other message to be wiped away and this new one left in its place. There were no signs of erasure, no smears of chalk. And she was not a believer in Alma's haunt.

Mallory walked up to the board. There was no give when she pushed the sides of the blackboard, no yield when she pulled on the wooden frame. Turning to the stage manager's desk, she grabbed up a sheet of paper and slid it between the slate and the wood—and then slid it halfway through the wall—the *false* wall—and it was ripped from her hand.

She stepped back.

"Took you long enough," said the muffled voice of Axel Clayborne.

The slate revolved on a center pivot, turning round until one thick edge jutted out in a vertical line down the middle of the wide frame. And now she had a split view of the space behind the blackboard, a small, enclosed room, as narrow as the hidden staircase—but there were no stairs.

"Hel*lo*!" Smiling, Clayborne leaned through one side of the opening, propping his arms on the sill of his odd window. Small metal cylinders protruded from one closed hand.

Dowels? Yes. She saw drilled holes of matching width on an inside edge of the frame. The dowels, once dropped into their sockets, would keep the slate from moving until the chalk messages were changed.

So Alma Sutter was not crazy. And Mallory had already tired of this trick of spinning slate.

"If you'd like to join me," said Clayborne, "just go back down the stairs, climb the ladder and push on a ceiling square, the one with a stain in the shape of— No? It's *very* cozy back here."

One hand rode on her hip to tell him that he should not annoy her one more time.

"Okay, have it your way." The actor climbed out through one side of the opening to stand before her, not contrite, but a bit surprised to see her gun leveled at his gut.

"Can't take a joke?" Clayborne turned to face the gopher. "I need a few minutes with Detective Mallory—*alone*." He smiled again, so condescending, regarding the baseball bat held in the ready position for a head-slamming swing—and the one who held it—as *insignificant* threats.

Mallory lowered her gun and leaned down to the little man at her side. "Don't hit him unless you really want to. Clayborne's *harmless*. . . . You know the type." She shot a quick glance at the movie star's face, pleased to see him wince at this insult, this payback for the slight to her wingman.

The baseball bat dropped to the floor. The gopher's shoulders slumped. His head ducked low.

Goodbye, Alan Rains.

It was Bugsy who scrambled off to quick-climb distant stairs. Between the hanging sandbags and loops of rope and cable, she caught a glimpse of him running along the high walkway toward the safety of his dressing room.

A door closed.

Axel Clayborne smugly regarded his handiwork on the blackboard. "Clever, isn't it?"

"So you're the ghostwriter. . . . I'm shocked," she said, not at all shocked. No one on the squad had even bothered to place a bet against him.

The actor lightly slapped the blackboard. "When I was

a kid, the old man who built this place was still alive. A bit of a practical joker—*and* a voyeur. Well, I figured out the trick. Caught him in the act. He swore me to secrecy, and then he wrote me a letter of introduction to a Hollywood producer."

"You only *think* I'm listening." Mallory holstered her gun.

"I can be miles more entertaining. Here's the deal. I'll answer all your questions—*if* you let the show go on tonight."

An easy bargain. Permission had already been granted, but no one had told this actor that the politicians, the *amateurs*, were running the NYPD today.

"Deal." She nodded at the chair behind the stage manager's desk. "Sit!"

He pulled out the chair, saluted her and sat down.

"You lie to me—*one time*," she said, "I'll shut this play down for good."

He rocked the chair on two back legs, grinning at her, so happy to comply. "First question?"

"Years back, when you were working in Rome, I know you went to prison for Dickie Wyatt's drug bust. How did he get you to do his jail time? Did Wyatt have something on you?"

Clayborne lost his grin. The chair tilted back toward the wall, and he was clumsy when he righted it to save himself. "No, it was nothing like that. . . . Dickie told me he'd rather die than kick heroin in jail. . . . I believed him. So *I* went to jail."

She recognized the sound of a true thing. And *now*

she believed he had loved Dickie Wyatt. That man's death was an open, bloody sore—something useful. "So when you came up with the ghostwriter scam, you called in that old favor."

"No, I offered him a share of the profits. He would've made a—"

"But he turned down the money, didn't he?" Yes, she was right. The actor would not meet her eyes. So Dickie Wyatt's agent had been right to label her client as "a stand-up guy"—until it came time to pay off his debt to Clayborne. Now any question she had for this man would be a welcome change of subject, and she said, "Tell me how long you've been torturing Alma Sutter."

"From the beginning. She was all wrong for the part."

"I know you didn't write your play during rehearsals. If I go looking for the copyright—"

"You'll find it under my mother's maiden name."

"But you gave Dickie Wyatt all the credit, right? You told Peter Beck—"

"So I lied to Peter." He raised his eyebrows to ask, *What of it*? "I couldn't have him following me around, nipping at my heels. Too distracting. But Dickie was accustomed to taking abuse from neurotics. That's a director's job."

"And what did you say to the Rinaldi twins? Did you tell them Wyatt was the one who ripped off their lives?" Mallory waited for a look of surprise. But the actor only found this funny, a punch line to a joke—on *her*. "You *knew* they were—"

"Psychos? Killers? Oh, yes. The boys *gave* me their story,

and they'll get a nice cut when I sell the film rights. Our contract was drawn up a year ago." Grief forgotten, mercurial Clayborne was enjoying himself again. "At first, they tried to pitch me a screenplay. It was absolute crap—only bare bones of the massacre. Not enough for an eight-minute slasher film. The character of the invalid was *my* creation. So was the dialogue, the plot—everything. I only used that massacre as backstory for—"

"Did you keep their original script?"

"*And* their handwritten notes. It's all yours—*after* tonight's performance. I invited a Hollywood super-agent, and I want him to get the full effect *with* the twins onstage. Real psychos playing psychos. Wonderful, aren't they? There's nothing quite as scary as the genuine article."

"So they confessed."

"No, they're not quite *that* stupid. It was the way they pitched the story. When I suggested a minor change, one of them said, 'But it doesn't happen that way.' His brother elaborated . . . talking about the way a tiny body goes on moving . . . after a little girl has lost her head. It scared me shitless. That was the moment when I fell in love with the whole idea. . . . You *are* planning to put them away, right?"

"Count on it."

But not today.

Even if she could get Clayborne's evidence at gunpoint, it would not be enough to charge the Rinaldi brothers with the Nebraska massacre, not without James Harper's cooperation, and there was no chance of that. The sheriff's John Doe warrants were in her back pocket, but if she served them without that lawman's positive ID, the

twins would be back on the street long before curtain
time. "If anyone gets hurt tonight . . . while you're jerk-
ing me around?"

"You'll shoot me," he said. "Understood."

"I don't need a gun to mess you up."

Axel Clayborne rocked the chair on its back legs, smiling again—and too wide. Mallory's hand flashed out and
slammed the back of the chair into the wall. The actor
knocked his head against the blackboard—*hard*.

And painful. *Good*.

His knees in the air, the actor's torso was almost horizontal and tenuously balanced. With a nudge of her foot,
the back legs of the chair were sliding out from under him.

A dangerous position.

He laughed.

This was *fun*.

"Those little psychos will be on best behavior tonight."
Clayborne placed one hand on his heart. "I promise you,
it's guaranteed. They know there's a movie deal in the
works, and the agent needs to see *all three acts*."

Such a happy smile.

Mallory let go of the chair, unwilling to hurt him
anymore—since he *liked* it. She walked away, laying plans
to keep Clayborne's bargain and break it, too.

SUSAN:	You didn't tell me how your grandmother died.
ROLLO:	No wounds. They only had to lift the bat and the axe. She died of . . . anticipation. Oh, but you should have seen her face.

—<u>The Brass Bed</u>, Act III

31

Riker owed his partner twenty dollars for a lost bet. How had Mallory known that the commander of Crime Scene Unit would make a personal appearance for a carton of old chalk?

No hellos were exchanged as the detective stepped to one side, and Heller lumbered past him, demanding to know "Where the fuck is it?"

Though Riker was outranked here, he had never been one to snap to attention. He closed the alley door and locked it. Then, in no special hurry, he led the man to the staircase inside the false wall.

Only a few minutes passed before Heller emerged from the stink hole below. He was angry, an excellent strategy for survival in Copland. Always shoot first. "My guys were supposed to work the audience area. *Maybe* the stage. But *not* the whole damn building! If the supervisor hadn't busted his appendix that night, you guys never would've gotten away with expanding the crime scene."

Riker's turn. He would not contradict this man with the mention of larger crime scenes in years gone by. No, he only needed to say, "That door wasn't marked on Clara Loman's diagram."

Heller did not pull out a weapon. So far, this was going well.

Mallory joined them in the wings by the blackboard, armed with a girlie, pink hairbrush. She seemed surprised to see the CSU commander—as if she had not placed a bet on his visit. "What're *you* doing here?"

The angry man shot a quizzical look at Riker, who was *not* faking surprise.

Heller turned on Mallory. "Your partner called me. He said you needed the damn chalk picked up for testing."

"Oh, I could've dropped that off." She reached out to the stage manager's desk and picked up a small plastic evidence bag containing a single box of chalk from the carton downstairs. Handing it to him, she said, "No rush. I already know Axel Clayborne's prints are on that package. In fact . . . I'm not sure I really need it." And now she toyed with the pink hairbrush, idly picking strands from the bristles.

Heller was a slow-moving bear of a man, but his brain could work at frightening speeds. If Mallory had no need of the chalk, then the hidden door, the one overlooked by his old mentor, might never find its way into a report.

Clara Loman would not lose face; she would never even know about this.

And Heller would never find out that the flawed crime-scene diagram had been drawn *before* Loman had arrived to take over the crew of CSIs.

In the pantheon of extortion scams, this one was beautiful. All that remained was the matter of Mallory's price. Riker stared at the hairbrush in her hand. Alma's brush? Alma's hair? He shook his head to warn Mallory off. No way could she get away with this. Heller would *never* put one foot wrong. Evidence was not for sale.

Mallory stared at the door that led down to her chalk supply. "You're right about the expanded crime scene. If Loman had replaced that supervisor *just* a little earlier, it never would've happened. And I'm the one who ordered the CSIs to search upstairs. Loman stopped them. She found out the actors had keys to their dressing rooms."

"And an expectation of privacy." Heller stared at the pink hairbrush in her hand, an item that had most certainly come from one of those off-limits dressing rooms.

"Right. We can't get a search warrant until we charge somebody." She plucked one hair from the brush and held it up to the light. "When Dr. Slope does strand tests, he doubles the usual lab requirement. He takes a hundred hairs for the sampling. . . . You, too?"

"Slope gets his samples from bodies, not brushes," said Heller. "That kind of evidence won't stand up in court."

"Of course not," said Mallory. "Take *this* brush, for

instance. No idea who it belongs to, but she sheds like a collie. Must be two hundred strands here. I found it on the floor backstage, right out in plain sight."

Was Heller buying that? No, of course not, but Riker did notice the man's slight nod to say he was following her train of thought all the way to hell.

"You're right," said Mallory. "A sample from *this* brush would never be admissible as evidence. . . . It wouldn't even be worth an entry in a CSU log—or an official test in the Police Lab." She reached out and took the bagged package of chalk from Heller's hand. "Don't waste time on this. Riker took down Clayborne's statement. Let's forget I ever found the chalk."

When Heller left the theater, he was carrying a tox-screen sample, a small bag of Alma Sutter's hair.

One bet lost, Riker's wallet was a bit lighter when he sat down beside his partner, center stage on the brass bed. It could have been worse. Given the chance, he would have made a second wager and bet his pension that Mallory could not win a lab test with no paper trail.

His pension, the moon and maybe a bottle of bourbon. *Sucker.*

He could hear Lou Markowitz ragging him all the way from the boneyard. Riker felt that he had let that old man down, but any lecture he gave to Lou's kid right now would only sound foolish and hollow. And *knowing* this, he said, "Kid, there were other ways of handling—"

"It was *fair*," said Mallory. "The CSIs crippled us from the start, and Heller knows it."

"So why not get Loman to run that hair-strand test?"

"Off the books? She'd never do it," said Mallory. "Rules of evidence are her religion. Not in the beginning, though. I think she got rigid as she got older."

"*Her* religion . . . but not Heller's? That guy lives for the—"

"He owes *everything* to Clara Loman. She probably cleaned up his early mistakes. I figure Heller must've made at least one *huge* screwup in his rookie days. That man knows ten ways to kill me without leaving evidence. He'd do that and worse to save Loman's job."

His partner had a gift for sussing out weaknesses in people—all the soft places where they could be hurt, and she would apply that talent to puppy dogs and felons alike. She had no sympathy for any living thing.

In sidelong vision, Riker caught a flash of movement on the other side of the stage, and now an orange cat was creeping toward them with a limp rat in its teeth. This catch was deposited at Mallory's feet, followed by a soft meow, and then the tabby slowly backed up before turning tail to make a run for the wings.

Shaking her head, uncomprehending, Mallory stared at the dead rat on the floor.

Riker guessed that she had never received a present quite like this one. He had grown up with cats in the house, and he knew they only left these gifts out of love—or fear. The orange critter had run off with no limp, no obvious sign of injury, and so he had to ask his partner, "What did you *do* to that poor dumb animal?"

Empty deli bags and paper cups littered the lieutenant's private office, and he was now on Jack-and-James terms with the Nebraska lawman. The door was closed, as were the blinds for the window on the squad room, and the wall clock told him the timing would be close for his end run around the NYPD chain of command.

Jack Coffey's stomach was still knotted up from a meeting with Commissioner Beale. He had volunteered the autopsy results on Dickie Wyatt and Peter Beck, but the commissioner and his buddy, the councilman, had decided that Slope *might* be mistaken about these two calls of murder. In the case of the junkie director, the commissioner had argued that drug mules swallowed heroin, did they not? And, yeah, they did, when the drug was safely encased in balloons, but *nobody* ever used heroin as a chili ingredient.

Idiots.

However, with luck and good timing, the lieutenant could shut down that play before it began. No one else would die, not tonight.

A dejected Sheriff Harper turned the last page of the ghostwriter's play. "So this whole town knows all my case details?"

"Only what's in the first act," said Jack Coffey. "Those photos you brought us are crap—useless. And all the bio material on the Rinaldi brothers was made up by a studio publicist. So we're gonna need a positive ID tonight."

"Can't help you there. If those two actors are the Chalmers boys, they've changed a whole hell of a lot."

"Then I'm sure you'll wanna help us locate the third survivor—the cousin. A family member's ID would work better anyway." Coffey was damn sure the sheriff had that witness stashed somewhere handy. A bedridden boy could not travel far. "So, maybe you could make a few calls to your sources . . . ask around?"

"My cell phone's dead. If I could charge it up—"

"Use my desk phone. I'll give you some privacy." As Jack Coffey left his office, he knew the sheriff would only rack up long-distance charges for the sake of form. Harper would want to give the *appearance* of cooperation.

The lieutenant stood outside his office door, looking out across the squad room, where his men were running down the leads of juvenile traffic accidents in Nebraska and every bordering state, though the old police reports would not be generous with details like the kind of injury that would make a teenage boy into an invalid.

Riker was back at his desk, and he held a telephone receiver to one ear as he gave the lieutenant a nod and a grin.

So the lady in Nebraska had finally returned Riker's call, and the news was good.

Seven hours till curtain time. Time enough?

When Mallory entered the incident room, the squad's expert on all things narcotic handed her a toxicology report.

"This one's for Peter Beck. It's a present from the ME's Office . . . addressed to you." Sanger regarded her with mild curiosity, but he would not ask how she had won the deluxe ninety-day drug screen for a corpse with a slit throat.

She scanned the paperwork, noting that the lab test had been ordered the morning after the poker game. "You read this?"

"Yeah. No drugs in Beck's system, not even over-the-counter stuff."

And now she could write off the possibility of a previous poisoning attempt on the playwright. Despite the odds, she was left with two different motives for the murders of Wyatt and Beck.

"There's something else you gotta see." Sanger led her down the wall to the sheets of cell phone and landline connections. "Your list of throwaway phones is panning out big-time. The guys in Narcotics are your new best friends." He touched one printed line. "Here's where the stagehands connect with a dealer under surveillance. And that guy's numbers are a damn bonanza—but not for us. Nothin' to support a trafficking charge on Garnet and Randal."

Next, he pointed to Alma's calls sheets, their catalog for the stagehands' prepaid cell phones. "But look here. Three days into rehearsals the actress makes a drug buy. A few days later, another one. This goes on for weeks—the buy pattern of a recreational user."

His pointing finger moved down the phone history and stopped. "Here, ten days into rehearsals, and Alma's making lots of calls. She's got a habit." He tapped a line in the third week. "Down here, it's getting heavy. Six weeks ago, our girl was a user, but she hadn't found a drug to fall in love with. But today? I *know* she's got a habit she can't support—and no rich boyfriend to pick up the tab anymore." Sanger pinned up statements for Peter Beck's bank and credit cards. "Looks like the guy cut her off weeks ago."

"And Alma took a big cut in pay," said Mallory. "They all did. Except for Clayborne. He got payment up front." But the actress was dead broke, and drugs were a cash-and-carry trade. "Somebody's paying down her tab with the stagehands."

"Clayborne? That fits with the stagehands visiting his place," said Sanger. "We know he wasn't making a drug buy that night."

Would that work? Could the movie star be Alma's bogeyman—*and* her Santa Claus?

Sheriff Harper emerged from Jack Coffey's office to see the whole squad in a partying mood, passing pizza cartons from desk to desk, and tabs on soda cans were popping everywhere.

The lieutenant handed him a slice piled high with toppings of meats and mushrooms and dripping with cheese. "*This* you won't find in Nebraska. What you got out there in the boonies? That's only a *theory* of pizza."

"Thanks," said the sheriff. "Sorry to say I came up dry on my calls. No luck with the third survivor."

"Oh, the cousin? Don't worry about it," said Coffey. "We found Billy."

Janos placed a soda can in the sheriff's hand. "Would've

happened a lot sooner if you'd remembered the guy's right name. But, hey, nobody's perfect."

"Yeah," said Riker. "If the state troopers get Cousin Billy on the next plane, he might make it to the theater tonight. If not, it's all on you, Sheriff."

"I may not be much help with the ID." James Harper knew that for a fact. He was not about to surrender the twins to any New York cops. "What if I can't—"

"We don't care," said Riker. "We're hoping the Rinaldi brothers remember *you*."

Lieutenant Coffey slapped him on the back. "Sheriff, all you have to do is sit in the front row and look pretty."

SUSAN: (standing by the window)
It's getting dark. (turns to
the door) They're so quiet
out there.
—The Brass Bed, Act III

32 Nan Cooper was the first to arrive. Off with her coat, on with the backstage lamps and wall switches. They had been plagued with electrical glitches, and so she should not have been surprised when the ghost light flickered out, leaving the stage in darkness as she approached the brass bed. An unlucky omen? In one pocket of her mind, it was easy to believe in things unseen—for half a minute.

She switched on the table lamp and stared at the bedding. Stains? She sniffed the sheets. Booze. No ghost, but some living soul had been making use of this bed. She stripped the mattress and went off to find clean linen. Behind her, the ghost light turned itself on again. Maybe someone was having a bit of fun with her? No, the theater had a dead feel to it. So quiet. Stale. Not even a draft to move the air.

Thirty minutes later, nearly done with her rounds of the dressing rooms, she was hanging clean wardrobe in the last closet when she heard Gil's big feet slapping metal steps, climbing the catwalk ladder. The crew had arrived. Downstairs, the two wheelchairs were on the roll, lights flickering, the gopher running to and fro, and the stage manager shouted out the time. *Now* the place had a pulse. And the actors were coming, the stage door opening, again and again, air rushing in—breath and life.

Time for a smoke.

One hour before curtain, when no one was looking her way, Nan unlocked a door near the end of the row of dressing rooms. Passing the makeup table, home to a Styrofoam head that held her new blond wig, she went to the closet and picked through the pockets of her coat. It hung beside the clothing bag with her own stage wardrobe.

The pack of cigarettes was found. Now where did she hide that ashtray? She opened a drawer, and at her back, she heard Detective Mallory say, "A wardrobe lady . . . with a *dressing room?*"

Nan turned around with a smile for the cop. "You gotta love those union contracts."

"Yeah, *right.*" Mallory reached out to touch the blond wig on the table. "I know the stagehands delivered drugs to your place the other night."

"And now you'd like to search my apartment for dope? Fine." Nan fished her keys from a pocket. "The place is all yours. Have a party. Try not to drink *all* my booze."

"Waste of time," said Mallory. "The drugs walked out with your wigmaker. You didn't tell Adolpho about the security camera in the elevator. We have film of him snorting cocaine on the ride down. I hear he's an old friend of yours from the Hollywood days."

Nan's pack of cigarettes fell to the floor. "So you took a hostage. Very smart. . . . Girl, what do you *want* from me?"

"The stagehands supply Alma Sutter, too. Somebody's supporting her drug habit. Maybe you want her part so bad you'd—"

"I *do* keep tabs on her, okay? But I don't pay for her drugs."

The detective sat down in the corner armchair and stretched out her long legs, as if she planned to stay awhile, maybe all night. "Where else would Alma get that kind of money?"

"You mean—since Peter died?" Nan copied Mallory's smile as she leaned down to retrieve her fallen pack of smokes. "Pretty women like her don't *need* money in this town."

"You *know* what that habit costs Alma. The stagehands would've told—"

"Okay, you got me for gossiping with teenagers." Nan fired up a cigarette and blew a perfect smoke ring. "Book me or shoot me. I can't *stand* the suspense."

The looking glass above Axel Clayborne's makeup table spanned a whole wall, and by the closet stood a full-length mirror with three panels, multiple views for the man who could not get enough of himself.

Riker watched him add ten pounds to his face, packing

his cheeks with cotton wadding. "Your doorman says the stagehands come by a few times a week. They usually stay forty minutes to an hour. What do you guys talk about?"

"Rumors mostly." The actor coated his face with makeup on a sponge. "I like to know what's going on backstage. Movies or theater, I always make friends with the crew. They hear things, useful things."

"So you're a control freak."

"Guilty." Clayborne mussed his hair into flyaway strands on the top and the sides, then patted it down in the back, aiming for the flat pillow-head effect. "Where the hell is Nan? She's—"

"You control Alma Sutter's drug habit, too? Maybe you subsidize it? Somebody's workin' that girl like a pharmaceutical yo-yo."

"I wouldn't wish that on a cockroach." The actor rose from his chair and reached out to a hook on the closet door. He pulled down the lower half of his fat suit and set it on the floor, where the thick pajama-clad legs assumed a crouching position. "Drugs killed my best friend. I'd never—"

"Well, now I'm confused," said Riker. "Your *new* good buddies, the stagehands—they probably supplied your old friend Wyatt."

"No, you're wrong about that." Clayborne dropped his robe to the rug. "When Dickie started getting high in rehearsals, that's when I took a real interest in those kids. I'd chat them up for hours, always circling back to Dickie. They didn't sell him any drugs. They never lied about that."

But Riker was dubious. Men parading around in nothing but skivvies so seldom conveyed credibility. "How would you know? You got a polygraph machine?"

"I know because they're *kids*." The actor pulled on the pant section of foam. "They lie about lots of things, but not very well." After donning the top half of the suit, he had gained at least four hundred fake pounds. "Garnet, the one with the pimples? He won't look me in the eye when he talks about his prowess with women. And the other one does this silly double take to see if I bought *his* last lie. That's how I know they spend all their money on women, getting them loaded on drinks and drugs. But they never get to take the ladies home." Clayborne made a curt bow, then raised his eyebrows and spread both hands, as if to prompt another question.

Or was he expecting praise?

The detective was not impressed. It must have showed. The actor turned somber.

"So there you have it." Clayborne buttoned his pajama top. "They can't lie worth a damn. And *that's* how I know they did *not* sell drugs to Dickie."

Riker was not insulted to be taken for the kind of fool who might believe in this nonsense. He knew that Clayborne believed in it.

The actor, gargantuan now, admired his bulk in the mirror, and then turned a satisfied grin on the detective. "I know what you're thinking. You're wondering how I'll fit through that door." His hands dropped to his sides to easily compress the foam girth as he made a hasty escape from the dressing room.

And Riker's actual thoughts?

He was only wondering if he should have the wizard of poker tells take a run at the stagehands. But not this evening. Charles Butler had declined a front-row seat to watch a woman get slammed in the teeth with a baseball bat one more time.

Live theater was not for everyone.

"You got a real fancy lighting booth," said Detective Gonzales. "All the bells and whistles. Who's got the key?"

"I do. But I don't use the booth." Gil Preston opened the large fuse box on the rear wall so the cop could examine rows of switches during this tutorial on lighting. "I work the stage lights from a panel up on the catwalk. Now for the blackout cues—" He pointed to a block of levers. "I have Bugsy switch off these fuses. They control the backstage lights, the lobby and—"

"Detective!" Cyril Buckner stepped between them and pointed to the wings, where a uniformed officer was standing behind an open scenery door. "That cop—will he be standing there all night?"

"You bet your sweet ass," said Gonzales.

The gopher sped by, nervous and jumpy and checking a wristwatch. And the stage manager shouted, "Bugsy, where the *hell* have you been?"

The detective turned his back on them to hail a young officer guarding the alley door ten feet away. "Hey! Where's your partner? He should be standin' right here. Nobody goes near the fuse box tonight."

"Hold it," said Buckner. "We have to cut the backstage lights. The stagehands wear night-vision goggles. They'll go blind if one bulb gets left on."

"Then you should be real careful about turning them *off* . . . the regular way," said the detective. "Nobody touches the damn fuse box!"

Riker had a better seat tonight, not dead center, but not near the wall, either. The sheriff sat in the aisle seat, constantly turning his head, looking back to the lobby doors.

The third survivor of the massacre had not yet arrived at the theater, though Nebraska State Troopers had loaded the twins' older cousin onto a plane bound for Manhattan, and that airliner should have touched down by now.

"Don't worry. Cousin Billy's on the way." Riker knew this was the last thing James Harper would want to hear.

"How *did* you find him? Your boss wouldn't say."

"Well, a search of old accident reports got us a few likely names, but we were runnin' outta time." Riker glanced at his watch. In thirty minutes, the play would begin. "Your deputies were no help at all. I don't think they were holdin' back. I didn't get that vibe from them. I figured you were holdin' out on your own people. . . . So I called your ex-wife."

ROLLO: Too late. Those are the
scariest words.

                    —<u>The Brass Bed</u>, Act III

No ordinary headache.

Needles of searing pain jabbed Alma Sutter behind her right eye, which pulsed like a beating heart in the socket. *This could not be happening, not tonight!*

She had Oxycontin in her purse. Should she risk it? No, not with four lines of cocaine up her nose.

Best to tough it out?

Maybe just *one* tablet.

Alma was not in charge of her hands anymore. She watched her fingers work the leather bag's clasp, as if someone else had told them what to do. *What was—*

The small, light purse dropped to the floor and landed at her feet with the loud *whomp* of a fallen sandbag. The volume control in her head was ramped up high, and plastic pill bottles spilled out across the floor, clattering like rolling hubcaps. Behind her, the knock on the door was a volley of cannonballs, and when Bugsy called out the time, she clamped her hands over her ears. *Make it stop!*

A conversation on the other side of the door ratcheted up to a roar. One eyeball throbbed to the rhythm of a marching band. And her brain was shot through with pain.

Panic time.

She walked toward the closet to fetch—what? The distance of four feet was too far. Off balance, she leaned against the wall for a moment, and then set out again on wooden legs, swing-out, jerk-and-drop puppet legs.

The roaring stopped. The world went silent. Alma stood still in the center of the room, calm and floaty. Her journey to the closet was forgotten.

Perfect peace.

She could feel the planet turning on its axis, moving through space. She looked down at her bare feet with a sense of awe. The boundary of skin fell away. Alma and the moon, the door and the floor, inside and outside, they were all one—the actress and the universe. She could not find her way across the room, yet everything in creation was known to her.

Euphoria.

Tingling now. The buzzing of flesh.

Flooding her breast in a strong wave, a million bee steps whooshed up her throat. She snapped back into the solid, dangerous world. Shock. Pain unending. Stabbing, stabbing. Alma folded down to the floor and fumbled with the fallen pill bottles. One would fly her up, and one would take her down. Which one would kill the pain? The labels were meaningless ciphers of squiggles and lines.

Pick one!

She held a pharmacy bottle in her hand, but she had no idea how to remove the cap. Her other hand was useless.

And outside the door, she heard Bugsy say, "Curtain in fifteen minutes."

Axel Clayborne was about to walk onstage when he heard Cyril Buckner's hoarse whisper of "Oh, shit!" And then, in an egregious breach of backstage etiquette that demanded quiet, Detective Mallory yelled, "Is that ambulance still parked outside?"

Axel stepped back into the wings and turned toward the staircase.

Oh, *big* trouble.

Bugsy was leading a wobbly Alma Sutter down the steps. She was barefoot, wearing only a robe and not a jot of makeup. One of the actress's arms was draped around the gopher's neck and the other one hung limp at her side.

Mallory stood at the bottom of the stairs, shouting commands to bring the ambulance down the alley. Now she called out to another detective, "Gonzales! Grab those stagehands!"

Gentle as a nanny, Bugsy settled Alma down on a trunk.

She was trying to talk to him, but her mouth only worked on one side, and all her words were strangled gibberish.

The ambulance crew barreled through the alley door.

Axel turned to a clock on the back wall. Ten minutes to curtain.

One of the medics guided Alma to a gurney, while the other man in white talked to Mallory, raising his voice to ask, "What *kind* of drugs?"

"I'll find out," she said.

Ted Randal and Joe Garnet were dragged before her, and she pointed at the actress being strapped to the gurney. "She's stroking out! Tell me what fried her brain! What did you give her?" And when she got no response, she said, "Gonzales! Cuffs!" And the man promptly twisted Garnet's hands behind his back to put him in handcuffs. Another detective stepped in to do the honors for Randal.

"Follow the ambulance to the hospital," said Mallory. "On the way, find out what they sold Alma tonight."

Axel wondered if Cyril Buckner might blow out his teeth trying to hold back a scream. That reddening face was an early warning sign of—

Ah, here it comes. *Kaboom!*

The stage manager sprinted toward Mallory and made a game attempt to yell at her while whispering, "You're *insane*! The stagehands can't leave *now*!" He threw up both hands, as if to ask how this fact could *possibly* have eluded her. What was she *thinking*?

The young cop ignored him to watch the parade of

medics, teenagers and cops filing off toward the alley door.

Buckner grabbed Bugsy's arm, saying, "You're working the props with me tonight." Then he pointed up the stairs to the dressing rooms. "Get Nan down here."

Seven minutes to curtain, the actor in the fat suit walked out onstage to take his place on the brass bed in the spotlight, where he arranged his blanket and waited for the curtains to part.

"Get out of our way, kid." The whispering wardrobe lady sported a change of clothes and her new wig, the blond one. "We go on stage in five minutes."

The Rinaldi twins hung back, their eyes on the detective, regarding her as if she might be a live bomb.

Mallory, feeling no urgency at all, stood in the wings, blocking the doorway in the scenery. "*Very* quick change." She assessed the woman's stage costume, an expensive improvement over what Alma had worn for the part. And the makeup was expertly applied—time consuming. "All this on a few minutes' notice."

"Yeah, I heard a rumor that Alma died. A little premature, but what the hell."

The electronic squeak of a public address system was followed by Cyril Buckner's voice announcing a replacement actress, Nanette Darby. The audience cheered and applauded this famous name from another era. There was no mention of the other actress, the one taken away by ambulance.

And good night, Alma.

Mallory casually reached out to touch the older woman's cashmere lapel. "I like the blazer."

"Thanks. I should've gotten the name of your tailor, but I guess it'll do. Four minutes to curtain. You're waiting for a heart attack? Wouldn't it be quicker to stab me?" The blazer was opened, exposing her breast for a target.

Damn. Too much moxie. No show of nerves. Not *yet.*

The detective glanced back over one shoulder to see the stage manager standing in the doorway on the other side of the set. He lifted three fingers to her, signaling only three minutes to go. "Nan, you miscounted." Mallory turned back to the actress—who was *smiling.*

She must fix that.

"Buckner thinks you're me." Nan Cooper raised both hands to frame her face in a check-me-out gesture. "Recognize yourself, kid?"

"No, I don't see it." Mallory dipped one hand inside her blazer and pulled out the revolver. "The gun makes all the difference." With equal weight to every syllable, she said, "It changes the way you walk—the way you talk." She had not expected fear from this woman, but there *was* jacked-up anxiety. Finally—something useful.

"You're *arresting* me?" The woman's spread hands moved up and down like pump handles as she said, "What? What's it gonna take?" She shot a look at the clock. "Two minutes to go."

And Buckner would not hold the curtain. He believed that Nan was already in position—in the doorway—where the detective stood.

Nan, are you frantic yet?

Getting there.

Mallory raised her eyes to the dressing rooms above. She spoke in the slow and easy way of opining on the weather. "I can almost see you sitting up there, all dressed to go onstage . . . waiting for something to happen to Alma." She smiled at the older woman. "Sort of like a spider."

"Buckner's idea. Alma's been getting more screwed up every day. Tonight, he wanted me ready to step into the role." Nan snapped her fingers. "That fast." She turned to the clock. *"We're down to one minute!"*

And *now* Mallory stood aside.

The houselights went out. Riker leaned toward the man from Nebraska. "Showtime, pal."

The sheriff's badge was pinned to his lapel, and it gleamed as the curtains were drawn to expose the brightly lit stage.

Before the actor on the brass bed could say his first line, he won a round of applause just for being famous. Then Nanette Darby made her entrance by a door in the scenery, walking backward to another round of applause and closely followed by the Rinaldi brothers, who were herding her onto the stage.

The impersonation of Mallory was spot-on tonight, and Sheriff Harper was startled.

Riker's cell phone vibrated in his pocket. He checked the text on the small screen. The plane had arrived on time, but Janos and his passenger were stuck in traffic.

———————

Onstage, Axel Clayborne shouted his line, "Find a chair for our guest!"

In the semidarkness of the wings, a pair of doors in the scenery opened onto the lights of the stage. One of the Rinaldi brothers reached in and rolled out the empty wheelchair.

When the other twin had closed the doors, the new stagehands, Bugsy and Cyril Buckner, watched the actors through the louvered slats. Each of them had a pair of night-vision goggles slung around their necks by straps. Behind them was the second wheelchair that held the mannikin, and behind that—a surprise.

"You *always* knew about Alma's drugs," said Mallory.

Buckner turned around, saying softly, "No talking backstage. I *told* you—"

"Then you better start whispering fast," she said, making no effort to tone down her voice.

"It was a gradual thing," said the stage manager, barely audible. "I didn't see it in the beginning. Alma didn't drop lines at first, but Dickie was on her—"

"Who got stoned first, Dickie or Alma?" Mallory rolled one hand to say keep talking—or *she* would do the talking, and she would be loud. This threat worked better than bullets.

He whispered, "Dickie. The first time he got high, we were starting the second week of rehearsals."

"Yeah," said Bugsy, "then Alma went nuts a few days

later. That's when she saw the first threat on the blackboard."

So Axel Clayborne had lied. He had not gone after
Alma from the beginning. Everything hung on that second week.

Only a few lights burned backstage. Soon all of them
would be turned off. The slightest light would blind them
during the blackout scenes. All of this was explained to
Mallory when Buckner learned that every detective out
in the audience and those backstage carried flashlights.
"Don't cripple us, okay? That's all I'm asking."

Mallory was not listening. Eyes on the louvered slats,
she watched the twins exit by a door on the far side of the
stage, where Detective Washington would pick up the
surveillance. The play had already gone on for too long.
What was keeping Janos?

Riker checked his watch. *Damn.* The timing would be
close.

Where the hell was Janos and their witness?

The Rinaldi brothers stood by the window in the scenery, and the actor on the bed explained that they were
gathering dead flies from the sill. "Every boy needs a
hobby," said Clayborne.

Riker's cell phone vibrated. He glanced at the small
screen, and then turned to see Janos coming through the
lobby doors.

Preceded by a flashlight beam, the large detective made
his way down the aisle, pushing a passenger in a wheel-

chair toward the front row. Janos parked the chair next to the sheriff's aisle seat. And then he made a production of fussing with a lap rug, draping it over the Nebraskan's withered legs. The young man's wan face bore a passing resemblance to the Rinaldi brothers.

The sheriff turned to the invalid. Each nodded to the other in the way of old acquaintances passing on the street.

Onstage, one of the twins was watching. With no prompt of a word or a nudge, his brother turned around to stare at the new arrival in the audience. And Riker smiled. These two had silently identified their Nebraska cousin, Wheelchair Boy, who now returned this favor with a look of fear.

Janos, the consummate deal closer, whispered to the young man in the wheelchair, "They're *still* scary, aren't they, Billy?"

And the invalid nodded.

Close enough.

They now had a positive identification. As the twins made their stage exit, Riker texted his partner a simple message, GREEN LIGHT. This was her cue to execute the John Doe arrest warrants.

The stage lights went out. A spotlight came on over the brass bed. And the detective settled back to wait for the scene with the baseball bat—and the arrest—with no worries.

In the blackout darkness, a uniformed officer stood by the fuse box, listening to sounds, tiny ones. Clicks? He had the sense of someone close by, and he reached out into space, but touched nothing. The feeling passed off.

Cyril Buckner, in night-vision goggles, rolled Nan backward into the wings. Bugsy replaced her onstage with the mannikin in the second wheelchair. After locking the wheels with a stage brace, he ran back to the wings and whipped off his own goggles. And now the three of them watched the stage lights come on, flickering through the slats in the scenery doors. Onstage, Axel Clayborne swung the bat. The mannikin's head went flying, and the audience cheered until they were plunged into total blackness once more.

Behind Nan's wheelchair, the stage manager and the gopher put on their goggles again. Now a bright light was trained on their eyes, and they stifled cries of pain.

The goggles were ripped from Bugsy's head. All he could see was the afterimage of twin suns scorched into his retinas.

Cyril Buckner's goggles were also stolen. Eyes on fire, his blind, probing hands found the wheelchair. He felt his way down Nan's arm and pressed a cigarette lighter into the palm of her hand, saying, "You have to collect the bat and the mannikin head. Get another pair of goggles from the prop box. Run!"

She flicked the lighter, and by that little flame, made her way around the stage set.

Onstage, the bat was ripped from Axel's hand. On this cue, and by memory of pace, the sightless actor turned and counted his steps back to the brass bed.

The only light was green, a wavelength seen through the night-vision goggles as the twins flew down the steps, armed with a metal pipe and a baseball bat. The audience sat in darkness, facing the stage, their unseeing eyes wide with anticipation, waiting for the light, oblivious to the goggled predators closing in on the young man in the wheelchair.

Hello, Billy boy. Long time no see.

Weapons rising, another thought was shared between the twins: *Oh, won't he be surprised?*

One brother could not help himself. He giggled.

The lame cousin, stone blind in the dark, turned his face toward them. Startled. Frightened. He *knew* that sound.

Another beam of green crossed theirs, and the twins turned to see Mallory wearing goggles—and holding a gun on them.

The detective watched the backs of them running off in the quick-scrabble way of insects—down the front row of seats—up the stairs to the stage. She ripped off her goggles and yelled, "Runners!"

Five stalks of yellow light appeared in the audience, and detectives ran down the aisles.

Riker flashed a strong beam on the sheriff. "Wheel Billy into the lobby. Make sure the uniforms got the top of the alley covered. *Run* for it!"

Backstage, Mallory yelled, *"Gil! Lights!"*

Gil Preston flicked on a penlight and madly flipped the switches on his board. *Nothing* worked—*zip!* He grabbed the rail of the catwalk and looked down on yellow beams crisscrossing the stage. It had to be the fuse box. Penlight in his teeth, he climbed down the catwalk ladder.

Ushers in the aisles were also brandishing flashlights, and the sheriff grabbed one as he pushed the wheelchair into the lobby to see uniformed officers standing before the street door. "You got the alley covered?" And one answered, "We got a man inside the alley door. Big guy. Nobody's gettin' past *him*."

One man. An *inside* man.

Backstage, Gil Preston approached the rear wall, and a uniformed officer waved a flashlight to ward him off, saying, "Nobody touches the fuse box!" And Gil said, "Are you nuts?" Oh, poor choice of words. The cop shoved him.

Bugsy's fingers were pressed to his eyes, no relief from the balls of light that killed his vision. He felt a blow to his back, and lost all the air in his lungs. His legs were hit with something hard, and he heard the sound of his own bones breaking. Hands were on him, dragging him across the floor, and he was sliding into shock, no thought of calling out. Over the floor, under the hanging clothes of the wardrobe rack, out the other side by the wall. Another crack to his legs. Fresh pain! Oh, *God*! Now his arm. Crack and splinter. His head was awash in a warm flow of blood. It ran down his face. Into his eyes. His mouth.

"Scream," said a whispered voice in his ear. "Scream *loud*," said the other Rinaldi brother.

And Bugsy *howled*.

Footsteps—so many. Pounding, *pounding*. They all came running.

The uniformed officer who blocked the stage door left

his post, and so did the cop by the fuse box. Well, *finally*. Gil popped the metal door open and flicked all the levers, resetting every fuse. Now the wall switch. And there was light.

The wardrobe rack was pushed aside. Mallory looked down at the writhing gopher. Bleeding. Broken. Crying.

Eyes closing.

Quiet now.

The sheriff stood alone at the mouth of the alley. He had never drawn a weapon in the line of duty, only on the firing range, and he was no great marksman. But it might not come to that. His hand rested on the grip of his sidearm. Ready. Waiting. *If* they got away—they'd come *this* way.

At the other end of the alley, a door flew open. The twins ran out. The sheriff drew his gun and hollered, "Hello, boys! We got a plane to catch!"

What the hell was wrong with those two? They were grinning at him. Daring him to fire? Damn boys and their games. One skinny runt held a baseball bat, one held a pipe—red with blood, and there was splatter on their clothes.

What have you done?

Both their weapons raised to swing, they walked toward him, shoulder to shoulder, like they planned to come right through him. For a second, he thought maybe they could. Little monsters, scary like the dead of night when a cockroach twitches out of a drain in a bathroom sink—ice-for-blood scary. "That's far enough." They kept on coming, grinning, slow-stepping. Coming to get him. One made a practice swing with his bat.

"Stop!" yelled the sheriff. "I'll drop you if you don't—"

Oh, *hell*! Where did she *come* from?

There was Mallory creeping up the alley, witched up out of thin air. And where was *her* damn gun? He had no shot. She held no weapon. And the young cop was in no hurry, either.

Damn it, girl.

The twins were closing the distance, bat and pipe at the ready, fixing to strike him dead. He looked down at his gun—useless till they got within a safe range for placing two bullets and missing the girl. If they put on some speed, one of them would get him for sure.

The young cop was right behind them! A tall one, she had some size on them, but girls had no muscle for—

Mallory raised both hands. *No—call 'em claws.* The sheriff thought his lungs would burst, and still he did not draw a breath. His firearm was on the rise. Steady, steady. Taking aim. *No* shot. The girl was too close, right on top of them, her face full of hate. In a move almost too fast to follow, she ripped the baseball bat from the hands of one twin. And now, in a rage unholy, she made a mighty swing—and slammed both their skulls with one crack.

A sick sound.

They dropped like dead weight at her feet.

The bat clattered to the pavement.

Past anger now, she watched them for an idle moment as blood pooled round their broken heads.

Satisfied, girl? They're not goin' anywhere.

Yes, she was done with them, strolling back down the alley, calmly issuing orders into her cell phone—just another night in New York City. And the sheriff's heart was hammering. *Oh, my.* He had to get out of this town.

SUSAN: When?
ROLLO: I didn't think you'd want
       to know. . . . I wouldn't.
                    —<u>The Brass Bed</u>, Act III

34 There were no screams on this floor of the hospital. The patients of the intensive care unit were the quiet ones, the critical cases who *might* live. Most of the civilian visitors had left the waiting room, gone off to sleep in beds provided for family members.

No sleep for the police.

Riker sat down beside the sheriff's chair and leaned back. *Easy* does it. Janos and Washington remained standing; they had other rooms to visit, other traps to spring.

Sheriff Harper closed his magazine. "Did she have to crack their damn skulls?"

"You think she should've used her gun?" Riker shook his head. "Naw, Mallory's no backshooter. Too much paperwork. You got no idea what cops go through to spend a bullet in this town." And Internal Affairs would have confiscated her weapon pending a hearing. But one cop up against two armed killers? Breaking skulls would probably get her a commendation for restraint. "Hey, the damage looked a lot worse than it was. No brains leakin' out, nothin' like that."

"So the twins are alive."

Janos smiled. "Oh, better than that, Sheriff. They're awake. Our guys are taking their statements right now."

"Yeah." Detective Washington also smiled down on the out-of-towner—as if that might be true, though it was only half a lie. The Rinaldi brothers *were* awake, but they lacked the proper incentive to incriminate themselves.

Riker's head rolled back. He closed his eyes, playing harmless when he said, "Looks like we're gonna wrap up your massacre tonight. . . . The boys were what—twelve when they killed their family? Damn shame. They'll get tried in kiddie court for sure." Eyes only half open, he turned to the sheriff. "I got twenty bucks that says you can't nail 'em for more than six years' jail time."

Harper seemed more relaxed. And relieved? Oh, he was definitely buying into the idea that they might actually let him take those monsters home to stand trial in Nebraska. The man lightly slapped one knee in a silent *hallelujah*. "So where'd you stash Billy?"

"Wheelchair Boy? He's in good hands." Riker loosened his tie, as if he might be winding down for the night. "Billy's the one you really care about, right?"

The sheriff sat up straight, eyes narrowing. "Exactly *what* did my ex-wife tell you?"

"She said Cousin Billy wasn't in a wheelchair back then. He was bedridden." Riker had enjoyed that cozy interview. The lady's obscenities were colorful, and her memory was long. "So, after the massacre, you put him up in your guest room. But your *wife* was the one who had to nursemaid Billy. And she was the one who got that kid into physical therapy—so he could use a wheelchair—and wheel it the hell out of her house." Though the woman had not used any four-letter words as tame as *hell*. "But even after she got Billy a job and a place of his own, she *still* had to cook him dinner every damn Sunday for years. *Your* idea."

"Did she say anything else?" The sheriff, a man still in love with his ex, had a lot riding on that long-distance conversation.

"What *could* she say?" Riker picked up a magazine and slowly turned pages. "You never told her the houseguest was a stone killer."

The sheriff was silent. And this was as good as a guilty plea with respect to the cousin's part in the massacre. Riker gave the nod to Janos and Washington, and the detectives strolled down the hall on their way to interview the twins—to play them against their wheelchair-bound conspirator.

Riker tossed his magazine on the table and picked up another one. "The twins weren't all that smart. But their cousin spent two years in that bed, spinning his plans. . . . It was the perfect alibi that got to you, wasn't it?"

"That *did* get my attention," said Sheriff Harper. "Billy hadn't been out of that house in years. And then, that night of all nights—"

"Yeah, you knew he was in on it."

"Damn right. Little kids don't kill for insurance money they can't spend, a house they can't sell. But their cousin had just turned eighteen, old enough for guardianship status. I guess he didn't count on another relative popping up outta nowhere to claim the twins. Who'd *want* 'em, right? Billy thought he'd get control over all the—"

"And Billy could stand trial as an adult. But you needed his cousins to rat him out in court." And now for the bad news. "You'll have to wait a few years for the twins. New York's got first claim."

"That ain't *right*!" An angry Sheriff Harper rose from his chair. "Mass murder trumps assault any day. They only *beat* that man tonight."

"The charge is assault with intent to kill," said Riker, "and the night's not over yet."

The sheriff had departed for the station house in SoHo. As a courtesy, he would be allowed to sit in on an interview with the twins' cousin—while the NYPD wrapped his old murder case.

The hospital waiting room was littered with cast-off coats, paper cups and candy wrappers. Mallory's shearling jacket was draped on the chair next to Riker's. He glanced at the white envelope protruding from a pocket, surprised to see the seal still intact. Heller had personally delivered this illicit lab test on Alma's hair. After extorting the man to get it, how could his partner have forgotten to read it? She was not in the game anymore—barely present. She had taken to haunting a stretch of the hallway outside the doors to the intensive care unit.

Charles Butler had arrived only to discover that Bugsy would be allowed no visitors tonight. And so he was given another job, translating medical jargon for the police. The psychologist stood at the center of the room, scanning a chart *borrowed* from Alma Sutter's berth in the ICU. "She's listed as critical. It might be hours before they know if the brain damage is permanent. She has to be awake for the—" Charles looked up from the chart. "There's a possibility that she'll never wake up."

This was not what the detectives wanted to hear, and five men finished the dregs of their coffee in silence.

Leonard Crippen was another visitor turned away from the gopher's bedside. He sat in a far corner of the room with only a potted plant for company. By Riker's lights, this man had taken the news of Bugsy's pain and suffering all too well. The theater critic rose from his seat and tried to introduce himself to Charles Butler—the perfect gentleman—who turned his back on the old man's extended hand and walked away from him to stand beside Riker's chair. The tired detective looked up to ask, "What's that about?"

Charles would not say. He only shook his head. It was an easy guess that the man's silence must be on Mallory's account—another damn game of keep-away. What did she have on that critic? What might she be holding back tonight?

She drifted into the waiting room, pausing now to watch snow falling past the window, and then she aimlessly wandered on.

"We'll stay," said Riker, "me and Mallory. You guys go home. Get some sleep."

Gonzales and Lonahan rose from their chairs and shrugged into their coats.

Detective Sanger kept his seat and crushed an empty paper cup in one hand. "I count *four* first acts. Does anybody know how this damn play ends?"

"I do." Charles Butler's worried eyes were following Mallory's travels up and down the corridor. "You won't *like* the ending."

And when no more was volunteered, Sanger pointed an accusing finger at Janos. "I know *you* read it!"

"Oh, let *me* tell it," said the grinning drama critic, *completely* recovered from the distress over Bugsy's injuries. "It's all about seduction. That's the foundation, the—"

"Hey." Sanger turned his bloodshot eyes to Crippen. "The *short* version, okay?"

"Yes, of course. In the second act, the twins open the window . . . and you *know* someone has to go out that window."

Gonzales and Lonahan sat down.

The critic continued. "The tension is unbearable—a truly frightening scene. The terror builds into the third act. And then it stops. Rollo and Susan turn to each other for comfort, ultimately seeking physical contact and solace. He takes her hands in his, a *very* tender moment." Crippen sighed and placed one hand on his breast. "The heart breaks." Done with heartbreak, he smiled. "Rollo offers Susan the protection of his arms.

He won't let them take her. The moment she climbs onto the bed, he enfolds her in an embrace. They kiss. . . . The heart *soars*."

The critic was on his feet, both hands clenched. "And then Rollo shouts, *'Geronimo!'* The twins rush into the room. They swing the bed around on its wheels and ram it toward the window. Rollo spreads his arms, as if to fly. The bed stops short. *Susan* flies backward. *Out* the window she goes. And you hear her scream taper off as she falls to her death. Then Rollo laughs and yells, 'Bring me another woman!'"

The old man made a deep bow from the waist. "And . . . curtain."

The detectives stared at him, incredulous, till Sanger said, "That's *it*? That's *all*?"

"Well, it's very dark comedy, true," said Crippen. "But you—"

"I'm outta here," said Gonzales.

Three detectives rose in unison and filed out of the waiting room.

Leonard Crippen turned from Janos to Riker. "Tough audience. Perhaps they didn't like the end because the actress looks so much like one of their own." He turned his eyes to Mallory, who paced the hallway outside the ICU. "They identify with *her*."

"Naw, it's just a crummy ending," said Riker. "When civilians see the whole play, they won't like it any better."

"Oh, but they *will*." Crippen waited for Riker to bite—but that was never going to happen. The critic sighed. "You see, Detective Mallory let me read an early version of the ghostwriter's play, and it had one grave flaw. The role of Susan was originally written for a *sympathetic* character."

Down the hall, Mallory caught Riker watching her. She turned her back on him, not inviting any company, and he knew better than to offer it. He had a memory of her when she was ten or eleven, a child-size island in a schoolyard teeming with kids at play. All alone. Always. She was only taller now.

"On opening night, and the next night," said Crippen, who would *not* shut up, "the audience *liked* the character of Susan. When she was struck with a bat in the first act, they were stunned—dead quiet. None of them would've applauded her death in the final act. In *that* version, the ending would never work. But then, along came Detective Mallory."

The ghostwriter's muse.

Riker knew what was coming next. Had it already occurred to her? Maybe not. He hoped not, for he was in the camp that believed she could be hurt.

"On the *third* night," said Crippen, "when the actress took on the cold, somewhat *cruel* persona of Detective Mallory, a character *no one* was rooting for . . . the audience only sympathized with Rollo. That's why the crowd cheered when he knocked off her head in the first act. Well, *now* you can see why the ending *will* work. The audience is going to *love* it when she—"

"*Don't* say it!" Charles Butler, double fisted, stood before the drama critic and leaned down, eye to eye with the old man. "Don't *print* it!" And he never had to add

the words, *I'll kill you if you do.* His face was not so comical right now. Anger looked good on him.

"So, Charles," said Riker, "wanna borrow my gun?"

Mildly distracted from murdering the critic, Charles
was now watching Mallory in the hallway, where she stood
deep in conversation with an ICU nurse. She turned her
head, surprised to see him standing there. He raised both
hands, silently wondering if she needed anything. And
she responded with a tilt of her head to ask, *Why are you
still here?*

The elevator doors opened. Mrs. Rains stepped out on
the run, coattail flapping, hair flying, hurrying toward
the doors of the ICU, where Mallory held up both hands,
a traffic cop's warning to stop. And Bugsy's mother did
stop. She stood a bit off balance, listening with a slow
shake of the head.

Riker could not hear the words, but he knew all the
signs of denial: Hands rising. No, it *can't* be! One hand
to the breast. Not *my* child! Tight fists. You're *wrong*!

Then Mrs. Rains doubled over, as though she had
taken a sucker punch to the gut. Mallory raised her up by
the shoulders, and the older woman flung her arms
around the young cop's neck. Holding on tight, Mallory
broke the mother's slow slide to the floor.

35

Assigning blame for tragedy was blood sport in New York City.

Reporters were gathered outside the SoHo station house, lying in wait to ambush the detectives of Special Crimes. Tomorrow the bloodletting would escalate when Dr. Slope officially released his finding of murder in the deaths of Dickie Wyatt and Peter Beck. The news media would scream incompetence for allowing the play to go on, and they would demand a head on a spike or, at the very least, a public flogging.

The watchers' room was now a midnight war room of visiting VIPs, the politicians who had botched this night. They were laying schemes to get clean away with it, and Mallory knew that her boss would be their chosen sacrifice—the sin eater.

She ended her cell phone conversation with the lieutenant as she walked down the hospital corridor alongside
her partner. "The stagehands won't stop talking, and the
DA's sweetening their deal every six minutes. Coffey says
they *know* who killed Peter Beck."

"Good. So . . . where to now?"

"The station house," said Mallory. "And then we go
shopping. We need a sin eater."

Riker only nodded, as if this might make sense to
him—eventually.

Janos was waiting for them at the end of the hallway.
He volunteered to stay behind for updates on Alma's
condition. "And I might have another go at the twins,
maybe *tweak* their statements a little."

As Mallory followed Riker into the elevator, Janos
leaned in to startle her with a parting gift—a tissue. Was
this a joke or an insult? The tissue was withdrawn as the
sliding doors were closing. Mallory raised one hand to
her cheek. It was wet. She had splashed cold water on her
face in the ladies' room.

And Janos had taken tap water for tears.

Apparently, so had Riker. The elevator began its slow
descent, and his voice was gentle when he said, "No,
you can't go back up there and shoot the witness." He
glanced at his wristwatch. "It's late, kid. Sanger's gone
home, and Clara Loman's workin' solo tonight. Wanna
call her off?"

"No, she'd keep going anyway—just to make the point
that she doesn't work for us."

Detective Sanger had ruled out this area of TriBeCa as a likely place for Dickie Wyatt's last meal, arguing that an addict only days out of rehab would not go near an old drug buddy. Even a stroll through Axel Clayborne's neighborhood might have triggered a relapse. Sanger's logic had been unassailable, born of his years in Narcotics.

However, Clara Loman was not hampered by that detective tonight.

She sat in the studio apartment of a young man who lived within walking distance of his job in a local restaurant. The hour was late, but the waiter was still wearing his work clothes, dark pants and a white shirt stained with chili.

He was *so* young. So stupid. Though she had shown him her badge, he had invited her in, confident that his air-freshener of canned pine trees masked the aroma of cannabis. An underlying scent was the insect spray that seemed to have no effect on cockroaches. Bugs scattered as she spread her expanded photo array on his rickety coffee table. The waiter looked at each picture carefully, taking his time. He did everything slowly.

He was stoned.

Yet he had no trouble identifying Dickie Wyatt's dinner companion.

The two detectives stood by the lobby doors. Beyond the dark expanse of theater seats, a bright bulb, caged in wire, hung down to light up the center of the stage—and the man sprawled out on the brass bed.

"So that's a ghost light." Riker kept his voice low, minding the acoustics that allowed sound to travel everywhere. "How long has *this* been goin' on?"

"He's been sleeping here since his friend died," said Mallory. "Bugsy never saw him, but he heard the footsteps every night, every morning."

This might be her most subtle punch line. So that was how she knew Dickie Wyatt had died in Axel Clayborne's apartment. The actor could not bear to sleep there anymore. Her other clue had been the dead man's suit, the one worn at the wake, and Riker thought he *might* figure that one out, too.

They walked down the aisle and parted ways at the front row. While Mallory climbed the steps to the stage, Riker chose a seat in the audience. Before sitting down, he donned his bifocals, and now he could clearly see the bedside table laid out with the makings of a private party: a wine bottle, half full, *no* glass, and small, plastic pharmacy containers.

Was every man, woman and child in this town on drugs?

Riker held up a palm-size device and a small microphone for the actor to see. "We gotta record the interview. Okay by you?"

"Fine, whatever you need." Axel Clayborne propped himself up on one elbow and smiled to see Mallory walk out of the shadows to stand beneath the ghost light. "Hel*lo*."

She held up a Miranda card and read the first line of

the actor's constitutional rights. "You have the right to remain silent."

"Allow me," he said. "I've played a lot of cops. I can also have an attorney during questioning. *And*, if I don't keep my mouth shut, anything I say can be used to savage me in court. Did I miss something?"

"No, that's the gist of it." Mallory placed the card on the table and handed him a pen. "Just sign at the bottom to waive the attorney . . . unless—"

"Anything for you." Clayborne swung his legs over the side of the bed and signed away all his rights with a flourish and a smile.

That was way too easy. How wasted could this man be? Riker hit the recorder's rewind button to play back the last few words, but Clayborne's voice betrayed no slurs of booze or drugs to taint the interview. The detective relaxed into a slouch. *On with the show.* Soon the actor would forget that he was being taped. Even hard-core felons tended to forget—when there was no lawyer around to remind them.

Clayborne pulled up his legs to sit yoga style. "So this is about the Rinaldi twins. You're pissed off, right? Sorry about the carnage. Well, I kept my word. I took that old script and their notes to the station house after—"

"I know." Mallory sat down in the only chair, the wheelchair. "Thanks."

He smoothed back his hair, primping for her. "Will I be a witness in court?"

"For the massacre? No, that won't go to trial." Her hands worked the wheels, and she rolled the chair back and forth. "A Nebraska sheriff is on his way home with three confessions."

"Three?" His head turned to follow the slow progress of the chair wheeling to the other side of the bed.

"The twins did all the slaughtering," she said on the roll, "but the massacre was planned by an older kid . . . an invalid. That would be *your* character, the one you made up for the play. He was a cousin, not a brother, but you were close." She wheeled the chair behind the bed and into the shadows beyond the glow of the ghost light.

Clayborne twisted around to grip the brass bars at the head of the bed frame. "A *third* survivor."

"Just like your play." She piloted the wheelchair back into the light.

"Art inadvertently imitating life." He turned around again to face her. "So I was—"

"Another killer . . . playing a killer." She rolled up close to the bed.

He lost his smile.

She rolled back and away.

Axel Clayborne rose from the mattress and followed her across the stage.

Riker wished the recorder could catch this. It was almost like slow dancing.

"You think *I* murdered Peter?"

"The twins didn't do it." Mallory turned the chair in his direction. "Those freaks only know one way to kill. It has to be brutal. It has to be *fun.*" Spinning the wheels, she circled around him. "Beck's murder was quick. No fear, no pain. *Not* their style."

"Well, it wasn't me." The actor slowly revolved to watch her as she wheeled around and around him in a widening orbit. Now he stood still, eyes focused on nothing. He snapped his fingers. "It had to be Alma." He turned to the wheelchair—the *empty* chair.

Mallory stood in deep shadow. "*Alma?* A *junkie* with split-second timing?"

"She managed that kind of timing in every performance. Speed was never her problem. Her cocaine was probably *laced* with speed."

"It *was.* . . . You should know." The young cop walked into the pool of light. "You're the reason Alma took all those drugs. Hiding in the walls, scratching on the blackboard. Threatening her—*torturing* her." Grabbing the back of the wheelchair, Mallory aimed it at him and gave it a shove. "Was that *fun* for you?"

Clayborne never tried to get out of the way. Riker glanced at the bedside table and its stash of drink and drugs enough to dull the reflexes. Was this why his partner had wanted audio only, no video tonight? Had she paid a visit to the actor's neighborhood pharmacy—and maybe a few liquor stores as well? Riker could never ask. *Plausible deniability* was his mantra now.

The empty wheelchair rolled to a stop a bare inch short of touching the actor, who was *acting* sober when he said, "Alma's the logical choice."

Mallory sank down on the edge of the mattress. "And you know that because . . . you played *cops* in the movies." She thumped the table with her hand. Once, twice, three times.

Riker smiled. Cats did that with their tails. First, this warning. Then the claws. The teeth.

The actor, obviously unacquainted with any cats, stepped up to the other side of the brass bed, so confident when he spoke to her back. "Peter ordered Alma to walk out on the play. He told her to do it *on opening night*."

"Yeah, *right*," said Mallory, all but yawning.

"I was hiding in the wall. I heard everything—well, Alma's end of it. She was on the phone with Peter—hysterical—and with good reason. She'd never get another shot at a Broadway play. *No* talent. And the little dummy's just barely bright enough to understand that. But her boyfriend was hell-bent on shutting us down."

"Was he?" Rising from the bed, Mallory pretended interest in the wine bottle's label. "All Beck had to do was bow out. Without his name on the contract, the Chicago investors would've shut you down—and sued you. They financed *his* play, not yours. Who throws money at hack amateurs?"

Struck dumb, Axel Clayborne mimed the word, *WHAT?*

Charles Butler had made the right call: This actor *was* a flaming narcissist with an ego that had no boundaries. So the loss of financing had never occurred to Clayborne. How could the backers fail to fall in love with the ghost-writer's play? And Riker could see the man had it in mind to challenge Mallory on that account.

But now Clayborne shrugged off her insult. "Peter threatened to blow up his contract twice a day. Ask anyone. He had this little bit of power, but he could only use it once."

"It kept him in the game," said Mallory. "He was fighting for his play."

"No, no, *no*." The actor shook his head, as if saddened by this foolish child—who carried a gun. "You miss the point. *Peter* was torturing Alma, *extorting* her. And when she *didn't* walk out on opening night, she knew he'd— Oh, wait! Here's another motive—she's in Peter's will."

"I don't think that'll work, either." Mallory's smile said it better: *You lose.* "Peter Beck's lawyer got the revised will today. He would've had it sooner, but the snowstorm backed up mail delivery. The man left everything to his favorite bartender."

"But *Alma* didn't know that."

"She was *damn* sure he wrote her out of the will. We've got her sworn statement. Alma even got the date right for the *new* will."

"Well, that was smart. She probably goaded him into it. She was laying plans to—"

"Alma's smart or she's dumb," said Mallory. "Pick one. Stick with it."

"*I* didn't murder Peter."

"You murdered *Alma*," said Mallory, as if she might be correcting him on a matter as small as the time of day. "She's brain-dead. We're waiting for her parents to fly in from Ohio and pull the plug on her respirator. Five minutes later, we charge you with—"

"She fried her own brain with drugs! You were *there*!"

Riker's eyes darted from one to the other, keeping up with the volley of salvos flying across the brass bed.

"It would've been kinder to slit her throat," said Mallory. "You just *had* to drag it out."

"What p-possible reason—"

"Your best friend wanted her out of the play. *There's* a reason. I know he was on her back every day in rehearsals. Dickie Wyatt put her through hell."

"No, Alma was just too stupid to appreciate a gifted director. She hated him for—"

"That's the way you saw it? Alma *hated* him?" Mallory folded her arms, and it was only her stance that said, *Prove it.*

Dig a hole.

Fall in.

"She resented him from the first day," said Clayborne. "Pill-popping ingrate, she—"

"That early on, you *knew* she was using?" And Mallory knew it, too, but now her hands were riding her hips to call him a liar.

"Well, she wasn't exactly a junkie, not then anyway. But I know she was scoring Ecstasy, some weed and—"

"Party drugs," said Mallory. "Just a recreational user. And *that's* why you blamed her for Wyatt's relapse?" By her tone, she might have asked, *Are you a moron?* And now, done with sarcasm—a touch of pure incredulity. "You figured she dosed him to get even?"

"I *know* she did." He was smug, the one with all the answers, so happy to guide the young cop who was leading him. *Hold it.* The actor had the look of a man who had dropped something, lost something. What was he missing? When, exactly *when*, had he accused Alma Sutter of doping his friend?

Ah, New York City rules: You lose your breath, you lose your turn.

And Mallory said, "So Wyatt was getting high on drugs. When? In the second week of rehearsals? That's when Alma got your first threat on the blackboard." She rounded the bed, closing the distance between them. "And the twins say that's when you set them loose on her." Mallory stopped short of striking distance. "The Rinaldi brothers only have one trick—they scare people."

Clayborne had no comeback line, but that look in his eyes said *caught* to every cop ever born.

Mallory's cue. "Between you and the twins, Alma was scared all the time. Nerves shot to hell. And the stage-hands always had pills for that, lots of them. Garnet and Randal could hardly wait to rat you out. You paid them so much cash—a drug scholarship for Alma. They sold her dope for next to nothing."

"I never—"

"You had them take notes on every damn thing they gave her. That sounds like an itemized bill to me. Their list has a drug that didn't show up in Alma's hair-strand test. So I know a few of her early buys were for somebody else— the same drug that got your friend high in rehearsals."

"I *knew* it!" He stamped one foot to punctuate the *damn* in "God, *damn* her!" Eyes rolled up, Clayborne raised a fist. And Riker, film buff extraordinaire, was reminded of one of the actor's old movie roles, that of a hellfire preacher.

"That *bitch*," said Mallory in a guttural tone of *Yay, brother, I hear you*. Mirroring the actor, she clenched one hand on the rise. "What she did to him was *sick*!"

Clayborne nodded his amen to that. "Twisted *bitch*!" Still playing the righteous role, he raised his eyes to the catwalk, as if a prop god might be perched up there. "I'm glad she's dead!"

"She had it coming," said Mallory. "Payback! Eye for an eye!"

And now, brother, *testify*.

"Damn *right*!" Startled, Clayborne took a step back, waving one hand, fast and jerky, trying to erase his words from the air.

Riker counted out three beats to Mallory's kill shot.

"But Alma was innocent. She's not the one who dosed your friend."

Punch line.

"Dickie Wyatt was God to her," said Mallory. "Alma would've slit her wrists to please him. And you *missed* that. You miss everything that isn't *all* about *you*. You never saw how hard she worked just to make him smile. She took every damn thing he could throw at her. Alma was *happy* to take it. She wanted more. . . . I saw her cry the night we found his body."

Clayborne shook his head. What was he missing now? "I don't—"

"After you and the twins went to work on her, Alma

was screwing up, forgetting lines. She needed coke to focus, pills to sleep. And *more* drugs, *killer* amounts, just to get her through the days. But it was taking her so *long* to OD. She wasn't dying *fast* enough, and you couldn't figure out why."

In a telling gesture, he raised his eyebrows to ask if Mallory had the answer to that one, and she waited him out until he said, "But *you* know."

"The *play* was keeping Alma alive. All she had—all she *wanted*—was her part in that play, and she held on tight. Alma *couldn't* let go of her life."

On that note of actual feeling, Riker was stunned. Pity for a junkie? From Mallory?

"You were wrong about Alma's perfect timing." Now every human quality was gone from her voice, and Mallory the Machine said, "During the blackout, the stage-hands noticed she was a few seconds late getting back to the wheelchair . . . wearing night-vision goggles. . . . Yeah, you got that one thing right. Peter Beck still wanted his play back—*and* his girl. He never signed the papers to break his contract. He was still holding it over Alma's head, the one thing that would've done her in. That's how she saw it. Life or death. And she killed Peter Beck . . . before he could kill the play."

Axel Clayborne was slow to grasp this—his own lie come true. Clearly, he had never believed that the actress could have murdered the playwright.

"Alma was pretty far gone when she slit Beck's throat," said Mallory. "The doctors say she was brain damaged before she stroked out. Judgment shot to hell. Hopped up and half dead from all those drugs. And *so* scared. *Your* work. The way I see it . . . you killed them both."

Mallory drew a cutthroat line across her neck to end the taping.

Almost poetic.

Riker nodded and depressed the stop button on the recorder. "Thanks for running your mouth," he said to the actor. "That's all we need."

"For what?" Clayborne watched him wrap the microphone wire around the recorder. He had forgotten that he was being taped. "*I* didn't kill anyone."

"You *murdered* them." Mallory sounded weary. How many ways did she have to say this? If not for Axel Clayborne, those two people would be alive tonight. "We didn't expect a confession. The tape is for the medical examiner. He's doing Alma's psychological autopsy. We need one for your grand-jury indictment."

"If you wanna plead out on that count," said Riker, "the movie-star deal is usually eight, maybe ten years to life. But that only covers Alma. Trial number two—ricochet rules apply for Peter Beck. You took your best shot at the actress, and a ricochet killed the playwright."

"And then," said Mallory, "there's complicity in the murder of Dickie Wyatt."

What? No, the DA had turned Mallory down on this score. No formal charge could be made in the death of the dead director. But the recorder was no longer taping this. Riker turned to her, silently asking, *What are you*—

"Dickie? No, he wasn't *murdered*." The actor turned

from Riker to Mallory. "I opened my door . . . he fell into my arms and died. It was a drug overdose."

"Murder," said Mallory, "and it's all on you."

"No! I *loved* him!"

"I know you did." She said this with no sarcasm, no irony. "You wanted him to live forever."

He held out his hands, begging her to make sense of this. And she said, "When Bugsy—"

"The *gopher*? You blame *me* for—" Clayborne nodded. "Well, I suppose that one almost makes sense. The twins are *my* monsters, aren't they? I'm sorry that little man got hurt tonight. I'll cover his medical bills. I'll get him the best—"

"He's *dead*!" One tight fist was on the rise, and Mallory brought it *down* on the table. So hard. A *hammer* fall. The flimsy table broke. The pieces of it crashed to the floor with the pills and the bottle, and splashed red wine pooled around the splintered wood. Clayborne stepped back, colliding with the wheelchair. Balance lost, he landed in the seat, the chair rolled backward, and Mallory closed in to stand over him. No way out of that chair.

Riker watched the rage leach out of her face—her fists. Calm again, dead calm, she said, "Back when Alma was only doing party drugs, she scored heroin for her *boyfriend*. I don't think she knew what he was planning. The stagehands watched her hand it off to him. But Beck's tox screen was clean for the past ninety days. You get it now? *He* did the dosing. Dickie Wyatt was enforcing the ghost-writer's changes, and Beck wanted a new director so he could put his play back together again. He only wanted Wyatt *gone* . . . not *dead*."

Mallory moved behind the wheelchair. "Peter Beck was a great playwright." She leaned down close to Clayborne's ear. "Dickie Wyatt always thought so. That's what his agent said at the wake. And *you*? By comparison, you're a monkey who managed to find the right end of a pencil. . . . Did you think Wyatt didn't *know* that?"

Shaking his head, Axel Clayborne tried to rise from the chair.

She placed her hands on his shoulders and pressed down hard. "Even before you pitched him the ghostwriter scam, Wyatt *knew* you were a hack. Years ago, you rewrote that old movie script and made a hash of it. Then you let your friend take the blame. Goodbye Hollywood, goodbye career."

"I made it up to him."

"I know. You pled guilty to Wyatt's drug charge. You went to prison for your best friend. So, when you say you loved him, I believe you. But this time, he only backed you up because he *owed* you. Maybe you thought he *liked* what you did to Peter Beck? When Wyatt left the play, he never said where he was going . . . because he was *done* with you."

"That's not true! When he OD'd, he came to *me* for help."

Mallory put more pressure on his shoulders, vise tight, and ever so softly, she said, "No, that's not what happened. He was two days out of rehab, clean and sober, when he got a phone call . . . an offer to share a meal. Wyatt had a conscience. He couldn't say no. Tonight, a waiter picked Peter Beck's face from a photo array. Odd-looking guy, hard to forget. And he acted strange, too. The waiter remembers him coming in an hour before the dinner crowd. The man had his choice of tables, but he took the worst one—in a corner near the kitchen, and he ordered two meals. He wanted them served before his guest arrived. Beck sat with his back to the room. Nobody saw him doctoring a bowl of chili with a lethal dose of heroin. . . . I guess he believed you when you gave Dickie Wyatt all the credit . . . for driving him *insane*."

Mallory relaxed her grip on Clayborne. He sagged in the chair like he had no bones. And his face was pale—no blood left, either.

But she was not quite done with him. "When Dickie Wyatt left that restaurant, the snowstorm was in full swing. No cabs on the street. So he heads for the subway— *your* neighborhood. He's feeling sick and high. He *knows* he's been drugged, and he knows why he's dying. Can you see Peter Beck walking alongside him, totally crazy, *explaining* it to him? But Wyatt can't call 9-1-1. No cell phone. He left it at home. And every storefront was locked and gated early that night. Now here's the part that'll just . . . *kill* you. He walked right past the subway, where he could've gotten help. He didn't even try to save himself. What was the point anymore? Thanks to you, he could *never* get clean again. . . . So he just kept walking. The more he walked, the faster he died."

Clayborne's mouth opened wide, and though he made no sound, Riker fancied that he could hear the man screaming, and that was the way he would remember this night.

Mallory stepped away from the wheelchair and looked down at the fingernails of her gun hand, examining them for imperfections, so bored with the act of gutting a man. Then the hand dropped to her side, and Riker could only read her expression as *Oh, what the hell, one more cut.*

"You know *why* Dickie Wyatt walked all the way to your place? . . . He *knew* you loved him, and he thought it might kill you . . . to watch him *die.*"

The actor's words came out strangled, and he had to say them again. "I *did* love him."

"I know." Mallory hunkered down beside the spill of pharmacy drugs. "I can see you've been grieving." She picked up one container to read the label. "Happy pills for the sad man." After emptying the tablets into her hand, she counted them. "Not many left. You're way over the dosage." The other bottles were held up to the ghost light. "Uppers, downers. You're already walking around in Alma's junkie shoes."

Eye for an eye.

"I warned you," said Mallory. "I *told* you I didn't need a gun to mess you up. When Bugsy died, I called the Chicago investors. They want their money back. They'll get a court order to freeze your assets. And *that's* when I'll come for you. How will you make bail? . . . Not much time left to *grieve*—and get stoned." She took his right hand, filled it with pill bottles and closed his fingers round them—with a *squeeze.* "I've got a bet with my partner. I say you've got no reason to live."

There had been no wager on Clayborne's life. She had lied about that. What rube would bet against her?

Mallory exited stage left, and Riker refrained from applause.

 There was no clock in Charles Butler's kitchen, but a window on the change of seasons kept rough track of time. It was spring.

All his trust issues put to rest, he happily drank the coffee—even though Kathy Mallory had poured it for him. This morning, she had come politely knocking on his door, rather than pick the lock to scare him with another shattering round of Heart Attack Express. They had not played the game in a long time.

Had she tired of it?

Mallory had brought him Sunday editions of every newspaper in the city, a concession to his love of smudgy newsprint, his distaste for the sterile glow of computer text. And he was touched by this gesture.

At first.

Charles set down his cup and picked up the tabloid, not his personal choice, but it lay on top of her stack. The obituary began on the front page, and there he learned that the man's body had been discovered yesterday. However, death had occurred some time ago. Nearly a week had passed since the recluse of recent months had released his bowels and died. Days of decomposition had added to the stink of fecal matter, but within the first hour, flies had come slipping under the door. Maggots had bloomed and multiplied until the neighbors had complained about the incessant buzzing of a thousand insects—so loud, they said—and oh, the smell, so godawful.

Lovely. A touch of horror on the Sabbath.

Well, this *was* a theater town, and he supposed that even a natural demise behind closed doors must have some drama. As he reached out for the second newspaper, he read the headline: *SCARED TO DEATH.*

Mallory refilled his cup. The hairs on his forearms were rising. Why was that?

Charles turned his eyes to the opening paragraph. It appeared that, prior to withdrawing from the world, the deceased had put on bizarre public displays, running down Broadway, running for his life, though with no pursuer in sight, and panicking pedestrians by yelling, "She has a gun!"

Mallory poured cream into Charles's coffee—a perfectly innocent act.

No witness to these scenes could account for any gun, much less a woman to wield it. The frightened man had also been observed tearing through the streets near his apartment. And, finally, too fearful to leave his home even to walk the dog, the drama critic had given his poodle away to a neighbor.

A noted cardiologist was quoted here, blaming stress as a major cause of heart failure, but adding that, given the victim's age and sedentary life, more damage had been done by the physical exertion of escaping the woman who frightened him. The old man's fear had apparently forced him to run a far, fast pace.

On to page two. An unnamed source at the NYPD had leaked the identity of Leonard Crippen's stalker, though the woman had always approached him from behind, and the critic, too scared to turn around, had never seen her face. Even so, he had named her.

Mallory sipped her coffee. Charles's cup was suspended in midair.

The article went on to say that, in numerous police reports, Leonard Crippen had accused the mother of a murdered actor, claiming that she was the only one with motive to kill him.

Oh, no. That poor woman? Oh, *yes*.

On the night of Bugsy's death, Charles had driven the grieving mother home, and he had stayed with her awhile in that house of mourning, replete with a mantelpiece shrine, a reminder that she had lost her son long before the Rinaldi brothers killed him.

Crippen's carnage had been more insidious to her.

But the critic had refused to tell authorities what the mother's motive might be. And yesterday, following this tantalizing lead, reporters had flocked to the Connecticut home of Mrs. Rains, a frail, soft-spoken lady unlikely to own a gun, let alone menace anyone, and she was dismissed as a player in the tragedy. As yet, police had found no credible gunwoman, if indeed one had ever existed.

In Charles's view, the reporters had given up on their only suspect too easily, and logic was on his side. In his own conversations with Mrs. Rains, she had not been shy in castigating the critic. Yet she had passed up an opportunity to posthumously and quite publicly expose Leonard Crippen as a monster.

Fear of self-incrimination?

Doubtful. Absent any witnesses, no case could be made against her, and so rancor should have held sway. But the lady had evidently found satisfaction elsewhere.

Motherlove could be fierce, and Bugsy's mother had the requisite hatred for an obsessive stalker, but she lacked the makings of a murderess. Like most ordinary people who were neither soldiers nor police, she might form the intent to kill, but he knew she would surely hesitate before pulling a trigger to end a human life. And this fitted well with the critic's habit of taking sudden flight, quite literally outrunning bullets.

The last newspaper at the bottom of the pile was the only one to include the fact that the mystery woman had never failed to whisper a threat, a shock to make her victim's heart race and bang. According to the police source, this offered no clue to identity since there could be no voice recognition in whispers.

Though the actual words might be helpful.

Turning back to the story's beginning on page one, he

found the familiar byline of Woody Merrill. In the past, this reporter had been the recipient of tips fed to him by the late Louis Markowitz, and now Charles looked up from his newspaper to consult Mallory, the most likely source of this exclusive detail. "It says here that the woman threatened Crippen. But there's no mention of what—"

By Mallory's slow smile, he could tell that they were onto a different brand of sport today. This was the smile that iced his blood. This was a game that would last all his life, and he named this one *What Have You Done?*

Against his will, he could not help but wonder.

Had there ever been a gun in play? Leonard Crippen might have succumbed to the mere idea of a weapon, perhaps a sensory suggestion that came with a cold touch at the back of his neck—and the whispered endgame line: *You're dead.*

And so he was.

Charles Butler would live to an extreme old age. Well into his nineties and long after the death of Kathy Mallory, he would often go wandering through all the rooms of his mind, pausing in the kitchen, where he kept so many memories of her and kept her alive. Here, he would summon her up from the ether to ask if she had worn a liar's smile that day.

Or had she been touched by the gopher's madness and his sorry life?

Had Bugsy affected her in some tender, get-even way that might, in a stretch, pass for humanity? *No, scratch that*. Leonard Crippen had died in a cruel fashion. *And scratch again*. On Mallory's planet, mercy was unheard of; she gave none and got none. And so it would all fit—for a moment or two.

And the next thought on this carousel? Had she ever *needed* a reason to play that scary game?

Ah, *games*. Back to the possibility of a lying smile. Perhaps she had only seized the advantage of circumstance and the props of obituaries to make him a little crazy on that long-ago morning—*just for fun*; sometimes Charles clung to that one. And then, in alternating hours, he would find her capable of anything. Over time, so corrupted was he by a ghost in the kitchen, all he had left of her; a theater critic's death via Heart Attack Express was refashioned as nobility, and Mallory became the gopher's champion.

Though she *might* have been innocent.

Charles would die as he had lived, an ardent player and a fool for love. Near the end of his days, a great-grandchild would come to him on tiptoe and perform her little errand of turning off his bedside lamp, extinguishing the light but not the enigma, as he lay dying, still trying to fathom a single smile that was only one of Mallory's enduring games.

FROM THE *NEW YORK TIMES* BESTSELLING AUTHOR

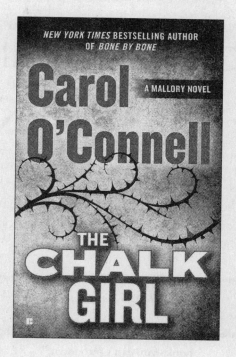

Praise for the Mallory novels:

"O'Connell has raised the standard for psychological thrillers." —*Chicago Tribune*

facebook.com/KathyMalloryBooks
penguin.com

M1456T0214

An astonishing new novel of family secrets
from an author who "has raised the standard for
psychological thrillers" (*Chicago Tribune*).

FROM *NEW YORK TIMES* BESTSELLING AUTHOR

Carol O'Connell

BONE BY BONE

Brothers Oren and Josh disappear into the
woods. Only Oren comes out. Twenty years
later, he must solve the mystery that has haunted
him for years. Because Josh is coming home—
bone by bone.

"Ingenious…dizzying…[a] serpentine story."
—*The New York Times*

"Pulses with a gothic noir…this is one of those
books you can't put down."
—*The Boston Globe*

"An author who can raise goosebumps with
both her plot and her prose."
—*Detroit Free Press*

penguin.com

M1057T0412

FROM *NEW YORK TIMES* BESTSELLING AUTHOR

Carol O'Connell

THE JUDAS CHILD

In a quiet New York suburb, three days before Christmas, two little girls disappear. It's a calculated and chilling reminder of a crime that happened once before, fifteen years ago to the day. The victim was Detective Rouge Kendall's twin sister. But if the crime was solved, that killer apprehended, then who is playing games with a haunted man's terrible memories and unforgettable fears?

"A brilliant twist...mesmerizing."
—*Minneapolis Star Tribune*

"[O'Connell's] most stunning novel yet...more chilling, twisted, and intense with each page... [a] soul-shattering climax."
—*Booklist* (starred review)

penguin.com

M1058T0212

Penguin Group (USA) Online

What will you be reading tomorrow?

Patricia Cornwell, Nora Roberts, Catherine Coulter,
Ken Follett, John Sandford, Clive Cussler,
Tom Clancy, Laurell K. Hamilton, Charlaine Harris,
J. R. Ward, W.E.B. Griffin, William Gibson,
Robin Cook, Brian Jacques, Stephen King,
Dean Koontz, Eric Jerome Dickey, Terry McMillan,
Sue Monk Kidd, Amy Tan, Jayne Ann Krentz,
Daniel Silva, Kate Jacobs...

You'll find them all at
penguin.com

*Read excerpts and newsletters,
find tour schedules and reading group guides,
and enter contests.*

Subscribe to Penguin Group (USA) newsletters
and get an exclusive inside look
at exciting new titles and the authors you love
long before everyone else does.

PENGUIN GROUP (USA)
penguin.com

M224G0909